Rock College

Rock College

An unofficial history of Mount Eden Prison

Mark Derby

MASSEY UNIVERSITY PRESS

For John Ringer — survivor

All royalties from this book go to the criminal justice reform organisation JustSpeak — www.justspeak.org.nz

Author's note

The first prison on the Mount Eden site was popularly known as the Stockade but officially named Auckland Gaol. By the time its successor on the same site was completed in 1917, its name was Auckland Prison. When the maximum-security institution at Paremoremo was completed in 1968, it acquired the name Auckland Prison and the older building became Mount Eden Prison. It has also been known to its inmates at various times as the Stone Jug, Rock College, the Rock and (by Māori) Mautini, a transliteration of 'Mount Eden'.

For the sake of simplicity and clarity, the building completed in 1917 will be generally referred to in this book, regardless of era, as Mount Eden Prison, the name by which it was and still is most commonly known.

As in other prisons around the country, during the nineteenth century Mount Eden was under the overall authority of a governor. In 1854 that position was renamed 'superintendent'. From the early 1990s the most senior role in the prison was known by generically administrative terms such as 'general manager'.

Contents

Introduction: **Bringing up the bodies**   11

1: **Feculent hovel:** 1841–1865   21

2: **Paste-board gaol:** 1855–1876   53

3: **Stone Jug:** 1877–1909   91

4: **Brutal Bastille:** 1910–1922   125

5: **Rock College:** 1923–1946   149

6: **The Meccano Set:** 1947–1962   183

7: **'Burn, burn, burn':** 1963–1969   223

8: **Death on remand:** 1970–2011   259

Epilogue: **Releasing the ghosts**   295

Notes   309

Bibliography   345

Acknowledgements   353

About the author   354

Index   355

Introduction
Bringing up the bodies

'It was midnight — torrential rain, lightning. And all these kaumātua standing in the exercise yard, doing their karakia. A row of coffins on the ground, open. And the prisoners were yelling at us from inside to shut up.'[1]

That eerie, rain-lashed night in 1989 was the first time 23-year-old Te Kahautu Maxwell had been inside Mount Eden Prison's daunting walls. He had travelled there from his home in the Bay of Plenty in a convoy led by elders of the Ringatū faith. They were a solemn, determined, ritualistic group, safeguarded at every stage of the journey with incantations and prayers for their spiritual protection. They bore the weight of their mission's profound cultural and historical significance. More than a century earlier, on a single morning in May 1866, five of their forebears had been hanged in the prison, and now the group had come to exhume the men's bodies and reclaim them.

A row of stone slabs, each incised with a single initial and set into the asphalt along the north wall of the main exercise yard, marked the location of the hanged men's graves. Prison authorities had strung a tarpaulin above the site, placed a wooden coffin beside each of the tombstones and erected floodlights that threw harsh beams through the driving rain. Guards and prison officials looked on uneasily at the chanting elders and younger men, numbering nearly 80 in total, who were disrupting the routine of this circumscribed, enforced community.

Once the old people felt that the preparatory rituals had been appropriately carried out, they withdrew to rest before ordaining the next stage of the arcane practice of hahu, or disinterment. Maxwell and the younger companions remained to carry out the physical side of the work. Each of them was under strict tapu: 'no food, no water — just digging'. They had been selected for this task in part because they shared the same tribal affiliations as the hanged men — Whakatōhea, Ngāti Awa and Tūhoe from the Bay of Plenty. Two others had arrived from Taranaki, on the other side of the island, to exhume the body of Horomona Poropiti, hanged along with Mikaere Kirimangu for the murder of a government agent, James Fulloon. A tōhunga from Parihaka, a sacred settlement for the Taranaki people, had prepared the way for them to do so. A third group were Ngāpuhi from Northland, there to offer guidance, as they had recently recovered the bodies of several of their own ancestors who had been transported in the 1840s to imprisonment in Van Diemen's Land, as Tasmania was then known.

The young men set to work with crowbars and pickaxes. 'The graves were dug up in order,' remembers Maxwell. 'You didn't touch anyone else's — just worked on yours.' The remains of the Taranaki prophet Horomona were the first to emerge from the earth. Maxwell and another Whakatōhea man then began disinterring their chief, Mokomoko, who, on the same day as Horomona and Kirimangu, had been hanged alongside Heremita Kahupaea and Hakaraia Te Rahui for the murder of Carl Völkner, an Ōpōtiki missionary and government spy. Mokomoko had protested his innocence until his last breath, and Maxwell had grown up listening to stories and songs of his wrongful execution. The chief's remains, coated in yellow quicklime to encourage decomposition, were encountered a little more than a metre beneath the surface of the exercise yard. They were reverently lifted and placed in a special coffin, handmade from native timber without the use of nails or screws, supplied by the Ngāpuhi men.[2]

Through the night more bones were uncovered and moved to other waiting coffins. An Auckland archaeologist, Simon Best, was present to witness this seldom-seen procedure. He believes that the five bodies were originally buried in full-sized coffins some 60 metres from the boundary wall, and moved to their new gravesite in the late nineteenth century to make way for rebuilding work. They appeared to have been reburied 'in wooden containers about half the length of a standard coffin'.[3]

The scope of the job suddenly and unexpectedly expanded. 'We'd be digging down,' says Maxwell, 'and the wall of the hole caved in and there was another skull — more bodies in there. And they were, like, "Take me too." So we had to get more coffins for them.'[4]

As the team worked methodically along the line of marker stones, the rocky ground beneath the tarseal proved too much for the hand tools they had brought with them. Jackhammers were ordered but, out of consideration for sleeping inmates, the men waited silently until 7 a.m. before using them.[5]

'Some of our relations were in that jail,' says Maxwell, and in the morning several of these men were permitted to work alongside the diggers. They included the heavily dreadlocked 'Diesel Dick' Maxwell, held for burning down a number of churches around Ruatoria, on the East Coast, in the early 1980s. The enlarged digging party worked on until the early afternoon, watched from behind concrete barriers by dozens of other inmates. Eleven bodies were eventually recovered, some of them not immediately identifiable. Best believes they had all been relocated from older gravesites around the prison and placed in a common trench.

When no further bones or other human remains could be found, the kaumātua returned to oversee their removal. Their karakia resounded down the prison's stone corridors as Te Kahautu Maxwell and others carried the first of the fully loaded coffins. 'They were heavy,' he says. 'We walked them out through the prison to the front entrance, back and forth ... And all the Black Powers and them trying to touch the coffins. All those hands reaching out from those pens. Some were crying.'

The coffins were loaded 'into a big truck, like a furniture truck, all stacked on racks'. Only the remains of the Taranaki prophet Horomona were placed in a separate vehicle, since he would be taken to an entirely different final destination. The first stop after the vehicles left the prison gates was the suburb of Panmure, where a Māori-owned firm of undertakers had hosted and supported the hahu party since it arrived in Auckland. Wailing, prayer and tears filled the air as the truck's roller door rose to reveal the stacked coffins. 'They were welcoming them back into the tribe,' says Maxwell. 'Those old people — my grandmother was doing the karanga — they were wailing and collapsing. The emotion, eh. Because they had grown up with the story, and now they were seeing the return of Mokomoko.'[6]

The return journey to the Bay of Plenty next morning was protracted and indirect. The midnight exhumations had become a nationwide news story and the Māori Queen, Dame Te Atairangikaahu, sent a request for the coffins to lie on her principal marae of Tūrangawaewae in the Waikato. After mourning ceremonies there, a roundabout route was taken, bypassing other marae that might also choose to welcome them, to avoid further delays. The truck was eventually unloaded at the Ngāti Awa marae of Taiwhakaea in Whakatāne.

In a striking example of cultural reconciliation, all the bodies carried to the Bay of Plenty, with the exception of Mokomoko's, were reburied together, even though some were almost certainly Pākehā. They had lain alongside each other in death for the past century, and the Ngāti Awa felt they should not now be separated. In the cemetery alongside the meeting house, the coffins were lowered into 'one huge trench like they bury whales', with a single rope to bind them together.

It was two in the morning when the last coffin, containing the Whakatōhea chief Mokomoko, was unloaded onto the marae at Waiaua, overlooking the Bay of Plenty. For the local people who received his remains, feelings of joy and propitiation were mingled with mourning and anger. Their chief had gone to the scaffold at Mount Eden expecting his body to be returned home immediately after death, but the prison authorities had refused to release it to his relatives. Generation after generation of his descendants took on the duty of honouring his final wish, a grim obligation they carried for 123 years. For the same length of time they wore the stigma of his alleged leading role in the ceremonial execution of the missionary Völkner. That stain was not erased for several more years, until in 1993 Justice Minister Doug Graham apologised in person to Whakatōhea, and to the descendants of Mokomoko in particular, for his wrongful conviction and execution.

| | |

The sombre exhumation in Mount Eden's main exercise yard was the first of its kind, but it may not be the last. According to former prison officer Phil Lister, the bodies of other inmates, including those who died there by suicide, illness or violence as well as by execution, may lie in the same northeast corner of the prison grounds, a spot chosen because under ancient Christian tradition it was the least sanctified and therefore the most suitable resting place for evildoers.[7]

There can be little doubt that a penal institution that has occupied the same site for over 150 years, for much of that time with limited official oversight or regard for the rights of its inmates, must hold many strange secrets. The tight-lipped old establishment itself, at the foot of Mount Eden's volcanic cone, is not altogether to blame for the atmosphere of mystery that cloaks it. Thousands of Aucklanders drive past its walled-in buildings every day, yet few seem to know that the prison has lain empty and unused since 2011, and almost none are aware of the influential role it has played in forming, and perhaps deforming, New Zealand's colonial history.

A prison first opened on the present site in 1856, and for more than a century it served as the country's highest-security penal institution, holding the longest-serving and most demonstrably violent and escape-prone criminals. From its first years, women, young children and those convicted of minor offences such as public drunkenness were also held there.

This book records the history of each of the prisons at Mount Eden, and also of Auckland's first jail, in Queen Street, which dates from 15 years earlier. It predated and therefore served some of the functions of the town's first mental hospital. The later prisons continued to confine the mentally ill, and by the 1980s Mount Eden Prison was notorious for its horrifying rate of suicides, predominantly by young Polynesian males.

Dramatic and disruptive events such as suicides, executions, escapes and riots drew nationwide attention to the prison and its inmates, but for those imprisoned there, they occurred amid the curious combination of tedium and camaraderie common to other enforced communities. For most of its long life, Mount Eden was simultaneously the country's toughest prison and also Auckland's all-purpose lockup, taking in drunkards, debtors, 'disorderly' women, and other short-term and first-time offenders. It acquired a unique and contradictory character, simultaneously forbidding and familiar, punitive and parochial.

Over its 150-year lifespan the changes to Mount Eden Prison's facilities, regulations, customs and inmate population have reflected the country's responses to criminality, and to changing social patterns more generally. The proportion of Māori, for example, was at first very small, and the most prominent among them were those such as Mokomoko, sentenced for essentially political offences. That composition changed markedly during the twentieth century as the number of Māori inmates increased in line with the urbanisation of the wider Māori population, until they comprised an overall majority.

Regardless of race, inmates have always been drawn overwhelmingly from the poorest sections of the community, with notable exceptions such as the draft resisters and conscientious objectors who were incarcerated during wartime in the twentieth century. The administration of the prison dutifully followed national penal policies that have fluctuated between retribution and rehabilitation, between simply containing prisoners and also aiming to change their behaviour.

Even as the society surrounding it altered fundamentally, the stone prison's dour contours remained almost unchanged. The Rock, or Rock College, or the Stone Jug, or Mautini has been a remarkably resilient and immutable feature of Auckland and national life, and the exterior of the main buildings still looks much as it did when completed in 1917. Until its closure, no matter whether penological theories favoured the harshly punitive or the optimistically rehabilitative, every cell in this impractical, intractable institution was usually fully occupied.

The prison survived numerous calls for its demolition, the first of them when it was barely finished, and has been reviled as unsightly and dehumanising not only by prisoners but also by its neighbours and by political leaders of all shades. A frenzied riot in 1965 gutted the interior but failed to permanently shut down what remained. Yet when the prison was finally decommissioned in 2011, the closing ceremony was an occasion for nostalgic regret by its staff and also, apparently, for many of its last remaining inmates, who had come to regard it with the affection shown towards a tough, irascible but irreplaceable old identity. While researching this book, both Corrections staff and ex-inmates typically said they agreed to talk to me primarily because the remarkable stories that Mount Eden holds deserve to be recorded and better known.

The Department of Corrections now finds itself responsible for maintaining an abandoned and echoing relic occupying a large area of the most valuable real estate in the country. The prison's battlemented towers and cruciform wings have the highest possible heritage classification, ensuring that the department's options for repurposing the buildings are strictly limited; they now stand empty and decaying as they await a new long-term use. It was this indeterminate, limbo state that, above all, convinced me that the long and harrowing history of the prison, and of the two less durable institutions that preceded it, would be worth telling.

| | |

That project has turned out to be more prolonged and complex than originally expected, even though I quickly decided that the circumstances of individual prisoners, and especially the actions that led to their imprisonment, would not be my primary focus. Rather, I have chosen to trace the lifespan of the prison itself — a peculiar walled community with its own culture, traditions, eccentrics and shameful secrets, a rough-hewn hostelry shaping and shaped by the lives of the tens of thousands of men and women, and some children, who lay in its cells and walked its corridors.

Mount Eden Prison in the 1950s, photographed from Auburn Street looking towards Boston Road. AUCKLAND LIBRARIES HERITAGE COLLECTIONS, 7-A17598

I have drawn heavily on published first-person accounts of prison life, especially by Mount Eden's first psychologist, Donald McKenzie, and by ex-inmate and later sociologist Greg Newbold. Interviews with former inmates and staff have been invaluable for describing the later years of the institution. The Department of Corrections has cooperated generously by giving me access to the prison and to members of its staff but has not funded this publication, nor has any such funding been sought. The findings and conclusions given here, and any inadvertent errors, are all my own.

I cannot claim direct personal experience of the inside of Mount Eden, either as an inmate or an officer, but I have aimed to do justice to the experiences and memories of those who lived or worked there, while giving others some understanding of one of Auckland's most prominent, recognisable, historically formative, yet least-known institutions (as well as its two long-vanished predecessors). Since no one now faces the possibility of enforced familiarity with the interior of Mount Eden Prison, I hope this book provides a less harrowing experience of passing through its towering, iron-bound wooden gates, under the carved stone portal above the main entrance, and into its sunless and austere back corridors to do some time.

1:
Feculent hovel

1841–1865

Saturday night, when both the inclination and opportunity for drunkenness are at their height, is the worst time of the week in a metropolitan jail. The violent, judgement-impaired and purely unfortunate are admitted in a sullen stream that overloads the regular muster of inmates, and the atmosphere is sour with recrimination and despair.

Some time after nine on the night of Saturday 8 April 1842, Auckland's newly built jail (or 'gaol', as it was generally spelt at that time) became so intolerable that head gaoler George McElwain took the extreme step of summoning his superior, James Coates, from his home. The cells were overflowing, McElwain insisted, and two of his prisoners were 'very violent and appeared to him to be deranged'.

The gentlemanly Coates held the ancient title of High Sheriff, yet he had no prior experience of the penal system. In 1842 Auckland was barely a year old, the makeshift and largely hypothetical capital of a brand-new colony, and its government posts were shared around among the mainly young and under-qualified men available to take them. Coates was just 27 when his gaoler sent the frantic request for his presence. Sensibly, he asked the older and more experienced Colonial Surgeon John Johnson, whose responsibilities included the health of gaol inmates, to accompany him. The two officials picked their way awkwardly by lamplight through mud and dung to the soggy lower end of Queen Street, where the town's wooden gaol stood. McElwain showed them to the larger of its two cells, where they found a scene from a nightmare.

The No. 1 cell, the size of a modest modern-day bathroom, held 14 prisoners. There was not enough room for them all to lie down, and a hammock had been strung beneath the low ceiling, further reducing the minimal ventilation. The second cell, even smaller, contained 12 men, and while the two observers were present another was admitted, so violently drunk that his handcuffed wrists had to be tied to the bars over the window. Another man became contorted on the floor of the cell with fits so intense that it took the efforts of most of the other prisoners to hold him down. Someone had evidently just vomited, and Sheriff Coates found that 'the stench was insufferable'.

Next day Coates reported these appalling conditions to the Colonial Secretary, the capital's highest-placed official apart from its governor, William Hobson. The sheriff did his best to absolve himself and his staff of blame for the scene he had witnessed. Coates explained that the cells 'are cleaned out every day that the weather will permit of so doing and every precaution is used to ventilate them during the day, but the number of prisoners confined in so small a space renders it inoperative . . . On Wednesday next I anticipate the introduction of 20–25 debtors, where I am to place them I cannot possibly imagine.'[1] This was the incontinent state of Auckland's only penal facility 18 months after the colony's capital was relocated from Kororāreka in the Bay of Islands to a thinly populated stretch of scrub and fern beside the Waitematā Harbour.

Kororāreka (later known as Russell) was a notoriously lawless former whaling settlement, and during 1840 a large proportion of its seafarers, ex-convicts, defaulting soldiers, needy women and gamblers followed the governor and his officials south to the promising territory of the new capital. Auckland therefore had immediate need to contain its most unruly and dishonest elements. In the first year this facility was a raupō lockup, a flimsy structure divided into a room for the turnkey and a single 3 x 3.5 metre cell capable of holding eight prisoners at most. A total of 82 inmates were held there in the town's first year, most of them charged with misdemeanours but 17 classed as felons, or serious offenders, and therefore likely to be serving lengthy terms.[2]

In early 1841 construction began on a larger and more secure gaol. The site selected was at the lower end of a gully opening into a sheltered section of the harbour recently named Commercial Bay, since it was where most of Auckland's supplies were landed. The tree-lined and tidal Waihorotiu Creek ran down the western side of the gully, and alongside this lay the town's main thoroughfare, the grandly and optimistically named Queen Street. At that time it was no more than a muddy track ending in a morass of mudflats and swamp through which new arrivals had to stumble ashore. About 200 metres up from the original shoreline, Queen Street was intersected by Victoria Street. This marshy junction, lying well below the properties beginning to appear on the surrounding higher ground, was the unfavoured piece of real estate chosen for Auckland's first gaol — a single-storey, wooden, shed-like building on the left-hand side of Queen Street as it ran down to the shoreline. The Waihorotiu Creek, then a clean and attractive little stream, ran directly behind the gaol, supplying a source of fresh water and a means of disposing of its waste. It was inevitable, however, that in Auckland's moist and fickle climate the stream would periodically overflow its banks and flood the gaol — a recurrent problem throughout the life of the institution.[3]

The gaol was not yet finished, and still lacked a roof, when in July 1841 its first prisoners were transferred from the temporary lockup.[4] They fell into the category of felons, since they included Thomas Brown, convicted of assault, and Donald McNaughton and Patrick Sharkey, who had attempted to free a companion from police custody using a sword and gun. Police Magistrate Gilbert Dawson was among those who had been attacked with these weapons, but in a letter to Lieutenant-Governor Hobson he attributed all three men's offences primarily to intoxication, and appeared concerned mainly for their health while they were held in the unroofed building: 'Considering the state of the gaol these unfortunate men may be subject to severe illness in their confinement and I would therefore recommend that the humane intentions of your Excellency should be extended to the whole of them.'[5] This generous appeal apparently succeeded, and three months later McNaughton and Sharkey were fined a shilling each and released.[6]

Once completed, the primitive gaol consisted of a single cellblock that included the two shared cells and three smaller single cells grouped around a central kitchen and dayroom in a yard surrounded by a two-metre-high wooden fence. Its staff comprised McElwain the gaoler, two turnkeys, and an overseer for the male prisoners sentenced to hard labour. Those inmates worked outside the prison on public works — collecting firewood for government offices, road-making, stone-breaking, and carting sand or lime. It was not possible to house different categories of prisoners separately, so hardened criminals, drunkards and those awaiting trial were held together with female and very young offenders. Some were already veterans of tougher prisons in other British colonies, and were especially hard to manage in the crude conditions they found in Auckland.[7]

Women inmates were acutely vulnerable to abuse from both fellow prisoners and the all-male prison staff. In June 1842, Arin Waite accused assistant gaoler William Kean of 'assault with intent to take improper liberties with her', and of using obscene language. Her complaint was dismissed for want of evidence. Kean was, however, found to have supplied her with liquor, and magistrate Felton Mathew considered his conduct 'highly reprehensible'. Remarkably, Kean was not immediately forced to leave his post, and two years later he accepted a bribe of £40 to enable another prisoner to escape.[8]

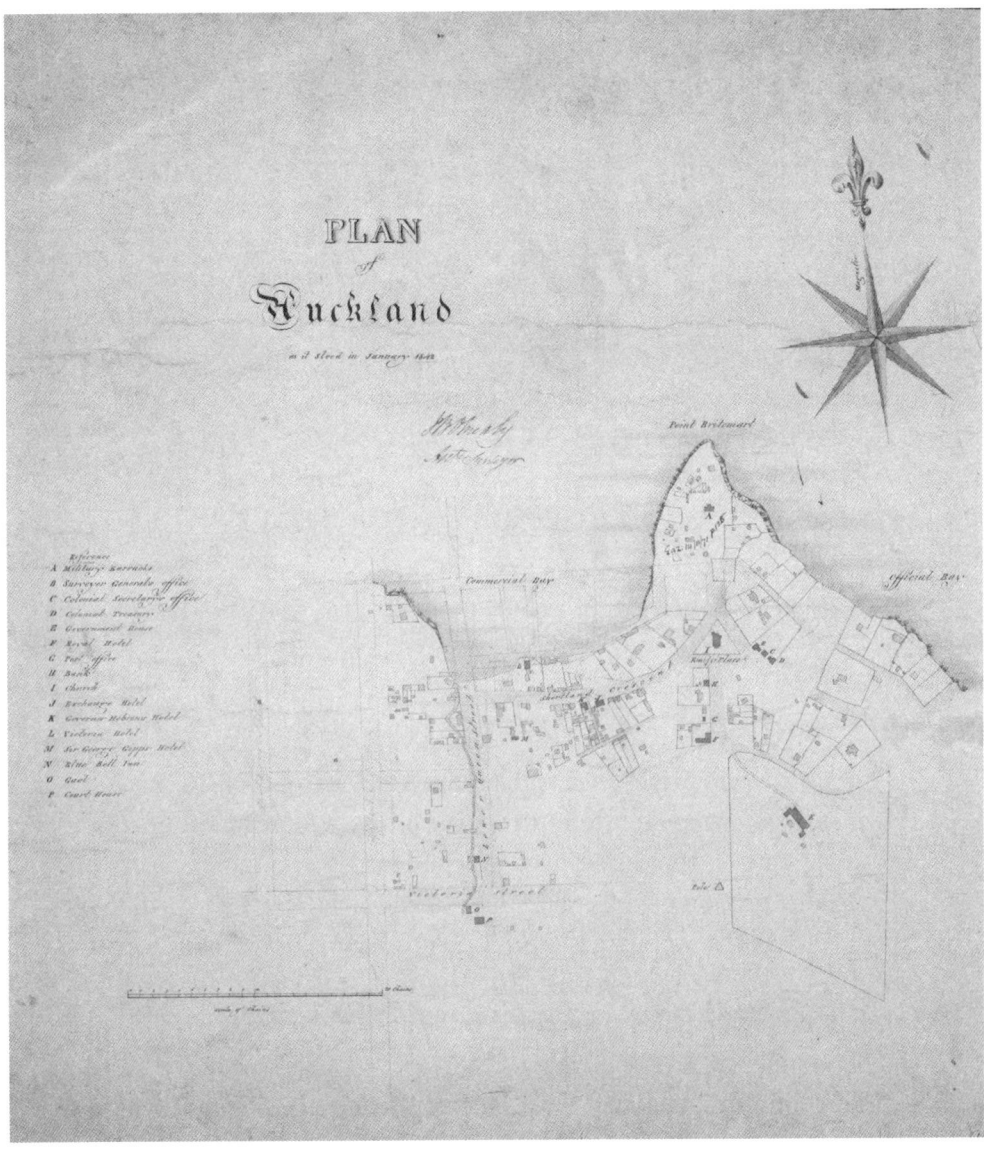

Above: On this map of Auckland from January 1842, the town's first gaol and the adjacent courthouse are shown at the southwest corner of Victoria and Queen Streets, alongside the Waihorotiu Creek. *TĀMAKI PAENGA HIRA AUCKLAND WAR MEMORIAL MUSEUM, G9084.A8*

Next page: The institutions of law enforcement in Auckland, c.1845. This early drawing shows the pillared courthouse (left) and gaol, surrounded by its flimsy fence. Outside this, to the right, on Victoria Street West, are the town's scaffold and its stocks, where miscreants were held for the amusement of passersby. *AUCKLAND LIBRARIES HERITAGE COLLECTIONS, NZG-19101207-32B-1*

In the town's earliest years, perhaps one in four of its business premises was a grog shop, and their patrons became regular inmates of the gaol.[9] One Queen Street resident expressed the outrage felt by 'the respectable portion of the community' at the sight of drunks hauled off to gaol by Māori who, being less prone to drunkenness than the European population, were hired for this purpose to assist the local constabulary. The writer's sympathies lay entirely with the 'poor unfortunates' treated in this manner by 'a set of savages'.[10]

Those unfortunates may have included women, who were typically charged with either drunkenness or 'vagrancy' (a euphemism for soliciting and prostitution). If unable to pay a fine, they were held for up to 48 hours in a lean-to in a corner of the main cellblock, which was not fully secured from the other cells. Police Magistrate Felton Mathew noted the 'very great inconvenience being continually felt from the want of any place within the Gaol which can be appropriated to the confinement of females'.[11] After Arin Waite complained of her treatment by assistant gaoler Kean, a police magistrate recommended that a matron be added to the staff to manage female prisoners. Governor Hobson thought the expense unnecessary.[12]

Soon after the gaol opened, construction began on the larger and more

ostentatious courthouse alongside it. This building would eventually be used for sittings of the Supreme Court and other lofty legal purposes, but meantime it stood in 'a perfect sea of mud, quite impassable unless a person walked carefully along a single line of boards placed end to end over the semi fluid'.[13] The local newspaper asked rhetorically how 'the Chief Justice, the Law Officers, and all connected with the Court, will contrive to get to it in wet weather — to pass and repass from the Court House to other parts of the town, with decent facility, will be out of the question.'[14]

III

Like the gaol, the courthouse was still unfinished when a landmark case compelled its immediate use. The defendant was a tall, 17-year-old Māori from a chiefly Northland family. Maketu Wharetotara was charged with murdering five settlers at Motuarohia Island in the Bay of Islands in a fit of rage after being repeatedly abused by one of them, a farmer named Thomas Bull. His lethal retaliation may well have been regarded with sympathy by his own people, and in former times been dealt with under traditional tribal processes of justice. The Treaty of Waitangi had been signed shortly before the Motuarohia murders, however, and notwithstanding the Crown's obligation to share governance with Māori, all New Zealand's people had become subject to a penal system introduced from Britain. After certain inducements were offered to them, Ngāpuhi chiefs agreed to deliver the young man over to this system, and he was held in a condemned cell in Auckland's gaol for several months until his trial. During that time he covered the walls with images of canoes, men and horses, perhaps to remind him of his home.[15]

The trial in the new courthouse was brief and decisive. Maketu was found guilty and sentenced to hang, and Sheriff Coates was required to organise the colony's first official execution. This was to be a public spectacle, and a gallows was erected directly outside the gaol gates. The hanging was scheduled for noon on 7 March 1842, the same time as an important sale of Crown lands. This auction was therefore postponed for an hour 'to enable intending land purchasers to witness the event'.[16]

Maketu, described as 'a fine young man, whose stature was upwards of six feet', was brought from his cell at the appointed time, wearing 'a blue blanket, of native manufacture'.[17] With the gaol bell tolling, he was led to the scaffold under the gaze of a thousand spectators who were kept at a suitable distance behind a strong guard of armed troops. A reporter noticed that very few Māori were among the crowd. Although capital punishment was well established in Māori tradition, it was generally delivered summarily, immediately after sentencing. Maketu's fate under the new judicial system was apparently accepted by his people, but they were distressed at the long and, they felt, unnecessarily cruel delay between his arrest and his execution. Whether for this or some other reason, Māori remained much less inclined than the European population to attend future public hangings.

Once the execution was concluded, Maketu's relatives asked to take his body back to the Bay of Islands, but they were refused and he was buried without ceremony within the grounds of the gaol. Ten months later, his father Ruhe begged again for his son's bones and this time the governor acceded to the request. The body was exhumed and carried back to the north for reburial.

It was in the month after this hanging that Sheriff Coates witnessed the dismal state of the cells on an April Saturday night, and urged the Colonial Secretary to make funds available to relieve the crammed and insanitary conditions.[18] His appeal stirred the administration to action, and a basic lockup, where offenders could be held overnight before being dealt with in court, was added next to the courthouse. This small cell, the first port of call for most gaol inmates, was later described by gaoler McElwain as 'not fit for any civilised community', a 'mere hole where men and women are thrown in drunk and wet on a floor, without light or anything else, until the morning'.[19]

Police Magistrate Felton Mathew, who was said to be 'possessed of stern piety', was notoriously hard on the town's many drunks.[20] He imposed fines of £1 5s, the equivalent of several hundred dollars today, on offenders, and those who could not pay were placed in the stocks outside the courthouse.[21] This medieval form of punishment required offenders to sit on a bench with their legs placed in holes cut through two heavy planks locked one above the other. The bench was somewhat lower than the planks, so the position was not comfortable.[22] It was a particularly undignified posture for women offenders, and Auckland's respectable citizens expressed disgust at witnessing 'the indecent and disgraceful exhibition of a female sitting in the public streets in a position and under circumstances of the most indelicate nature'.[23] These stocks are clearly visible in early illustrations of Queen Street, and remained in use until late in 1845.

Jurors hearing trials in the courthouse were subjected to conditions little better than those faced by offenders in the gaol next door. In June 1842, a jury sat on a defamation case brought by Sheriff Coates against his superior, Colonial Secretary Willoughby Shortland.[24] To consider their verdict, the jurors were locked in the gaoler's small bedroom at the rear of the prison. They could not reach agreement on the case and when they returned to court the following day were placed in one of the cells to continue their discussion. No food was provided, and they were obliged to beckon through the bars and hand a passerby some cash to buy them bread and cheese.[25]

For its first five years Auckland had no hospital, and certainly no facility for caring for the mentally ill. The gaol therefore fulfilled this latter function, to no one's satisfaction. In May 1842, Dr Johnson advised Governor Hobson that a man named Joseph Hale was held in the gaol, 'having been found wandering about in a state of mental derangement . . . it is highly necessary that he should be removed from the Gaol for at present he occupies one of the two cells allowed for the prisoners, who are thereby crowded most incommodiously into one cell, to the probable detriment of their health'.[26] The only option available was to place him in a subterranean cell beneath the courthouse, and to direct one of the hard-labour prisoners to act as his keeper while he received treatment from Dr Johnson. This cell was so damp and rat infested that Coates did not consider it fit for habitation even by a lunatic.[27]

| | |

A unique and intriguing figure among the early gaol inmates was an English-born chancer named William Phelps Pickering. He had arrived in the colony in March 1841 by way of Australia, where he had spent the previous four years as a small-time and not always scrupulous businessman, eventually serving six months for debt in Van Diemen's Land. He then sailed for the Bay of Islands but soon followed the exodus south to the new capital in Auckland. There he represented himself as agent for an Australian bank and attempted to secure funds under its name. The deception was uncovered, and in October 1841 the 25-year-old Pickering, described as an unmarried merchant, was charged with false pretences. His jury found him guilty but with a recommendation for mercy. The interim Attorney-General, Francis Fisher, was unmoved, and sentenced Pickering to the maximum available penalty — transportation 'beyond the seas' for seven years.

To the judges who ordered it, and to most of the offenders thus sentenced (they were then officially termed convicts to distinguish them from felons and petty offenders), transportation was the most severe penalty in law short of a death sentence. William Pickering was the first New Zealand resident to receive such a sentence from a local court, and the press and public were outraged at this exceptionally harsh treatment of a man of some distinction.[28]

Van Diemen's Land was then the only Australian colony prepared to accept convicts transported from New Zealand, so Pickering faced a return to the place where he had been imprisoned two years earlier. While the sheriff negotiated with ships' masters for a suitable rate for his passage, the young fraudster spent two months in the fetid Auckland gaol, although he was permitted to walk up and down outside its walls during the day.

Eventually the schooner *Sisters* agreed to carry him, and in December 1841 he was led down the short and squalid stretch of Queen Street to the waterside with irons on his legs. Pickering had become known and liked in the town during his confinement there, and Aucklanders who witnessed this humiliating spectacle decried it as a 'judicial display of cruelty'.[29] Certainly, leg-irons were a severe punishment in themselves. They could weigh 14 kilograms and, according to another prisoner, as they were fixed in place, 'each stroke of the riveting hammer causing a sensation of pain something like toothdrawing'.[30]

Pickering's fate, however, was not yet sealed. En route to Australia his ship called at the Bay of Islands for firewood. By then he had evidently been released from his irons and acquired accomplices on board. He and a companion slipped down the ship's side and made for shore in its dinghy. Pickering spent several weeks at large before he was captured and returned to Auckland Gaol, his ship having long since sailed. He then faced a second and much more tedious wait behind bars while a new passage was found for him. As an escaper, he was kept inside the gaol at all times and not permitted beyond its walls either for exercise or to work with the hard-labour men. He appears to have made use of this enforced idleness with his customary imagination and energy.

The town's Anglican clergyman, Reverend John Churton, made regular pastoral visits to the gaol and conducted a Sunday service in one of the cells. Although he was 'frequently gratified by finding a desire for spiritual knowledge and improvement' among the prisoners, he was alarmed to discover that few of them, even the most devout, could read and write. In an early attempt at prison reform, Reverend Churton urged the acting Governor, Willoughby Shortland, to introduce literacy classes in the gaol and offered to personally provide 'all books that may be required for the above purpose'.[31]

Shortland was cautiously encouraging, and invited the sheriff to respond to Churton's offer. Coates suggested that all prisoners serving more than nine days should in future be required to attend classes in the gaol between six and seven in the evening. That extra time would be found by cutting their breakfast and supper times by half an hour each, so that 'the hours of labor [*sic*; i.e. hard labour outside the gaol] may not be interfered with'. The schoolmaster, who would, it was presumed, be one of the inmates, would also conduct compulsory morning and evening prayers, and a Sunday Bible reading if the chaplain was unavailable.

Sheriff Coates advised Shortland that:

> [A]t the present moment there is one person in the Gaol fully capable of undertaking the charge of the School, but his sentence is seven years transportation. The individual I allude to is 'William Phelps Pickering.' He has now been confined for thirteen months in the Gaol at the expense of the Government, during that period I have found him obedient and orderly, and with the exception of his escape from the vessel in which he was forwarded to Van Diemens Land I have had no cause of complaint against him. I would therefore humbly suggest that His Excellency might be induced to take the case into his consideration and to commute his sentence to imprisonment in this Colony with hard labor for such period as His Excellency may deem proper.[32]

This plea for mitigation of Pickering's sentence was echoed by the local paper, which urged that 'His Excellency might shew [sic] a little mercy. We understand [Pickering] has been very useful in gaol, in teaching the other prisoners to read and write ... We trust Mr. Shortland will take this opportunity of manifesting that he has the wish, as well as the power to exercise the Divine attribute.'[33] Later, Pickering even claimed that while held in the gaol he had saved the life of an assistant gaoler.[34]

At that time an intervention by the governor was the only provision, short of a royal pardon, that could give a convict early release from a sentence of transportation.[35] Shortland advised the sheriff, 'Whilst the convict Pickering shall remain in the Gaol at Auckland his services will be temporarily made use of at School ... But I cannot provide him a pardon — his offence being greatly aggravated by his attempted escape.'[36] This decision deprived the inmates of any further chance of education and ended Reverend Churton's hopes for their school. In May 1843, Pickering was placed on board a Hobart-bound vessel for the second time; with him were 12 other men, most of them sentenced for relatively petty dishonesty offences. This time the voyage was without incident, and Van Diemen's Land received its first New Zealand convicts.[37]

III

During his two terms in the Auckland gaol, William Pickering was popularly regarded as an ill-treated victim of the justice system who deserved more lenient treatment on the grounds both of his crime and his class. A similar dispensation was often extended to another category of offender, the debtors, who made up a significant element of the gaol population from its earliest years. They could be imprisoned for up to three months, the term generally being scaled to the amount they owed, and in that time could expect to receive better treatment than the common criminals.[38]

Sheriff Coates had requested separate accommodation in the gaol for debtors since at least March 1842, and several months later two debtors' cells and a dayroom were added to the southern end of the prison.[39] The debtors were still obliged to share cooking and dining facilities with the other prisoners, and the sheriff regarded this situation as quite inappropriate for offenders of their status. In 1843 he reported that they 'will not, nor can it be expected that they should, associate with Felons to cook at their fire'.[40]

The following year a self-contained debtors' prison was built just behind the main cellblock, along the bank of the Waihorotiu Creek. The perimeter fence there was low and insecure, so that 'a very trifling hindrance is presented to the obstruction of the fugitive'.[41] However, the debtors do not appear to have taken advantage of the opportunity for easy escape, and confinement was apparently not dreaded by the town's defaulters. One early report describes 'several flashy young men there, chatting, smoking, in a most enviable state of insouciance'.[42]

No separate provision at all was made for young offenders, whose numbers increased sharply after the unexpected arrival during 1842–43 of two shiploads of 'Parkhurst boys'. These were former inmates of Parkhurst Prison on the Isle of Wight, Britain's first and at that time only juvenile prison. In an especially heartless display of bureaucratic ineptitude, about 120 of these hapless boys, aged from 11 to 20, were transferred directly from Parkhurst to the other side of the world.[43] The Colonial Office did not see fit to consult New Zealand's fledgling administration over its decision, and citizens of Auckland were astonished and dismayed at the sight of so many undersized and unaccompanied new migrants trooping down the gangplank. 'The chances are ten to one against them in such a country as

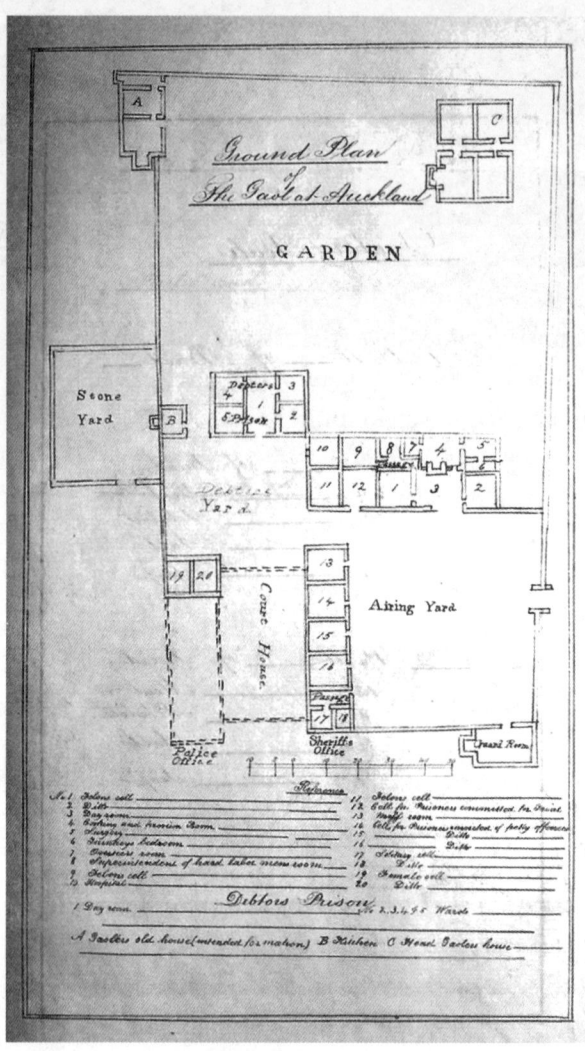

Auckland Gaol at its most expansive. This 1855 ground plan shows Queen Street running from left to right across its lower edge and Victoria Street West along the right-hand side. *ARCHIVES NEW ZEALAND, BLUE BOOK OF STATISTICS, 1855*

this, where temptation and opportunity are so frequent, and so inviting,' the *Daily Southern Cross* fulminated, 'and being from early youth trained to vice, they naturally betake themselves to it with an appetite sharpened by the temporary restraint [of their emigration passage] . . . We are now being put in the position of receiving everything that is offensive in the convict system, without any advantage whatever.'[44]

The boys had been given some trade training while in prison in England but found no demand for their skills in the nascent township. Without support or funds they were left to fend for themselves, and the same newspaper report predicted that 'when they are detected in their bad practices among the Europeans, they will immediately find their way into the native settlements'.[45] Some destitute boys did indeed seek support from local Māori and were reported to be 'living with the Natives at the native pahs in almost a state of nudity, or at best but covered with a rag of an old blanket'.[46] Others were sent to labour in the copper mines on Great Barrier Island, and the more fortunate found work on Auckland's roads, where, however, they were soon reduced to working in bare feet. 'This is not by any means proper,' declared the press. 'If the Government work them, they ought to keep them in food and clothing.'[47]

Britain's Colonial Office had earlier promised that no convicts would be transported to New Zealand, and this distinction over Australia was highly prized by Auckland's respectable citizens. Since the Parkhurst boys had been released from prison under a conditional pardon, they were, strictly speaking, not transported convicts, but this point of law meant little to aggrieved Aucklanders. However, the colonial government was then critically short of funds and Shortland could do little beyond requesting the British government send no further shiploads of crime-prone youths. He reminded the House of Lords that while New Zealand was colonised 'on the faith that it should never be inundated with a convict population . . . the inhabitants of Auckland are now in constant dread of thefts and robberies from the "reformed convicts"'.[48]

Indeed, and unsurprisingly, many of the boys quickly resorted to vagrancy and petty thievery. For the first time since Auckland was established, bolts and bars were in demand to secure shops and houses, and the term 'Parkhurst boy' became 'a proverb for lawlessness and vice'.[49] The gaol received so many of them that by 1843 more than half its inmates were aged under 18. Dr Johnson found that they arrived there 'in a most filthy state and generally out of health', and some, at least, may have wished they had never left the relatively well-run conditions of Parkhurst.[50]

In December 1843, one young recalcitrant escaped from the lockup three times in succession and was sentenced to the rare punishment of a whipping. Thomas Somerville, the superintendent of the hard labour prisoners, was ordered to administer this sentence and, to his lasting credit, refused to do so. His humane insubordination was applauded by the local paper, which pronounced: 'No man possessed of any self-respect could be expected to degrade himself' by inflicting 'such beastly and degrading punishment'.[51] The paper's editor questioned whether it was even lawful for the magistrate to order anyone 'to be flogged in a free country'.[52] Gaol records show that the whipping was carried out nevertheless.[53]

III

As it struggled to accommodate such unforeseen pressures as the influx of Parkhurst boys, the gaol's regulations and physical structure evolved in a piecemeal and haphazard fashion. Management of the country's gaols had not yet been placed under the control of any central authority, so it was left to individual and local initiative to determine how each institution should be run.[54] Auckland Gaol was fortunate to come under the direction of a dedicated and, by the standards of the day, humane sheriff who developed regulations that were later emulated at other prisons throughout the country. This man was Percival Berrey, who replaced James Coates as sheriff in September 1843.

Berrey evidently had some legal training, as he had earlier been considered for the post of Auckland's Crown Prosecutor. He drew up a comprehensive set of regulations designed to improve standards of order and hygiene. These listed the bedding and clothing allowance for each prisoner, including a 'smock-frock' or long over-shirt.[55] The protocols for admission and discharge of prisoners, their routine tasks and obligations, and general rules of discipline and behaviour were laid down. Singing, conversation and 'angry expressions' were forbidden, as were 'games and amusements of any kind', and tobacco. The regulations changed very little over the next 10 years, although they were slightly relaxed from 1849, when the ban on talking was restricted to prohibiting 'loud conversation'.[56]

The specified daily food ration consisted of four ounces (a little over

100 grams) of meat, 24 ounces of bread, 12 ounces of maize meal and 8 ounces of vegetables. Especially well-behaved prisoners, and those recovering from illness, might be permitted a larger ration of meat. Those in solitary confinement or facing some other punishment were limited to the daily bread ration and water. This spartan and monotonous diet remained largely unaltered until the 1860s. The midday meal was invariably a soup or stew made from the cheapest cuts of meat and cooked by inmates chosen for this task. Breakfast and supper consisted simply of bread and water. Not surprisingly, illness was frequent and medical authorities expressed repeated concerns at the nutritional inadequacies of the prisoners' diet. In 1844 Dr Johnson applied successfully for 'medical comforts' — tea, sugar, rice, oatmeal, sago and wine — for his sick and convalescing patients.[57]

If the gaol's regulations are a reliable guide, the daily routine, like the diet, was unchanging year-round. It began at 6 a.m., when the turnkey made his rounds, unlocking each of the cells. Inmates then had 15 minutes to dress and another 15 to sweep and wash their cells, 'during which time the bedding is to be suspended in the airing yard and then folded in the smallest possible compass'.[58] From 6.30 they washed themselves thoroughly under the observation of the officer on duty. At 7 a.m. they were assembled for roll call and a short prayer service by the gaoler, followed by the bread-and-water breakfast.

At 7.50 the hard-labour men were mustered by their overseer and issued their tools before setting out 'in couples and in orderly fashion' for the day's work, either in the prison's own stone-breaking yard or on public works beyond its walls. They were under the command of overseers who permitted no talking, especially to the public. Meanwhile the other able-bodied prisoners, including all women, carried out regular gaol duties such as cutting firewood for the cookhouse and preparing the midday meal.

In 1843 a prisoner named Tolley refused to go to work because 'his shoes were so much broken he was afraid of hurting his feet, and exhibited his shoes to the court, which were certainly very bad'.[59] Sheriff Berrey later obtained tools and materials for making the heavy hobnailed boots issued to the men who were engaged in stone-breaking, laying ditches, building jetties and other public works.[60] Prisoners who possessed the skills to make and repair boots were greatly valued.

The men worked from eight until noon, and then returned to the gaol for their midday meal, when they were required to have 'clean hands and face'. They worked a further four hours in the afternoon, then washed up and unrolled their neatly stacked bedding. A roll call at 5.45 was followed by more prayers and Bible readings and a search for contraband, succeeded by a final meal of bread and water. The prisoners were then locked up until morning. Apart from those sentenced to solitary confinement, prisoners of every kind — first offenders, hardened criminals, juveniles and the mentally unwell — spent the next 12 hours in each other's company.

The only variation in the weekly routine was on Thursday, when the chaplain led a prayer service from 4 till 5 p.m., and Saturday, when the work day ended at noon, leaving the men the afternoon to wash and mend their clothes and generally prepare the prison for the following day. Sunday was a rest day, apart from the compulsory morning divine service. This ritual was held in a cell, there being no designated chapel, with the women, remand prisoners awaiting trial, petty criminals and felons seated on forms in separate groups. Ironically, this was one of the only occasions during this period when prisoners were ever classified into these categories.[61] The Anglican chaplain led the service, although a Catholic priest visited every Saturday and 'dissenting' ministers occasionally.

The hard-labour men's tasks were allocated by one of the town's more influential officials, the Superintendent of Public Works. His entirely unpaid labour force should, in theory, have made a substantial contribution to the never-ending need for new works and maintenance. In practice, the hard-labour gangs achieved relatively little. The superintendent could never be sure how many men would turn up for each day's duties, since most were sentenced only to short terms. The incidence of sickness among them was so high that at times half the potential labour force was in the gaol's rudimentary infirmary. Those who did shuffle out to their appointed tasks were often, and understandably, unenthusiastic about performing them. Māori, in particular, 'can seldom be trusted upon the road', Berrey found, presumably because of the increased opportunities for escaping, and he suggested they should be put to dressing flax and weaving mats instead.[62]

'The quantity of work performed by the men convicted of hard labour has not been more than equal to half the number of days they have been employed,' the superintendent complained in 1843, and he recommended introducing 'some coercive measure' to improve the output.[63] The sheriff had a range of such measures available to him, including the use of irons, the bread-and-water punishment diet, solitary confinement for up to

14 days at a time, or some combination of these.⁶⁴ Berrey acknowledged that these penalties might not be sufficient to control his worst troublemakers, especially as he could not prevent other prisoners from supplementing the bread-and-water diet of men under discipline. He proposed adding a new refinement to the punishment regime, borrowed from British gaols — a heavy treadmill on which prisoners would be required to trudge for a fixed number of hours each day. As a bonus, he said, the treadmill could also grind corn for the prisoners' meals, saving almost £3 a week on the food bill. At that rate, he estimated, the human-powered mill would pay for itself in eight months.⁶⁵

This ingenious plan was not approved, and instead the sheriff was provided with two secure solitary cells beneath the courthouse. They were known as dark cells, suggesting that they had no windows or other light source. For as long as the town had no other facility for treating the severely mentally ill, these patients were also routinely held in gaol even when not charged with any crime. In 1849 William Yates, a 40-year-old 'free person', was held there 'that he might have the benefit of attendance of the Colonial Surgeon'.⁶⁶

I I I

As the thrusting little capital expanded in size and sophistication, its gaol sluggishly followed suit to eventually include a room for measuring, searching and recording new arrivals; a surgery; bedrooms for the turnkey and hard-labour overseer; and a house for the head gaoler. The prison yard was overlooked by a watch-house for the town's police force, which also provided armed guards when required. A number of doves were housed on the premises, perhaps because their gentle cooing soothed the prisoners, 'who found in feeding the birds a relief to the monotony of their existence'.⁶⁷

More raucous barnyard noises came from the pound in a corner of the prison yard, a vital facility in a town whose properties were rarely fenced and where dogs, cattle, horses, goats and pigs roamed the streets at all times. Unclaimed animals were sold at auction, and 'if a dog was not claimed within a day and a night it was killed'.⁶⁸ Unclaimed goats, however, were released on Rangitoto Island, where they thrived and multiplied in the scrub-covered gullies.⁶⁹

Sheriff Berrey frequently pressed the Colonial Secretary for further funds to improve his facilities, but there was little anyone could do to ameliorate the unhealthy conditions, given the gaol's location in a damp valley floor, beside a stream whose waters had deteriorated to become an open sewer named the Ligar Canal. Diarrhoea and dysentery featured constantly among the complaints on the list of prisoners too ill to go out to work.[70]

When, in 1844, Governor FitzRoy asked his Colonial Surgeon to account for the constant sickness among the prison population, Dr Johnson ascribed the fault equally to the state of the prison population and to its site, compounded by 'crowded and ill-ventilated cells and irregular food'. Some prisoners, he said, were 'men of dissolute habits and enfeebled constitutions, most of them convicts from the other colonies whose sentence had expired'. These already debilitated men were further weakened, he acknowledged, by heavy labour in the cold, wet Auckland winter, and by their confinement in a gaol 'on a swamp which although drained must certainly create damp in the buildings — also that the water at one time was unwholesome being impregnated with decayed vegetable matter, but it has been improved by sinking the well deeper . . . without doubt the various diseases have been prolonged from want of a proper hospital room and nurse.' FitzRoy declared himself satisfied with these explanations, and appeared to feel that no further action was necessary.[71]

The gaol's unhealthy surroundings were not noticeably improved after the walls of the polluted Ligar Canal collapsed and was rebuilt as a stone-lined and enclosed drain. This watercourse still ran through the gaol yard, directly behind its main cellblocks, reeking in warm weather and dank in winter, and periodically overflowing after heavy rain. In July 1845 a heavy flood carried away part of the fencing around the gaol. The Superintendent of Public Works directed the hard-labour men to replace the fences, but a few weeks later another winter flood caused more damage.[72]

By this time the outbreak of war in the north had filled Auckland's streets with troops, and with refugees from Kororāreka who often spent their time 'hanging about the town and getting drunk'.[73] To accommodate further detachments of British troops sent out from Australia, the Albert Barracks was constructed on the hill above the gaol. A senior officer observed that of the 67 Māori who laid the stonework for its walls, all but one were both literate and sober.[74] His own men were less reliable, and gaol records show that troops served terms of hard labour for offences such as 'indecently exposing their person in a public highway with intent to insult a female'.[75] In October 1847 the gaol held 21 soldiers serving hard-labour sentences, many of them, according to Berrey, 'very desperate characters'. He pleaded to be able to transfer his military prisoners to the more secure Albert Barracks, and this request was eventually approved.[76]

Prison authorities made intermittent and tentative efforts to recognise the distinctive customs of Māori prisoners. For two years, between 1844 and 1846, Māori were exempted from imprisonment for debt on the grounds that their ignorance of the law meant they could not 'justly or safely be subjected to the more severe penalties thereof'.[77] When 'Temenia', a Ngāti Whātua man of some rank, was sentenced to three months with hard labour for stealing a cap from a general store, he was allowed to remain in the dock while his friends approached to hongi and cry over him. They took advantage of this opportunity to spirit him out of the courtroom before Berrey and his constables could do anything to prevent it. Armed troops from the barracks immediately launched a vigorous but ineffective search, and a few days later Temenia handed himself in. The incompetence of the military and the probity of the chiefly offender provided proof, said an Auckland newspaper, 'that the inhabitants of this colony would be much safer under the actual protection of the natives as formerly [i.e. before the signing of the Treaty of Waitangi], than under the present nominal Government of England'.[78]

In 1848 a prisoner named Ruaki was given six months with hard labour for stealing one of a pair of boots, his Pākehā accomplice stealing the other. After four months in gaol, Ruaki was gravely ill with dysentery and tuberculosis. 'He appears to pine away under confinement and unless a change takes place I have no hesitation in asserting that his life is in danger,' said Dr Johnson. Sheriff Berrey petitioned the governor to discharge this offender so that he could be cared for by his own people; Ruaki's conduct had always been 'unexceptionally good', he wrote, and Governor George Grey agreed to the request.[79]

Some years later another Māori prisoner was also discharged early because of illness. Te Waere was gaoled for assault, although he had been declared insane some months earlier by two Auckland surgeons. Berrey pointed out that the town's newly opened Hospital for the Insane was full but that Te Waere's relatives were anxious to take him back to Rotorua where he could remain in their care. Again the governor agreed to a pardon, observing that the case had 'caused some excitement among the natives'.[80]

In both these latter cases, it was to the advantage of the gaol staff to have the problematic prisoners removed from their care. In other circumstances where prisoners faced unjust or inhumane conditions, they had few means to complain of them or to apply for remedy. In 1846 the first 'Ordinance for the Regulation of Prisons' was enacted, authorising the appointment of Justices of the Peace to visit each gaol at least monthly to validate the punishments imposed within them, to hear complaints of unjust treatment from prisoners, and to send quarterly reports to the governor.[81] Few such appointments seem to have been made in Auckland for the lifetime of the gaol, although grounds for complaint by the prisoners were not lacking.

For some months in 1848 the gaol held a woman whose adult life had been marked by degradation and misery. Irish-born Margaret Reardon lived with a former naval carpenter named Joseph Burns, and the couple and their two small children led a destitute and marginal existence marked by heavy drinking and violence. Local Māori felt sufficiently sorry for Reardon that they offered to help her plant a potato crop if she left Burns.[82] In late 1847 Burns, familiar with naval routines, robbed a naval lieutenant named Snow of his pay. In the hope of throwing suspicion of the crime on Māori, Burns killed Snow and his family, mutilated their bodies and burned down their house on Auckland's North Shore.[83] Reardon fled from the shack where they had been living, taking their children with her, but Burns found her and attempted to cut her throat with a razor.[84] Under further duress from her husband, she gave evidence in court that implicated a friend for his crimes. However, she later recanted, and her revised evidence saw Burns executed. In a theatrical demonstration of judicial retribution, the hanging was carried out on the site of his murders, before a crowd who had sailed across the harbour for the occasion in a flotilla of small vessels.

Four months later Reardon, whom newspapers referred to as Burns' 'miserable concubine', was tried for perjury. She had no lawyer to defend her, and was found guilty and sentenced to transportation for seven years. She begged to be imprisoned in Auckland instead, even for an indefinite term, so that she could remain near her children. Chief Justice William Martin was unmoved, proclaiming that her earlier attempt to implicate others in the murders showed a 'frightful degree of depravity'.[85] Margaret Reardon was shipped to Van Diemen's Land with seven other convicts in October 1848, the only woman to receive a sentence of transportation from New Zealand.[86]

III

By 1849 two rooms in the original Auckland Gaol cellblock had been converted into hospital rooms, one for regular patients and the other for the insane. The quality of care given to those patients was dependent largely on the other inmates selected to provide it. In February 1849 the post of 'cook and nurse tender' in the hospital was held by a court-martialled soldier of the 58th Regiment named Edward Sayers. Three months later his commanding officer, Lieutenant-Colonel Wynyard, complained that Sayers was being indulged with special privileges such as tea and sugar, and was generally treated with 'such leniency as amounts to an encouragement for crime'.

Inquiries revealed a very different story. The Colonial Surgeon reported that Sayers was 'the most attentive man to his duties (which are extremely arduous) of any who has had the like to perform', and explained that he had ordered Sayers to be given the tea and sugar 'as medical comforts, deeming it necessary for his health whilst engaged in such severe duties'. Gaoler McElwain believed that the job of cook and nurse tender in the hospital was 'the most severe duty to which any prisoner sentenced to hard labour could be put to' and that 'not a man in the gaol would do the duties that Sayers does'. Some idea of those duties was provided by McElwain's turnkey. Sayers, he said, 'is continually obliged to get out of his bed at night to attend the sick' and 'is very often up all night'. Furthermore, he had to clean the hospital thoroughly every day, a duty made particularly unpleasant by an insane patient 'who is constantly dirtying the floors by relieving himself in the room'. Wynyard apparently declined to pursue the matter further.[87]

Conditions for female prisoners in the gaol improved very slightly with the addition of two women's cells, excavated from a cellar space on the south side of the courthouse. They were tiny, very dark and poorly ventilated, with a ceiling height of less than 2 metres, yet by 1851 they were required to hold as many as three female prisoners at a time. These might include women breastfeeding their children, or 'in daily expectation of confinement' (confinement in this case meaning giving birth).[88] Those using the courthouse complained strongly of the noxious odours rising through the floor from the bodily wastes of the inmates housed beneath it. Chief Justice Sir George Arney said that after Supreme Court sittings there he experienced 'lassitude, vertigo, and a total prostration of bodily and mental vigour', so the effect on those held in the cells themselves must have been far worse.[89] The gaol still employed no matron or female attendant, and provided no separate area for women patients in its hospital cells.

Sheriff Berrey struggled vainly to defend such facilities and his administration of them. The subterranean women's cells had been built, he said, to hold 'a particular class of prisoners, namely drunken women with short sentences', yet they were now occupied by women serving up to two years for crimes such as theft. The sheriff's greatest concern was that 'contact with male prisoners cannot be prevented', since the fence surrounding the female cells was no longer adequate for its purpose.[90] The truth, however, was that the entire gaol was a dilapidated facility and entirely unfit for its function. Its low-lying position alongside a drain choked with sewage and other wastes, and the constant overcrowding that saw criminals and lunatics packed together in cramped, shared cells created severe health risks, especially for those serving the longest sentences.[91] During 1852 the annual inmate total reached almost 400, and in November of that year alone Berrey had 39 prisoners under his care. Although each of them was nominally entitled to two blankets, he had only 53 blankets to issue in total.[92]

These conditions were seen as a disgrace in a town now making self-conscious claims to respectability. In an 1853 editorial on 'that inhuman kennel the Queen-street Gaol', the *Daily Southern Cross* spared its readers no unpleasant detail of 'the barbarous and perilous manner in which criminals and lunatics still continue to be packed within its narrow and fetid cells', including the appalling odours released when the turnkey opened up those cells each morning. 'In its very best condition, [the gaol] was but a confined and ill-contrived wooden structure. In its present, it is a rotten and ruinous hovel, overrun with rats, and only fit to be used as a place of torture.'

The article was a bitter corrective for those pious colonists who liked to think their young country had learned from the evils of England's workhouses and prisons. Conditions in Auckland's gaol compared dismally, claimed the newspaper, with those in England or even with the notoriously brutal Port Arthur penal settlement in Van Diemen's Land: 'We have received communications describing the state of the Auckland Gaol as absolutely revolting to humanity . . . One important measure of relief may, we believe, be easily and immediately afforded, and that is by removal of the insane to the Asylum provided by public benevolence for their reception.'[93]

Auckland's long-promised Hospital for the Insane, within the grounds of the general hospital in Auckland Domain, had just been completed, and was presumably in a position to relieve the gaol of some of its most troublesome inmates. The criminal and violent mentally ill, however, were still held in the gaol 'during Her Majesty's pleasure' (that is, indefinitely), rather than in the hospital. Justice Arney reported that one of these unfortunate men made a useful contribution to gaol hygiene, since he 'indulges his propensity to sweep away or gather up every particle of incumbrance [sic] from the ground of the airing yard or the flooring of the rooms'.[94]

III

Later in 1853 one of the most significant developments in penal policy to that date contrived to add a much greater burden to the already overloaded gaol facilities. Ever since William Pickering stumbled down Queen Street in irons in 1843, the practice of transportation had enabled the colony to decant its most troublesome and longest-serving convicts offshore. New Zealand preserved this useful outlet for disposing of its least desirable citizens even as it firmly refused to accept the transported convicts of the mother country. The Parkhurst boys who arrived in 1842–43 were a deeply regretted and sole exception to this, one of the colony's central principles. In 1845, and periodically thereafter, the British government asked New Zealand, as well as Australia, to accept shipments of convicts under the ticket-of-leave system. These were prisoners who, after long periods of hard labour in Britain, were released to the colonies under strict conditions specifying where they could live and work. New Zealanders objected strongly to this request. The paroled convicts could not be controlled, let alone reformed, in New Zealand, they cried, but instead would escape into the trackless bush. Governor Grey was especially opposed to receiving Irish political prisoners who, he thought, would have 'an irresistible temptation' to make their way to remote Māori communities and cohabit with their women.[95]

The idiosyncratic Grey also noted the hypocrisy of 'sending our convicts from our own shores to those of another colony, at the expense of Great Britain, protesting at the same time against the felons of other countries being sent here'. He suggested that if New Zealand retained its most serious offenders within its own penal institutions, the colony would have much stronger grounds for refusing to accept hardened criminals from Britain and Ireland.[96] However, transportation to Van Diemen's Land was a politically popular option, and the courts continued to impose this sentence for some years in the face of the Colonial Office's rising indignation.

Men were transported for years for nothing more serious than stealing small articles of clothing. The theft of farm animals was treated more harshly still, and in 1849 Justice Martin gave a total of 35 years' transportation to an Auckland butcher for what he called 'great and mischievous' crimes — the theft of four cattle.[97] A man could even be transported 'for the term of his natural life' — a sentence imposed on a 20-year-old corporal of the 58th Regiment for killing another soldier in the Auckland barracks. Another convict, Jeremiah Cooper, described in the court report as 'a man of colour', was sentenced to transportation for life for the attempted murder of Captain Abner Tucker in the Bay of Islands.

Auckland Gaol often held convicts from other parts of the country, since an affordable berth to Van Diemen's Land was more likely to be chartered in Auckland than in any other port. These convicts were thus separated from their friends and families during the grim weeks and months while they waited for their departure, with little to do but contemplate their fate. In that time they received harsher treatment than other inmates. They were not permitted to work outside the gaol with the hard-labour men for fear they might escape, and in the earliest years were not even permitted to exercise in the yard.

This state of tedium and torment proved the undoing of a young Nelson man, the father of three children, named Owen Connor. He was sentenced to transportation for 10 years for stealing a bullock for food, and sent up to Auckland for several months to await a vessel bound for Port Arthur. Just one day before his ship was due to embark, Governor FitzRoy issued him a pardon. It came too late, since Connor had by then lost his mind.

Although now technically a free man, Connor seemed likely to remain in gaol indefinitely.[98] He required the constant attention of a keeper, said

Sheriff Berrey, as it was not just unsafe to approach him 'but he keeps the prison and its neighbourhood in an uproar day and night'.[99] In May 1846, while he and his cell were being cleaned, Connor escaped by rushing around to the debtors' yard and leaping the fence. The gaoler quickly recaptured him, although 'at considerable risk to his life'. The medical attendant thought Connor 'permanently insane and of a most ferocious temper' and suggested 'some strong man [i.e. another inmate] to have the charge of him and to have authority to procure a straitjacket for him'.[100] Connor does not appear to have died in the gaol, but his eventual fate is unknown.

In 1850 the British government informed its high-minded South Pacific colony that transportations to Van Diemen's Land must cease from 1853. The colony's Attorney-General responded by drafting the Secondary Punishment Act, which replaced transportation with a new sentence of penal servitude, meaning imprisonment within New Zealand while 'employed on the roads or public works, or otherwise . . . kept to hard labour'.[101] The recommended terms for this new sentence were longer than the conventional hard-labour sentences already handed out for regular felons, although somewhat shorter than the terms they replaced. Transportation for up to 10 years, for example, was replaced by penal servitude for four to six years. In both cases, however, a life sentence meant nothing less than that (unless commuted by exercise of the royal prerogative of mercy, i.e. by order of the sovereign's representative, the Governor-General).

The Secondary Punishment Act would ensure that New Zealand's penal policy for its serious offenders finally conformed to Britain's stipulations. However, the Act would also require the size and security of existing prison facilities to be greatly expanded to enable them to manage these long-serving, escape-prone prisoners. The country's prisons, including Auckland Gaol, were at that time under the control of their various provincial governments, which baulked at the expense of such remedial work. The Act was therefore deferred until 1855 to give the provinces time to carry out the vital upgrading.

In the interim, New Zealand judges handed out the dreaded sentence of transportation more freely than ever. The convicts thus sentenced were not subsequently transported, but held in gaol awaiting transfer to the planned new facilities where they would serve out their replacement sentences of penal servitude.¹⁰² In June 1854, a Māori named Taraiwaru was given seven years' transportation for theft, one of the last convicts to receive this sentence from a New Zealand civil court. Three months later the practice of transportation 'beyond the seas' was formally ended by the implementation of the Secondary Punishment Act.

Taraiwaru did not survive for long after his sentencing, dying after just a few months in Auckland's gaol. He had been a 'strong, hale man' when he entered the gaol, and a year later Māori in his district of Hauraki continued to feel troubled at the circumstances of his death.¹⁰³

The passing of the Secondary Punishment Act had a further outcome, equally problematic for the overcrowded, understaffed and poorly equipped Auckland Gaol. It immediately became apparent that the long-established practice of sending hard-labour prisoners outside the gaol to carry out useful public works was not legal, since the power to order this activity was held by central government, while the gaols themselves had passed under the authority of provincial governments. For the next two years, until new legislation authorised the outside projects, the hard-labour men remained within the gaol at all times and spent their working hours crushing rocks in the stoneyard.¹⁰⁴ The gaol's annual returns record this dramatic transformation in the daily routine. During 1852 a total of 303 men worked at hard labour outside the prison's walls. Two years later none did.¹⁰⁵ Instead they milled around inside the yards, seeking to avoid the overseer's eye and speculating about what they could expect from the new prison under construction on the southern fringe of the town.

III

Although not much more than 10 years old, the gaol was clearly beyond hope of renovation, and both its inmates and staff longed for the day when it was vacated. Until then, its decrepit state made escapes easy and tempting. Breaking through the perimeter fence was as simple as pulling away the boards, since in places the uprights were 'too rotten to hold a nail'.¹⁰⁶ Men broke out knowing that recapture, followed by solitary confinement and bread and water, was almost inevitable.

On a Sunday morning in the spring of 1855 the exercise yard held more than 70 prisoners, including 13 convicts who would formerly have been transported and who had 'the highest pre-eminence in crime'. A remand prisoner named Wilson was awaiting trial for larceny and was permitted to work at his trade while in gaol in order to support his family. He could also receive meals from the outside. On this Sunday his wife arrived as usual with his breakfast. As the assistant turnkey opened the gate to the exercise yard to receive the steaming plate, Wilson and four other inmates rushed through it. The unfortunate turnkey, 'a steady, sober man', was forced to remain at his post to ensure that none of the other prisoners followed them. The police were called out immediately and by the end of the day four of the men had been recaptured, but the fifth, John Noble, was still at large a month later.[107]

In his report on the incident, Sheriff O'Brien attempted to describe the near-impossibility of maintaining security in the period after transportation. 'I labor [sic] under disadvantages which my predecessor did not; with an increased Gaol establishment and criminals of a deeper dye to watch over, every vigilance should be used.'[108] It must have been a considerable relief when, in 1856, the first of the penal servitude and hard-labour men were transferred to a brand-new prison. Yet it strains credulity to note that the huddle of decaying wooden structures in Queen Street remained in constant use for a further 10 years, congregating the town's drunks, prostitutes, petty thieves, vagrants, lunatics, debtors and children together, as many as 14 to a cell.

Auckland's coroner revealed that the Queen Street Gaol inmates 'are in danger of their lives by night for the buildings being of wood, in the event of a fire breaking out many of them would be roasted alive before the jails and cells could be entered and the inmates rescued'.[109] A few years later the prison doctor suggested that a conflagration would be welcome if it could be confined to the gaol alone, since '[i]ts total destruction would be of greatest service'. Another doctor stated that it was 'disgraceful to put people there, particularly poor debtors . . . being built beside a large open sewer, they must suffer from malaria'.[110] Perhaps the most damning account of all came from Chief Justice Sir George Arney, who made a visit of inspection to 'the revolting place with its foul odour and its promiscuous intermixture of men and women. Every kind of sexual activity from rape to sodomy punctuate the night-time lockup [and] for want of available facilities prisoners had to urinate and defecate on the cell floor.'[111]

The inmates at this time may have included four boys serving two months with hard labour for stealing from a house in Official Bay. The youngest was only eight, and in the dock his head barely showed above the railing. The magistrate noted with regret that when boys of this age went to gaol, they 'came out worse than they went in, in consequence of the impossibility of keeping them separated' from the older prisoners.[112]

The austere and precise Justice Arney went so far as to measure the gaol cells to ensure that his excoriations were soundly based. The two female cells beneath the Supreme Court, he discovered, each measured '11 feet 9 inches by 5 feet 2 inches, and are six feet from floor to ceiling'. Three or four women were sometimes confined in this space, leading Arney to conclude that 'they must be packed almost as merchants pack herrings, lengthwise'. His persistence ultimately saw a matron, 'a highly respectable woman', appointed to take charge of the female inmates, but she could do little to improve the living conditions of those women whose cell overlooked the 'filthy ditch' running through the yard, choked with the refuse of the gaol's privies and 'the accumulated offal and sewage of the surrounding neighbourhood . . . As many as six and eight have at times slept therein at night, with a child or two, as it may happen, at the breast.'[113]

Many of the cells leaked in rainy weather, yet when one desperate debtor cut a small hole in the floor to drain off the foul water that had accumulated in his cell, he was severely punished and forced to sleep out in the passage where, Justice Arney said, quoting an imprisoned debtor, 'four men are nightly packed like swine'.[114] Why the Provincial Council continued to tolerate such conditions in a town whose wealth and population were rapidly increasing was a subject of mystery and speculation, but Justice Arney himself suggested that the Council hoped to purchase the gaol site and in the meantime was unwilling to carry out any improvements that might increase the value of the land. 'Nor will the plea of economy hold good, since they have expressed themselves willing to spend from £10,000 to £20,000 on a new Supreme Court.'[115]

This civic abomination continued to serve as the site of Auckland's public executions. On four occasions during the 1850s a condemned man was marched to a gallows erected outside its gates, and from the scaffold, above the bayonets of the armed guard arrayed in front of him, looked out at the crowd of spectators assembled to see what the *New Zealand Herald* called 'the extreme penalty of the law' carried into effect.[116] The last of these men, John Killey, was executed in 1858, and public hangings were abolished later that year.

On a night in December 1863 a summer storm sent a flood of water a metre deep through the cells. 'By 11 o'clock the water rose so high that men of 6 ft stature made their way to the safety of the guardhouse with difficulty, while persons of minor inches had to swim for it. A child of four years of age had a very narrow escape, it being extremely difficult to rescue him in the dark.'[117] This incident prompted yet another crusading editor to flex his pen and deploy his choicest adjectives against this ongoing affront to public decency: 'Under its pestilential roof the Court undergoes some of the sufferings of the Black Hole of Calcutta. When is this filthy and feculent [i.e. stinking] hovel, a disgrace to the finest street of the finest city of New Zealand, likely to be removed?'[118]

The answer, it transpired, was almost two wretched years later, in November 1865, when the last prisoners were moved to the new prison.[119] The following year local businessmen arranged to use the yard of the abandoned gaol for a temporary market, but before the first stalls could be put in place a macabre excavation was required. The six men hanged outside the gaol had all been buried in its yard and only the body of the first of them, Maketu, had later been removed. 'Respect for public decency,' thought the *New Zealand Herald*, 'should prompt the removal of the graves and the disturbance of the remains which they enclosed.' Accordingly, in a strange precursor to the midnight exhumations of 125 years later, a group of men entered the gaol yard 'between twelve and one of yesterday morning', presumably a time chosen to spare the feelings of passersby. They disinterred the bodies and reburied them 'in a remote and unused spot in Symonds-street cemetery'.[120]

That late-night ceremony finally brought to a close one of the most shameful and reviled institutions of the town originally named for Governor Hobson's English patron, who held the title of Earl of Auckland. In a further tribute, Hobson gave the Earl's attractive family name to the truncated extinct volcano, with a conical crater at its heart, which overlooked the town's southern fringe. This gentle and accessible summit, the chosen location for the new prison, was named Mount Eden.

2:
Paste-board gaol
1855–1876

'The site best adapted for the erection of the proposed Stockade for hard labour men,' pronounced Auckland's provincial architect William Mason in 1855, 'is a portion of the Mount Eden reserve.'[1] His reasoning was not stated but can be assumed to include the large scoria deposits lying just beneath its surface. By climbing to the modest summit, Mason could observe that Mount Eden is penetrated to a surprising depth by a steep-sided and remarkably regular inverted cone created by an ancient eruption, lava from which eventually cooled and solidified into brittle yet intractable scoria basalt.

Over millennia, earth and foliage built up on the rock until, by the mid-sixteenth century, the land was fertile enough to support a community of some two thousand people, a section of the Waiohua confederation of tribes. They named the peak Maungawhau for the dominant tree species that grew there. The Waiohua were displaced in the mid-eighteenth century by invading Ngāti Whātua, who were themselves ousted in the following century by musket-bearing warriors from further north. The small and shapely mountain lay abandoned, its rich gardens overgrown by regenerating mānuka and bracken, when the British arrived to build their new capital in 1840.[2]

After renaming this prominent landmark for a British naval lord, the government soon auctioned off much of the land surrounding the summit to settlers and speculators. Once cleared of scrub, its pure volcanic soil produced vigorous pasture, and crops of grain and European vegetables. An area on the northwest face of the lower slopes was withheld from sale as a site for future public facilities, and Mason's 1855 report convinced the central government to allocate this land for a 'permanent gaol reserve'.

The driving reason for Mason's instructions to locate a site for a new and more secure prison on Auckland's fast-expanding periphery was the abolition of the sentence of transportation. The 1854 Secondary Punishment Act provided substitute sentences for the most serious crimes but also highlighted the insecurity and general inadequacy of the colony's early gaols, including the eyesore in Auckland's Queen Street. For a decade after its inadequacies became a public scandal the gaol survived as a blight on the town, since most of its inmates served comparatively short sentences and were not serious and dangerous offenders. However, the abolition of transportation meant that the most hardened and desperate individuals in the colony must thereafter be held under the same roof

In its earliest years, the Stockade stood in isolation from the town of Auckland behind its low and rickety wooden wall. The small building to the right may be a guardhouse. AUCKLAND LIBRARIES HERITAGE COLLECTIONS, 4-1214

for years on end. The location and impregnability of that roof suddenly became a matter of urgent concern to Aucklanders.

The year before Mason recommended Mount Eden's suitability for a convict prison, a parliamentary committee delivered a report intended to determine the management of such prisons throughout the country. The committee's chair, Chief Justice Martin, set the tone with his introductory views. The main object of a judicial system, he intoned, was 'the repression of crime by the dread of punishment; the reformation of the convict is not the primary object, except . . . in the narrow sense of a discontinuance of criminal acts, produced by the motive of fear'.

Accordingly, said Martin, the most suitable regime for a convict prison would be a local version of Britain's 'separate system', under which each prisoner was held in isolation and contacted only by prison staff, ministers of religion, and 'discreet and trustworthy visitors of other classes'. This regime, he noted approvingly, was 'greatly dreaded by criminals'.[3] It also effectively ruled out collective labour of the type carried out by the work gangs of the Queen Street gaol.

Others consulted for the report saw the situation somewhat differently. Lord Grey, Britain's Secretary of State, from his panoptic view of the penal systems in various British colonies, came down firmly in favour of 'hard labour on public works', so long as the convicts thus engaged were separated from each other overnight.[4] This model held more appeal to both the central and Auckland provincial governments, since convict labour might recover much of the cost of building and maintaining the new prison, and Lord Grey's pragmatic position prevailed.

Despite the legislative urgency for a convict prison, Auckland's Provincial Council squabbled and stalled over the project for much of 1855. The system of provincial government, instituted three years earlier in the hope of soothing ferocious regional rivalries, was thrown into disarray in Auckland by the sudden resignation in January 1855 of its superintendent, immersing the council in 'party strife and bitterness'.[5] Nevertheless, £1500 was voted in April 1855 to build a 'Stockade for Hard Labour men', an amount soon increased to almost £2000.[6] Construction began on the prison in late 1855, and a further £1000 was voted early in the following year to finish it.[7]

The resulting building, invariably known as the Stockade, proved unworthy of its commanding site. It was a gaunt and unsightly barracks-like structure of two low-ceilinged storeys — a slightly grander version of the disreputable gaol it was intended to replace. Like the gaol, it was constructed entirely of wood, including the shingled roof, so its inmates were permanently at risk from an outbreak of fire. Each floor was divided into 12 individual cells about the size of a present-day car-parking space. The lower floor provided a convicts' messroom and officers' kitchen, with a five-man dormitory for the guards on the floor above. This flimsy and provisional-looking structure was completed in July 1856, and 16 of the toughest penal-servitude men from the Queen Street gaol, including three lifers, were transferred there in September.[8]

It was apparent almost immediately that the new building, although planned to house long-serving criminals, could not deliver them even a barely adequate supply of fresh air. Each cell was ventilated by a small grating in the outside wall and another above the door, barred with iron rods about 12 millimetres in diameter. The gratings on the upper floor were further impeded since they were overhung by the roofline. The convict yearning to breathe free of the odours from his brimming chamberpot could find further ventilation only through the corridor outside his cell, and since this was barred at intervals by open ironwork gates, the cell doors could potentially be left open without compromising security. In practice, the foul air emanating from the cells was so offensive to the guards sleeping in the upstairs dormitory that they preferred to keep all cell doors locked overnight.[9]

A further hazard to health was created by the primitive water supply. Mount Eden had few springs or streams, and the prison's first water supply came from casks for rainwater and a small well situated outside its walls, to which the prisoners walked carrying buckets. At times one in every 20 prisoners was engaged all day in this tedious, essential routine.[10] Twenty years after it opened, the prison could provide its inmates with only a single cold-water bath.

The physical feature that came to be most closely and derisively associated with the Stockade was its wooden boundary fence, little more than two metres high and of such crude construction that it repeatedly blew down in strong winds. In October 1856 the fence was reported to be 'kept up by the assistance of the prisoners' themselves.'[11] This feeble

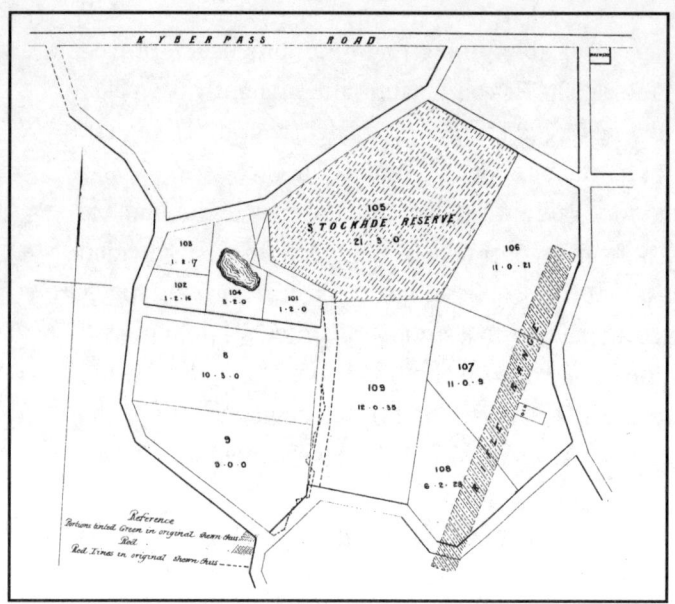

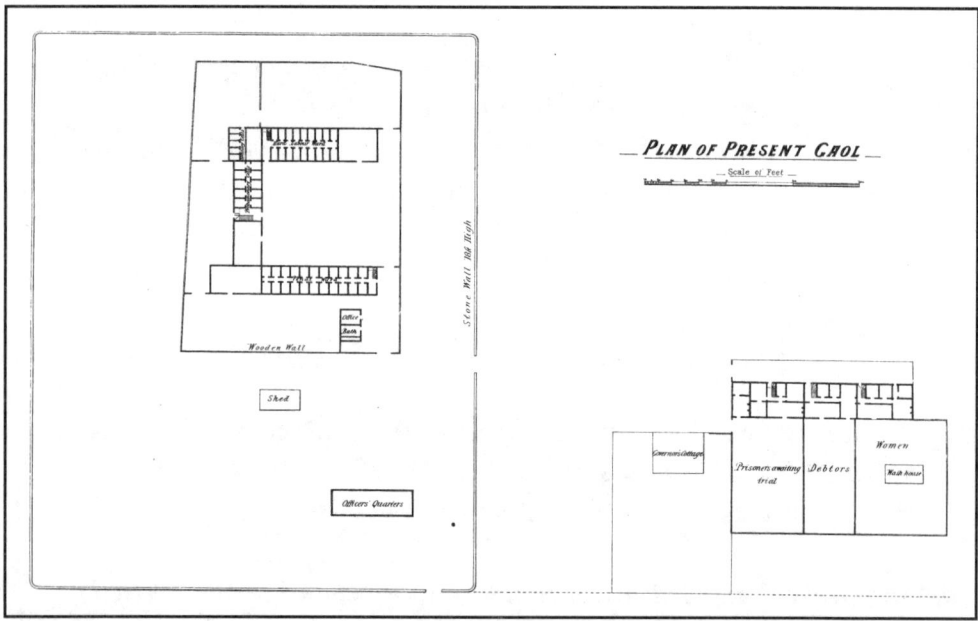

Above: The land on which the Stockade stood, reserved in 1840 for military and penal purposes, is shown on this 1877 plan hemmed in by streets and adjacent land blocks. Mount Eden's cratered summit lies to the west of the reserve.

Below: Twenty years after it opened, the Stockade had grown to encompass three cellblocks inside the perimeter wall and a separate block for remand, debtor and women prisoners outside it. *PAPERS PAST, AJHR, 1877, H-30*

barrier was defended as 'a very temporary constraint on the prison inmates' that would be replaced as soon as those very inmates 'should have constructed a stone wall in lieu of it'.[12] Like many such interim measures, it remained in place in some form for more than a decade and, in spite of the vigilance of armed guards, afforded irresistible opportunities for escape. The first of these took place just three months after the earliest prisoners were admitted. Two of them, Owen McCabe and Patrick Lang, fled southward, pursued by armed and mounted police. They managed to reach Waikato and found employment at Maungatautari, south of present-day Cambridge, before their recapture after two weeks.[13]

In 1858 a second building was erected parallel to the first and some distance from it to house the hard-labour men from the Queen Street gaol, and the perimeter fence was extended to surround both structures. Externally, the hard-labour wing was almost identical to its neighbour but its upper floor was divided into six large shared cells. Here the prisoners slept in groups, supposedly of about six but later, as the prison became heavily overcrowded, of a dozen or even more. The ground floor was divided into 18 'one-man' cells (in practice, often holding three prisoners each), a messroom and kitchen, and a hospital and surgery. This floor had two punishment cells for men sentenced to solitary confinement, although eventually these cells were also used to hold the overflow of regular prisoners, and by 1864 seven men were occupying them. The total prison population by then numbered 136, in buildings designed for a maximum of about a hundred.[14]

Most of the hard-labour prisoners faced shorter sentences than those of the convicts, usually no more than two years, but otherwise there was little difference between their conditions, and when allowed outside the two groups were not separated in any way. The daily routine for both revolved around physical labour on the slopes behind the prison — exposing the stubborn basalt found two metres under the earth, dynamiting and breaking it in movable boulders, and shaping the broken material in the stoneyard nearby. The men worked in this way from 7.30 in the morning until six at night in the summer months, and from eight to five in winter, with an hour for lunch. As at the Queen Street gaol, their Saturday afternoons and Sundays were free time.[15]

Prison physicians insisted that to maintain the prisoners' health under a regime of such hard labour, their daily diet must be nutritious.[16] The prison's medical officer, Dr Philson, believed that '3/4 lb to 1 lb [340 to 450 grams] of animal food a day is necessary to maintain a labouring man in a fit state for work'.[17] The Provincial Council calculated the cost of such a diet against the income it might receive from prison labour, estimated the potential added expense of treating men who fell ill from under-feeding, and approved the recommended changes.

The work of quarrying and stone-breaking was as demanding as the most punitive politicians could wish, since Mount Eden's scoria proved exceptionally dense, heavy and difficult to handle. It required considerable skill to cut up the rock using a hammer, cold chisel or special axe, and to shape it into blocks for uses such as the wall surrounding the Albert Barracks, a remnant of which can still be seen in the grounds of Auckland University. The less skilled prisoners crushed the leftover rubble into road metal.

This onerous work persisted at Mount Eden for almost a century, as the rock faces surrounding the crater's northern slope were progressively exposed and mined, and in time the road running up the mountain itself became known as Prisoner's Hill. Quarrying is a dangerous activity, particularly when carried out by inexperienced labour under duress, and accidents were frequent and sometimes fatal. William Neill, a military prisoner, was killed in 1861 when a boulder weighing several tons fell from the quarry face and 'crushed him in a dreadful manner'.[18]

While the large majority of the Stockade's inmates were always employed in the quarry and stoneyard, others were required to carry out routine tasks. One fortunate convict was employed to cook for the officers of the gaol and to keep their rooms clean, and others served as cooks and cleaners for their fellow prisoners.[19] Eventually several workshops were established to produce equipment and materials for the prison and the town's other public institutions, and skilled prisoners were employed at these as carpenters, shoemakers, tailors and blacksmiths.[20]

| | |

Sheriff Loughlin O'Brien, now in charge of both the Auckland Gaol and the Stockade, drew up comprehensive regulations for his new prison, placing heavy emphasis on tighter security. Prisoners were searched before and after each shift in the quarry and stoneyard, and marched to and from their workplaces in a double file and in strict silence, apart from the melancholy clanking of irons on men regarded as extreme escape risks. Each guard who accompanied them was armed with a musket and bayonet, and a pistol with 12 rounds of ammunition, and prisoners were required to keep at least 10 paces distant from their guards at all times. Anyone who attempted escape, or assisted in an escape, risked having further lengthy terms of hard labour added to their sentence.

To discourage escapes, the prisoners' outer clothing was marked 'MEG' for Mount Eden Gaol, and all but the shortest-sentenced men had their hair cropped close to the skull.[21] This uncomfortable and degrading monthly ritual was much resented by the prisoners. They were not provided with headgear at work, and found the summer sun on their exposed scalps a torment during their long hours in the quarry. In the final month of their sentence they were permitted to regrow their hair, although even this modest privilege was sometimes overruled by the guards.

O'Brien's regulations established a carefully calibrated system of rewards for good behaviour and demerits for offending. Each prisoner was placed in one of three classes, and promotion between them earned extra comforts or privileges. First-class prisoners were entitled to write letters every two months, and receive a visit on one Saturday a month. Outside their normal working hours these elite inmates were permitted to perform further work on their own behalf and keep the income from it. In the earliest years, this self-employment appeared to consist mainly of carving figures from bullock horn to sell to visitors.[22] These items, 'covered with portraits and designs . . . during many a weary hour's incarceration', were for some time popular among Aucklanders as home decorations, but the practice of making them was later banned 'as contrary to the policy of prison discipline, and calculated to militate against the deterrent effect of punishment for crime'.[23]

Breaches of prison regulations by first-class prisoners might be punished with a reduction in class and a loss of their earnings, while men in other classes might be subjected to 24 hours in solitary confinement and a reduction in rations. The most severe offences earned a month in solitary, a similar period in irons, a whipping, or some combination of these.[24]

Within a few years it became evident that O'Brien's regulations gave a misleading impression of the practices taking place within the Stockade's walls. At least a quarter of the inmates, and probably several of the guards, were illiterate and therefore unlikely to abide by rules they could not read. Most Māori prisoners were literate only in their own language, and no translation of the regulations was provided for them. Māori were further disadvantaged in that none of the guards could speak their language.[25]

In 1861 that indefatigable reformer Chief Justice Arney paid a visit of inspection to the Stockade as part of a wider inquiry into a nationwide system of prison management. His report was refreshingly frank and tinged with dry humour. 'The palisade wall rocks in the wind, but as the situation is sheltered, the erection will probably not be blown down at present . . . Imprisonment within its circuit endures so long as a prisoner lacks ordinary ingenuity to scale the palisades.'[26] He described one such attempt when

> a prisoner simply upset one of the hand carts used for carting stones, and resting the shafts against the palisade, he ran up them, reached from the cross-bar to the top of the paling and at once sat astride the prison walls. Thence he dropped easily on its outer face and disappeared from the gaze of two guards, who stared at an adventure which they were too bewildered to prevent, although they held, one, a loaded carbine, and the other, a six-chambered revolver.[27]

Before presiding over a trial at Auckland's Supreme Court, Justice Arney made a practice of first visiting the Stockade and then delivering a vivid account of his impressions to the jury who faced the solemn responsibility of dispatching an offender there, perhaps for years on end. Before the 1862 trial of two recent escapers from the Stockade he reminded the jurors, who were all male and drawn from the upper ranks of the city's business community: 'A wealthy constituency, in which one sees . . . thousands and hundreds of thousands of pounds accumulating in the banks, and every department of business manifesting the greatest prosperity, should provide better for the custody of its prisoners.'[28] A well-run prison, he insisted, should contribute to reducing crime through reforming and rehabilitating its inmates, and the government was acting unjustly in refusing to spend the sums available on that objective. In another caustic indictment two years later, he reminded jurors that the Stockade was 'part of a system to which alone you owe your prosperity: therefore, I say you

Chief Justice George Arney, photographed in the 1860s.
ALEXANDER TURNBULL LIBRARY, PA2-0918

have no right to hold merchant palaces in Queen-street save by the law ... And I say that a community which thus outrages the law and outrages the first principles of natural justice does not deserve to have the prosperity which awaits it.'[29]

Such condemnation from the highest tier of the legal system produced no evident improvement. As the decayed state of the Queen Street gaol convincingly demonstrated, upgrading penal establishments was not a politically popular use of public funds. Furthermore, Auckland and other North Island provinces were engulfed throughout the 1860s by the fiscal and human costs of war against a large element of their Māori population. By March 1862 gaoler George McElwain was so short of supplies that 23 prisoners were unable to work in the quarry because they lacked proper clothing and footwear.[30] The following month about half the entire prison population was said to be in this situation, 'their labour lost, because men could not be put to work half naked or shoeless'.[31]

The war economy posed multiple strains on the provincial government's finances. While it starved public amenities such as the prison of funds, it also added substantially to the costs of imprisonment. As troop numbers in the colony rose, more military prisoners were dispatched to the Stockade, and regular troops had to be added to the number of guards to control the prison population.[32]

Auckland's respectable citizens appeared to take a keen interest in their new prison only during occasions of great drama. They turned out in large numbers for the first execution there, in September 1863. The condemned man was a Queen Street butcher named Richard Harper, found guilty of murdering his wife with the primary tool of his trade. Under the newly introduced Execution of Criminals Act, public hangings were abolished and the sentence was required to be carried out inside the prison walls, with a strictly limited number of approved witnesses present.[33] The Act, however, did not take into account the Stockade's location, directly beneath Mount Eden's steep but accessible upper slopes.

From very early on the morning of 22 September, as Harper was led in irons from his cell, the slopes were crowded with onlookers. The scaffold was surrounded on three sides by a high screen, but the unofficial spectators had a clear view from above as Harper was led towards it by the hangman — a fellow prisoner who had agreed to perform this duty in return for a sum of money and a reduced sentence. To conceal his

THE EXECUTION OF HARPER.

At a quarter-past six o'clock yesterday morning, Richard Harper, butcher, aged thirty-three years, suffered the extreme penalty of the law at the Mount Eden Stockade. The crime for which he suffered was that of murdering his wife Jane Alice Harper, on the 16th of June last, in Edwardes-street, and as there may possibly be many of our readers unacquainted with the details of the tragedy, we avail ourselves of this opportunity of recapitulating the leading facts. For some time previous to the 16th June, Harper carried on business as a butcher in Queen-street, and his wife Jane Alice Harper lived separate from him. She had borne two children to him, the eldest being now about 18 months and the youngest an infant. He frequently visited her, and on the Sunday previous to her death he was with her some time at her lodgings. Before he came away they appeared to have quarrelled, and Mrs. Harper ran away from him into a neighbour's house, and there stated that he had exhibited a knife to her and threatened to kill her. On the succeeding Tuesday evening, the 16th June, he again called at the house, and expressed a wish to the landlady, Mrs. Baker, to see his wife. Mrs. Harper endeavoured to conceal herself from his view, but ultimately came and spoke to him at the back door, and afterwards put on her hat and cloak and passed into the yard with him. They remained standing conversing together for about ten minutes, when Harper stabbed her with a butcher's knife in the breast and back, and death must have been almost instantaneous. Harper afterwards assisted to

The execution of Richard Harper on 22 September 1863 was the first to take place at the Stockade. Although public hangings had been abolished, a large crowd of onlookers observed from the slopes of Mount Eden. *PAPERS PAST, DAILY SOUTHERN CROSS, 23 SEPTEMBER 1863*

identity his face and head were covered in black cloth, and a slouch hat was drawn down to his ears. He was, however, visible to other prisoners peering through the gratings of their cells, and they recognised him 'from some peculiarity in his gait . . . His appearance was the signal for a perfect Babel of yells, hooting, curses, and the most terrible threats of vengeance.'[34] Despite this unforeseen disruption, the hanging went ahead as planned.

Harper was apparently popular with his fellow prisoners; after his body was buried within the Stockade walls, they created a modest memorial on the gravesite, placing a border of upturned bottles around it, and planting geraniums and other flowers on the mound.[35] This small monument survived for at least a year before the head gaoler removed it, while admitting that the prisoners who had known Harper 'will not let the man's memory so easily die out'.[36] It seems likely that Harper's body was among those exhumed in 1989 and reburied at Whakatāne.

Hangings attended by lively crowds of onlookers became a regular feature of prison routine. A year after Harper was executed, two Māori were hanged together. One, a young chief named Ruarangi, said to possess 'a very intelligent countenance', was convicted of the murder of a woman and her daughter in Kaipara, a crime he denied until his final breath. The other, named Okeroa, had been sentenced for a killing in the Bay of Islands, although he was described in the *New Zealand Herald* as 'evidently idiotic and has indeed been known to be so for this ten years past'.[37] Okeroa's trial was delayed while his fitness to plead was considered.[38]

After the judge decided the case could proceed, a petition signed 'by a very respectable portion of the citizens' asked the governor to exercise clemency.[39] No reprieve was granted, and both men were led out to the scaffold early on an April morning in 1864, observed by a dozen official spectators within the prison walls and about three hundred others outside them. Again the hangman was concealed beneath a black veil. Okeroa's body was buried within the prison walls, but Ruarangi's body was given to his relatives for burial in his home territory. This privilege was not always granted when Europeans were executed, causing some observers to question whether 'there are to be two laws — one for the Maori, and another for the European'.[40]

This double hanging had a bizarre sequel. On the evening of the execution, a man named John Thomas accosted a well-known Ngāti

Whātua leader, Paora Tuhaere, in central Auckland. Several times Tuhaere ordered the man to leave him alone, and finally Thomas threatened, 'I'll hang you by the neck.' He was charged with assault, and at his trial was revealed to be the Stockade's recent hangman. He had been immediately released from prison as a reward for dispatching his two fellow inmates, but his unseemly behaviour saw him swiftly returned there to serve a further sentence.[41]

III

These periodic spectacles aside, the prison's regular routines had become settled and productive. The cobblers' workshops made boots not only for prisoners but also for sale, at a third the regular price, to inmates of the provincial lunatic asylum and hospital. The work of stone-breaking was made more efficient by a steam-powered engine that kept seven horse-drawn carts busy removing the crushed metal.[42] The *New Zealand Herald*, in a complaint that is regularly echoed to the present day, was outraged at 'how plump and happy these jail-birds are . . . The Province feeds and clothes these men well; why should not the Province have some real return from them in the shape of profitable labour?'[43]

Such musings gained force in 1864, by which time the prison's initial population had doubled. The Stockade's governor, Flynn, and his head gaoler, Joseph Tuckwell, had a more practical understanding than the *Herald* of the realities of imposing forced labour, and they employed a system of financial incentives. Prisoners who met a daily quota qualified for a payment, known as exertion money, calculated at a third of the amount they would have received for the same work outside the prison walls. 'The money thus earned may be appropriated to the purchase of extra clothing under the control of the authorities, and the balance will be handed to the men at the expiration of their terms of imprisonment.'[44] In certain cases hard work and good behaviour could also bring remission of part of a prisoner's sentence. This incentive scheme was understandably popular among the inmates and was extended to those who carried out the routine maintenance work of the prison itself — the office clerk, cooks, barber, hospital nurse, cleaners, woodcutters, water-carriers (always a numerous category) and, when a suitable candidate could be found, the schoolmaster.[45]

By the mid-1860s the financial returns from prison labour regularly exceeded the modest sums spent on the prisoners who performed it.[46] Yet the Provincial Council's tightfistedness with regard to its prison remained apparent in the miserable conditions and wages of the warders, and in the inadequate facilities for prisoners. To prevent outbreaks of disease the cells were kept scrupulously clean, with whitewashed walls and well-scrubbed floors, yet they remained stubbornly infested with various vermin. In 1865 prisoners were reported to be 'busily engaged in whitewashing and "puddling" — putting lime into the gaps between the boards to discourage the bugs'.[47]

Nothing effective was done about the site's lack of fresh water and its poor sanitation facilities. Apart from the chamberpot in each cell, the prison's only toilets were crude and inadequately screened pits out in the exercise yards. Although iron tanks had been installed to catch rainwater, the main water supply for all inmates was a single pump in the main exercise yard, unwisely sited near the main latrine and the site where executed criminals were said to be buried. Visitors reported that 'the olfactory senses are annoyed with a stench' from both the latrine and an open drain carrying the prison's wastewater out to the garden at the rear of the buildings.[48]

The Stockade was never seriously regarded as a place for reformation of its inmates, but it also failed to meet the fundamental requirement to securely contain long-sentenced penal servitude prisoners. By early 1865, 34 convicts and 137 hard-labour prisoners were being held in 'a pasteboard [i.e. cardboard] gaol . . . nothing better than a wooden box, and in many respects a very ricketty one'.[49] The 'wooden apology for a wall' that surrounded the two cellblocks was reinforced at intervals with props on both sides. These sloped from the ground to about a third of the wall's height, affording excellent purchase for a leap over the top.[50] Twenty-six escapes were recorded between 1856 and 1864, and one persistent bolter, Richard Dumfrey, carried out at least five of them, on the last occasions wearing heavy irons intended to prevent him doing so.[51] Most escapers were swiftly recaptured, but of more than 20 in 1865 alone, 12 remained at large by the end of that year.[52]

To deal with one of the most desperate and incorrigible escapers, the prison superintendent was apparently willing to contemplate a lethal ambush. His chief warder testified that this unidentified inmate, while working in the quarry, was given 'an opening to escape if he was disposed to attempt it. Nothing was said about challenging him.'[53] Instead a guard, armed with extra shells for his rifle, was placed in a concealed position just outside the prison. If the prisoner was seen to make a run for freedom, 'the orders were to shoot him'.[54] But the inmate could apparently not be lured into another escape attempt, and avoided the extra-judicial execution planned for him.

In March 1865 the frequent escapes, and gathering rumours of serious disciplinary problems, compelled the Auckland Provincial Council to 'inquire into and report on the condition and management of the Mount Eden Stockade'. The inquiry found that the Stockade 'has been conducted in a very loose manner, such as must be subversive of all discipline', with 'too much leniency shown to the prisoners'.[55] Governor Flynn insisted that he had increased the number of overseers at the quarry and supplied more weapons to the guards.[56] These efforts did not satisfy the public demand for a scapegoat, and Flynn resigned as soon as the inquiry findings were made known.[57]

He was replaced by his second-in-command and head gaoler, Joseph Tuckwell, a stern disciplinarian with long experience in the police force of Victoria, Australia.[58] Tuckwell soon discovered that loaded carbines and revolvers were stored in an office beside the hard-labour yard, where they could be seized by a determined body of prisoners, and he removed the weapons to his own house outside the prison walls. As a further precaution against prisoners arming themselves, day-shift warders carried truncheons rather than firearms while on duty in and around the prison buildings, and only those guarding the quarry and tradesmen's shops were heavily armed at all times.[59]

Tuckwell also ordered raised platforms to be built at the corners of the boundary fence overlooking the exercise yards, from which armed warders kept sentry duty day and night.[60] Their cry of 'All's well!' rang out every half hour during their six-hour night watches. If a warder saw a prisoner escaping, he was required to challenge the man before firing but not permitted to chase him for fear of allowing others to escape. Instead, an alarm bell was rung and a four-man flying squad, 'picked from the smartest runners amongst the warders', was sent in pursuit.[61]

By late 1865 the hard-pressed superintendent faced a large additional intake of inmates, the remnant population of the now defunct Queen

Street gaol. These were mostly remand prisoners awaiting trial, debtors, female prisoners, and short-sentence offenders such as drunks. Another wooden wing was built for them at right angles to the earlier two, forming the third side of a roughly paved yard about 15 metres square.[62] Their arrival saw a number of changes to the prison regime.

One corner of the prison's new wing contained four punishment cells, ventilated only by small openings near the ceiling and with their walls painted black to make them as dark as possible. Insubordinate prisoners were held there for up to 30 days on bread and water, although these punishment rations were illegally supplemented by other prisoners who, 'by that dexterity which is a marked characteristic of "old hands"', slipped them part of their own precious ration of meat or tobacco.[63]

Like other prisoners, the women were required to spend their days in hard labour and also qualified for exertion money, but their work was of a domestic nature. Large washtubs were installed in their airing yard and each week more than 900 articles of clothing and bedding from the prison, the hospital, the asylum and its associated Old Men's Refuge, 'much of it in a most filthy condition', were scrubbed clean by hand.[64] Their other main occupation was sewing and repairing clothing and bed linen for the inmates of these institutions. Only occasionally, when the supply of this work was insufficient to keep them occupied, were female prisoners set to the uncomfortable and tedious task of oakum picking — untangling strands of tarred hemp rope.[65]

A number of women prisoners were accompanied by their newborn and very young children, and the prison's diet scale specified a daily ration for children aged two and under, and those aged from two to eight. The wooden cell walls were far from soundproof and the proximity of these very small inmates is likely to have disturbed other prisoners, but some loosening of the regulations was allowed for them. Well-behaved female prisoners were allowed a visit from their husbands and friends once a month, but mothers and children could visit at any time.[66] Even the exacting Justice Arney conceded that '[t]he females are now well provided for; they have airy rooms and an airy yard, and are kept entirely distinct from the other sex. Likewise there is a person who devotes her services to that department, and admirably discharges her duties.'[67] This was Mrs Andrewartha, the prison's first matron, whose duties also included overseeing all searches of female prisoners. These were carried

The redoubtable Mary Colclough, pioneer prison reformer. *PRIVATE COLLECTION*

out by the all-male staff of warders, and the matron's presence is likely to have made them less unpleasant for the women concerned.[68]

Matron Andrewartha held the view that 'severe punishments ... have a bad effect on prisoners', and she could recall only one woman under her charge who was handled especially harshly. This 'very refractory' prisoner, Ellen McLean, was apparently suffering from delirium tremens, a symptom of alcohol withdrawal.[69] Her uncontrollable behaviour saw her sentenced to seven days' solitary on bread and water, and as a further and rare punishment the gaoler ordered her hair to be cropped as close as the men's.[70] McLean furiously resisted on the entirely valid ground that this punishment could be imposed only by order of a Visiting Justice. She was shorn anyway, with two warders to tie her arms and hold her on the stool.[71]

More sadly typical of the women's ward inmates was Jeannie Finney, who looked far older than her 19 years when she was admitted in November 1865 for 'keeping a common brothel'. She was in a weakened state but it was not immediately apparent that she was also pregnant. Finney went into labour early in the new year, and delivered a healthy girl in the prison hospital. Her own condition, however, did not improve, and although Dr Philson supplied 'wine and other nourishment' she died two weeks later.[72] Such incidents prompted Auckland's early feminists to point out that female prison inmates were subjected to poorer conditions than the males, and to demand changes to the regime in the women's wing.

The most vociferous on this theme was a diminutive firebrand named Mary Colclough (pronounced Coakley), who began visiting women inmates regularly from 1871 and besieged the newspapers with letters on the necessity for reforms.[73] Her sharpest barbs described conditions in the women's so-called exercise yard which, as she pointed out, was so overcrowded that no meaningful exercise was possible within it. In one corner women who had overflowed their dayroom picked oakum under a tarpaulin. Much of the remaining space was used to wash and dry institutional bedding, often 'disgusting and pestiferous ... Now just think of the condition of some twenty-five to thirty human creatures shut up among these infected clothes, with no other air to breathe ... than that impregnated with their pestilential odour.'[74]

Colclough pointed out that the women's upstairs dormitory could be used during the day as a schoolroom where girls could learn to read, write and sew. In the longer term she wished to see a separate women's institution opened, 'to be a Refuge for the Repentant'. She energetically raised funds for this purpose, meanwhile housing recently discharged women in her own home while they adjusted to life beyond prison walls.[75] But the Women's Home and, apparently, her other proposed improvements failed to find favour with prison officers and city fathers alike, and women like Ellen McLean and Jeannie Finney continued to scrub, sicken and serve their time without benefit of training or other reformatory efforts of any kind.

I I I

The makeshift wooden buildings spreading across the seaward slopes of Mount Eden represented a low-cost and interim response by the Provincial Council to the Auckland region's rapidly growing prison population. Prisoners of all types were held there and it proved impossible to segregate the 'young neophyte' from the 'old and incorrigible offender'.[76] Separating the very young and the female prisoners was hardest of all since their relatively small numbers made it especially difficult for the warders to find independent accommodation for them. A female debtor, regarded as more refined than other female prisoners, was therefore obliged to overhear conversation among convict prisoners housed next to her — conversation that one sentencing judge, Justice Moore, warned jurors was 'likely to be most objectionable'.[77]

In late 1865 Chief Justice Arney acknowledged: 'We must still regard our prison as a temporary expedient . . . well adapted for temporary purposes, and wholly unfit for a place of penal servitude. It was utterly impracticable to effect reformation in it.'[78] He and others recognised that such an object could only be achieved in a well-designed and strongly built prison capable of adapting to the changing needs of future decades. To this end, plans for 'a new and substantial gaol on the most modern and improved construction' were drawn up by the Provincial Council's chief engineer, and inmates prepared a supply of stone for its materials under the instruction of a convict who had learned the skills of masonry in various prisons in Australia and New Zealand.[79]

That project did not proceed much beyond the preliminary stage for the rest of the decade, although both central and provincial governments were well aware of the growing need for it. Prisons have never been a popular target of public expenditure, and the ponderous processes of provincial government magnified the difficulties of raising the necessary finance. Auckland province expected the central government to take financial responsibility for those convicted of serious crimes, but politicians in Wellington continued to resist building and maintaining an expensive central penal institution.

The government did, however, set up a committee to study existing prisons and consider their suitability for a 'general penal establishment for the colony'. Mount Eden, along with several other possible sites around the country, was regarded as highly suitable for this purpose, but the cost of transporting prisoners to and from a secure central prison, as well as the loss to each province of the value of the labour from their relocated convicts, caused the committee to advise against such a facility.[80] This inertia ensured that the inadequate wooden Stockade remained in use for many more years.

Prison inmate numbers continued to expand, and the daily average rose from 87 in 1861–62 to 220 by 1866 as warfare across the North Island continued to ensure a large intake of court-martialled troops, and also of their opponents. In the first months of 1866 there was an event unprecedented in the prison's history: the admission of 31 Māori remand prisoners from the Bay of Plenty, followers of the Pai Mārire or 'Hauhau' movement. They were charged with offences connected with the deaths the previous year of the Ōpōtiki missionary and government spy Carl Völkner and the government interpreter James Fulloon. Although their ages are not known, most of these prisoners were too young to have received the tā moko, or facial tattoo that signified adulthood, when they arrived 'sad and haggard' at the Stockade after a sea journey from the Bay of Plenty.[81] One very young man named Penetito wept unceasingly during his first day at the prison. Another, Ngatihoko, was so ill with consumption that he had to be assisted to walk to his cell, and died of the disease without leaving the prison.[82]

During early April 1866 these prisoners, handcuffed together in pairs, were transported daily between the Stockade and the courthouse in two horse-drawn omnibuses, with a strong guard of armed police sitting on top of each vehicle.[83] Five of them received death sentences. While their trials were in progress another prisoner, a former soldier named James Stack, was hanged for an unrelated murder. His executioner was an inmate named Mills, sentenced for robbing several city hotels, who was rewarded with the sizeable sum of £10 and a free pardon.[84] However, like his predecessor in the hangman's role, Mills returned to the prison a short time later after committing another robbery. He boasted that this would give him the opportunity of hanging the Ōpōtiki prisoners, but his fellow inmates responded to his reappearance among them with 'a most extraordinary demonstration of disgust'.[85]

The five condemned men were all hanged on 17 May 1866, the largest number ever executed at once in this country. At eight in the morning the Whakatōhea chief Mokomoko and the elderly Taranaki man Horomona Poropiti (Solomon the Prophet) were led out of their cell to the tolling of the gaol bell. At least 150 people held tickets to view the spectacle at close hand, and a much larger number watched from the hills above. Horomona had been conspicuous at his trial for his long white hair and beard, but he was shaved close for his execution. He prayed continuously in his own language as he was marched, with his arms tied, towards the scaffold. Mokomoko, who had persistently denied his involvement in the murders, was less sanguine about facing his death sentence. The morning was clear and fine, and he looked above the prison wall and called, 'Hei konei rā, te ao mārama' ('Farewell, the world of light'). A reporter observed: 'His features seemed distorted with his emotions, and the muscles of his face were twitching in a way painful to look at.'

The hangman, shrouded to the waist in black, fastened a rope around the neck of each man as Mokomoko continued to loudly proclaim his innocence. In words clearly recalled among his people today, he told the hangman, 'Tangohia mai te taura i taku kakī, kia waiata au i taku waiata.' ('Take the rope from my neck, that I might sing my song.') The execution proceeded as arranged, although the hangman found the experience so distressing that he was unable to perform his duty on the other three condemned men and a replacement had to be called in. Of those three — Heremita Kahupaea, Hakaraia Te Rahui and Mikaere Kirimangu — the first two were large and heavy, while Kirimangu was 'merely a boy, slightly-built, and emaciated to a skeleton'. His execution was consequently horribly bungled, and he was reported to have struggled for several minutes before the second hangman completed the task by pulling several times on his legs.[86]

To hold the bodies of the five men, a single large pit had been dug within the gaol yard alongside the grave of Richard Harper, hanged two years earlier. After the bodies were laid down and covered with quicklime, the mass grave was marked by six stone slabs into which the initials of each of the dead men had been chiselled.[87] Burial within the prison was a fate that Mokomoko, at least, had sought strenuously to avoid. Before the hanging, some of his Whakatōhea relatives had asked the sheriff to have his body handed over to them, as in the cases of several other executed men, including James Stack the previous month. This request was denied, but the refusal was kept secret from Mokomoko, who went to the scaffold believing that his body would soon be returned to his people in the Bay of Plenty.[88] His relatives undertook to fulfil this wish at a later date and did so more than a century later, as described in the introduction to this book.

| | |

Tuckwell's regime of stern discpline combined with carefully graded rewards for good conduct appeared to be working well by the mid-1860s, but there were occasional discordant notes in the otherwise glowing accounts of his reforms. Although the hard-labour wing housed more than 150 inmates, its one messroom was capable of serving only about 40 at a time and, as a result, 'scraps of meat and potato skins bestrew the passages and staircases, wherever the prisoners can find a spot to sit down and take their meals'.[89] The punishment cells were gloomy caves where men were confined for up to 30 days on end, with half an hour's exercise morning and evening when they were marched in a circle in total silence.[90] Very young offenders such as Alexander Buchanan and Celicia Phillips, both 11, were jailed for absurdly petty offences, in their case the theft of a nightgown and a dozen pairs of stockings from a shop. There was no way of segregating them from 'the most hardened and abandoned' offenders, and the sentencing judge suggested that a whipping might be a more appropriate punishment.[91]

Perhaps most disturbing of all for the people of Auckland was that every year, despite Tuckwell's heightened vigilance, determined prisoners succeeded in escaping the Stockade. In 1866 there were three such escapes, including two by an Irish-born former trooper named Isaac Robinson.[92] After his first breakout he was placed in heavy irons, but these were later removed to allow him to work as a stonemason, an activity at which he was one of the most skilled in the entire prison.[93] The Provincial Council's chief engineer 'wrote officially to the Visiting Justices, pointing out the desirability of keeping this man to stone cutting, in order to expedite the wall which was so much required'. This request was approved, and Robinson took advantage of it to escape a second time.

The other 1866 escaper, Frederick Plummer, wrote a letter while at large which, to Tuckwell's impotent fury, was published in the *New Zealand Herald*. It was addressed from 'Safety Villa' and described how Plummer had eluded the armed guards searching for him by hiding in the flax and scrub behind the quarry.[94] He had still not been recaptured in late November 1866 when the prison's two Visiting Justices, Thomas Beckham and Hugh Carleton, delivered an approving annual report to the Auckland Provincial Council. The 'state of discipline in the gaol bears testimony to the watchfulness and general efficiency of the gaoler', they announced. They also praised the new warders' dormitory built just outside the prison gate 'as tending to destroy that familiarity between prisoners and warders which has existed so long'.

The prison's most urgent requirement, thought the Justices, was better accommodation for women and juveniles and, of course, a suitably formidable stone boundary wall. While initially expensive, such a wall could be expected to pay for itself through savings on the number of guards employed.[95] The Provincial Council had not long received this encouraging report when its findings were called into question by rumours suggesting that Superintendent Tuckwell subjected inmates to extraordinarily brutal punishments that breached prison regulations, and that the Visiting Justices colluded with him to ensure these were carried out.

Whipping, although listed in the array of punishments officially available to the prison authorities, was seldom inflicted at the Stockade. The exceptions appear to be in the case of young offenders for whom whipping was regarded as more humane than confinement alongside older and hardened criminals. As early as 1854 Chief Justice Martin had proposed 'private and inglorious and severe' whipping as a suitable punishment for juveniles.[96] When another two young boys were admitted to the Stockade in 1866, Visiting Justice Beckham ordered them to be whipped with a birch rod. The long-serving warders instructed to carry out this sentence both refused to do so, and Beckham fined them 14 days' pay for misconduct, along with an undertaking to obey such an order in

from them again. If I occupied the position of Mr. Tuckwell, and had the same amount of men to dispose of at my command, rather than put chains upon the prisoners, for such purposes as he does at present, I would reverse the order of things, and chain myself until I could form able plans for keeping them in without chains. As things were managed when I was a member of the establishment, there was every chance for one to make himself scarce. Two or three of the young men that were placed as sentries over us at times used to amuse me exceedingly. After taking a short tour on the platform outside one would seat himself in the box, and indulge in a quiet nap; when, if there had been no punishment for so doing, I should have expressed my warm feelings, by giving him a bucket of cold water, to help to stimulate him to greater exertion in his duty. After rousing himself up, he would again take to the platform, holding his rifle in such a position as I never saw one put before, and, with head thrown slightly back, he would amuse himself with a selection from some grand opera, or an attempt at Sims Reeves. One of them was making a trial of

Soon after escaping from the Stockade, the elusive and defiant convict Frederick Plummer wrote to the *New Zealand Herald* from a secret address he called 'Safety Villa', derisively reporting on conditions on the inside. The editor said his letter 'bears every indication of having been penned by the escaped prisoner himself, the calligraphy agreeing in every particular with a communication which the prisoner addressed whilst in the unconvicted part of the Stockade to a gentleman in town, and who has kindly permitted us to compare the documents'. PAPERS PAST, DAILY SOUTHERN CROSS, 19 NOVEMBER 1866

future. One boy was later sentenced to a second whipping, and this time one of the warders resigned rather than carry out the order. A younger colleague named George Dreardon agreed to whip the boy because, he said, 'I could not afford to disobey.' On Beckham's recommendation Dreardon received an additional two guineas for 'zealous conduct'.[97] He later stated that if he had known before taking up employment at the prison that 'such a service might be required of me, I would not have accepted the appointment'.[98]

This and other alleged abuses drove the Auckland Provincial Council to the exceptional step of commissioning an independent inquiry into its prison, which extended to the actions of its own Visiting Justices. The grotesque and sensational evidence amounted to more than 80 pages. Among the findings of this 1867 inquiry were that convicts John Wright and Isaac Robinson had been gagged while held in the solitary cells, at Tuckwell's orders and in his presence. Robinson testified that he had been punished in this way 'for singing out'. He was first 'knocked down with heavy bludgeons', then had his arms 'pinioned behind me until my elbows nearly met' and was finally gagged 'with a horse's bit being put across my mouth, and pulled that tight until I was black in the face'. He was left in this state for 24 hours. Wright was gagged with a heavy rope formerly used by a prison hangman. Warder Karl Nash observed that Wright 'appeared in great pain. There was froth on both sides of his mouth.'[99]

The most experienced warders recognised that such brutal punishments did not result in improved discipline. In his 14 years in an English gaol and three more at Mount Eden, chief warder Thomas Young had never before known a prisoner to be gagged. 'Lenient punishments,' he told the inquiry, 'have a more salutary influence on the conduct of prisoners, and tend to improve them, more than harsh and irritating punishments.'[100] Dr Philson was likewise opposed to the use of the gag, but on medical grounds. It was more dangerous and severe than a flogging, he told the inquiry, and he would on no account sanction such a punishment.[101]

At almost every point the inquiry's findings rebutted the emollient statements supplied by the Visiting Justices. The prison's own regulations, it appeared, were not properly made known to the prisoners. 'Some of the rules clash, the interpretation of others appear doubtful, and where such is the case, prisoners have not had the benefit of the doubt interpreted in their favour.' The warders had asked, without success, for the rules to be translated for the benefit of prisoners literate only in Māori.[102]

It became strikingly apparent that far from providing a means for prisoners to register complaints of ill-treatment, the Visiting Justices conspired with the superintendent and other staff to ensure that these complaints were ignored or even punished. One group of prisoners, in the spirit of Oliver Twist, took the bold step of objecting to the quality of the midday stew, which even chief warder Young admitted contained meat of 'inferior quality, composed of necks and shins, and when boiled becomes very hard'.[103] When this complaint was presented to Justice Beckham, he thundered, 'How dare you convicted felons complain of good rations which hundreds of honest men would be glad of?' and sent the complainants to solitary for four days to repent of their ingratitude.[104]

With prisoners unwilling to lay complaints before the Visiting Justices, cruelties could be inflicted on them in breach of both prison regulations and the general law, such as placing men in heavy irons for weeks on end.[105] Chief warder Young told the inquiry that men emerged from these prolonged spells of solitary confinement in a very weakened state, yet they were expected to immediately carry out the same labour as their fellow prisoners. 'I do not think the solitary-cell system has had the effect of humbling, taming, or making prisoners more tractable,' he said, 'but, on the contrary I think it makes them more reckless.'[106]

Māori prisoners appeared to be among the better behaved in the prison, but they were more prone to illness, and in winter the clothing and bedding supplied to them proved to be quite inadequate. 'They seem to suffer more from cold than Europeans,' noted one warder. A prisoner named Te Huri told the inquiry that three of his fellow Māori had died 'from working too hard, and when sick they are compelled to lie on the boards [on the floor of their cell] waiting for the doctor. Sometimes they are sent to work, and sometimes to hospital, whence they are taken to their graves.' One of those he referred to, a Whakatōhea man named Paraharahara, was, according to warder Dreardon, 'treated in a more severe manner than I ever saw any other man treated'.[107] While suffering from a weeping abscess, Paraharahara was put to work in the stoneyard, where he collapsed.[108] Dr Philson later found him unable to leave his cell and admitted him to the sickroom, where 'he appeared to despond' and died several weeks later.[109]

The inquiry found that Superintendent Tuckwell ran the Stockade like a personal fiefdom. He kept pigs near his house outside the boundary fence, and admitted that they were regularly fed on leftover stew from the midday meal, although he disputed prisoners' claims that the stew was deliberately watered down to ensure a surplus for this purpose. Prisoner Daniel Burke told the inquiry that he had lost a coveted job in the cookhouse because 'I would not give Mr Tuckwell food for his pigs, poultry etc'.[110]

The evidence of sullen prisoners and resentful warders against those in authority might be regarded as self-serving and unreliable, but the Provincial Council decided that the inquiry findings were more than sufficient to convict Superintendent Tuckwell of gross cruelty and negligence. 'Cast out the evidence of the prisoners altogether, as worthless, and the remainder justifies us in believing that the interior discipline of the Mount Eden Goal is a matter of public reproach and scandal to an enlightened and Christian community — that within its walls tyrannous acts of cruelty and torture have been committed, the existence of which no such community could tolerate.'[111]

Like his predecessor, Tuckwell was dismissed as soon the inquiry's findings were made known. Some defended him on the grounds that restraining vicious and dangerous criminals within an inadequately funded institution must lead inevitably to brutalities by its staff. There was certainly some truth in the basic charge that no one individual could be held responsible for a systemic failure. Whoever replaced Tuckwell, it was generally agreed, should temper harshness with mercy and provide reformative measures as well as punishment so that 'prisoners should know that it is desired not merely to punish them for the past, but to train them, so as to give them the means of earning an honest living for the future'.[112]

The next prison governor was a former army officer, Robert Ayre, seemingly a humane and conscientious man who was later found to have worked for a year without taking a single day off.[113] Among the developments that followed his appointment was the first effective school in the Stockade's history. Several desultory attempts at prisoner education had been made in the past, always reliant on the willingness of a well-read inmate to act as teacher. The prison population usually included several interesting potential candidates, often sentenced for crimes such

An armed prison guard stands on duty at his watchtower, overlooking the quarry, in 1900. *NEW ZEALAND HERALD*

as forgery or embezzlement. One unidentified convict could, after a day spent swinging a sledgehammer, return to his cell in the penal-servitude wing to devour a shelf-full of books that included works in Latin, French and Arabic.[114]

During 1868 another such prisoner, also not identified, was employed to teach four daily classes of about 10 prisoners each, grouped by their levels of literacy — the entirely uneducated, those with basic literacy, a class for 'Natives' who were mostly illiterate, and an advanced class for those who could already read and write well and sought further education. This elite class learned arithmetic, 'Euclid' (i.e. geometry), algebra, history, geography and grammar. After six months, all 47 pupils of the Stockade school showed pleasing improvement.[115]

III

Another victim of the devastating findings of the inquiry was Visiting Justice Thomas Beckham. He had been Auckland's resident magistrate for more than 20 years and wielded exceptional influence within its judicial system, yet he could not survive evidence that he had, for example, threatened both prisoners and warders with retribution if they testified against him. Although forced to resign as the prison's Visiting Justice, Beckham retained his magistrate's post for several more years, until his retirement from the bench.

His replacement was the magnificently named Ponsonby Peacocke, a former British army officer. Paora Tuhaere, the highly respected Ngāti Whātua chief who had been accosted three years earlier by the inmate and hangman John Thomas, was assigned as Peacocke's adviser on 'affairs relating to the native people in the province of Auckland' — an early instance of bicultural consultation.[116] Lieutenant-Colonel Peacocke and Auckland's police commissioner James Naughton were each also appointed to the newly created post of 'inspector of gaols and prisons in the province of Auckland'.[117]

In that capacity, Naughton took part in yet another inquiry into the colony's existing prisons, finding, predictably, that all of them served to 'harden old offenders; to demoralize, corrupt, and debase those who have recently become criminals, and innocent persons waiting for trial; and to afford opportunities for instruction and confederation in all kinds of crime and vice'.[118] The answer to these evils, the inquiry found, was to build a national high-security prison under the control of 'a gentleman of education, who has had considerable experience of prisons in England, Ireland, or the Australian Colonies'.[119]

This inquiry went further than its predecessors in making the case for such a prison, but the provincial government system continued to stall its implementation. Prison reform had become 'too vast and complicated, and too expensive for the provinces to deal with,' pronounced the *Southern Cross* newspaper, yet the central government lacked both the resources and the political will to take the initiative in this area.[120]

Escapes from the Stockade therefore remained commonplace, and only occasionally was one so unusual that it attracted special attention. This was the case in March 1869 when Heremia Te Wake, an athletic and authoritative Māori leader from north Hokianga, fled from the quarry pursued by a flying squad of officers and a hail of bullets but nonetheless succeeded in returning to his home community.[121]

This achievement seems less remarkable given the circumstances of his conviction. Te Wake had entered the prison the year before, charged with a murder committed during a land dispute between his Te Rarawa people and their Ngāpuhi neighbours. It was understood that he had not personally carried out the killing, but as the senior Te Rarawa present, and in accordance with Māori custom, he accepted responsibility for it and gave himself up, expecting a nominal punishment. Instead he received a death sentence, later commuted to penal servitude for life.[122] 'No one, not even the judge and jury . . . believed that Te Whaka [sic] was morally guilty of murder.'[123]

As a result of the sentence, tensions between Ngāpuhi and Te Rarawa rose to the brink of outright war. The government was desperate to avoid such a crisis at an already tense stage in the various concurrent conflicts further to the south, from which the northern tribes supposedly provided a united bulwark of safety for the citizens of Auckland. The authorities may therefore have unofficially connived to enable Te Wake's bold escape, his eluding of pursuers, a canoe voyage across the Manukau Harbour and his return to his tribe, where he was eventually pardoned.[124] More than a century later Te Wake's daughter, Whina Cooper, made the return journey from Northland via Auckland to Parliament at the head of the 1975 Māori Land March.

III

It was only in the early 1870s, after warfare between Māori and the Crown declined, that a massive stone boundary wall finally encircled the Stockade's pitiful wooden fence.[125] This imposing barrier, which still surrounds much of the Mount Eden prison complex today, had been planned and intermittently progressed from at least 1863, when a local paper described it as the first truly enlightened use of prison labour. 'No more serviceable plan could be adopted than that of compelling [prisoners] to erect a wall of such height as to prevent their escape, and so render the Stockade secure.'[126] The wall rose in a slow and halting fashion for the rest of the decade, but by 1872 its final form could be discerned and the *Auckland Star* announced that 'when finished the establishment will not be only a prison in name but also one in reality'.

This dominating and undeniably impressive work of Victorian penal architecture was designed with several features to render it unclimbable. Although the outside surfaces were rough-hewn, all the wall's interior faces were dressed smooth and its corners were rounded, as 'nimble prisoners have been known to "wriggle" themselves up a corner of a gaol wall built entirely square'.[127] The wall's thickness tapered from 1.2 metres at the base to 60 centimetres at its full height of 5.6 metres, where it was topped with a coping of smoothly dressed stone to resist grappling irons or frantically grasping hands.[128] Tunnelling underneath the wall was never a realistic possibility given the site's volcanic rock substratum.

The quality of construction, by gangs of prison labourers overseen by highly skilled stonemasons, is apparent more than 140 years later, as the wall still stands tall, straight and regular in all dimensions. Its large blocks of dark-grey basalt, quarried and dressed on site and cemented with lime made from ground and burned seashells, lend it a suitably sombre appearance, reinforced by the formidable arched gateways. The monumental structure's completion in early 1874 meant that half-a-dozen sentries could be dispensed with, announced the *Star*, 'and the saving in that alone will recoup the outlay on the wall in course of a few years'.[129]

That prediction, like most others made about the Stockade's level of security, proved somewhat overconfident. In March 1872, when the wall was well advanced but still incomplete, the expert stonecutter Isaac Robinson, who had contributed more than most to its construction, passed through it with ease. He was then one of the longest-serving convicts in the prison, having escaped from it twice already. He committed a highway robbery during his second attempt and had many years of penal servitude added to his original sentence. However, after a long period of exemplary conduct he was relieved of his irons and assigned a job as cleaner in the debtors' ward where he discovered a suit of clothes and boots belonging to a warder named Martin.

To Martin's profound discredit, his loaded revolver was lying nearby. Thus armed and disguised, and presumably with cap pulled well down and heart pounding, Robinson, one of the most feared and desperate criminals of his century, strolled unchallenged through the gates of the prison to make his third bid for freedom.[130] Later that day a pursuing detective spotted him on a bush-lined track, entering the Waitākere ranges. He fired his revolver at the fugitive, but Robinson dived off the track and was never officially seen again, either dead or alive.[131]

The public furore caused by this flagrant breach of security drove the prison authorities to undertake further measures to restrain their other long-serving and high-risk inmates. Two months after Robinson disappeared, his fellow recidivist escaper Frederick Plummer and seven other long-sentence men, including five lifers, were removed from the Stockade in chains.[132] They were shipped under heavy guard to Dunedin where a solid stone prison had been built in the early 1860s, when Otago's provincial government was flush with funds from the gold rushes. The Auckland council agreed to pay its southern equivalent the vast sum of £250 a year for hosting its most dangerous convicts. This proved a poor investment. Just three months after his arrival in Dunedin, Plummer, while part of a road gang, made yet another escape from custody.[133]

It was not so much the erection of the boundary wall as the decline in prisoner numbers after the New Zealand Wars that produced a period of greater ease and order in the Stockade in the early 1870s. The long-overdue Imprisonment for Debt Abolition Act of 1874 further reduced inmate overcrowding, and the debtors' ward became available to the traditionally poorly served juvenile and female offenders. The system of paying exertion money to hard-working inmates, and remitting part of their sentences, was by then well embedded in prison routine. Many prisoners took pride in out-performing others, and goal commissioners pointed out that in the hard labour of cutting and shaping the scoria blocks, 'the rivalry to obtain the maximum credit at the end of the week is so keen that results in excess of the best free labour are obtained'.[134] The sums paid for this enforced labour were increased during 1874, although this had the unintended consequence that the most industrious students of the prison school abandoned their studies to concentrate on income-earning activity in their free time.[135]

Some elements of prison life remained stubbornly, uncomfortably familiar decade after decade, regardless of adjustments to the internal regime. Remand prisoners awaiting trial faced conditions often worse than for those found guilty. In 1873 they were held four to a small cell for 16 hours a day, and even longer on Sundays and holidays. The *Auckland Star* reported that they were not allowed 'the use of tobacco or any newspaper, and no books are supplied, although by the 14th condition of the Government regulations they are required to provide books'.[136] More than one-third of the 1874 prison roster were described as drunkards, and the Visiting Justices suggested that an inebriates' home would be more suitable for these unruly inmates serving relatively short sentences: 'Such sentences are too short for the discipline of the gaol to make any impression on the person committed, while the last vestige of independence and self-respect is destroyed.'[137]

That sorry fate had apparently not yet befallen two sisters, Kate and Mary McManus, when they appeared in court together in October 1873. Kate was 19, Mary a year older, and both had already accumulated lengthy criminal records for prostitution, indecent behaviour, vagrancy and public drunkenness. When given a further 12-month sentence they were so unmoved that Mary called out, 'Oh! I can do that comfortably.' Both sisters then 'laughed immoderately, and danced out of Court'. This spectacle was observed by Auckland's mayor, who was so enraged that he complained to the Minister of Justice that imprisonment for prostitutes and female vagabonds was quite inadequate in effect; he proposed that any woman with at least three such convictions should face the further punishment of having her hair cut off. A terse note to this letter pointed out that this deterrent 'would require a fresh prison regulation', and the mayor's vindictive suggestion was not implemented.[138]

From 1875 the daily average number of prisoners began to rise again, and the prison staff, whose numbers had been reduced when the boundary wall was completed, became strained to breaking point. Matron

Maria Martin claimed that she had 'not had an hour's respite since her appointment three years ago', and the Provincial Council approved the employment of an assistant for the women's ward.[139] The male staff had even stronger grounds for complaint: their wages and conditions had barely shifted in two decades and were regarded as scandalously poor throughout most of that period.

As early as 1861, Chief Justice Arney found that the guards were 'ordinarily on duty fourteen hours per diem' and frequently also had to work a night shift, making a 19-hour working day. For this they were paid the miserable salary of £100 a year.[140] Seven years later the proportion of prisoners to warders at the Stockade was 13 to one, a level at least double that of any other prison in the colony, and the warders were described as suffering 'a most unjustifiable amount of overwork'.[141]

In 1874, all 21 warders and guards at the Stockade petitioned the Provincial Council for 'an increased salary and relaxation of present hours of duty'. Governor Ayre fully supported his men's claim. Their working hours, he thought, were 'unequalled in this or any other country'. They were granted only one Sunday off in 18, and received no 'retiring allowance or gratuity according to service and conduct, which is provided for in other provinces'. Their rate of pay was 'far below that of an ordinary labourer, whilst they are obliged to support a respectable appearance, and perform duties combining trust and responsibility'. Unless their pay was increased, he warned the council, a number of his staff would leave for the Thames goldfields, which offered 'many opportunities for more lucrative and less harassing employment'.[142]

The self-evident rationality and justice behind this pay claim, like the many earlier arguments for a better-designed and -resourced prison, failed to overcome the provincial government's sluggish short-term planning. Neither the warders' nor the prisoners' conditions improved significantly until after 1876, when the abolition of the provincial government system allowed a fresh and vigorous approach to reforming Auckland's and the country's other prisons.[143]

By 1882 the Stockade was dwarfed by its new stone perimeter wall. Houses, businesses and other properties are now evident in the surrounding area. *AUCKLAND LIBRARIES HERITAGE COLLECTIONS, 4-1068*

3:
Stone Jug
1877–1909

The dismaying bleakness of the penal institution at Mount Eden presents a daunting literary challenge to a writer. Few heartwarming and uplifting anecdotes emerge from such places, so those that do deserve particular mention.

In early 1877, Mary Ann Kane, aged 20, entered the women's section of the prison. The facts of her crime were plain, and cruelly common. She had migrated from Ireland three years earlier and found work as the chambermaid of the Thames Hotel in Coromandel. In 1876 her employer gave her notice to quit, suspecting from her pale and trembling appearance that she was pregnant. In fact, the young Irishwoman was discovered to have just given birth to a baby girl in her room, and its corpse was found there in a carry-all.[1]

The crime of infanticide, although far from unusual in that time, carried the death penalty. However, Kane's otherwise unblemished character moved the judge to show humanity. Since no evidence had been produced to prove that the baby had been born alive, he said, the charge should be reduced to one of concealment of birth, and he handed down a 12-month sentence.[2] He added that he would greatly have preferred to punish the accused's seducer instead, and offered the hope that the Mount Eden gaoler would 'keep her apart from the hardened classes of criminals'.[3]

There was little prospect of that. Women inmates were held in the most overcrowded of the old wooden buildings, a dilapidated structure standing outside the stone wall to the west of the main prison and housing anywhere from 25 to 50 inmates. With no provision for separate cells, even for the sick, they were simply 'huddled together' in fetid conditions, and may have been glad of the chance to work out in the yard where the washtubs stood, and where some two thousand items of bedding and clothing from the town's lunatic asylum, hospital and Old Men's Refuge were washed by hand each week.[4]

At all times, indoors and out, the women were required to keep at least 100 yards from any male prisoner. Nonetheless, by some unknown means Kane managed to attract the attention of one of them. His name was William Smith, also from the Coromandel district, who had been convicted of 'forging and uttering', the quaint legal term that in his case meant passing bad cheques.[5] Although by temperament an eccentric and dressy individual, Smith spent his days in the quarry and stoneyard wearing the coarse and shapeless convict's uniform of moleskin trousers and yellow jacket.

The couple's mutual affection was expressed through ferried messages, as well as wordless glances when they were in sight of each other. Eventually, and in spite of the very considerable odds, one of those messages contained a proposal of marriage, which was accepted. When her time was served and Mary Ann Kane was due for release, gaoler and governor Loughlin O'Brien, who knew nothing of her secret romance but recalled her former occupation at the hotel (and probably shared her Irish origins), offered her a job in his own household. His large house stood alongside the prison and was therefore a convenient place from which she could maintain the clandestine courtship.

As a well-behaved inmate Kane had become popular with the prison staff, and as O'Brien's servant she was free to roam about the rambling institution almost at will. This enabled her to plant further fond messages in a crevice in a far corner of the quarry, assuring Smith that she would wait for him as long as necessary. In reply he told her that he was due to inherit a sizeable property soon after his release, and would support them both. Innumerable prisoners convicted of dishonesty offences have made similar assertions, but Kane had faith in her fiancé's good intentions.

Finally the day came when William Smith was permitted to pass out through the prison wall's great arched gates, jauntily attired for the occasion in plum-coloured pants and a wide-brimmed hat. Two days later the couple were married, and in the following months, improbable though it seems, the groom apparently did inherit some family property.[6] His very common surname has meant that all traces of their later life remain lost within the archival record and we can only hope that their union, formed in such grim and unpromising surrounds, was a long, happy and fruitful one.

The squalid state of the women's quarters was noted at this time by government architect Edward Mahoney as part of his vigorous campaign to replace the Stockade buildings with a secure and permanent stone-built prison. All of the existing facilities, he declared, were 'unfit for the ordinary purposes of a prison'.[7] Both of the Visiting Justices endorsed this view. Visiting Justice Thomas Cheeseman told the Justice Minister: 'There are no separate rooms for females waiting trial, and although they may be found innocent of the charges preferred against them, yet they have to associate with the old *gaol-birds*— some of whom may be classed with the most depraved and abandoned of their sex.'[8] His colleague, Mr Barstow, was more specific and said that every woman inmate on remand, 'and therefore still presumed to be innocent, is necessarily obliged to herd with the most debauched prostitutes. Young girls, whom painful necessity compels to send for a first time to gaol, are associated with veteran brothel-keepers; the consequences of such contaminating influences can readily be imagined.'[9]

Barstow also drew the Minister's attention to the dire medical facilities in the women's ward. 'There is no female hospital, and women are regularly delivered of children in cells occupied by three or four other women. Any woman with a cough disturbs the rest of the occupants; the consequences of diarrhoea are of course very disagreeable.' Chronic overcrowding greatly worsened these conditions. Barstow found that 'from thirty to forty women are penned together in one yard for work or exercise, one room for living and eating, and six cells for sleeping accomodation. I have known the number of female prisoners to be as high as 47 — nine and ten sleeping in the larger cells.'[10]

A sizeable proportion of these women were imprisoned under the 1866 Vagrant Act for nothing worse than advanced age and destitution. In 1880, 83 female inmates and another 94 males were held under this Act, including several who, noted the prison governor, 'were committed to prison for the sole purpose of giving them food and shelter and it is much to be regretted that these can be provided only by classifying such old or sick people with criminals'.[11] These aged 'vagrants' were unable to work while in prison, and therefore could not offset the cost of their maintenance, making them even less welcome in the eyes of the staff.

While the women's division boasted its own wash-house, only one cold-water bath was provided for the rest of the inmate population, and the toilets consisted of earth-closets in the exercise yards; these were not connected to a sewerage system. The Stockade's hastily constructed wooden buildings were in a poor state by the late 1870s and the shingled roofs, in particular, were leaking and beyond repair. 'The rain comes through,' Governor O'Brien informed the Justice Department, 'and is causing damage to the interior. Some of the cells are unfit for occupation in consequence of this, and as the accommodation is exceedingly limited it is necessary that something should be done to the roofs without delay.'[12]

The hospital, which Mahoney described as a 'miserable makeshift', was sited directly above the kitchen and therefore subject to continuous heat and cooking odours. Most alarming of all, to Mahoney and many others, was the extreme fire risk from the wooden buildings whose cramped corridors and primitive water supply would condemn inmates to be burned alive before warders could unlock their cells. In 1877 O'Brien estimated that it might take 20 minutes to remove all prisoners and their bedding from the penal ward alone.[13]

The following year fire did indeed break out, in the kitchen of the remand ward, but by good fortune it was extinguished before any serious damage was done. 'If the fire had extended a very little more than it did,' declared O'Brien, 'the consequences would have been most serious as the only water obtainable would have to be drawn from the tanks by a tap.'[14] This near-disaster provoked the Department of Prisons to unusually prompt action, and within months a piped water supply, including a fire hose, was laid on from the Khyber Pass reservoir.[15]

Mahoney's damning assessment of the state of the Stockade buildings was provided to yet another commission of inquiry into the prison, and its members unanimously agreed that the facility was 'not only unsuitable in construction and faulty in arrangement, but utterly inadequate for even the present number of occupants.'[16] They endorsed Mahoney's proposal to progressively replace most of the wooden buildings with 'erections . . . of a permanent character', using both the local stone and the large and largely unpaid inmate workforce.[17] This 1877 commission reported to the central government rather than to its torpid provincial equivalent, and therefore stood a rather better chance than its predecessors of having its recommendations acted upon. Its report was accompanied by two sets of sketch plans for the proposed stone prison — one by O'Brien and a more detailed version from Mahoney. They were floor plans only, with no indication of how the exterior structure might look, but both appeared severely functional. They employed a roughly hexagonal design with cell blocks circling a central administration area, and separated by exercise and recreation yards.[18]

The completion in the late 1870s of the impressive perimeter wall added weight to the case for a newly built prison on the Stockade site. Nevertheless, bureaucratic inertia and perennially stretched budgets meant that although a large supply of dressed building stone accumulated during the decade, it lay unused as prisoner numbers increased in line with a rapidly growing general population.

Two years after the commissioners had firmly endorsed Mahoney's proposed new designs, the *New Zealand Herald* observed that the town's gaol was still 'utterly and hopelessly inadequate and unsuitable'.[19] Lack of finance could not convincingly be advanced as the excuse, as the colony was experiencing a surge of growth prompted by massive public borrowing for railways, roads, immigration and public buildings. Yet it remained unwilling to find the funds for such a disfavoured purpose as adequate accommodation for criminals.

| | |

The country's numerous prisons and lockups had, like many other features of a frontier society, developed in an ad hoc, highly localised and often chaotic fashion. In 1878 a commission of inquiry into the country's goals observed: 'Every gaol in the colony is . . . managed to a great extent according to the views and experience of the gaoler.' As a result standards of discipline, prison regulations, wages and conditions for warders, and all other features of prison operation and management varied widely across the country. 'The first essential step towards a reform in prison discipline and management,' declared the inquiry committee, 'is an efficient system of Government inspection. The inspector should be a man thoroughly trained in the soundest principles of prison management, and should not have been connected with any gaol heretofore established in New Zealand.'[20] Similar bodies had voiced the same view since at least 1861, but following the dissolution of provincial government in 1876 action was finally taken to bring consistency and order. Julius Vogel, New Zealand's Agent-General in London, was instructed to seek suitable applicants for the prison inspector's position. After a tortuous selection process, the successful candidate arrived in Wellington with his large family, then embarked on a nationwide tour of the country's prisons to familiarise himself with the scale and scope of the task ahead of him.

Mount Eden Prison staff knew that their institution would change beyond recognition when, on a February morning in 1881, a stiff-backed, bristling-moustached Englishman arrived to make his first inspection of the premises. This was Arthur Hume, the country's first Inspector of Prisons, who would hold this position for the next 28 years. Hume's reputation as a ferocious disciplinarian, tactless and intolerant with

Arthur Hume, the country's first Inspector-General of Prisons, and the primary instigator for the creation of Mount Eden Prison.
ALEXANDER TURNBULL LIBRARY, 1/2-32219-F

subordinates, had preceded him. He noted with cold disapproval the lack of sanitary arrangements in the gaol, and ordered the immediate construction of a new bath-house. More significantly, he approved the longstanding proposal to replace the wooden buildings with a capacious and well-designed new prison using locally quarried stone and prison labour.[21] Hume considered that in coming to this distant colony, his role was to transform its multifarious and loosely managed prisons into a nationally consistent system closely resembling the one he had left behind. The battlemented towers he imagined rising within the grey stone perimeter wall were to look as nearly as possible like those of his home country.

Captain (later Colonel) Arthur Hume had joined the army at 19, straight from a minor public school. He served in India with the 79th Highlanders before entering the prison service, and rose within it to become deputy-governor of a succession of convict prisons, including several of the most notorious in Britain such as Dartmoor and Wormwood Scrubs.[22] By the time he accepted the appointment in New Zealand, he had spent almost his entire life either under strict command or exerting command over others, and had developed an iron will and fierce powers of self-discipline. These characteristics were compounded by a lack of imagination, a vindictive disposition, and an expectation of instant and slavish obedience from those under his control.[23]

Hume's arrival was opposed by a fractious group of local prison officials. In an early instance of counter-imperialist nationalism, they demanded to know why New Zealand's prisons should not be inspected by one of its own citizens, and proposed the highly experienced and well-liked James Caldwell, head gaoler of Dunedin prison, for the position. In addition, Visiting Justices who, since the abolition of provincial government, had held sole authority to impose punishments for offences committed by inmates, felt their powers undermined by 'the pretentious protégé of Sir Julius Vogel', and also registered strong protests against Hume with the Justice Minister.[24]

Hume did not help his own case by the bluntness of his opening attack on the existing prison system. In his first annual report he announced that the daily diet was too generous and that prison schools should be abolished ('a man who has performed his day's allotted task of hard labour cannot possibly benefit by attending school in the evening'). Inmates who offended against discipline should be punished by whipping with a birch rod, since his British experience had shown him that this had 'a humiliating effect, and therefore is deterrent, and a valuable addition to the cat' (the 'cat-o'-nine-tails' or multi-stranded whip). Hume was also of the view that many warders were 'too old and slovenly', and that governors should be successively replaced by retired naval and military officers.[25]

In the longer term Hume hoped to introduce the 'silent system' common in British prisons. This meant providing single cells for all prisoners, who would be forbidden to communicate with each other apart from very limited conversation among work parties. Most New Zealand prison staff regarded the silent system as cruel and inhumane; in any case, it was impossible to introduce unless almost all the existing prisons were replaced.

A journalist who applied to tour the Stockade in late 1881 found himself prevented from doing so 'by a new ukase [i.e. order] issued by Captain Hume', and instead wrote a cutting critique of the inspector's penal theories. 'The captain is an enthusiastic believer in two theories as a means of effectually reforming criminals — the "silent system" and the birch. These he regards as the most effectual means of degrading the self-respect of criminals . . . and reducing them practically to the level of wild beasts.' Hume was so enthusiastic about the 'silent system', claimed the aggrieved journalist, that he was now extending it to the press, 'and perhaps the severe comments of the newspapers . . . have filled him with a desire to try the virtues of the birch as a further aid to the enforcement of his favourite reformatory regime'.[26]

The war of attrition between Hume and his critics straggled on for years, with both sides recording small victories. Although gaoler Caldwell had not become Inspector of Prisons as his advocates had hoped, he was transferred from Dunedin to become governor of the Stockade after the long-serving Loughlin O'Brien retired in 1882.[27] Hume withdrew his opposition to prison schools after a year but was able to make interim progress towards his 'silent system' by ending the custom of prisoners associating freely in the exercise yards, and requiring them instead to walk silently in circles.

Despite his stated commitment to seeing the Stockade rebuilt in stone, the Inspector-General regarded a national high-security prison as a more urgent priority and believed it should be built in Wellington, where he himself was based.²⁸ From 1882 construction of a massive brick prison began at Mount Cook, the low hill just south of the capital's centre. Hard-labour prisoners were transferred to Wellington from throughout the country to help with construction, but progress was glacially slow and further obstructed by public opposition. The town's citizens objected vigorously to having an unsightly structure on such a prominent and valuable site, and after it was completed in the early twentieth century the prison remained empty and unused. It was later named the Alexandra Barracks and converted into the country's defence headquarters, and was demolished entirely in the 1930s to be replaced by a national war memorial and museum.²⁹

| | |

For the first years of Hume's tenure as Inspector-General, therefore, life carried on much as usual in the flammable, insecure and increasingly ramshackle Stockade buildings. Hard-labour men worked alongside penal-servitude convicts in the quarry, distinguished only by dark-grey jackets for the former and yellow for the latter, known therefore as 'yellow-tails'.³⁰ Both groups, and the much smaller numbers who worked at bootmaking, blacksmithing and carpentry, wore prison garb well spattered with the broad-arrow markings that were the stigmata of their state — 27 arrows on the outer clothing and 16 on the inner, leading old hands to refer to the outfit as the 'butterfly suit'.³¹

The system of exertion money introduced by Loughlin O'Brien was retained by his successors because it produced sustained effort and obedience among the inmates, and provided modest sums for rehabilitation on their release. In the stoneyard and quarry especially, warders noted approvingly that the system encouraged vigorous rivalry among inmates who might otherwise be shirkers or troublemakers. Exertion money was paid only for work carried out in excess of a stated daily standard, and the sums involved were pitiful even by Victorian standards. Once women had fulfilled their stipulated seven hours in winter and eight in summer of sewing or washing, they received just a penny for each further hour's work: at that rate the prison undoubtedly made a tidy profit on their labour. Even so, highly motivated prisoners compiled significant sums, in the range of £5 (the equivalent of about $1000 today), in the

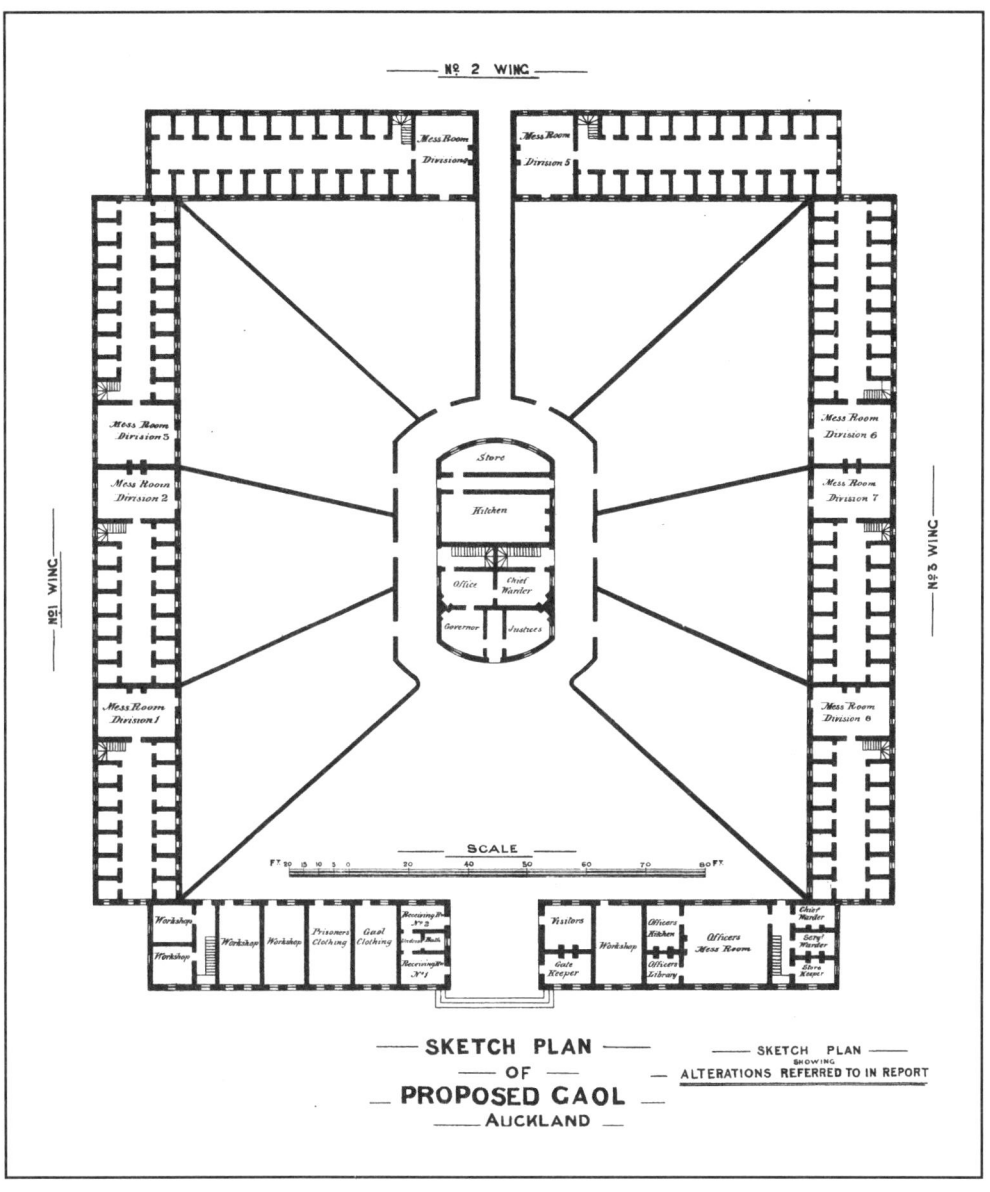

Government architect Edward Mahoney refined an initial design by prison governor Loughlin O'Brien and produced this severely functional 'panoptic' design for a stone prison to replace the Stockade. The plan was rejected in favour of a cruciform design that could be built and occupied in stages. *PAPERS PAST, AJHR, 1877, H-30*

course of their sentences. Some arranged to have this money paid to their spouses, and many used it to buy comforts not supplied with their prison uniform, such as socks and warm underclothing.[32]

From the first few years of Hume's tenure, the exertion money system was accompanied by a parallel system of marks awarded for effort and good behaviour, or deducted for lack of them. Inmates could use their accumulated marks to have up to a quarter of their sentence remitted, so a well-behaved prisoner with a one-year sentence typically served no more than nine months and 23 days. This system proved so effective at Mount Eden that it was implemented nationwide.[33]

In keeping with its paltry remuneration, the only work available to almost all Mount Eden inmates was arduous and unskilled.[34] The few prisoners who already possessed trade skills such as carpentry were permitted to practise them for the benefit of the prison but no trades were taught within its walls, and Hume was adamant that no rehabilitation programme would be introduced under his authority. Instead he introduced a regime of rigid classification according to security risk and behaviour. Staff had discretion to transfer inmates to higher or lower classes, and therefore acquired additional authority over them.[35]

Among the various privileges that might be extended, restricted or denied altogether under the classification system was that of writing and receiving letters. Depending on the class in which they were placed, prisoners were entitled to send a letter and receive the reply every one, two, three, four or eight months, and to receive a 20-minute visit on a Saturday afternoon at the same monthly intervals. The head gaoler read all inward and outward mail, and the gaol regulations stipulated: 'All letters of an improper or idle tendency . . . or containing slang, or other objectionable expression, will be suppressed.'[36] Since no member of the prison staff could understand letters written in Māori, these were automatically destroyed, whether inward or outward, and irrespective of whether correspondents could write in any other language.[37]

These restrictions particularly troubled one of the prison's more notorious yet pathetic residents in this period, a Timaru land agent named Thomas Hall, who was serving a life sentence for attempting to poison his wife (who, however, remained loyal to him throughout his prison term). Hall was 'by far the most interesting prisoner detained within the walls of Mount Eden gaol', thought the *Auckland Star* some years into his time there. 'His quick intelligent glance and the habitual look of . . . indescribably hopeless woe on his face at once interests the most casual observer.'[38]

By 1894, a decade into his life sentence, 45-year-old Hall had qualified for a letter and a visit at three-monthly intervals. He wrote at length to Arthur Hume, pointing out that since he had no friends or relatives in the Auckland region he received no visits at all, and pleading to be able to write and receive more frequent letters instead. 'My letters are divided equally between my wife who lives in England and my father and mother in New Zealand,' he wrote. If those correspondents happened to live nearer each other, he explained, one of them could pass his letter on to the others, but this was not possible in his case, so he was forced to wait several lonely months for a communication from any of them. Hume was unsympathetic and declined to make an exception to the regulations, although he advised the head gaoler that Hall might occasionally be permitted to write a 'special letter' if he could justify doing so in each instance.[39]

This uncompromisingly punitive attitude marked most of Hume's reforms to prison management and discipline. From 1883 he banned the use of tobacco by prisoners, causing many of them intense discomfort — and creating a thriving black market. His enthusiasm for birching and, in more serious cases, for flogging was opposed by the 1883 Prisons Act which, to his strong disapproval, ended corporal punishment as a means of disciplining adult inmates (although young people's training centres could continue to punish their inmates by whipping until 1936). The 1883 Act also banned most of the imaginative punishments inflicted by Joseph Tuckwell, and restricted warders to punishing inmates by means of the bread-and-water diet, the solitary cell and loss of privileges. However, the courts could still impose flogging as part of the sentence for certain crimes, and prison staff were then ordered to administer it.

In 1884 Henry Goodward was dealt with in this way for the rape of a young woman. A description of his punishment was leaked to the press, which reported that the gloomy faces of the two warders who performed this duty 'showed clearly that the task was not a congenial one'. Another warder 'sent in his resignation sooner than lay himself open to be called upon to perform an action so revolting to his sensibilities'.[40] Goodward was given 25 strokes of a knotted whip, and the warders took turns to deliver them. His back was left striped and bleeding but he uttered no sound throughout the procedure.

The incident was raised in Parliament some weeks later. Several MPs pointed out that warders ordered to flog an inmate risked retaliation from their superiors if they refused, and from other inmates if they obeyed. Sir George Grey, by then an ageing but still formidable backbencher, proposed abolishing flogging completely, as this would 'attain to a better state of civilization than has hitherto prevailed in the British Empire'.[41] His was a lone parliamentary voice on this issue, and flogging, primarily for sexual offences, continued in prisons for another 50 years.

As a staunch upholder of Britain's imperial traditions, Hume was resistant by temperament to innovation, and he brought few lasting changes to New Zealand's prison system. Among these, however, perhaps the most valuable was in raising the status of its staff.

In 1878 Mount Eden prison's warders worked a routine 13-hour day, including on weekends, for less pay than their southern colleagues. MPs praised the prison as 'the best and cheapest managed' in the colony, but able and dedicated staff could not be recruited on those terms.[42] From his first years as Inspector-General, Hume determined to replace ageing and incompetent warders with strict, mature and incorruptible men. Reflecting his own background, he favoured recruits with military training, and in the first years of the new century took on veterans of the Boer War.[43]

Once employed, officers living in the prison had to be in bed by 10 p.m. unless on night shift, and required permission from their superior before marrying — a privilege frequently withheld since it meant one fewer officer sleeping on the premises. To compensate for these unappealing conditions, Hume also introduced uniforms and an improved salary scale, with bonuses and long-service pay. Promotions became fairer and more frequent, and by the turn of the century staff were given two training periods a week.

I I I

The other consequential, and still visible, outcome of Hume's long spell at the head of the prison service was a phalanx of new prison buildings.[44] In Auckland particularly, almost all the construction work was carried out by inmates themselves — a form of hard labour of which Hume greatly approved. 'There is no labour more suitable for prisoners,' he thought, 'than their employment upon buildings rendered necessary by their own misconduct, more especially if it can be proved that the cost of erection is minimised.'[45] He rejected the floor plan drawn up by Edward Mahoney, and in 1882 ordered a new design from another architect, P. F. Burrows, who produced a plan more closely modelled on the British 'panopticon' prisons that Hume was familiar with, with cellblocks radiating from a central control point.[46]

The design was in the form of an irregular cross, with its vertical arm forming the administration and central surveillance wing. The horizontal arm crossed the vertical towards its lower end, and an additional wing stood at a right angle from each end of this horizontal arm. This allowed, at least in theory, for 220 prisoners of different types, including women and debtors, to be confined separately while supervised by a relatively small number of guards. A useful feature of this modular design, as Mahoney had originally noted, was that each wing could be built in succession, with prisoners from the Stockade moved into it as soon as it was complete, while further construction carried on alongside.

Hume rejected the more elegant features of Burrows' design for the exterior of the prison in favour of a stark and forbidding gothic style. The final plan included a large basement floor with two-storeyed wings above it, except for the central wing, which rose to three storeys, topped by a handsome hexagonal tower reached by a spiral staircase. Smaller turrets giving panoramic surveillance rose from the ends of the cellblocks, each topped with a pointed roof, which, the *Herald* suggested optimistically, would 'relieve the somber aspect of the structural mass'.[47] The use of iron roof girders, concrete floors and other inflammable materials relieved the extreme fire risk that daily threatened the Stockade.

By late 1882 Burrows' revised plans were approved, and prisoners set to work in the open ground alongside their rotting wooden cellblocks, excavating the foundations for the buildings that still stand on Mount Eden's lower slopes.[48] For the next 25 years, apart from breaks when state finances ran short, prison-building was the dominant daily activity for most inmates. For much of that time only a foreman and two instructor stonemasons were employed on the construction, while prisoners supplied all other labour. 'It is very rarely a stonemason gets "ran in" [i.e. imprisoned], and his services become available gratuitously to the State,' the *Herald* revealed. 'The prisoners employed on the work have the melancholy satisfaction of knowing that their labours are all tending to one remit, namely, making their own bondage more secure.'[49]

The entire external structure was built from the dark-grey basalt that the prisoners quarried nearby. Although much modified, damaged and surrounded by newer structures in the following 120 years, this is fundamentally the same louring edifice that Aucklanders drive past daily on the Southern Motorway, which now passes closely beside it at the height of the second-storey windows. The first section to be started was the north wing. The basalt blocks for its walls, typically measuring about 30 x 45 centimetres, were laboriously passed by hand up the levels of scaffolding until they reached the blocklayer. Much larger blocks weighing up to three tons were also used at certain points, and must have required a block and tackle to hoist into position. Every door and window opening was topped by an arch with a central keystone, although these magnificent examples of Victorian stonemasonry were mostly replaced later by concrete beams.

The windows were heavily barred, and the wrought-iron cell doors pierced with a small window. Cells were equipped with hammock beds and an 'indicator' — a button the inmate could press in an emergency to release a small hinged arm that swung out into the corridor and alerted the warder on duty. At the end of each corridor, hot and cold baths were installed, and prisoners were required to use them weekly.[50] An unfortunate dogleg entrance to these bathrooms obscured them from the view of warders in the passageways, and they were favoured locations for numerous rapes and beatings, sometimes fatal, in years to come.[51] The building had no heating, insulation or damp-proofing and proved bitterly uncomfortable in Auckland's dank winters.[52]

The first occupants of the new prison, mostly long-serving penal-servitude men, were installed in the ground floor of the north wing in 1888, while construction of its upper floor was still underway. It took a further six years to fully complete the wing, and in that time the problems caused by combining a penal facility with a construction site created onerous security headaches for the staff. At some points the outer walls of the new wing reached to within three metres of the perimeter wall, and the scaffolding that surrounded the unfinished structure narrowed this gap further still. A warder with a loaded carbine patrolled the gap during the day, and after the evening lockup an unarmed night watchman replaced him. Escaping from the unfinished building was difficult, but a sufficiently determined and agile man could break into it.

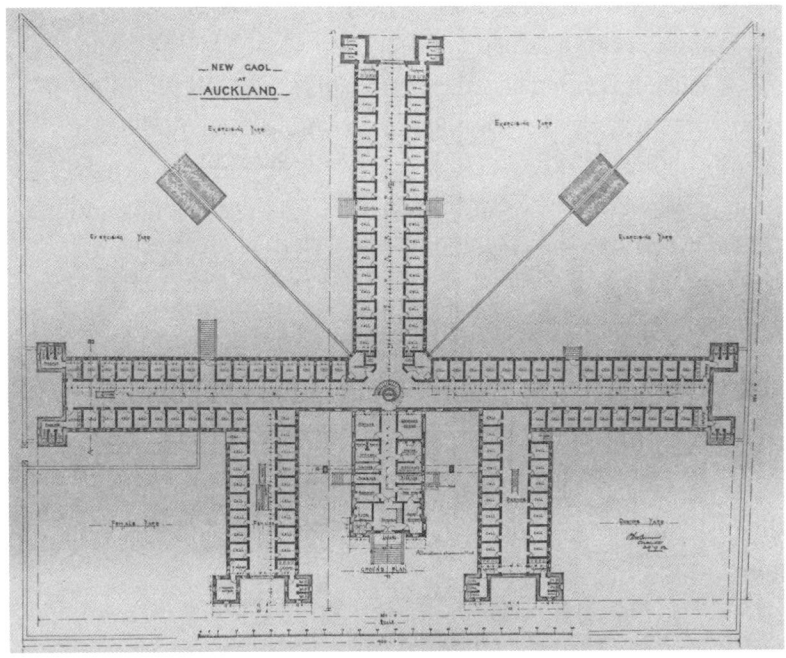

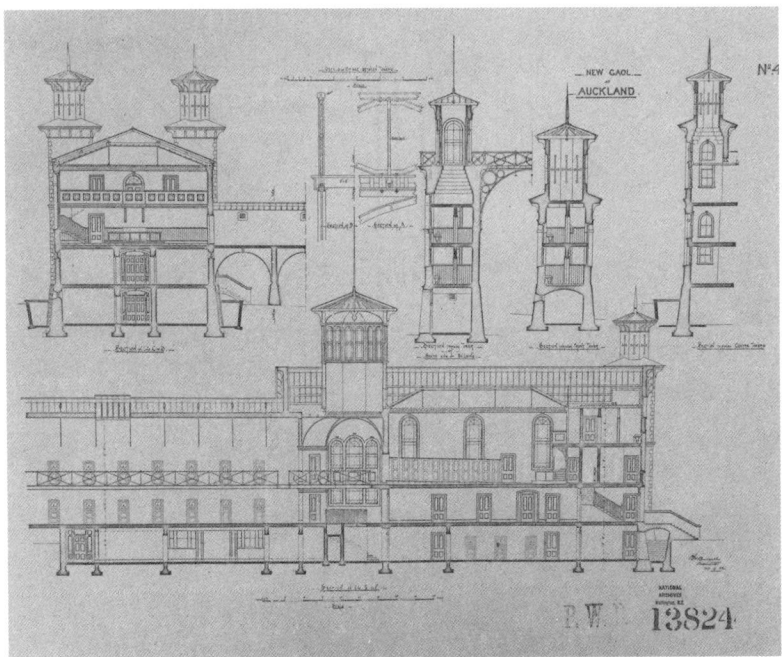

Architect P. F. Burrows' plans were adopted in 1882, but the proposed exterior design was rejected in favour of a more traditional, dour, gothic style. The hexagonal towers were replaced with rectangular crenellated turrets. The central tower, however, survived. *ARCHIVES NEW ZEALAND, ABKK W4358 24411, BOX 141*

Just on dusk in March 1889, a skilled housebreaker named Joseph Hood, released a week earlier from his three-year sentence, surreptitiously approached the outer side of the boundary wall with a long ladder. He climbed to the top, hauling a heavy sack, waited until the night watchman had ambled out of sight, then swung down onto the scaffolding and concealed his load in an unfinished cell in the upper floor before returning by the same route.

Next day the excitement among inmates working in that area aroused the suspicions of the foreman of works and other staff. After lockup that night they searched the site and discovered a treasure trove hidden under lime-sacks. Tobacco, tooth powder, sugar, cheese, butter, apples, jam, preserved milk, pepper, writing paper, postage stamps, currant cake and other delights had been smuggled in by the philanthropic Mr Hood. He had even included a flask of brandy 'for the use of one of the female prisoners'.[53] Hood was picked up shortly afterwards for a jewellery theft, but although police suspected him of smuggling in the contraband they were unable to prove it in court. He was given a further four years on the theft charge and returned to the prison, presumably hoping for another benefactor on the outside.

The constant presence, within reach of alert inmates, of building materials and half-completed structures resulted in the first escape from the new prison in 1896. A young burglar and recidivist escaper named Alley spotted a long plank lying near the boundary wall and found the temptation too much to resist. He propped the plank in a corner of the wall, crawled up it, and dropped the full five and a half metres to the ground on the other side.[54] This impromptu feat brought him several days of freedom, before a detective arrested him at the home of an accomplice.[55]

Once completed in 1894, the north wing's solid outside walls reassured visitors and nearby residents. However, some were disturbed at the prison's bleak appearance and feared that it would soon appear outdated. Premier Richard Seddon made a visit of inspection and told the House that he thought the new structure resembled a fortress. He would have preferred a more attractive, better-lit building, 'one more in accordance with modern ideas, and constructed by free labour'.[56] This impression was insightful, and anticipated many later comments on the prison's already outmoded design.

In addition to his new building's deliberately dispiriting appearance and

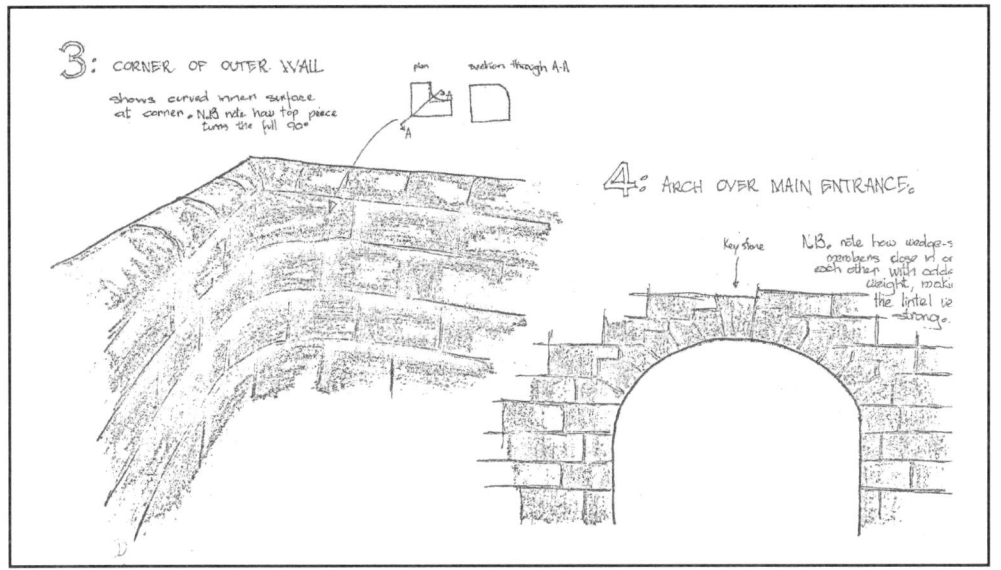
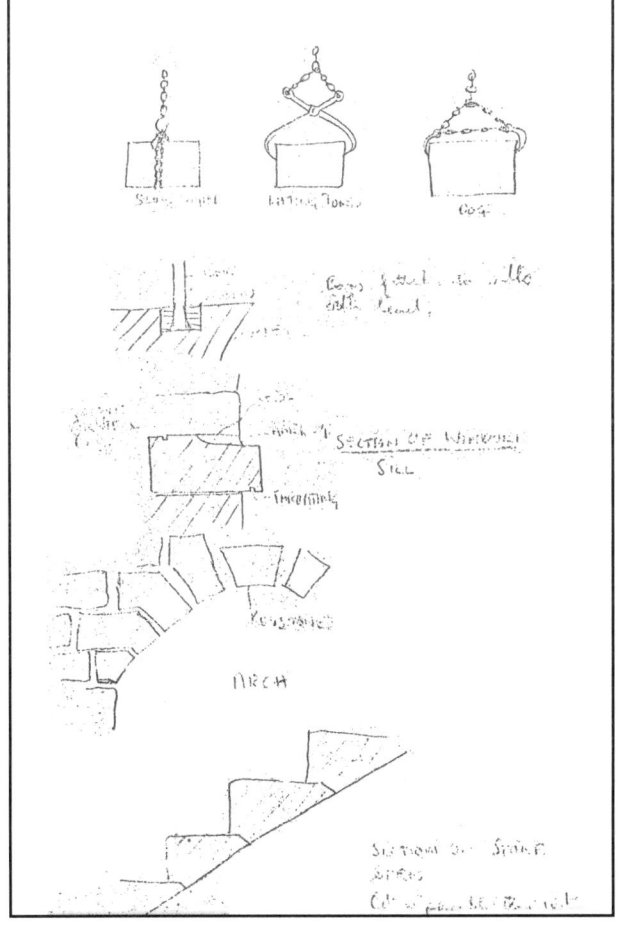

Details of the prison's impressively complex stonework. *DEPARTMENT OF CORRECTIONS*

lack of comforts, Hume favoured a cell layout that kept prisoners apart as much as possible, on the grounds that any association would lead them to further corrupt one another. This lack of common spaces created endless problems for later generations of staff, and was a disadvantage not shared by the Stockade, whose design included large shared cells. One of those became known as 'the Pa', since it was occupied for many years by the Māori prisoners who, until well into the twentieth century, made up only a small proportion of the total inmate population. They were typically sentenced for minor dishonesty offences such as cattle-, sheep- or horse-stealing, or for crimes stemming from cultural differences in matters such as the age of sexual consent. 'When in single cells, they are rather given to fretting,' a fellow inmate reported, and placing them together in the Pa was found to be the most suitable arrangement.[57]

I I I

As early as 1879, before work on the stone prison had even begun, a distinguished visitor toured the Stockade and asked to speak to its Māori inmates. The fully tattooed Waikato chief and military leader Rewi Maniapoto gave the 13 Māori then in residence a stern lecture. 'It is right that those who break the laws should pay the penalty ... but if you remain quiet, patient and obedient, you will be allowed to return to your homes, and I advise you to sin no more.'[58] The previous year the old chief had made a peace treaty with the government, and this speech may have been intended to impress his hosts with his loyalty.

A few years later, one of Rewi's kinsmen, a tempestuous Maniapoto chief named Te Mahuki, was admitted to the prison to serve 12 months with hard labour. He and his followers had vehemently opposed government plans to build the Main Trunk Railway through their tribal territory, and a surveying team that entered the district to mark out the route was ambushed and captured. For this crime Mahuki was regarded by the other Māori inmates as a political prisoner rather than a criminal, and they referred to him as 'the prophet'.

During one Sunday morning church service he gave them a memorable lesson in equal rights. Archdeacon Clarke conducted the main service, attended by Māori as well as Pākehā, and then announced, 'My white brethren will now retire; the Maoris will remain, as I will hold a short

Inmates in the stoneyard prepare materials for the new prison, 1906. The decrepit Stockade stands behind them, with the first wings of the new prison to its right. *NEW ZEALAND POLICE MUSEUM*

service for them in their own language.' Mahuki rose to object. 'Why make a difference?' he asked. 'We Maoris have sat all through the pakeha service, not understanding a word... let the pakeha sit through the Maori service.' When the archdeacon translated these words, 'there was a sort of general "Good on you, Mahuki!"'[59]

A second Māori prophet and military leader whose name and reputation were known throughout the country spent a short period in the prison in 1890. Te Kooti Arikirangi Te Tūruki, a former guerrilla commander later pardoned by the government, had been arrested near Ōpōtiki while leading an unarmed cavalcade to visit followers of his Ringatū religion. He was convicted of breaching the peace and ordered to pay sureties amounting to the enormous sum of £1500. While his supporters sought the means to pay this amount, he was transported to Auckland and held at Mount Eden for two weeks. Other Māori prisoners were exceedingly deferential to this elderly and near-legendary figure. 'He spoke little to anyone. At a [church] service he never looked to the right or left, or moved, sitting on a form by himself.'[60]

In the final years of the century, several Hokianga Māori were imprisoned for their armed resistance to paying a deeply resented dog tax. Their leader and four others were sentenced to 18 months' hard labour in mid-1898 but released less than a year later for good behaviour and after political agitation on their behalf. During their time in prison they received enforced medical treatment from the now very elderly Dr Philson. He insisted on vaccinating new inmates and particularly Māori, whom he believed were widely infected with tuberculosis. Any prisoner who could not show the scar of an earlier vaccination on his arm was liable to receive the doctor's attentions. The five 'dog tax' prisoners may have been given a faulty dose of vaccine, as their arms became so severely infected they were unable to go out to work in the quarry for some time.[61]

III

For several years in the mid-1880s a small and dismal auxiliary penal facility, occupied only by women, stood alongside the Stockade. This was the Lock Hospital, established under the Contagious Diseases Act 1869, which empowered city authorities to compulsorily detain suspected prostitutes and, if necessary, treat them for venereal disease. One patient,

Mary Alice Eggerton, was just 10 years old. The women's clients were not subject to the same restraints, and feminist agitation eventually forced the repeal of the Act in 1910.⁶²

Women inmates of the Stockade itself were shifted to a new female division in 1893, when the second wing of the new prison became available. They found this accommodation more spacious than in the Stockade, in part because the number of female inmates had dropped to as few as 12 at a time.⁶³ This welcome development was thought to be due to the earnest efforts of the Salvation Army's Prison Gate Brigade and particularly of one of its staff, a Mrs Hutchinson. She offered short-term accommodation to women on their release, and often saved them from being swiftly re-arrested for drunkenness or other minor offences.⁶⁴ The first Prison Gate Brigade in the country had opened in Auckland in 1884, with the aim of helping all recently discharged prisoners 'towards employment and giving them fellowship'.⁶⁵ Hume, a father of seven sons but no daughters, had little faith in these efforts in respect of women since 'the female criminal population of the colony ... is, with few exceptions, of the most degraded class, and long past all possible chance of reformation'.⁶⁶

From the 1890s women's groups such as the National Council of Women and the Women's Christian Temperance Union added prison reform to their agenda of social concerns, and agitated for a separate women's prison in both the North and South Islands, and for women to be able to serve as Visiting Justices. Hume predictably scorned both proposals. He argued that the relatively small number of women inmates, mostly serving short sentences for drink- and disorder-related offences, did not justify separate institutions, although he conceded that women's prisons would inevitably be introduced at some future date. Female Visiting Justices, he believed, were also unnecessary since women committed few offences while in prison.⁶⁷ As late as 1907 he advised the government that:

> the extreme leniency shown to female offenders is a distinct menace to the health and morality of the community. Each of these women is a plague-spot in their neighbourhood, and from them vice spreads throughout the district, often beginning with their own daughters. No short term of imprisonment will ever reform these women, probably a

Prison guards photographed in 1903. Their work was hard and their pay poor, but most were proud of their profession. *NEW ZEALAND HERALD*

long sentence would be equally useless; but in the latter case society would be free from their baneful presence for some time, and they themselves would live a cleanly, useful life, for the worst women can be made useful in prison.[68]

The work of the Prison Gate Brigade was supplemented by an increasingly active prison chaplaincy. The Presbyterian Inner City Missioner, Duncan MacPherson, visited Mount Eden regularly, spending time in the prison hospital, the recreation yards and the women's division.[69] Inmates appeared to have particularly high regard for the diminutive Anglican chaplain, Reverend Hill, who, like Mrs Hutchinson, sometimes took discharged prisoners into his own house until they could find employment and accommodation. On his departure from Auckland in 1890 they sent 'the little parson' a heartfelt written tribute: 'As chaplain, you are the one official whom prisoners can be permitted to regard as their friend, and not one of coercion.'[70] Humanitarians such as these helped counteract the Inspector of Prisons' more bigoted attitudes.

Hume believed in making prisons so unpleasant that the poor would be deterred from entering them, and as the 'long depression' of the 1890s began to bite this policy had a growing appeal to political leaders. Ensuring that conditions within the prison were less attractive than those faced by even the most deprived sections of the unincarcerated community was known as the principle of lesser privilege. 'It is the duty of all interested in the reformation of criminals,' announced Hume, 'to set their faces against anything like luxuries or too good feeding in places such as prisons'; and from 1890 the allowance of bread and meat for boys under 16 was sharply reduced.[71] However, social conditions in Auckland grew so desperate that some homeless men made deliberate efforts to be admitted to prison. To discourage this practice, rations for those serving less than three months were cut further still.[72]

To Hume's credit, he recognised that some classes of inmate — drunks, lunatics and children — could not be held wholly responsible for their offending and did not deserve the harsh treatment imposed on the remaining prison population. Year after year he protested in his annual reports about the practice of imprisoning young offenders. Both boys and girls as young as 10 were routinely admitted to Mount Eden for up to three months, although, he advised, 'it is invariably found that the prison discipline has absolutely no reformatory influence upon them'. The only other options available to magistrates when sentencing these juvenile offenders were to discharge them or, in the case of boys, send them to the Kohimarama industrial training school.[73] Until 1887 no such institution existed for girls, so if they were found living in 'a wretched condition amidst squalid surroundings', they were imprisoned with hard labour for having no lawful means of support.[74] After an industrial school for delinquent girls opened in Auckland, where they were trained for jobs as domestic servants, the prison received fewer of these highly vulnerable inmates.

From early in his term of office Hume advocated for non-custodial sentences for children, and was gratified when a First Offenders' Probation Act was passed in 1886, long before any other country in the British Empire. It empowered magistrates to sentence first offenders to probation rather than prison, and appointed probation officers to monitor their activities. However, very few young offenders were treated in this way in the years immediately after the Act was passed, and for much of the 1890s a large number of young boys and girls continued to be admitted to Mount Eden's slot-like cells.[75]

Not everyone shared Hume's approval of probation as a diversionary sentence. The Mount Eden governor in this period, Francis Severne, thought the First Offenders' Act was 'responsible for a large increase of crime amongst youths and servant girls' because it encouraged them to believe they could break the law with impunity, thus launching them on criminal careers.[76] In 1904 Hume pointed out in response that of more than 1500 offenders placed on probation since the Act was passed, 85 per cent had not re-offended. He commended the probation officers for the way they performed their 'onerous and unpaid duties', and the Act itself for 'giving those placed under it a chance of redeeming the first false step'.[77]

Hume and Severne were in accord, however, in resenting the constant problems resulting from imprisoning alcoholics and the mentally ill. Habitual drunkards were the prison's most recidivist inmates, commonly spending less than 24 hours outside its walls between their two- and three-month sentences for disorderly behaviour and similar petty crimes. Hume was adamant that '[d]runkenness is a disease requiring a conscientious and judicious medical treatment', and 'to punish it with a fine or short imprisonment . . . is an expensive and useless cruelty'. He pointed out that this view was widespread in other countries, yet in New Zealand a chronic drunkard had 'not the slightest chance of being admitted to a hospital even when in a dangerous state of *delirium tremens*'.[78] Once in prison, these unfortunates were greatly over-represented in the punishment cells and infirmary and, with melancholy frequency, among those who died before their sentences expired.

Year after year Governor Severne denounced the inhumanity and inconvenience of imprisoning drunkards, and by 1906 his irritation on this matter had overcome his customary deference to higher authority: 'I suppose it is quite useless for me to again point out the necessity of providing a fitting place for the treatment of persons suffering from delirium tremens. It is quite obvious that a prison is not such a place; it is unfair to the patient, to the officers of the prison, and to the prisoners.'[79] In that year his pleas were finally answered by the passage of the Habitual Drunkards Act, which gave magistrates the power to commit alcoholics to institutions providing for their care as well as their detention. The Salvation Army set up the country's first 'inebriates' retreat' at Pakatoa Island in the Hauraki Gulf, and then added another facility on the larger, neighbouring island of Rotoroa. Thereafter drunks and drunken behaviour could still be found inside Mount Eden's walls, but not the distressing spectacle of men and women 'drying out' through agonised fits of delirium.

In 1891 the prison cannot have housed a more despairing inmate than the Italian-born Louis Chemis, aged 39 and serving life for murder. Two years earlier, he had been living quietly as a roadman near Wellington with his wife Annie and their five children. Then his neighbour was brutally stabbed to death and Chemis was convicted of the crime, although the prosecution case amounted to little more than an assertion that Italians were known to be excitable and to carry stilettos. Although he had no previous criminal record, Chemis, as a lifer, was sent to Auckland where the most dangerous and desperate convicts were held and where he was far removed from his family and acquaintances.

One evening he took the blunt tin knife issued to prisoners with their meal and hacked into a vein on his arm, losing a large amount of blood before he was noticed by warders and carried to the infirmary.[80] He was returned to his cell as soon as he was sufficiently recovered, and for the rest of his sentence received no special treatment apart, perhaps, from extra surveillance from sympathetic warders. He made a second and successful suicide attempt some years later, after his release.

By the late nineteenth century the nation's more floridly mentally ill could be housed in several large mental hospitals, but those whose symptoms were combined with criminal behaviour were held in prisons with no facilities or expertise for managing them apart from truncheons and straitjackets. Both Hume and Severne abhorred this situation, since these inmates created many of the same problems as drunkards, and often to a more extreme extent. In early 1900, within a few months of his appointment, Severne was obliged to admit 'a dangerous lunatic' who had committed a savage assault on a police constable.[81] Two years later he gave evidence that prisoners of unsound mind were regularly held in the prison 'and considerable difficulty was experienced in getting them removed to the lunatic asylum', which was often overcrowded.[82]

III

By 1901 the basement of the central wing, the core structure of the entire facility, was almost complete and the governor's only complaint with the work was that he could not find more prisoners to carry it out, especially as the old wooden cellblocks alongside were 'rapidly falling into decay, particularly the roofs'.[83]

Inmate numbers reduced somewhat in this period due to improving economic conditions, but also to slowly advancing theories of penal policy. Hume had come to realise that low-risk prisoners could be held in cheaper and less secure surroundings than a massive stone prison, and tree-planting camps were established in rural locations — the forerunner of today's prison farms. Within the wider prison system, Mount Eden's role was changing to become the nation's maximum-security institution, and the longest-serving, most dangerous and repeatedly violent offenders were progressively transferred to it from throughout the country. Systems for admitting and managing inmates had become more regularised and better documented from the 1890s, offering a more detailed picture of the daily routines.

On admittance, an inmate was placed in a cell furnished with a straw mattress; a set of tin bowls for washing, bodily wastes and food; a small shelf for books and a larger one for a table. At 6 a.m., and an hour later in winter, a clanging bell marked the start of a new day and cell doors were unlocked to allow their occupants to empty their slop tins into a sink in the yard. After breakfast they were allowed an hour's outdoor exercise, walking in circles in their separate classes — convicts serving three or more years, hard-labour inmates and 'short-timers'.[84] This was the only time of day when conversation was allowed. Their diet had barely changed from the days of the Queen Street gaol, with porridge, or 'skilly', and bread served for breakfast and dinner. The midday meal consisted almost invariably of a stew of boiled beef and vegetables, and potatoes (sometimes rotten).[85]

Meals were prepared in a subterranean kitchen, with individual portions ladled into mess tins and sent up in lifts to each corridor. By the early 1900s one small but treasured luxury had been added to the daily routine — each wing had a box of tobacco pipes, to be handed out by a warder for a 15-minute smoke.[86] The offices in the central administration wing included a room for the resident fingerprint expert and an armoury, with racks of ready-loaded rifles and revolvers awaiting use in an emergency. The chief gaoler's office contained a special feature, a shiny steel dock placed well back from his desk, in which an inmate seeking an interview stood at attention until invited to speak.[87]

By the early 1900s, about half the total prison population had been transferred to the new buildings, which boasted one undoubted improvement on the Stockade — each pair of adjacent cells was lit with a small gas lamp. The acute fire risk in the adjacent wooden buildings, where only shorter-sentenced inmates now remained, meant they had no form of lighting; 'next to the loss of liberty, being locked up in the cells in the darkness, from an early hour in the winter afternoons, is most keenly felt by the prisoners', the *New Zealand Herald* reported.[88] Reading and solitary study was a valued privilege, and the prison library's small stock of books was issued at the rate of one or two a week, depending on the prisoner's classification. Edward Bellamy's socialist-utopian classic *Looking Backward* was a particularly popular title after its release in 1888.[89]

In both the old and new buildings, infestations of lice and other insects were a constant torment. The staff blamed this problem on indigent new arrivals bringing vermin in their clothing. The usual remedy was 'to strip a prisoner to the skin and bury his clothes six feet under the soil as the only effectual means of exterminating insect pests'.[90]

As a consequence of the generally falling crime rate, and of growing public unease at the courts' practice of imposing death sentences for a wide range of crimes, the condemned cells at the southern end of the central wing were seldom occupied in the last years of the Victorian era. The machinery of execution, however, remained ready for use, and was significantly upgraded after the horrifically botched hanging in 1882 of Taurangaika Winiata. He was an Epsom farmhand who murdered a colleague and took refuge for several years in the King Country, from where he was captured and returned to Auckland. His execution in the prison, carried out by an ex-inmate named Lewis, was described as 'a shockingly bungled and mismanaged affair. The scene below the scaffold was brutal and revolting.'[91] These well-worn euphemisms referred to the hangman's failure to ensure a prompt death, so that he was obliged to add his own weight to the lurching body beneath the trapdoor until Winiata eventually expired.

A few years later a double hanging of the 'Great Barrier Island murderers' took place, with the usual macabre group of onlookers stationed on the hill above the prison walls. Although the task was again carried out by Lewis, an improved scaffold mechanism was employed, and it was afterwards asserted that 'no execution in New Zealand was ever carried through more smoothly or with greater certitude'.[92] This reliably lethal device was reassembled in 1893 for the final execution performed in the prison in the nineteenth century, and again it operated with impressive efficiency. The condemned man, Alexander Scott, became the twenty-third to be executed in Auckland since Maketu's hanging 40 years earlier.[93]

| | |

By 1905, with the second major stage of the building programme well advanced, Hume could claim that the 'Stone Jug', as hardened offenders now referred to it, 'bids well to shortly be one of the best prisons in the Australasian Colonies'.[94] Not all public officials were so enthusiastic. Auckland MP, William Napier, was concerned that even before it was finished Mount Eden was a prison 'of an obsolete type' and its proximity to the central city would come to be regarded as a mistake.[95] That prediction was borne out within a few years when the neighbourhood was subjected to a vociferous riot by inmates.

In late 1904 a shrewd career criminal named Thomas Ramsey, serving a 12-year sentence for robbery with violence and regarded by police as 'the most dangerous criminal in the colony', was transferred from Dunedin to the greater security of Mount Eden. Within a few months he and other prisoners attacked a warder and were placed in punishment cells in the north wing. These happened to overlook the railway line and Khyber Pass Road, and for the next several days people in that vicinity were assailed with 'a flood of the most disgusting language that the human tongue can fashion'. Using planks broken up from their beds, the prisoners smashed everything in their cells. They barricaded the doors to prevent the warders entering, and soon 'the whole prison was in revolt, and the furniture-breaking had become general'.[96]

Even after warders succeeded, with great difficulty, in removing the ringleaders to solitary cells in the basement, the uproar continued, and the following morning a culprit named Ashton was detected in an escape attempt, using 'a rope about as thick as a man's waist, contrived out of his cell blankets'.[97] It later emerged that the offenders had deliberately contrived to be moved to the basement cells to better their chances of making an escape.

This riot occurred, it was claimed, because Mount Eden 'has been made the dumping ground for the worst offenders in the colony — men of the most desperate character, whom it is not considered safe to leave in prisons less strongly built'.[98] The disciplinarian Hume reiterated his earlier call to allow flogging 'for insubordinate and mutinous conduct'.[99] More temperate voices pointed to the need for a special maximum-security institution, well apart from residential communities, where the most reckless and violent criminals could be held. 'A proper system of classification would remove such individuals altogether from the common gaol, and place them on an island where they could be subjected to a regime of sternness fitted to their temperament and disposition.'[100]

Given the investment in building the prison over the previous 20 years, there was no immediate likelihood of constructing a further high-security institution elsewhere, and instead legislation was introduced to deter a repeat of the alarming scenes of 1905. The Habitual Criminals and Offenders Act 1906 provided for the most serious and recidivist offenders to be imprisoned for an indefinite period, at the discretion of a Supreme Court judge. A law of this kind was already in force in New South Wales and it was believed, although with little real evidence, that Sydney's most desperate lags had fled across the Tasman to 'constitute the nucleus of a professional criminal class' in New Zealand.[101] In 1908, Mount Eden's new governor Thomas Pointon could count 11 inmates held under the Act, which remained in force for the next half-century.[102]

By 1909, two-thirds of the total prison population of about three hundred were housed in the new stone buildings. This was Hume's final year as Inspector-General of Prisons. After three decades of remarkably dedicated if uninspired effort, he could take satisfaction at the sight of Auckland's massive new prison, although tempered with disappointment that most of his reactionary penal policies had not been adopted by the New Zealand authorities. A later successor, Charles E. Matthews, described Hume's reign as one of 'discipline, discipline, discipline. Discipline means repression. Little wonder that such a system led to outbreaks of savagery on the part of men so treated with retaliation by warders.'[103]

The government had largely abandoned the practice, of which Hume himself was the prime example, of recruiting prison staff from the armed forces, and his replacement as Inspector-General came instead from a medical background. Dr Frank Hay had formerly been inspector of the country's mental hospitals, and he intended to draw on that experience to address the psychological elements of criminal behaviour. In his enthusiasm for reformative rather than purely punitive policies, Hay found a powerful ally in the new Minister of Justice, an eloquent liberal named John Findlay who hoped to 'restore a measure of self-respect to the criminal, to find out his physical and mental state, the temperamental conditions, the environment, the circumstances that led to the crime'.[104]

Findlay told parliamentary colleagues that 'the old method of punishment looked only at the enormity of the offence; it cared nothing for the criminal . . . No attempt was made to go beyond the crime and look into the character of the prisoner.'[105] As a preliminary step in this new direction, he ordered all prison cells to be equipped with lighting so every inmate had the opportunity to read and study throughout their sentence. The prison libraries, he found, were so poor that some prisoners had read every work they contained at least once, and he gave instructions to stock them with a larger and better-selected range of reading material, including popular journals.[106]

The new minister was greatly influenced by Reverend James Kayll, who had served as Mount Eden's Anglican prison chaplain in the early 1890s.[107] For prison to have any long-term beneficial effect, Kayll believed, inmates should be given opportunities for education that would return them to where they had departed from 'the social track', so that on release they would regard themselves as functional members of society.[108] Together, he and Findlay planned a system of specialised prisons to hold different types of offender, including one specifically for the criminally insane.[109]

As noted earlier, a large new prison building intended to become the country's main central prison had been constructed on the summit of Wellington's Mount Cook from about 1894. Effective local opposition to this proposed national prison appears to have been the main reason why Mount Eden remained in use for a century after it was first declared unfit for purpose. In spite of concerns at its gloomy appearance and oppressive design, Mount Eden was seen as an outstanding facility which, when its construction was completed, offered great promise for reformative projects. Its long history of putting prisoners to profitable work raised hopes that they could eventually be trained in a range of industrial skills.[110] Findlay promised a penal policy based on reformative rather than vengeful principles: 'A new spirit, and a new purpose, and a new measure of criminal punishment has arrived.'[111]

4:
Brutal Bastille
1910–1922

> The old wooden prison still existed [in 1912]. It hadn't been taken down . . . We slept on old straw mattresses and at night-time the bugs came out and had a great feast of us . . . And I can say this with every word of truth, that you'd be astounded at how happy prisoners were to get away from that old wooden building and to get into these modern stone cells. It just shows you how things change. To get into one of these stone cells was a remarkable thing and of course, there was only one man to a cell.[1]

In 1974 John A. Lee — one-time delinquent, war hero, political orator, bestselling author and one of Mount Eden's most distinguished former inmates — returned to revisit the institution that had played a formative part in his extraordinary career. More than 60 years on he recalled with acuity and bone-dry wit his early impressions as a defiant 20-year-old facing his first prison term after a year spent roaming the central North Island with a Māori mate he called Ned.

The two young larrikins had been arrested in Raetihi for sly-grogging and petty theft, and sent to Auckland for trial in early 1912. While on remand awaiting trial (bail was out of the question, given their history of absconding at every opportunity), they were not required to go out to work with the other inmates. Both chose to do so anyway because, as Lee said, 'remand rations were the barest of sustenance', and they preferred to qualify for the rather more generous hard-labour diet. The pair were split up straight away, with Ned marched off to the quarry to work alongside the short-time and less skilled, while Lee, although inside prison walls for the first time in his life, was assigned to a stone bench known as a banker in the penal yard, and put to work squaring blocks of stone with cold chisels and a heavy mallet.[2]

He found that he had arrived at Mount Eden during an era of 'long, brutalising sentences', and that his workmates included men serving 16 years and even life.[3] Lee had earned admission to their company by drifting into delinquency after a childhood spent in crushing poverty, and especially by running away repeatedly from the Burnham juvenile reformatory near Christchurch, where he was sent at age 15. The casual brutality and regimentation of Burnham was so intolerable that Mount

Eden appeared almost a sanctuary by comparison, and the thought of escaping from the prison apparently never crossed his mind.

However, one face in the penal yard already familiar to him from Burnham was that of an energetic young career criminal who thought of little else but his next escape. John Christie was a stylish crook, fatally attracted to fast motorbikes, safe-cracking and extreme risk. He had absconded repeatedly from Burnham, then from a five-year sentence for theft in Invercargill, before being sent to the supposedly escape-proof Mount Eden.[4] Within months he was discovered trying to break through his barred window.[5] He made several further attempts, and was re-admitted to the prison in 1917 as a habitual criminal. He went on to escape successively from several ships, the Avondale Mental Hospital and a moving train. In his final bid for freedom, in 1924, Christie followed the well-tried route of a plank propped against the wall of the Mount Eden stoneyard. He was seen by a warder, refused his order to stop, and was shot and killed. He was not yet 30.[6]

Within Mount Eden's rigid inmate hierarchy, the old lags in the penal yard ranked very near the top, and Lee felt both pride and trepidation at joining them. The experience proved surprisingly rewarding. 'I was in the yards between two fellows whose backs had been lashed with the old-fashioned cat of nine tails . . . Every time those two fellows talked to me, and they were very gentle fellows too, their constant refrain was, "You're a young man. Don't ever come back into this institution again." They were tireless in regard to it.'[7]

In this solicitous company, Lee toiled at the skilled and demanding work of shaping stonework for the few unfinished sections of the new prison. He quickly learned to meet his required daily output, then to exceed it, eventually producing double the amount of dressed stone expected of him. 'It wasn't long before someone was telling me to pipe down a little bit, you see. I was a youngster full of energy and with my chisel and my hammer I was probably trying to show what I could do. Suddenly the fellow who had about as much as 16 years to serve didn't want a pacemaker in jail.'[8] In time Lee learned to shape even the most complex and difficult pieces of granite masonry, such as the door-jamb stones. Sixty years later he could still feel a glow of pride as he inspected the old building's craftsmanship: 'All of my work is embedded in that grim fortress.'[9]

Even the experience of standing trial and receiving a 12-month sentence did not dampen the spirits of this novice inmate. While Ned was sent to serve his time in one of the low-security tree-planting camps formed in the final years of Arthur Hume's regime, Lee was regarded as a potential escaper, and was issued his broad-arrow prison uniform and placed in a wing occupied mainly by penal-servitude men.[10] Before locking him into his narrow single cell, a warder issued stern instructions not to communicate with any other prisoners. Soon afterwards Lee heard a cautious 'Hello' through the wall and, for fear of punishment, did not respond. Later, during his first spell of trudging around the penal-servitude exercise yard, a 'huge, tough man' approached him and introduced himself as the neighbour who had tried to make illicit contact. This proved to be another fortuitous acquaintanceship. The big man was a Mount Eden veteran and taught the young Lee the rules of survival in that strange and oddly companionable walled community. The sound of rattling keys, for example, let the inmates know when a warder was on their wing, and when that sound faded it was safe to communicate through the walls.

Lee's new guardian held the elite post of lead scaffolder on the construction works, and after a few weeks, when one of his gang was released from the prison, Lee was offered the chance to replace him. The work was sought after but extremely dangerous, and another scaffolder, a popular prisoner who had played at first five-eighth in Auckland's provincial rugby team, was killed when a plank he was passing up to the second floor slipped and fell on him. 'A great wave of emotion spread though the jail about that, and of course the average prisoner immediately said he was murdered.'[11]

For the devil-may-care Lee, however, erecting scaffolding proved less strenuous and at least as satisfying as the work of shaping stones. Descended from a line of vaudeville acrobats and circus tumblers, he discovered he could walk with ease along a two-by-three-inch plank some 10 metres above the paved courtyard. Erecting the topmost scaffolding also offered a greater degree of freedom, since few warders were prepared to venture up to the highest levels. At times Lee was able to climb to the turrets above each of the cellblocks and experience the rare gift of quiet solitude while enjoying a view that extended over much of Auckland city.[12]

After some months at this exhilarating activity he noticed from his privileged height that large crowds were regularly assembling outside the prison gates, waving flags and placards, and attempting to make themselves heard by those within. These protesters, he learned, were members of Auckland's vocal radical labour movement, gathered to support workers from the underground gold mines at Waihī that had been shut down for much of the year by an increasingly bitter strike. The police had chosen to bring matters to a head by arresting a number of the strikers, and eventually more than 60 of them, including union president Bill Parry, were held in Mount Eden.

Although they were required to wear prison uniform, the Waihī strikers were not given the option of hard labour and therefore had to sustain themselves on the more meagre diet provided to non-workers. They were offended by the hordes of biting insects infesting their bedding, and appalled at the 'disgusting' sanitary arrangements. Each man had a small bedpan in his cell and 'the covering being very defective indeed, the stench as it travelled down the passage-way and invaded the cells was beyond comparison'. A man who used his bedpan after lockup at 5 p.m. had to endure its smell during dinner and breakfast until 6.45 the following morning, when he was allowed to visit the outside lavatories. The weekly labour journal the *Maoriland Worker* commented: 'Fancy about a hundred-odd prisoners all congregating around one water tap, dodging one another in the effort to rinse and clean their slop basins.'[13] These insanitary conditions indicate that the proposed prison reforms promoted with such enthusiasm by John Findlay did not survive the 1912 general election, which produced a new Reform government headed by an uninspired conservative, Bill Massey.

The Waihī men were undoubtedly political prisoners, held for taking a stand on principle, since they could immediately obtain their release if they undertook not to repeat the protest activities that had led to their arrest. Although respectable and law-abiding in their former lives, they were denied privileges accorded to more routine criminals, such as newspapers that might enable them to follow the progress of the strike in their home town, and they were confined to their own area of the prison to prevent contact with other inmates.[14] They were also forbidden to smoke, although almost every other inmate smoked heavily during the exercise period and 'the jail currency really was tobacco'.[15] Nevertheless, much informal communication took place. 'Prisoners are always against the status quo,' wrote Lee. 'Large quantities of tobacco were gathered and donated to the strikers.'¹⁶ The poet Kendrick Smithyman, whose father was one of the radicals who orated, sang and shouted their support from outside the perimeter wall, wrote:

> By the end of September 1912
> the best place for a crash course in militant unionism
> was Mount Eden.¹⁷

These steadfast but fair-minded union men may not have anticipated how some students of their crash course would respond to it. In this period, a guard found in the stoneyard a handwritten charter urging the prisoners to form a union to defend their interests. It began:

> In view of the fact that the Screws of this prison have been having all their way lately, it is proposed to form a league, the object of which will be to protect <u>ourselves</u> against <u>them</u> and to stick together in all things. That in order to make the power of the League felt, it is suggested that an example be made of one of the worst screws by knocking him out and chopping an ear off.

No other evidence of the league's existence was found, but the charter was evidently taken seriously by prison authorities.¹⁸

Young Jack Lee, at that stage an unpoliticised member of the lumpenproletariat, was apparently unaffected by the mood of militancy and he never spoke with the Waihī men. However, on at least one occasion, from his eyrie in the scaffolding, he waved a red handkerchief at the demonstrators outside the perimeter wall, provoking wild cheers from the crowd. This 'was my first real act of agitation', he claimed later.¹⁹ The uproar outside was soon echoed by the prisoners themselves, until 'the prison staff interrupted work and locked all prisoners in their cells. Hysteria spreads easily in prison and cheering crowds could encourage bravado that might spark hysteria.'²⁰

Lee and the Waihī strikers shared the same view of one important aspect of prison life, its library. Lee found the selection 'wretchedly poor' but nevertheless read avidly from the moment he was locked in his cell at night until lights-out. The strikers, agreeing that '[t]he literature provided

WITHIN PRISON WALLS.
Semple and Parry converse, guarded by Cossack authorities.
(This is almost an exact representation of a scene in Mount Eden Jail on Monday, September 23.)

In 1912 the labour movement newspaper *Maoriland Worker* published this drawing of imprisoned Waihī strikers' leader Bill Parry, standing in the exercise yard accompanied by a hulking warder. The Federation of Labour's Bob Semple (a future Cabinet minister) is conversing with Parry through a hole in the perimeter wall. PAPERS PAST, MAORILAND WORKER, 4 OCTOBER 1912

for the prisoners leaves room for vast improvement', did the same.²¹ They also used the precious hours of illumination to write letters, at the permitted interval of one a month, to their supporters on the outside. In September, Bill Parry wrote to a fellow member of his union executive: 'Well, Comrade, I think it is time to conclude as my light is extinguished at 8 o'clock and I have only a little time to go . . . this is a typical home of the proletariat and makes an ideal industrial mirror, which enables one to see past, present and future.'²²

Two months after sending this letter, Parry's present circumstances seemed even less appealing, and for all of the 63 Waihī-strike inmates the future was suddenly a matter of the gravest urgency. Their seven-month-long dispute had been crushed, in an outburst of savage violence, by hired strikebreakers, and the remaining strikers and their families had been forced to leave Waihī under a volley of threats and curses. Parry told the press that these families 'were being terrorised'; accordingly, he and the other imprisoned men agreed to sign good-behaviour bonds that granted them their release. Bail for each of them, amounting to a hefty £1600, was advanced by a wealthy supporter, the brewery magnate Ernest Davis. The men marched out of the gates at nightfall to be met by more than one hundred men, women and children, most of them shouting and crying; the women, especially, were 'eager to tell their husbands, brothers, lovers, of the great change in the strike town'.²³

After some months Lee also left the prison — on transfer to the lower-security prison of Fort Cautley on Auckland's North Head in belated recognition of his age and minor criminal record.²⁴ He had spent long enough in Mount Eden, however, to experience one of the prison's most shameful executions, the hanging of a 16-year-old Northland youth named Tahi Kaka, who had murdered a gumdigger and stolen his savings to buy new clothes. 'There had been a big controversy about him, about whether he should be hung or not, just before I came into Mount Eden. And one thing that lives in my memory is the fact that on the wooden door of the remand yard, I saw his name there. He'd managed to write his name.'²⁵ Kaka's execution went ahead despite a public outcry, including a strong recommendation for mercy from the jury who convicted him. Described as 'of fine physique . . . with markedly boyish features', he went to his death after making a full confession, and with remarkable dignity. The last word he spoke as the hangman placed the regulation white canvas cap over his

Recent jailbird and future war hero and political legend John A. Lee on his discharge from prison in 1913. PAPERS PAST, POLICE GAZETTE, 7 MAY 1913

head was reported by the press as 'Hooray'.[26] It was almost certainly a cry of lamentation in his own language — 'Aue'.

Lee recalled: 'When the hanging occurred . . . nearly everybody battered on their iron doors. You could hear them ringing all over the place . . . Almost at any crisis in a jail — I don't know whether it's hysteria or just a desire to express some attitude — it's difficult to prevent nearly every prisoner in a ward starting to bang on the wall.'[27]

III

When Lee left Mount Eden in 1913, two months short of his one-year sentence in recognition of good behaviour, the prison building remained far from complete, with the west and south wings still under construction.[28] Inmates held in the near-derelict wooden buildings complained more bitterly than ever of insect infestations, and some woke with their eyes swollen almost shut from their bites, yet the growing number of inmates had to be housed somewhere.[29] The austere stone prison designed in 1882 was intended to hold no more than 220 prisoners, but by 1913 up to 300 might be in residence — one-third of the entire national prison population — and the unluckiest of them over-spilled into its decrepit predecessor.

The staff of 40 warders found the decaying wooden wing similarly uncomfortable, although this was just one of the grievances that prompted several of them to resign, and that made them hard to replace.[30] The disaffected men described a daily routine that began at 6.50 a.m., when they unlocked the cells for breakfast. Trusted inmates then delivered each man's porridge, bread and tea to his cell. An hour later all cells were again unlocked and the prisoners marched out to their day's labour. At noon they were marched back again, collecting their midday meal of soup or stew as they passed down the corridor. They were permitted a 20-minute smoke in the exercise yard before forming up again to be searched and marched back to work. The last bell at five o'clock marked the end of the day's work and the serving of the evening meal, a repeat of the breakfast. The warders therefore worked for 10 hours before they could sign off their day's reports. Two of them, on a fortnightly roster, remained on duty for the night shift, taking turns to catch a few hours' sleep.[31] Complaints about these long hours, poor pay and other working conditions were loud and frequent, but the Massey government had been elected on a fiercely

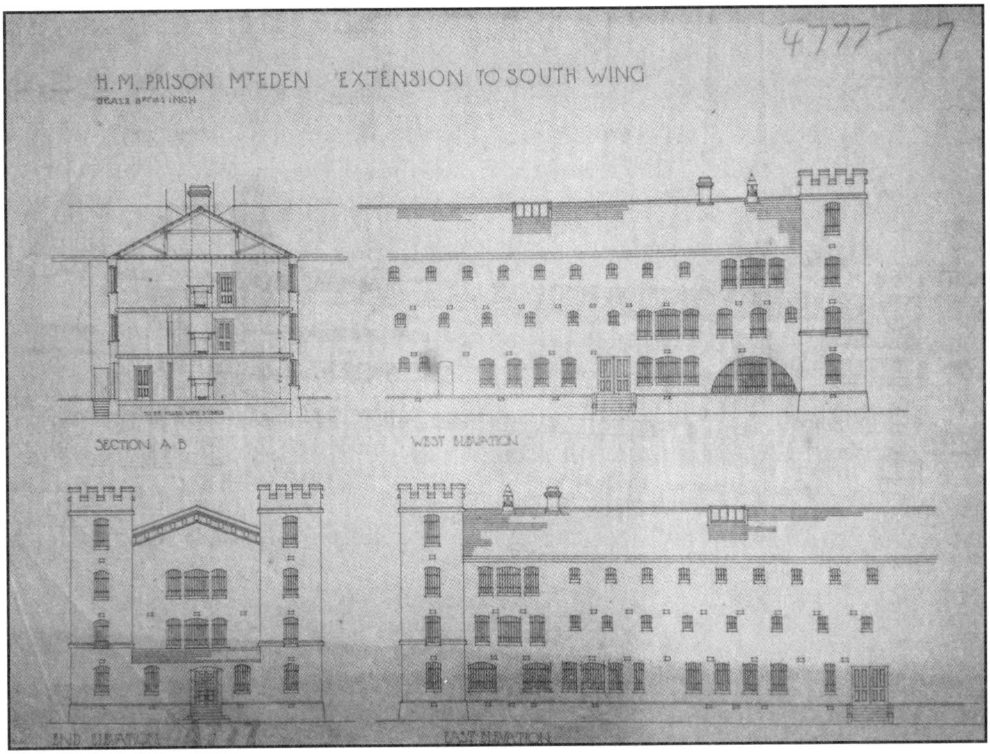

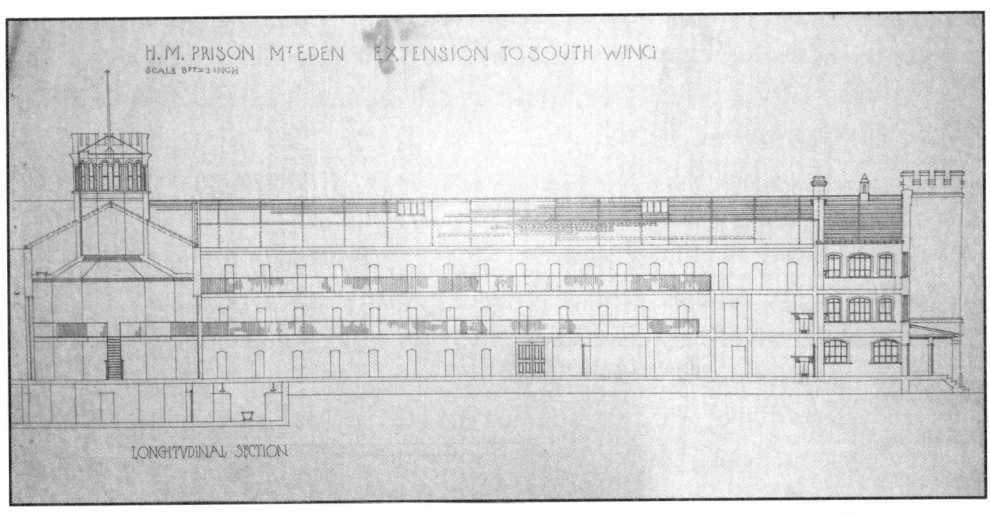

The first floor of the south wing was occupied by inmates from 1913. The wing was then extended to include a hospital, schoolroom, officers' quarters and more cells. This extension, the last part of the main prison to be built, was completed and occupied from 1917. *ARCHIVES NEW ZEALAND, BBAD A717 24137, BOX F86 ADO 777*

anti-union platform and made no concessions beyond progressing with the building programme.[32]

The Dome, the central control point housing the administration and the superintendent's office, was the radius for the four main wings of the new prison. Each of these wings rose up as a triple tier of cells around an inner atrium, ringed by walkways lined with iron railings. The unfinished west and south wings were occupied at the earliest opportunity, with the cell floors still 'left in a rough state'.[33] As the work progressed, the original plans were amended to provide facilities that had not been considered when construction began 30 years earlier, such as an adequate infirmary, dining and recreation rooms for the warders (but not the inmates), and a schoolroom. The internal design of the south wing was altered to incorporate these features at the cost of some individual cells.[34]

The final stages of construction were also able to take advantage of recent technological advances such as electric lighting, installed by a qualified electrician who was apparently also a serving inmate.[35] A hot-water supply was considered necessary, and the Public Works Department supplied the boilers and pipes, putting an end to the all-weather cold-water baths that, for over 40 years, had formed part of the admission process for every inmate.[36] The quarry was equipped with a mechanical stone-crusher producing road metal for sale, although its output was still supplemented by hand crushing carried out by old and infirm prisoners who could not manage the heavy work of the sledgehammer and drill.[37]

By 1915 the schoolroom in the new south wing was in regular use three nights a week, and for the first time classes were under the instruction of a state-certificated schoolteacher rather than an educated inmate. 'The progress of the prisoners attending is very satisfactory,' reported chief gaoler Ironside. 'They take a keen interest in their studies, and are grateful for the opportunity afforded them.'[38] Showing an assiduity that must have delighted their teacher, most students chose to continue their studies in their own cells in the intervals between school nights. However, the teacher reported his discouragement when 'men who are making good progress are removed to the prison camps where no primary-school work is taken'.[39] He described the lessons as primary-level reading and spelling, 'writing and English graded in difficulty according to the standard of the pupil, and geography of the British Empire'. The best progress was made by his Māori students and men due for release in a short time, as those with heavy sentences were inclined to 'brood over their troubles . . . [T]he long-sentence men value school only inasmuch as it makes a break in the monotony of prison life.'[40]

> The Maoris are for the most part quick and intelligent, but many are handicapped by the lack of even the little education the white men possess . . . Lack of self-confidence is apparent in most of the men, but a somewhat childish eagerness to appear well in the eyes of their fellows leads to many a subterfuge. For instance, one very weak reader, a Maori, was most anxious that he should be allowed to read a certain piece of poetry on the last night he was to attend class. He acquitted himself very well indeed, but it did not need very close observation to discover that he had learned the whole poem by heart, doubtless with the aid of some sympathetic friend. Still, he made a good impression.[41]

By 1917 the south and final wing was at last completed. The 'old wooden divisions that had been an eyesore and a menace for so many years' were accordingly demolished, presumably with great satisfaction by those who had recently been confined in them. The extra space created was used to increase the number of exercise yards to six, ensuring that prisoners could be more strictly classified and separated than ever.[42] The habitual criminals, for example, housed in the new south wing, were kept apart from all others outside working hours. This improved system of classification had become even more pressing as Mount Eden was by then routinely receiving a category of prisoners seldom seen before, and its staff and systems were wholly inexperienced at dealing with them.[43] These were men, often well educated and otherwise law abiding, who refused to join in the wave of patriotic fervour that swept the country once war broke out on the other side of the world.

The very first opponents to this mood of militarism had been admitted to the prison in March 1911, when two young men were jailed for breaches of the Compulsory Military Training Act.[44] Under this Act, all males aged from 12 to 21 were required to register for training. A determined minority refused to do so, and were at first fined and, if they refused to pay, eventually imprisoned for seven days with hard labour.

By May 1912 the jail held 12 of these 'anti-militarist youths', aged from 17 to 21. The young resisters had no prior criminal records and their parents were anxious that they should not be in contact with older and more hardened criminals who might corrupt them. The prison management was sympathetic to this view, and these youths, like the men from Waihī, were kept apart from other prisoners, although they were treated like them in all other respects — photographed, fingerprinted and required to wear the broad-arrow prison garb.[45] There were occasional failures of this segregation policy and at least one young resister, an Auckland student named Barton, was put to work on the rock pile alongside long-serving convicts.[46]

From late 1915 all New Zealand males between 17 and 60 were required to register their availability for military service, and conscription was introduced the following year, initially only for non-Māori. Hundreds of men were convicted for resisting these wartime regulations, and many more for condemning the war in terms judged to be seditious. These objectors, whose motives ranged from religious pacifism to Irish Republicanism, tended first to be warned and fined, then given relatively short sentences in military detention barracks. If those measures failed to subordinate them, they faced up to two years' hard labour in civil prisons such as Mount Eden. The first of these objectors appeared in the prison early in 1917. Some maintained their opposition to military service after their release and were returned to prison almost immediately, with a few serving as many as three sentences in succession and remaining inside long after peace had been declared.[47]

Like the young anti-militarists, these adult objectors tended to be first-time offenders, and rather more law-abiding than the average citizen: men who, if they found a £1 note on the pavement, would hand it in to the police as lost property. They included Harry Urquhart, an Auckland teacher and Christian pacifist who had written an anti-conscription pamphlet and was promptly charged with sedition. The magistrate considered the work 'so well-written as to be the more serious accordingly', and gave him 11 months. Perhaps in recognition of Urquhart's gentle and scholarly demeanour he was not sentenced to hard labour, but opted to serve his time in the quarry anyway.[48]

The appearance of these idealists, some of them devoutly religious, among the general prison population is likely to have proved insightful for all parties. The Prison Department acknowledged somewhat ruefully that: 'The advent of such a number of prisoners who, whatever their faults, were not criminals presented a somewhat difficult problem to the Department, which has hitherto had to deal only with offenders against the civil law. The position was met, however, by effecting a complete separation, wherever possible, between the civil and military prisoners.'[49]

However, every category of inmate at Mount Eden was required, from 1915, to take part in daily physical exercises under an instructor. The prison authorities noted the improvement that this regime produced 'in the erect bearing and general demeanour of the prisoners attending the drill parades'.[50] What the anti-militarists thought of this parade-ground activity is not recorded, but they are unlikely to have enjoyed it.

Nationally, most conscientious objectors (popularly known as 'conchies') were sent to prison camps in remote areas, including one specially built for them, but a few were sent to Mount Eden for committing offences in those institutions. A religious objector, Arthur Johns, escaped twice from Rotoaira prison camp near Lake Taupō and was given a further 12 months in Mount Eden. Robert Gould, a Wellington waterside worker serving two years in Waikeria for refusing military service, applied for a transfer to Wellington to see his wife who was in poor health. His application was refused and, in protest, Gould refused to work or eat. A fellow inmate, John Brailsford, joined the hunger strike in sympathy with him. Both men were then transferred to Mount Eden, where they were placed in solitary cells with nothing but 'a blanket and a Bible'. After a further seven days on hunger strike, Gould achieved his aim of a transfer to Wellington.[51]

Those objectors jailed on the grounds of their socialist views were more trouble to the prison authorities than the religious pacifists. Like the Waihī miners who had preceded them, '[t]hey could count on a stronger and more vociferous support from organisations and politicians than was afforded to the religious objectors. They were more demanding and readier to embroil the whole prison population in their protests.'[52] James Thorn, a Boer War veteran and prominent labour leader, was one of the best known of these socialist opponents of the war. In late 1916 he gave a public speech in Auckland against conscription and was charged with 'seditious utterance'. He was refused bail and while awaiting trial was held at Mount Eden where, he said, he was 'herded with the dregs of the country — the most depraved criminals, sodomists, whoremongers and brothel keepers'. He was given a 12-month sentence in their company by the magistrate, and an ovation by the crowd of supporters waiting outside the court.[53]

During his sentence Thorn was kept supplied with letters, food and other gifts from his supporters, who visited him as often as possible. A few months into his term he was joined by a group of nine Huntly coalminers convicted of sedition for carrying out a go-slow strike in support of their wage demand. Like Thorn, they were remanded without bail at Mount Eden during their trial, and supporters sent special meals to them daily. The miners were each sentenced to several months but spent less than two weeks in prison through the intervention of a well-known former inmate. Bill Parry, former Waihī strike leader, had been elected vice-president of the Federation of Labour while in Mount Eden in 1912, and he began working in that role on his release. He was ideally qualified to negotiate the miners' freedom in return for their commitment to take no further strike action in the following 12 months. John Jones, the miners' leader, was clearly relieved to be outside the jail walls but unwilling to dwell on the experience. 'I can tell you honestly we do not want it again. It was not so bad while the Auckland people looked after us so well with tucker . . . Of what happened after we were sentenced I will say nothing.'[54]

Miners were exempt from conscription because their labour was vital to the support of the civilian population, and this is likely to have spurred the wartime government into sending the Huntly men back to work. Thorn, by occupation a socialist agitator, was not so fortunate, and he served his full term with only the standard remission for good behaviour. An official history of the prison system notes that the more prominent socialist objectors often made use of the public interest surrounding their release to denounce the conditions they had just experienced and to urge for fundamental reforms.[55]

Thorn was not a man to let such an opportunity slip. On the night after his release he told a packed house at an Auckland theatre that his prison experience had convinced him beyond doubt that 'British justice laid down one law for the rich and another for the poor . . . The atmosphere of a prison reeked of every evil, and inevitably had a demoralising effect on the prisoner.' Crime resulted above all, he concluded, from social neglect 'and must be approached with quite new methods'. Sex education was one immediate requirement, 'and men must be secured in decent well-paid employment through a social transformation of industry'.⁵⁶

These were sound and even farsighted recommendations, but they stood no chance of being implemented under the exceptionally stringent wartime regime. The prison was severely understaffed because its most able warders had enlisted, and those who remained or replaced them tended to be older, less physically fit and unwilling to accept any innovations to routine. As a result, conscientious objectors, and particularly those who, in the words of the *New Zealand Herald*, 'decline to work or who are agitators and foment discontent among their fellows', could expect to be treated with great severity by prison staff who chose this means to express their own patriotism.⁵⁷ Labour leader Harry Holland, whose advanced age and limping gait enabled him to condemn such ill-treatment without risk of experiencing it himself, quoted a letter from a young schoolteacher held at an unnamed prison that may well have been Mount Eden: 'The jail is full of nothing but Objectors. The doctor asks the prisoners what they are in for. If they are Objectors, God pity them if they are ill.'⁵⁸

One victim of this institutional vindictiveness was William White, a religious objector held initially in Waimarino prison camp in the Tongariro district. There he became unwell and refused to work, and he was transferred to Mount Eden in January 1919. He was given no medical treatment and put to work in the quarry, although he was unable to hold down the crude regular diet. After six days he was found vomiting in agony in his cell. He was finally admitted to the prison hospital but died there soon afterwards. A coroner's inquest found that he died from natural causes, but several fellow prisoners told Holland they were prevented from giving evidence that would have contradicted this finding.⁵⁹ Long afterwards, other Mount Eden objectors recalled the terrible food, the 16 hours of daily confinement in their cells, and the utterly degrading experience of being woken in the middle of the night and held upside down for an anal search for hidden objects.⁶⁰ Treatment such as this was condemned by the labour weekly *Truth* in terms as strong as wartime censorship permitted, and its headline writers referred to Mount Eden, with their trademark alliterative flair, as the Brutal Bastille.⁶¹

A number of the religious objectors were Quakers, whose Auckland meeting-house was, and still is, sited a short walk from the prison gates. When reports of horrifying prison conditions reached them, the devoutly pacifist Auckland Quakers responded by sending flowers to every sentenced and convicted inmate on Christmas Eve 1918. They have maintained this tradition annually to the present day, despite periodic official attempts to end it.[62] At various times the Quakers also sent flowers to decorate the chapel, and during the war and for some years afterwards provided every inmate with a piece of Christmas cake. 'It was thought quite wrong to be sending a big piece of cake just to the COs,' remembered Quaker Athol Jackson, 'so we decided to send quite a generous piece to every prisoner. It involved quite an expense but no doubt it was appreciated.'[63]

As the numbers of articulate, principled men in the cells increased, and their supporters grew more vocal on their behalf, both the prison management and the central government grew uncomfortable about the potential impact on the war effort of the harsh policy towards objectors. Several means were tried to reduce their numbers without losing face. In 1918, the Defence Department reprinted a pamphlet by Germany's ambassador to Britain, Prince Lichnowsky, in which he expressed concern about the legal and moral validity of his country's actions. Copies were sent to every New Zealand prison for distribution to conscientious objector inmates in the hope of persuading them to drop their opposition. Mount Eden's superintendent received a hundred copies of this pamphlet. There is no evidence that any imprisoned objectors altered their stance after reading it.[64]

Nor were the conchies the only inmates who posed practical and moral difficulties for the hard-pressed Mount Eden prison staff. The prison also held a number of German nationals for various breaches of wartime regulations. At least 14 German civilians were kept in Mount Eden in mid-1918, and their situation prompted British authorities to inquire, on behalf of the Red Cross, 'what criminal deeds are they charged with and what sentences passed on them?'[65] No such uncertainty surrounded the brief but notable internment, in late 1917, of the flamboyant Count Felix von Luckner, an aristocrat and naval captain, one of Mount Eden's most colourful and charismatic guests, and possibly the only one entitled to bear a hereditary title. He and the crew of his pirate raider, the *Seeadler*, had been captured in Fiji and sent to Auckland as prisoners of war. They were placed in Mount Eden, presumably because their record of daring escapes required them to be confined in the most secure facility available.

Von Luckner, as a serving military officer accustomed to commanding other men, objected strongly to being held in a civilian prison. In a later and highly coloured narrative of his South Sea adventures, he described Mount Eden as 'a real jail, a hard bad prison'. Soon after he was admitted, a fellow inmate arrived to give him a shave. This man greeted the unusual new arrival with great respect and introduced himself as a lifer who had killed a woman. 'It's an awful feeling to have a murderer shave you,' von Luckner found, 'especially when the razor goes over your throat.'[66] Others have also noted that Mount Eden's convict-barbers, who were issued with folding 'cut-throat' razors, were typically serving long sentences for extremely violent crimes. 'You see, a joker isn't allowed a responsible job like wielding the razor until he's a trusty, been there a good long time, say ten or fifteen years. So . . . you'd know when you had your bristles taken off that the man stroking your jugular might be the same one who'd cut his girl's throat some time.'[67]

Von Luckner was not put to work, and had little to do all day except to observe the spiders spinning webs in his cell and to impose his considerable personality on everyone he met. 'In jail,' he advised his readers, 'you must make people respect you . . . The wardens wanted to give me tin plates to eat from, like those they give to all the convicts, but I said, "Get out of here, I want china plates." I told them they shouldn't treat an officer prisoner of war that way.'[68] It must have been a considerable relief for all concerned when, after just three weeks, he and his crew were sent on to various other camps and facilities, the Count himself ending up in the small military prison at Ripa Island in Lyttelton Harbour.

Although his demands for quality crockery were not met, von Luckner appears to have been treated with deference and even admiration during his prison term, even by the superintendent. The same was not true of another remarkable inmate, the Tūhoe prophet Rua Kēnana, whose term overlapped with von Luckner's. In the years before World War One, Rua had built up a following in the Urewera region and become notorious among the European population, including leading politicians, for his resistance to contemporary Pākehā culture and conventions. Once the war began, Rua, in common with several other Māori leaders, refused to encourage his followers to enlist. The pent-up hostility towards his community drove the government to send a large force of well-armed police into his remote bush settlement of Maungapōhatu. A deadly gun battle erupted before Rua and several others were marched in handcuffs to the nearest road, and from there by train to Auckland. A large crowd assembled at the Mount Eden railway station to obtain a glimpse of the prophet and his five co-defendants as they arrived. Each day for more than two months Rua, described by the press as 'broad-shouldered, tall and upstanding', was conveyed between his cell and the courtroom by horse-drawn carriage, until he received the unexpectedly harsh sentence of a year's hard labour and a further 18 months' 'reformative treatment'.[69]

In the prison workshops, the prophet, although aged over 40, was put to work as a blacksmith's striker, wielding the heavy hammer to shape and repair iron tools and equipment.[70] He may have had earlier experience at this trade, as horses were vitally important to the roadless communities of Urewera and he probably learned to make and fit horseshoes from an early age.[71] In his free time Rua read the Bible in a Māori translation, and wrote at least two waiata that are still sung by his people. One of these contains the line: 'Mekameka i aku ringa ka pai e te iwi ka rite ngā karaipiture' ('Although my hands are locked in chains, the people know the scriptures have spoken').[72]

Rua's conduct in the prison was exemplary and Superintendent Wilford supported the plea from a deputation of his followers that he should be released in early 1918, six months before his full sentence expired.[73] There is some evidence that the conditions of this early release required him to reverse his former opposition to enlistment and instead encourage the young men among his supporters to go to war. Some 80 of his Tūhoe followers did indeed enlist after his release, although none went on to serve overseas.

As a nationally known representative of unreconciled Māoridom, Rua's imprisonment was a source of satisfaction to the Pākehā community, and the press made a great deal of it. By contrast, the dozen or so other Māori defaulters who were admitted to Mount Eden Prison a few months after he was released made little impact on the public consciousness, even though their protest was arguably more politically significant. These were young men from the rural hinterlands of Waikato, followers of the Māori King (Kīngitanga) movement, and their actions had the full understanding and support of their local communities. For the Waikato people, the state that had invaded and attacked them a half-century earlier was now forcing their young men to fight on its behalf, and their resistance to this compulsion was unwavering.

In June 1917 conscription was extended to Māori in the Western Maori electorate, which incorporated both Rua's people and those in Waikato. Widespread resistance caused the police to make a number of arrests among the marae-based communities in the region. By mid-1918, 28 young defaulters were held in detention barracks in Devonport and another six were taken to the region's main military training camp at Narrow Neck on Auckland's North Shore. When they refused orders to put on uniforms, they were sentenced by court-martial to two years with hard labour. This sentence was pronounced in the most humiliating way possible, in front of an outdoor muster of 400 of their fellow recruits.

In both English and Māori, the punishment was read out to each of them in turn, followed by a notice from their commanding officer, Colonel Patterson. This referred to them as taurekareka (slaves), the lowest form of insult in the Māori vocabulary, and their elders were denounced as seditious traitors. The muster parade was a well-calculated piece of political theatre aimed at frightening the young defaulters, maximising the antagonism of their fellow recruits, and extending the army's condemnation to those with the highest status in their home communities. Yet none of the young men gave any indication of weakening, and maintained what officers described as 'their stolid, sullen demeanour'.[74]

After much official discussion it was decided that the first six defaulters should be held in the country's toughest prison as a deterrent to the others. Their treatment there was exceptionally harsh. One of the six, Here Mokena, later recalled:

> We were made to sleep on the bare boards with only two blankets. There was neither mattress nor pillow. We all felt the cold severely. Most of the time we were hungry because we were given only bread, and little enough of that, and water. We became covered in lice, and used to pass the time away by having races with the kutus. Men who had been in prison [before] told us that ordinary prisoners were treated better than we were because they at least had the usual comforts.[75]

The defiant Kīngitanga leader Princess Te Puea stood outside the prison every day as a silent encouragement to these men. The only place where she could be seen from their cellblock was one of the toilets, and the

Waikato men took it in turns to make trips there to fortify their resolve.⁷⁶ None succumbed to the extraordinary pressure to undergo their military training; and by the end of hostilities, and after more defaulters from Waikato had been jailed, eight were still held in the prison with more than a year of their sentences left to run.

III

As the rest of the country exulted in armistice celebrations, objectors of all kinds remained in Mount Eden and the other prisons and camps around the country. A Religious Objectors Advisory Board was set up to advise the Defence Minister on which of the men, if any, should be released before their full sentence. The board was inclined to grant early release to those objectors whose stance was based on 'purely religious grounds' but not to those, such as the socialist, Irish and Māori protesters, who opposed the war on other grounds. It proved difficult, and often impossible, to make such distinctions between the different categories.⁷⁷ In January 1919, the board advised Defence Minister James Allen that 'none of the Maoris who appeared before us objected to military service on bona fide religious grounds, but we are of the opinion that these cases merit your most earnest attention with a view to deciding whether in equity these men should be detained in prison'. The report quoted one of these objectors as representative of all of them: 'At the Treaty of Waitangi we signed to make peace and they put a Bible in our hands. They have now taken the Bible away and put a sword into our hands and wish to make us fight.'⁷⁸

Allen took no immediate action, but when a deputation of Te Arawa rangatira appealed to him for the Waikato men's release, he told the group that whereas the Pākehā prisoners were genuinely disloyal and he was not prepared to release them, the Māori prisoners were simply badly influenced and had little understanding of the motives behind their protest. Improbable as this seems, given the statement quoted above, Cabinet ministers agreed, and decided to release all Māori objectors, including the eight held in Mount Eden. The decision was not made public due to the government's refusal to release the remaining objectors. In May 1919, eight months after their court-martial, all the Waikato men were released, apart from four who had died during the previous year's influenza epidemic. The bodies of these four were not returned to their home marae — an act of bureaucratic inhumanity that brought further grief and resentment to their families and iwi.

Most of the remaining objectors in Mount Eden were released by September 1919 although a few, regarded as non-religious and therefore especially culpable, were held until the last New Zealand servicemen returned home in November 1920.[79] The harsh treatment handed out to objectors in Mount Eden may have had the unintended outcome of contributing to the faltering but inexorable impulse for penal reform by creating a highly articulate category of ex-inmates, some of whom would later shape the country's politics. Just seven years after miners' union leader Bill Parry walked out of prison in 1912, he was elected to Parliament for Auckland Central and remained an MP for more than 30 years. From 1922, in a truly remarkable instance of synchronicity, his benchmate in Parliament was John A. Lee, his one-time fellow inmate, now the MP for Auckland East, the electorate that incorporated the prison.

Despite a far longer commitment to parliamentary politics than either Lee or Parry, James Thorn was for many years unable to join them in the House. By executive decree in 1918, he and all other former conscientious objectors, or 'defaulters', were deprived of their civil rights, including their right to vote, for 10 years — a vindictive act that reversed many decades of progress towards a wider franchise. Since 1852 various categories of prisoner had lost the right to vote after completing their sentence, but typically for periods of up to a year. The extra-judicial 1918 decree was therefore unprecedented, and several of those affected by it pointed out the cruel irony of imposing it after a war fought, allegedly, in the name of human rights. Harry Urquhart told the chair of the Religious Objectors Advisory Board that conscientious objectors 'did not require four years of bloodshed to teach them the futility of war and because of their clear-sightedness you now propose to inflict a further penalty of ten years' disenfranchisement'.[80]

This sanction put paid to Thorn's hopes for a political career throughout the 1920s, but in 1935 he was able to join his fellow former inmates in Parliament.[81] The elevation in their social status in the years after release from Mount Eden owed nothing to the reformative effects of their confinement there.

5:
Rock College
1923–1946

A coal bin in a dusty corner of a prison workshop, used to store fuel for steam-powered machinery, is a relatively sophisticated hiding-place for contraband, given warders' likely reluctance to thoroughly search it. Nevertheless, during a routine search in early 1923 assiduous warders burrowed through the bin and discovered lengths of rope and wire, and a homemade hook for scaling the walls — strong grounds for presuming that an escape attempt was planned. The case was made stronger still because the man charged with the attempt, a 35-year-old ex-seaman named Tom Westlake, had a lengthy record. Since 1915 he had stolen a succession of pleasure yachts and taken them on long voyages, on one occasion right around the South Pacific.[1] For that theft he was sentenced to five years and declared a habitual criminal.

Westlake, however, flatly denied all knowledge of the escape apparatus and offered a novel defence. He had no need of such equipment, he told Magistrate Pointon, because if he wanted to escape from the prison he could do so easily without the use of such aids. He entreated the magistrate to give him the opportunity to demonstrate the truth of this claim and, remarkably, this request was granted.

The following morning the workshop filled with an intrigued but sceptical audience that included Pointon (accompanied by his fox terrier, Peter), the prison superintendent, a number of warders and several representatives of the press. The vertical bars across the window were inspected and found to be securely set in concrete, and six-and-a-quarter inches (about 16 cm) apart. Westlake, described as a dark, medium-built man, was led in between two warders, and stripped off his brown uniform jacket to reveal 'a slim body and wiry arms'. He jumped onto a table standing beneath the window, slipped one foot through the middle pair of bars, followed it with his left arm and then his head. 'It was all done so quickly that the eye could scarcely follow the movements,' wrote a reporter from the *Auckland Star*. 'For a second the prisoner was there between the bars, then there was a short gasp, a rapid twist of the body and — heigh presto! — he was free!' Westlake showed his audience how he could then climb onto another building, 'with my foot on that ledge, catch hold of that drainpipe, swing up to the roof and across to the top of the wall. Then I'd be out!' The magistrate was clearly impressed, and pronounced that he would give the defendant the benefit of the doubt and dismiss the charge against him. This was a humiliating outcome for the prison officials, and they assured assembled reporters that 'steps will be taken to alter the bars on this window, making egress impossible'.[2]

Although generally averse to press publicity, the Mount Eden administration recognised that it sometimes needed to counter damning reports of prison conditions from recently released inmates like the conscientious objectors. In 1919, therefore, the *Auckland Star* was invited to tour the prison. The resulting series of articles provides a strikingly partisan picture of the institution in the immediate postwar period. 'The first impression,' wrote the *Star*'s man after his escorted tour, 'was that of scrupulous cleanliness in the cells, in the corridors, in the kitchens, in fact everywhere.'[3] The building's interior was likened to 'the engine-room of a large steamer or battleship with its polished steel rails and companionway'.[4] This agreeable image ignored the sanitation facilities, which remained mired in the past. Every inmate's first task after rising to the 6 a.m. bell was to place their tin chamberpot in the passageway, where two of the least fortunate men emptied it into a 'slop-bucket', a cut-down 44-gallon drum slung from a pole carried on their shoulders.[5] This drum was occasionally dropped or overturned, creating an unpleasant duty for the man charged with cleaning that section of floor.

The one-man cells, known as 'peters', were furnished with a canvas hammock hung from two heavy ropes running from wall to wall. Four blankets were issued — five in winter — and remand prisoners also received sheets and a small locker to keep certain luxuries not permitted to convicted men. Every cell was scrubbed daily by assigned inmates, although long-serving and life-sentence men preferred to clean their cells themselves in their own time.[6] The cells were lit until 9 p.m., by gas in the older wings and electricity in the newer, enabling inmates to read the library books or weekly newspapers now supplied to them. They were also allowed to receive 'reputable newspapers or magazines' from their friends, to read and write one letter each week, and receive a weekly visit from up to three people at a time.[7] One especially prized privilege was the weekly allocation of an ounce of tobacco. Inmates were permitted to smoke in their cells only after dinner, and to prevent smoking at other times they were issued with a single daily match. Real experts, however, could subdivide the match to provide an astonishing number of unauthorised smokes.[8]

Each Saturday half-holiday a complete change of prison-made clothing, including such luxuries as a woollen singlet, underpants and socks, was handed out, and every man was required to take a cold bath. Wearing the same clothes and remaining unwashed for a week while toiling outdoors in an Auckland summer was clearly unwholesome even for labourers, and critics of the system asked prison superintendent Jim Dickison how he would find such a regime. He admitted 'it would not be altogether to his taste', and a twice-weekly bath regime was later introduced.[9]

The inmates themselves 'look well and fit', the *Star* reported, 'and in many cases put on weight during their sentence because of the wholesome diet and regular hours, combined with physical exercise, which is given every morning'.[10] The menu, however, was limited and monotonous. As in the past, the only substantial meal was served at midday when the inmates returned from their morning's work. No dining room had been provided in the men's quarters, so this lunch was eaten in their cells. Food prepared in the kitchens was served in individual, two-tiered tin 'dixies', with boiling water in the lower compartment to keep the meal hot. Meat, supplied as whole carcasses from the Waikeria prison farm and butchered on the premises, was now roasted as well as stewed, while men without teeth could usually expect mince.[11] Fish was available on Fridays for Catholics, and any left over was eagerly consumed by those of other faiths or none. The tea and porridge served at breakfast and dinner included a ration of sugar, salt and pepper, and the loaf supplied daily to each inmate was made alternately of white and wholemeal flour, and from the mid-1920s baked on the premises.[12]

Those who failed to thrive despite this diet could be treated in the prison hospital, described by its administrators as the equal of any in Auckland.[13] Its facilities did not, however, extend to humane and competent medical staff, and every inmate who reported sick was assumed to be malingering until their condition was serious enough to require in-patient treatment. As in the past, no special help was given to those with mental illnesses apart, perhaps, from spells in the 'silent cell'. Its heavily padded walls were lined with canvas stuffed with horsehair, and violent prisoners were placed there until they became quiet enough for staff to manage them. The injustice of confining severely mentally ill people in this way was apparent to all, but no better solution was available. A convicted murderer named Kit Matthews was admitted to the prison in 1921, with his death sentence reprieved on the grounds of lunacy. When questioned about the propriety of treating an insane man as an ordinary prisoner, Justice Minister Ernest Lee replied that 'Matthews was a man who should never be let loose on society', and offered the supposedly reassuring prediction that he would die in the prison 'within a comparatively few years'.[14]

From the early 1920s, in addition to the evening literacy classes provided by the schoolmaster (a post held, in the following decade, by a PhD from Yale), individual inmates could undertake more advanced study by correspondence.[15] They had to pay all fees themselves but were permitted a desk and an extra hour of light in their cells at night. Engineering, navigation, signwriting and accountancy were subjects especially encouraged by prison staff, and at least one inmate learned Arabic.[16]

Amid the thriving economy of the 1920s, several new cottage industries were introduced to make more effective use of the prison workforce. The workshop where the agile Tom Westlake was employed, and where the escape equipment was found, produced soap from animal fat supplied by the Waikeria prison farm. The traditional products of the quarry were expanded to include building blocks, ferro-cement telegraph poles and roofing tiles. These were supplied to government departments faced with a postwar population boom, and the blocks were eventually used in such sturdy public buildings as Newmarket School.[17] Both building materials and inmates were employed in constructing new staff houses in the vicinity of the prison. These included a two-storey house in Clive Road made in solid stone for the deputy superintendent. The construction work, electric wiring, plumbing, plastering and other finishing was all carried out by inmates under the supervision of prison officers.[18]

Similar attention to the economic value of prison labour is evident from the other industries introduced. In almost every case the output of the work met the needs of the prison and of other state institutions. The tailoring shop made inmate uniforms for all North Island prisons, as well as for patients and warders in its mental hospitals. The uniform at Mount Eden itself comprised 'white moleskin trousers and rough grey jackets. Since nothing was tailor-made... penal yard at assembly time was a gathering of identikit mannikins.'[19] However, prisoners hoping to look respectable on their discharge could, for a fee, have their own clothing made or mended by the tailors. The heavy boots issued to inmates were also made on the premises. Each night they had to be placed outside cell doors in case their laces were used to attempt suicide.[20] Mailbags, hammocks, tin pans, brushes, coir mats decorated with patriotic emblems — all were produced within Mount Eden's walls, for its own needs and to sell to other state facilities.

From 1921 prisoners received two forms of payment for their obligatory 44-hour working work, both of them very modest and not immediately available for their own use. Each working prisoner could earn up to eight shillings a day, equivalent to about half the national average pay rate. Half of this sum was deducted at source for the costs of their upkeep, and the remainder was paid to approved dependants — children, wife or mother.[21] A revised version of the old system of marks for good conduct and industry provided a tiny additional income. From the fourth month of their sentence all prisoners, regardless of classification, could earn between sixpence and eightpence a day (equivalent to about three dollars today). During their sentence they could draw on this accumulated sum only to contribute to the cost of their education. The remainder, less any marks cancelled for poor conduct, was handed to them on their release.[22] Under both systems, inmates earned the same daily amount regardless of the type of work performed. Even more dismaying for the prisoners, their earnings were stopped if they were unable to work due to sickness or injury, although the hazardous nature of dynamiting and other quarrying activities meant that incapacitating injuries were frequent.[23]

Other overheads from the prison's industries were kept as low as possible. Mechanised equipment was slowly introduced to the quarry, and to the bootmaking, tailoring and several other workshops, but the general working conditions were far worse than those considered acceptable by free labour. An inspection by Auckland Justices on a winter's day in 1935 found that '[t]he conditions under which the men are continuously busy washing blankets, mail bags, and clothes are, to say the least of it, no better than those of 50 years ago'. The inmates were not supplied with rubber boots and were unable to keep their feet dry. 'Apart from the men's own welfare, it does not seem good business to compel them to work under conditions which no Government inspector would tolerate in a commercial factory.'[24]

It may therefore have come as a welcome change for a dozen good-conduct prisoners when they were assigned in 1925 to travel to Rangitoto Island in Waitematā Harbour to cut roads and walking tracks out of its solid lava rock. For the next nine years, gangs of up to 20 spent months at a time on the lovely uninhabited island, building a road around the foreshore and up to the summit, and creating seawalls, shelter sheds, a tennis pavilion and a swimming pool.²⁵ They were housed in a camp of portable huts, equipped with woodstoves but no electricity, sited near the main wharf and shaded by pōhutukawa trees. Three warders accompanied them, and the public was assured: 'There is no fear on the part of the officials that the men will misbehave.'²⁶ On at least two occasions, however, prisoners succumbed to the temptation to creep away after nightfall and make for shore in a stolen dinghy. With no telephone, the warders had to resort to waving frantically to the naval signalman at Devonport, who then contacted the prison for a search party.

The introduction of new and marginally more skilled forms of industry made little difference to the daily routine for most Mount Eden inmates. The quarry and its associated activities of stone-breaking and gravel-crushing still employed more than all the others put together, as it had since the prison opened in the 1850s, when its quarry was the only one in Auckland. As the dynamiting and rock-breaking ate progressively into the slopes behind the prison buildings, the flat land created was turned into small garden plots that eventually produced almost all the vegetables, apart from potatoes, served for the midday main meal.²⁷

The expanding range of prison industries was proudly cited by politicians and officials as evidence that Mount Eden was slowly evolving a reformative as well as a punitive function. 'In general,' claimed one report, 'the change has been in the direction of providing work for every prisoner, of teaching him a trade, and making him self-supporting when his term is up.'²⁸ This inspiring vision did not stand up to analysis. Prisoners were typically assigned to work in skilled trades such as carpentry and electrical work only if they had experience in these fields before their sentence. Those with skills in less demand might, however, be permitted to practise them in their own time, and the New Zealand South Seas International Exhibition held in Dunedin in 1925 featured examples of their personal handiwork, such as 'a desk made of figured red pine, containing some exquisite inlaid and veneer work'.²⁹

The most telling rebuttal to the claim that Mount Eden prepared its inmates for a good job on the outside came from its own superintendent, Mr Ironside. On his retirement in 1920 he admitted that while some men picked up skills in the prison, 'few of them profited by it. The inevitable question, "Where did you learn your trade?", when the man left gaol and went to a union or an employer, was a hurdle to be faced by the prisoner.'[30] In truth, the work carried out in the prison was dictated above all by the economic and practical demands of the institution and of the wider community. During the economic depression of the early 1930s the government sought to cut costs in every area of the prison budget, including the weekly tobacco ration issued to all inmates. It instructed the Waikeria farm to add tobacco to the crops it produced, and the fresh leaf was dried, cured and cut at Mount Eden. Within a few years the tobacco requirements for the entire prison service were met in this way; instead of an annual cost to the Prisons Department of more than £1000, by 1934 'the Department was actually in credit on the sale of its surplus leaf'.[31]

Other prison industries fared less well, even given the advantage of low labour costs.[32] For many years competing businesses such as private quarries had complained of undercutting by the prison, which had come to rely on the sale of its road metal to local authorities as a crucial line in its administration budget. It sold its products at well below market rates and justified this on the grounds that the taxpayer was spared an equivalent portion of the total costs of imprisonment.[33] During the worst years of the Depression, however, mass unemployment, drastic price-cutting and bitter commercial competition meant that even the subsidised prison industries struggled to find a market for their products. Cash-strapped government departments could source institutional footwear and clothing at rates even cheaper than Mount Eden's, and the prison was forced to drop its prices.[34] Unsold road metal piled up in the quarry, as neither local authorities nor private contractors could afford it.[35] The resulting shortfall in the prison's annual budget was met, at least in part, by cutting back on conditions that may have taken decades of patient effort to achieve.

The number of women inmates at Mount Eden had dropped sharply after a special women's prison opened at Addington in Christchurch in 1913 and a women's reformatory in Wellington seven years later. When a new women's wing was provided at Mount Eden in 1923, barely half of its 24 rooms were initially occupied. Each of these was sparely but tastefully furnished with a wire bedstead, wardrobe, table, mirror and chair, and some small personal ornament. The new quarters even included a communal dining room.[36] For some reason, the women qualified for an addition to the standard ration — a serving of pudding after the midday meal three times a week. These, however, were token privileges in light of the women's very vulnerable and often harrowing circumstances. An especially distressing event occurred in 1921 when the charred body of a newborn male was found in the furnace of the laundry-room boiler. Matron Jane Poulton suspected the mother was inmate Flora Waite because of her recent unusual behaviour. She confronted Waite, who confessed that the baby had been born in her cell a few days earlier.[37]

Institutional domestic work such as laundering was invariably carried out by women inmates like Flora Waite, as it had been since the days of the Stockade. The only items they did not have to wash were the prison's own woollen blankets, since these were too heavy for women to manage when wet. 'These unfortunates live in a deadly monotony of routine washing and darning, perhaps all day,' noted a member of the newly formed Howard League for Penal Reform.[38]

An active New Zealand branch of this organisation was formed in 1924 by the eccentric Christchurch poet and suffragist Blanche Baughan, after she encountered the work of the parent body in Britain. Baughan was pre-eminent among a postwar generation of resolute penal reformers, mainly female, who insisted that prisons should be judged on their record of rehabilitation, and not on the economic value of inmates' labour. She visited prisoners, especially but not exclusively women, throughout the country, offered them temporary accommodation in her house after their release, and in a stream of writings urged compassion for those with mental illnesses and physical addictions. When she encountered a likeable Mount Eden inmate who attributed his lengthy prison record to a fondness for outwitting the police, Baughan encouraged him to turn his talents to writing detective stories and applied to the Prisons Department for permission to publish them.[39]

I I I

Reflecting the general population of the Auckland region, a wider range of races and cultures was found among Mount Eden's prisoners in the years following World War One. Asian inmates, previously rare, and usually sentenced for drug or gambling offences, became more common. Pacific Islanders, especially Samoans, arrived after conviction for serious offences in their own countries. Most of them were young, spoke little or no English, and found the cold and loneliness exceptionally difficult.[40] The most notable of these was the young high chief Tamasese, leader of the Mau movement campaigning for Sāmoa's independence from New Zealand colonial control. He was held for six months from late 1928 for resisting payment of a greatly resented poll tax.[41] Sāmoa's colonial administrator, Colonel Allen, insisted that the term for this relatively minor offence would be served in New Zealand. Tamasese 'is not a criminal but a spoilt child', blustered Allen, and ought to be 'subject to real discipline for a few months'.[42] Tamasese's followers believed, with good grounds, that their leader had been sent out of his country 'to give him an extra dose of punishment among strange people and strange surroundings'.[43]

The chief was seasick for much of the voyage to New Zealand and was admitted to the prison hospital on his arrival. Although it was high summer he found the cold unbearable, and in a letter to his wife, Ala, said he feared he would die by the winter.[44] The following month Ala and their three children arrived in Auckland to be near him, and visited the prison whenever possible. Ala found it 'very strange and unnatural . . . that they should be compelled to converse in a foreign language and also to have to obtain permission to greet or embrace one another in their own native fashion'. Their young children spoke no English, and although officially prohibited from speaking to their father in their own language they 'could not be restrained' from doing so.[45]

Tamasese struck a commanding figure in his radiant white lavalava with a blue bowtie and purple rosette, the colours of his political movement. The blatantly political character of his arrest, and his distinguished manner and appearance, meant he was befriended in prison by some of Auckland's leading citizens, who found him to be 'a pleasant, mild-mannered man with a perpetual smile'.[46] When his sentence was due to expire, Colonel Allen attempted to extend it but could find no legal grounds to detain the prisoner any longer.[47] A vocal crowd of about 40 local supporters gathered outside the main gates to celebrate Tamasese's release in June 1929. Their cheering was echoed by a gang of prisoners working near the stone-crusher, who had an elevated view of the welcome party. Six months later, the unarmed Tamasese was shot and killed by police while leading a Mau march in Apia. He was then about 28 years of age.[48]

Also evident among the work gangs and in the exercise yards was a growing number of Māori prisoners. Before World War One there was never more than a handful of Māori serving time for non-political offences, but the wave of urbanisation that arose after the war drove thousands of Māori from isolated communities into Auckland. The proportion of those who entered its prison gates closely tracked the tribulations of the economy, and the number of Māori inmates doubled between 1928 and 1932, the worst years of the Depression. 'This growth of crime among the younger Maoris, particularly in the North Auckland districts, is a disquieting feature,' stated the Prisons Department's 1933 annual report. 'Probation has proved to be largely futile, as this form of treatment is regarded by natives as equivalent to "getting off," and when on probation any constructive supervision is difficult to apply, as these offenders laze round the pas under conditions of indiscipline and idleness.'[49] A succession of magistrates noted with disapproval 'the large number of native prisoners' but could neither account for nor suggest solutions to it.[50] The great majority were put to work in the quarry rather than in more skilled activities, perhaps in recognition of their rural backgrounds.[51]

Herbert Thatcher, a young Auckland unemployment activist, encountered a group of young Māori while serving a three-month sentence in 1933:

> While I was there some Maoris were sent in for stealing sheep and sentenced to various terms from a fortnight to three months. They claimed they had killed and eaten the sheep because they were starving at the pah. They kept to themselves in the exercise yard and played many Maori group games such as the stick game or games played with the movement of the arms or hands. They seemed to think that the 'Mount' was a 'Kapai boarding house' but as they came from the north they missed the company of their friends and were pleased to get home again.[52]

III

By the 1930s, Arthur Hume's residual influence on the prison's internal layout had decreased to the point where a number of communal cells, known as association cells, had been created. These housed from three to 12 men each (two-man cells were out of the question, since they might encourage homosexual activity), and inmates with good-conduct records competed fiercely for the opportunity to transfer to them.[53] One, known as the 'old men's home', was described by the *Herald* as reserved for 'aged derelicts whose place is not really prison. They do no work, but potter about.'[54] Herbert Thatcher 'had rather a jolly time' in his association dormitory. 'On Saturday evenings we would start a "sing, say or pay" evening, when each prisoner in turn would recite, tell a story, sing a song or pay a forfeit (usually tobacco)', followed after lights-out by a community singsong until the warders intervened.[55]

Although visiting performers gave an occasional concert from the 1920s, the only regular public events at the prison were the Sunday church services, which were consequently well attended. Anglican and Catholic services were now held in succession in the prison chapel, and various other faiths, including the Rātana faith followed by Māori, held their own services in other corners of the building. During chapel services women were seated in the raised rear gallery, out of sight of the men on the floor.[56] The male-voice prison choir was a longstanding prison institution, much remarked on by visitors who admired the quality of their singing. The rest of the congregation also joined in lustily but were known to use this opportunity to make illicit communications with each other by matching their words to the rhythm of the hymns.

For many years the chapel's remarkably accomplished organist was a one-time bandleader and man-about-town named Eric Mareo who, in happier times, had lived just a short distance from the prison with his wife, Thelma, and their two children. In 1936 he was admitted to a condemned cell on a charge of murdering Thelma, and after several trials steeped in sensational evidence of transgressive sex and drug-taking, his death sentence was commuted to life imprisonment. Mareo spent 13 years in the prison's north wing among other long-sentence men while his many supporters battled to overturn a verdict they insisted, with strong support from forensic experts, was unjust.[57] On several occasions this consummate musician with a previously unblemished record was given hope for an early release but his case was deferred each time, for reasons that included the outbreak of World War Two. With his health failing, Mareo finally left Mount Eden in May 1948. He told his lawyer that he had been well treated by the staff there, the superintendent in particular appreciating his excellent service in directing the prison choir.[58] After just a few weeks

The circular walking tracks in the exercise yards, where inmates tramped daily in single file, are clearly visible in this 1930 aerial view of the prison, looking north towards Khyber Pass Road and Newmarket. *NEW ZEALAND HERALD*

of freedom Mareo remarried, and it is an indication of how the prison had changed during his time there that his bride was the first physiotherapist to have joined its staff; she had met him as an inmate and patient.[59]

The chapel was the only large common room in the prison and was used during the week for a variety of other purposes, including debates among inmates or lectures by outside speakers.[60] The films that had become the dominant cultural form in the outside world did not enter Mount Eden's walls until 1931, when *Balaclava*, a British historical epic about the Charge of the Light Brigade, was screened to a rapt audience of 400 in the chapel. Many of the men had been admitted to the prison during the silent-movie era and had never before seen a 'talkie'.[61]

During overcrowding emergencies, the chapel was also used for inmate accommodation. In 1925 it housed hundreds of striking seamen who had arrived in Auckland on British liners to find their employers in Britain had slashed their wages by almost half. Wildcat strikes then 'swept across British steamers wherever they happened to be across the seven seas of the world'.[62] For taking part in such a strike, almost 300 men crewing on ships berthed in Auckland were sentenced to up to three months' imprisonment. Mount Eden's chapel and schoolroom were hastily lined with mattresses to accommodate them. While local union officials negotiated with shipowners on their behalf, the strikers sprawled there with nothing to do but smoke and page through the tepid works in the prison library, mostly donated by churches or charitable institutions and accordingly emphasising 'temperance and penitential themes'.[63] The mariners were not permitted to go out to work and were sent to one of the exercise yards when other inmates returned to their wings for the midday meal, presumably to avoid any contagion of their dangerous views.[64]

The government, meantime, was wracked with anxiety that similar strike action by local unions might damage the country's agricultural export trade. A New Zealand branch of the Communist Party had been founded a few years earlier and was believed to be cultivating influence in the union movement.[65] Police surveillance of local communists was heightened, and during the final weeks of the 1925 Homeboat Strike, as it was called, the two leading members of the tiny New Zealand Communist Party were sent to Mount Eden for the rare crime of sedition. Banned literature had been found in the homes of the party's president, Oswald Bourbeau, and its secretary, Evan Thomas. Bourbeau, a printer by trade,

The prison chapel in 1931. *NEW ZEALAND HERALD*

was also charged with printing the party's newsletter, described in court as 'a document encouraging violence and lawlessness'. Both men had previous form for offences of this type and each was sentenced to several months.[66]

Punishment for offences committed while in prison could now be imposed only by Visiting Justices rather than warders, and was usually limited to stretches of no more than three successive days on bread and water, with the offender confined to his regular cell and only occasionally held in the 'dummy', or punishment cell.[67] The dummy contained nothing but a wooden plank bed with a raised headrest for a pillow. Only three blankets were provided, a severe penalty in the winter months, and even these were removed during the day. All reading matter except the Bible, and other privileges such as tobacco and visits, were forbidden, and exercise was restricted to a lonely half-hour in the adjacent execution yard.[68]

Reverend George Moreton, the prison chaplain throughout the 1930s, told the *New Zealand Herald* that 'the dummy knocks the fight out of any man . . . If he stays long enough he begins to break out in sores produced by the rubbing of the concrete; after four days he's either a murderous maniac or a broken piece of humanity — most men are broken.'[69] Another long-serving chaplain, Reverend E. C. Budd, supported Moreton's claim that solitary confinement 'tended to produce insanity' among the prison's inmates.[70] However, Superintendent Ironside defended the policy of bread and water and the dummy on the grounds that 'it was invariably successful with obstinate prisoners'. Yet even this noted disciplinarian felt no regret at the possibility of losing his former authority to impose floggings and other forms of corporal punishment, since these 'never did any good anyway'.[71]

Ironside's pragmatic view on corporal punishment was not shared by the local Labour MP, Henry Mason, who told the House in 1928 that it was the job of the Prisons Department to 'imprison, to flog or to hang, not to care for a man in any other way'.[72] At that time no flogging had taken place at Mount Eden for several years, so Mason may well have approved when the Supreme Court inflicted this punishment on two hit-and-run thieves in 1932. The judge described their carefully planned daylight attack as 'a crime of the gangster type' and ordered each man to be given 12 strokes of the cat-o'-nine-tails on top of their prison sentences.[73]

Mason's hard line was exceptional even by the standards of his day, and ran counter to the postwar trend for modest improvements in conditions at Mount Eden. The growing number of prison reformers pointed out the deeper truth: in spite of small gains, the prison's facilities and rehabilitation record were inferior to those in comparable countries and even to those of newer prisons elsewhere in New Zealand. After decades of entreaty, inmates around the country were now better segregated according to type and severity of offending, and a new generation of prisons was being designed for specific inmate types. 'Sexual perverts' (a category that included those convicted of homosexual activity) were held at New Plymouth, where they received treatment from medical and psychiatric specialists. Most short-sentence and low-risk inmates were sent to prison farms, women mainly to Addington, and young people, whenever possible, to borstal or probation.[74]

These institutions all recognised the necessity for reform as well as punishment. 'Only ignorant, unreasonable people clamour for a useless, expensive and wasteful penal severity for all alike,' declared Dr Mildred Staley, secretary of the New Zealand branch of the Howard League for Penal Reform, in 1927.[75] Mount Eden remained the archaic exception, the entirely punitive destination of last resort for the most dangerous offenders, and two years later it could be officially described as the 'only purely penal prison in New Zealand'.[76]

This was an inherently contradictory situation: the country's largest and most expensive prison was following a rigid punitive regimen while the country's penal legislation was directed towards reforming prisoner behaviour. Back in the brief heyday of Justice Minister John Findlay in the first decade of the century, the sentence of reformative detention had been established to encourage prisoners to develop habits of industry and good conduct in the hope of breaking their patterns of re-offending. Each inmate sentenced in this way was nominally considered on an individual basis for good behaviour and the promise of future betterment. A Prisons Board assessed their sentences quarterly and had the power to release them at any point, regardless of the length of time still to serve.

In practice, prisoners committed to Mount Eden for reformatory detention were treated identically to those sentenced to hard labour, with the exception of their uniforms — the former were outfitted in blue and the latter in brown.[77] In no other prison in the country was so little distinction made, and the benefits of a reformatory sentence were accordingly much reduced.⁷⁸ Jasper Calder, Mount Eden's outspoken chaplain in the mid-1920s, felt the Prisons Board also acted capriciously and often unfairly, siding with warders rather than inmates whenever their accounts conflicted.⁷⁹

In late 1926 a most unusual lifer was escorted out through the massive arched gateway of the prison. Fifty-one-year-old Charles Mackay had been released after just six years of his much longer reformatory sentence, on condition that he immediately left the country. Before his conviction he had been a well-respected Whanganui solicitor and for the previous 10 years had served as the town's mayor. It was known to his political enemies, however, that although he was a married man and had several young children he engaged in homosexual activity. On an afternoon in May 1920, a burning-eyed would-be poet named D'Arcy Cresswell called on Mackay in his office and threatened him with blackmail. In desperation the mayor fired a revolver at Cresswell, wounding him, and was sentenced to 15 years. The Prison Board's decision to release him after less than half that period was based on evidence that his mental and physical health were deteriorating, that he had lost both his profession and his family, and that his sister was willing to accompany him out of the country to start a new life elsewhere.⁸⁰ The same day he was escorted out of the prison, this shattered and ailing figure left Auckland by ship. He began a new life in Britain, working as a foreign correspondent for a daily newspaper, and was accidentally killed in 1929 during a shootout in Berlin between the police and left-wing activists.⁸¹

The tensions between the prison's ostensibly reformist policies and its stringently penal practices were further heightened by its highly diverse inmate population. Remand prisoners, first offenders and chronically recidivist drunkards mingled promiscuously with burglars, rapists, and those convicted of manslaughter and murder. The short-sentenced and low-risk prisoners were housed in different wings from hardened criminals and exercised separately during the week, yet every category of inmate came together for most of their daylight hours on the work gangs. Inmates of all types could also mill around on Saturday afternoons in the big main exercise yard where, since no organised sports or other recreations were provided, activity was limited to playing cards or draughts, gambling, and boasting of former glories. In this way Herbert Thatcher, the political activist short-sentenced on first offence, became

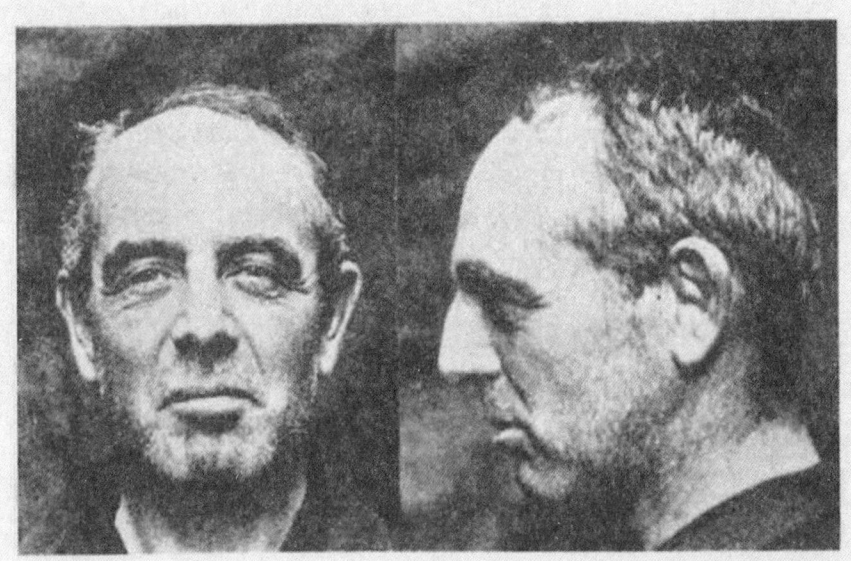

Formerly a well-liked mayor and prominent lawyer in Whanganui, Charles Mackay cuts a much diminished figure in his 1920 police mugshot, after his conviction for the attempted murder of D'Arcy Cresswell. *PAPERS PAST, POLICE GAZETTE, 1920*

acquainted with 'all classes of prisoners including "lifers" and "act men" or "dog collar men" (habitual criminals)'.[82] In the yard, he learned, '[c]rime is discussed in all its angles, from the prisoners' point of view ... Gambling on all the current races goes on openly or at least unchecked.'[83] Numerous other accounts confirm that 'Rock College', as it was known by inmates in this period, was 'a university of crime', whose syllabus offered everything from 'the art of appealing to a judge for a light sentence' to picking locks and blowing safes.[84]

These lessons were continually put into practice by inventive inmates determined to find loopholes in the prison's stony carapace. The mailbags sewn and repaired in one of the workshops gave an enterprising fraudster named Alfred Lamb the idea of using them to evade the censors. A postal clerk regularly delivered old bags and collected new ones, and in 1925 Lamb persuaded this remarkably naive official to smuggle contraband, including illicit letters that the clerk thoughtfully stamped and posted for him, in and out of the prison.[85] More secret letters passed to and fro in 1932, written invisibly on the backs of ordinary letters in a solution of sodium bicarbonate. 'By rubbing a warm iron over the letter the ink became visible.'[86]

In spite of Mount Eden's pre-eminence as the country's most secure prison, almost every year a few of its inmates, usually those working in the quarry beyond the high perimeter walls, would brave the shotguns of the warders and make a dash for freedom. Their prison clothing was no longer marked with broad arrows, but these escapers were almost always recaptured within hours, and sometimes within sight of those who lived or worked in the immediate neighbourhood. A 23-year-old named Seckington seized a moment in November 1929 before his morning march to the quarry and broke away in the direction of the Colonial Ammunition Company, just down the road from the prison. Warders' whistles shrilled, their rifles cracked, and Seckington was soon cornered near one of the company's buildings, under the enthralled gaze of its mainly female workforce. One woman found it 'a bigger thrill than a Wild West drama on the picture screen. "Such a nice, handsome young chap, too, he was."'[87]

Only the occasional escaper enjoyed more than a few days of freedom. One who did so, John Buckley, made a carefully planned overnight getaway with an associate in May 1928. The two men used a skeleton key to reach the roof of one wing, and worked along its steeply sloping edge and down a drainpipe until they reached the rounded top of the main wall. Both were injured after dropping to the ground outside, but Buckley succeeded in evading a massive police manhunt and holed up for some weeks in an out-of-the-way bay on Waitematā Harbour.[88] Police surprised him at his camp and he was re-arrested without a struggle, but two months later the impetuous 27-year-old made another dash across the prison yard and scaled the wall near Auckland Grammar School. He was fleeing across open ground when a warder shouted a warning, then delivered a blast from his Snider shotgun. Buckley collapsed from his injuries but recovered in hospital, and was returned to prison as an 'incorrigible rogue', with three years added to his sentence.[89]

I I I

These frequent if generally short-lived escapes took place as the environs around the prison were progressively transformed from a rural enclave to a busy suburb. Trains, trams and cars ran within metres of the perimeter walls; houses and industrial buildings pressed against them; and the long-ago decision to site such a large, sombre and turbulent institution in that locality became bitterly regretted. Residents of the suburb found that wherever they travelled around the country, their notorious prison was the one thing invariably associated with the name Mount Eden. 'Here we have a beautiful suburb which has to bear the stigma of having a prison named after it,' lamented borough councillor R. J. Mills.[90] The country's Chief Justice, Sir Robert Stout, had rejoiced at the completion in 1918 of this 'splendidly built stone prison . . . the finest building of the class in New Zealand'.[91] Fewer than 10 years later his booming commendation was replaced by pleas to move the dank and discrediting rockpile elsewhere.

In 1926 Mount Eden's mayor had suggested that the Waitākere Ranges would be an ideal alternative site: 'The gaol reserve would then become available for general use. It was admirably suited for factories or for business purposes.'[92] Once he became the local MP, John A. Lee took up the campaign to relocate the prison with vigour, although he acknowledged that the expense meant it would be a long-term project.[93] After every escape attempt, the prison's neighbours grew more vehement in urging the facility's removal. In 1928 the Minister for Prisons was forced to concede that if his department 'were starting over again it would not put a prison where the Mount Eden one was', although he defended the continuing value of the adjacent quarry both for forced labour and income.[94]

Many critics alleged that Mount Eden was not just poorly sited but also an archaic blight on the city and the country. 'If ever there was a battlemented relic to prisons past it is the Mount Eden Gaol,' announced one MP in 1929; he looked forward to the day of its closure.[95] 'Goodness knows we are none of us proud that the Prison stands where it does, or that it looks gloomy and forbidding,' admitted the defensive Superintendent Dickison.[96] By 1940, Auckland's mayor, Sir Ernest Davis, had taken up the call to remove the prison to somewhere less visible and populous. 'The building is not a thing of beauty, and its appearance has a depressing effect on the immediate surroundings. If the gaol were situated in open country it could be better guarded, it could be made self-supporting and it would impart an isolation influence to its inmates.'[97] His council voted to urge Labour's newly appointed Minister of Prisons, Dr Girvan McMillan, to relocate this ageing and unsightly landmark.[98]

Labour's momentous election victory in 1935 had given hope to interested parties both inside and outside the prison that long-awaited changes might finally be implemented. Practically overnight, former prison inmates such as John A. Lee, Bill Parry, Peter Fraser and Bob Semple were lined up shoulder to shoulder on Parliament's Treasury benches, and their commitment to penal reform had been signalled well beforehand.[99] The Labour Party had a longstanding policy of ending both hangings and physical punishments such as flogging, and some Labour figures had shown a particular interest in Mount Eden and its inmates.

In April 1932 a peaceful protest by the unemployed exploded into violence when police batoned the protest leader Jim Edwards. The chaotic Queen Street riots that followed impelled the government to send 13 of the so-called ringleaders to jail; Edwards himself, although evidently blameless, was given a particularly harsh and repressive two years with hard labour.[100] When Labour Party leader Harry Holland visited these men during their imprisonment, the Justice Minister informed him that 'care is exercised to prevent contamination through harmful association with the more undesirable class of criminals. Those desirous of pursuing their economic studies are permitted to do so, but literature of an ultra-radical or revolutionary nature is not permitted.'[101] Most of the alleged rioters were highly politicised radicals, prone to breaking out into choruses of

'The Red Flag'.¹⁰² Jim Edwards, although the longest-serving of them all, was by contrast a model prisoner, described as 'always affable, agreeable and pleasant to the gaol officials', yet he spent his term isolated from other inmates and was accompanied by two warders whenever he left his cell.¹⁰³ His young son witnessed this treatment during visits to the prison, and the sympathetic chaplain, Reverend Moreton, explained to the boy gently that, 'your father is a political prisoner, and he is considered to be an agitator. The authorities apparently fear that he might incite some kind of rebelliousness among the other inmates.'¹⁰⁴

In the short term, these stringent efforts to prevent Edwards and his fellow agitators from inciting rebelliousness succeeded in containing dissent. After the Labour victory of '35, rumours flew among Mount Eden inmates that their longstanding grievances might finally be addressed. Soon after the election, a vehement minority hoped to jog the government's elbow with a very public show of discontent. In April 1936, several large groups of inmates refused to carry out regular duties or return to their cells at the end of the Saturday afternoon exercise period. Police were rushed to the prison to assist its warders to restore order, and the insurgency was resolved peaceably.¹⁰⁵ Thomas Leggett, the prison's newly appointed superintendent, played down the seriousness of the incident, and the Inspector of Prisons arrived from Wellington to interview three leaders of the disturbance. They told him that their most pressing concerns were the unfeeling and arbitrary actions of the Prison Board and the implementation of the law declaring certain repeat offenders to be habitual criminals.¹⁰⁶

Leggett, a particularly harsh and unimaginative superintendent, gave no weight to these arguments and dismissed the entire disturbance as 'an incident engineered by hot-headed notoriety-seekers, whose sole object was to subvert the discipline of the prison'.¹⁰⁷ Girvan McMillan, however, an unorthodox and energetic Minister of Prisons, had a passion for reformative policies. He made a point of meeting personally with inmates at Mount Eden and elsewhere, accompanied only by a stenographer to record their conversations, and insisted that no warders or other prison officials could be present.¹⁰⁸ No government minister had ever gone to such lengths to investigate prisoners' complaints or demonstrated such confidence in the value of their testimony, and his willingness to sit down with them in this way may have given the more fractious inmates further ground for believing that his government was committed to more than cosmetic efforts at penal reform.

The first signs of change in this direction were disappointingly slight. By 1939 all prisoners were permitted to have flowers and pictures in their cells, and the regulation diet was expanded to include regular puddings and milk.[109] The new government also introduced the daily broadcasting of radio programmes through speakers in the exercise yards and via headphones in the cells of long-serving inmates. Music and 'instructive talks' were said to be popular, but the instant reporting of racing results is likely to have been especially important to inmates who routinely gambled their precious tobacco rations.[110] These authorised broadcasts eliminated a major element of prison contraband, as for years inmates had smuggled or constructed their own illegal radio sets, causing warders endless trouble to locate and remove them. One snap search after a 1932 church service had revealed 'a perfect miniature set coiled up' inside a Bible.[111]

McMillan's efforts towards reform might well have produced more significant changes in the country's most procrustean prison, but they were overtaken by a dramatic and shockingly violent escape in 1940 that provoked a public outcry against the government's penal policies and savage judicial reprisals against the offenders. The 'most daring prison break ever staged at the Auckland gaol' took place one evening in October 1940 after the inmates were released from their cells to attend a lecture on physical training. In a sequence of actions that had evidently been carefully planned, four prisoners, one of them convicted of murder, made a savage assault on one of their warders and seized his heavy bunch of keys. Two other warders who came to his aid were attacked with an improvised weapon.

The escapers had somehow arranged for a long ladder to be placed in position in an exercise yard, and they were able to scale the outer wall and lower the ladder to the other side where a getaway car was waiting. Throughout the night more than 50 detectives and constables combed the city and suburbs, while police officers across the greater Auckland area set up checkpoints at main roads and bridges, stopping and examining every car.[112] This fine-meshed dragnet succeeded in recapturing all four men after a week.[113]

The savage beatings delivered to the warders and the violent records of two of the escapers kept much of the population in a state of terror until their recapture, and caused fierce recrimination after it. Labour's alleged determination to look for the best in criminals, and especially McMillan's unconventional practice of communicating directly with them, were seen as a disastrous softening of former measures.[114] Highly placed critics such as Sir Hubert Ostler, the chairman of the Prisons Board, accused McMillan himself of inadvertently encouraging prisoners to become insubordinate.[115] Public outrage during the subsequent trials of the four escapers was particularly intense, as the injured warders were still in hospital, one of them in a serious condition. Twelve years' hard labour was added to each of the men's sentences, bringing the term for one of them up to a bleak 33 years.[116] A wartime defaulter, Ian Hamilton, observed the quartet, known as the Kelly gang, when he was admitted to the prison a few years later. Grey-faced and silent, they were shepherded along the halls by several armed warders. 'They work in a yard by themselves sewing mailbags,' he was told. 'They're not allowed to speak to anyone else. Two of them have gone religious. They make little images out of bits of bread and worship them.'[117]

Even these conditions were not sufficient to satisfy the public that justice had been served in this case. The judge who had increased the men's prison terms also ordered them to be flogged — an order that conflicted with the expressed policy of the wartime Labour government, which had long campaigned to abolish both capital and corporal punishment in prisons. McMillan and his Cabinet colleagues took the rare step of overruling the judge's verdict, and asked the Governor-General, Sir Cyril Newall, to remit this element of the sentence. Sir Cyril refused on constitutional grounds, and the government's only recourse was to delay the order to administer the flogging until it could pass a Bill abolishing both corporal and capital punishment. It did so in late 1941, just before the end of its second term, provoking further public outrage.[118]

The following year a small and explosive book delivered the most systematically damning critique of Mount Eden Prison's facilities and practices then published. It could not be readily dismissed as unreliable, since it presented the experiences and views of the prison's longtime, widely admired and internationally informed chaplain, Reverend George Moreton, who expressed himself with a bluntness not often heard from members of his calling. In *A Parson in Prison*, Moreton summed up the country's entire penal system as 'hopelessly archaic' and Mount Eden

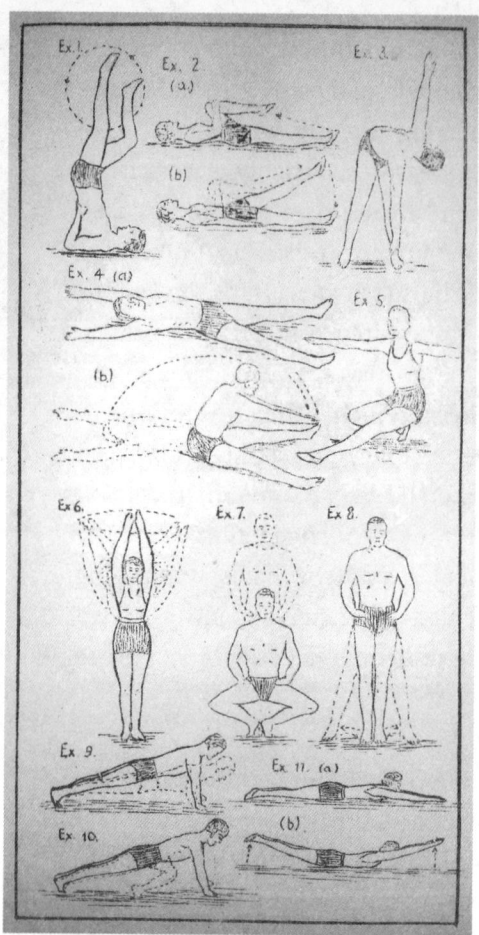

Left: Keeping fit in confined spaces is not easy, and this exercise chart was sent to Mount Eden and other prisons in 1939. 'The men should be able to practise quite easily in their cells,' advised Controller-General of Prisons Bert Dallard.
ARCHIVES NEW ZEALAND, R16362954

Below: On Anzac Day 1936, Mount Eden inmates refused the weekly shave on the grounds that it was a public holiday. Police were called to reinforce the skeleton staff on duty.
AUCKLAND LIBRARIES HERITAGE COLLECTIONS, AUCKLAND STAR, 28 APRIL 1936

itself as the country's last major monument to the unmourned tenure of Colonel Hume.[119] 'The men who designed that building should have been shut in it for the rest of their lives. It's hideous; and in an age in which responsible people are trying to approach the problem of crime intelligently, scientifically, it stands there like a brutal product of medieval ignorance.'[120]

As instances of an intelligent and scientific approach, the chaplain proposed better training for prison officers, and a pay rate that would attract skilled and insightful staff into the profession. Work performed by inmates should be meaningful, reasonably remunerated and carried out in safe conditions. More classes should be provided, both in technical and cultural fields, and inmates should have sports facilities rather than the nightly routine of synchronised physical exercises under the direction of a warder. Moreton welcomed the recent provision of radio broadcasts, but he noted that 'on five nights a week its use is restricted to "war news", after which it is switched off . . . Surely it would be an improvement if talks of educational value, lectures, drama, theatre and music were placed at the disposal of men at all hours on the weeknights.'[121]

The response from McMillan's successor as Minister of Justice and Prisons, Rex Mason, was swift and devastating. The minister claimed that the chaplain had revealed in his book information given to him by a prisoner in confidence, and as a result he was 'no longer to be permitted access to the prison'.[122] Moreton was given no warning and no opportunity to explain or defend this alleged breach of confidence, which he denied. 'My criticism of the prison system has cost me my job, and those who are moved by their consciences to speak critically of the administrative policy of the present Government must be prepared to face official punishment and to place their positions in jeopardy,' he told a reporter.[123]

| | |

At another time Moreton's well-founded condemnation of Mount Eden's treatment of inmates and his thoughtful suggestions for reforming them may have received a more measured hearing, but by 1942 the prison administration was once again struggling to cope with an influx of articulate and well-connected military defaulters. They were fewer in number than during World War One, when almost none of those resisting military service were acknowledged to be sincere conscientious objectors, but once again those who failed to share in the mood of militant patriotism were treated with greater intolerance than in almost any other Commonwealth country.

The first objectors to arrive in Mount Eden, from mid-1941, were those who openly opposed the government's wartime policy.[124] Soon they were joined by those who resisted conscription for active service, including five young men sentenced for refusing orders at Papakura military camp.[125] Others were given short terms of hard labour for breaches of military discipline such as refusing to submit to a medical examination. These military defaulters worked alongside other inmates in the prison but during exercise periods were kept segregated from 'the ordinary criminal offender'.[126] On the day of their release, many found a military van waiting beside the prison gates to return them to camp; if they did not cooperate, they faced immediate re-arrest.[127]

By the end of 1941, the thousands of predominantly young men who refused to submit to military orders were being sent to a network of detention camps around the country. An intransigent minority who continued to disobey orders or refused to work in the camps were later transferred to prisons such as Mount Eden. According to several studies of the detention-camp system, some of these recalcitrants were deliberately sent to prison to rid the camps of troublemakers, by, for example, giving them an order it was known they would refuse.[128] They had no public trial or right of appeal against their transfer, which was often made on the word of an embittered detention-camp guard. At least five such men were held in Mount Eden by mid-1942. Another, John Bayley, was sent to the prison for escaping from his detention camp, and then spent 10 days in the prison dummy for refusing to salute the medical officer or superintendent.[129] The punishment was repeated three times because he repeatedly refused to salute 'those jumped-up damned dictators'.[130]

Nineteen-year-old Neil Smith unwittingly repeated the words of World War One-era conchies on the subject of the prison's medical services. 'Ordinary, common physical illnesses seem to be the only ones recognised in gaol, and the doctor takes a completely impersonal, unsympathetic attitude towards prisoners.'[131] This doctor may also have been overworked, given that the prison was severely understaffed throughout the war as some men signed up to serve and others could not be replaced. The remaining staff were required to manage categories of inmates with which they were unfamiliar, such as 30-odd US servicemen who, according to the superintendent, gave 'considerable trouble' and 'required firm handling'.[132]

In these strained circumstances it was inevitable that security precautions were sometimes found wanting.[133] In 1944 two habitual criminals with records of violence took advantage of the manpower shortage by escaping in spectacular fashion though a hole they blew in the perimeter wall.[134] They were chased across vacant land towards Mountain Road but disappeared over backyard fences.[135] One of the pair, John Wilson, was at large for seven weeks before he was recaptured in nearby Kingsland with a loaded revolver. In court he pleaded for more opportunities for recreation and entertainment for himself and other long-serving inmates: 'For eighteen months I had been closely confined with only one hour's exercise a day.' The judge decided an additional three years on his sentence was the best response.[136]

By the final year of the war, the prison's contingent of conchies had grown in number and also in stroppiness. Some had spent four years in detention camps without trial and were inured to the various forms of punishment imposed on them. A few had escaped long enough to inform, and alarm, sections of the civilian population with their accounts of both camp and prison conditions. In February 1945, five of these men refused to parade for hard labour with the rest of Mount Eden's prison population, and when placed in solitary next to the condemned cells refused to eat the bread-and-water rations provided. All five insisted they were genuine conscientious objectors who had been treated for long periods as criminals; they also said that in a time of an acute national shortage of manpower they were prepared to work in essential industries on soldiers' rates of pay.[137]

Superintendent Leggett filed a report describing each of the men's characters in similar terms — 'a troublemaker and a nuisance at all times', 'a rebel whose presence was prejudicial to good order and discipline', a 'nasty type, impudent and rebellious by nature'.[138] To persuade the men to abandon the hunger strike, their meals were delivered to them hot each day from the kitchens, but the plates sat untouched on their cell floors. Eventually the regulation meals were stopped on medical advice, since they would prove harmful to men who had taken nothing but water for several weeks.[139] By the time one of the strikers, Harold McAuley, was admitted to Auckland Hospital, word of the protest had also reached beyond the walls of the prison and disturbed sections of the public, who asked why these men should be facing indefinite sentences.[140] Bert Dallard, the Controller-General of Prisons, replied that they were acting 'apparently in a desire to seek notoriety or to bask in the sunshine of martyrdom'.[141]

The hunger strike petered out undramatically as the men recognised they might be permanently damaging their health for little result.[142] They remained in the prison, weakened but defiant, and were joined by more objectors sentenced for carrying out collective protests in their detention camps. Some were highly distinctive and eccentric individuals, such as a proto-hippie who had not cut his hair or beard, or worn leather, for many years.[143] The rigidly traditionalist prison staff made no effort to understand principles such as these, and tended at first to treat such idiosyncracies as deliberate breaches of prison regulations.

None of the final batch of objectors proved as troublesome as a former lawyer from Christchurch named Jack Crichton. He had opposed conscription since its introduction in early 1941, and spent the intervening years in a succession of camps and prisons, isolated from other inmates to restrict his influence on them. By mid-1945, with the war with Germany at an end, Crichton decided to challenge the government's right to continue holding him for as long as it saw fit. At Mount Eden he was swiftly placed in the dummy. Insisting that he was held without legal grounds, he refused to wear the prison uniform and was treated so roughly by warders that most of the prison's other defaulters defied regulations in sympathy with him. He had become their de facto legal adviser, and won the admiration even of hardened criminals when, during an exercise period, he suddenly stripped naked, bundled up his uniform and hurled it over the outer wall of the yard.

Crichton remained a thorn in the side of prison officials, and several times forced them to acknowledge that their treatment of objectors was legally unsound. The Controller-General of Prisons warned Superintendent Leggett that his practice of repeatedly sending non-cooperating defaulters such as Nelson pacifist Harold Hansen to the dummy might expose him to a lawsuit. 'It is quite possible that an action for damages against both the Visiting Justice and yourself, particularly in Hansen's case, would succeed.'[144]

4 WEEKS WITHOUT FOOD!

CONSCIENTIOUS OBJECTORS HUNGER STRIKING MT. EDEN PRISON

URGE GOVT. ACTION BEFORE DEATHS

This page and next page: In February 1945, after three years in detention camps or prison, conscientious objector Harold McAuley refused work duties at Mount Eden Prison in protest at his indefinite imprisonment without the right of appeal. Justice Minister Rex Mason was unmoved, and McAuley and others began a hunger strike. Their supporters risked arrest to paste posters on lamp posts around Auckland. PRIVATE COLLECTION

HE HASN'T A
Belsen Horror Camp
BUT HE DOES HIS BEST WITH
Mount Eden Prison

HON. H. G. R MASON
Minister of Justice

Read the Facts of the Harold McAuley Case Overleaf

McAULEY IS FIGHTING FOR:

Recognition as a sincere conscientious objector.

The abandonment of the Government's policy to hold INDEFINITELY those men who are unable to convince Appeal Boards of their sincerity.

The rights of individuals against a growing totalitarianism which threatens to ruthlessly suppress every minority and non-conformist.

We Urge:

The immediate transfer of McAuley to hospital or, at least, the provision of facilities for independent medical attention.

An immediate enquiry, by an independent tribunal, into the facts of this case and the parts played therein by the Prison Superintendent, the visiting J.P. and the Prison Doctor.

A reconsideration of McAuley's claim to be a genuine C.O. If his sincerity is established he should be released immediately. If he is unable to "prove" his sincerity he should be sentenced to a **definite** period of imprisonment. (He has already served three and a half years.)

As the first postwar year dawned and the rest of the country exulted in peace and victory, the Mount Eden defaulters grew ever more rebellious. Several had been sentenced 'for the duration of the war', and the government had made it plain that it would decide this duration. In the first few days of 1946, Jack Crichton organised a protest that quickly made the national press. After the evening lockup, slogans and wordless cries were chanted in deafening unison. 'The war ended five months ago. We are still incarcerated without a trial,' the men roared. 'Their concerted "coo-ees" and prearranged choruses of complaint have echoed over a wide area beyond the limits of the prison,' reported the *Herald*.[145] For nights on end, nearby residents were deprived of sleep, and some complained that when they finally dropped off they were troubled by nightmares.

Superintendent Leggett must have been equally distraught. He had exhausted his legal options for punishing these men, and could now attempt to silence them only by shifting them to the most isolated precincts of the jail and sandbagging their cell windows.[146] The structural defects and systemic failings of his sturdy fortress had become impossible for those inside and outside its walls to ignore

6:
The Meccano Set
1947–1962

The Auckland War Memorial Museum's subterranean, climate-controlled storage rooms hold two large and well-worn wooden crates marked 'Secretary for Justice, Wellington, New Zealand'. They were shipped to this country in early 1952 from Britain's Prisons Commission to meet a sudden and urgent demand. Pasted inside the lid of each box is a list of its contents: 'Execution box: 2 ropes, 1 block and fall tackle, 2 straps, 1 sandbag, 1 measuring rod, 1 cap . . .' The objects inside are meticulously wrapped in tissue paper, with the smallest and most fragile at the top — a toy 'Zorro' mask made of black cardboard complete with the elastic thread to hold it in place, once worn by the government hangman to aid in concealing his identity. The juxtaposition of this item of children's make-believe with the more conventional accoutrements of capital punishment is chilling and bizarre.

The heavy rope nooses and other equipment in these boxes were required at Mount Eden Prison at short notice when, in 1950, a new government suddenly reintroduced hanging after a hiatus of 15 years. During that period the smaller and less durable articles of the hangman's trade had evidently disappeared or been disposed of, so replacements were sought from Britain where executions had been carried out without interruption throughout the 1940s. The locally made scaffold, however, required only to be removed from storage and given minor modifications at Britain's Wandsworth Prison to be fully functional again.

This unique item of custom-made machinery is also now held in the museum's basement storerooms. Stacked in dismantled form on several pallets, it comprises a mundane-looking heap of heavy kauri planks and iron plates and fittings marked with letters and numbers for easy assembly. It was built in the early 1920s to replace the wooden scaffolds that had once been constructed before every hanging and then destroyed. As an advance on that practice, the state railway workshops in the Hutt Valley produced this portable scaffold, designed to be repeatedly dismantled and re-assembled at different locations.

Truth reported admiringly in 1924 that it was 'excellently made, and reliable. The superstructure is of a neat tripod design in place of the previous large and cumbersome beams and overhead joist. The basement is tarpaulined off and the body, after the drop, is not visible.'[1] This kitset device, painted silver and referred to with what can only be termed gallows humour as the 'Meccano Set', remained in intermittent operation

One of two nooses included in the 'execution box' supplied by Britain's Prisons Commission in 1952. After the reintroduction of the death penalty in 1950, Mount Eden Prison was the site of the country's final eight hangings. *NEW ZEALAND POLICE MUSEUM*

for 40 years.² In the 1920s and 1930s it was shuttled by rail between Mount Eden and Wellington's Mount Crawford as required — for the execution of four men in each location. After World War Two, the Meccano Set was installed permanently at Mount Eden, the only prison in the country where executions were still carried out.³

The prison's east wing ends in a narrow, high-walled yard with the proportions of an open grave. In this permanently shadowed enclosure no visible trace of the scaffold remains, yet even half a century later it is not difficult to imagine, within the dank atmosphere and oppressive dimensions, the crash of the trapdoor. This was the sombre setting for all of Mount Eden's twentieth-century hangings — a total of 16. The crowds of shuddering, engrossed spectators who, in the previous century, had witnessed the spectacle of an execution from the slopes overlooking the prison were eventually denied that opportunity, and from 1911 the public's knowledge of hangings at Mount Eden was conveyed only through the moralistic accounts of newspaper reporters. A handful of pressmen were among the select group invited into the prison on execution days, both to amplify the deterrent effect of the death sentence and to satisfy morbid curiosities.

Through the nineteenth and the early twentieth centuries, their reports prompted little public outrage, as the moral justification for the death sentence remained largely unquestioned. Taking a life as punishment for murder and other heinous crimes was generally regarded as justly and necessarily retributive, and more humane than a long period of imprisonment. By comparison with any other method of execution, hanging was said to deliver an instant and relatively painless death, and so provided a deterrent to others without unduly tormenting the victim.⁴

Within the prison itself, however, this periodic disruption to routine was never lightly accepted. Although all other inmates were confined to their cells before an execution, they learned of the moment of death when the clang of the final drop resounded through the corridors, and as John A. Lee observed in 1912, that noise triggered a deafening outburst from the entire inmate population. Many prison staff also seem to have experienced dread, shame and profound unease as the date of an execution approached, and those responses can be traced back to some of the earliest hangings on this site.

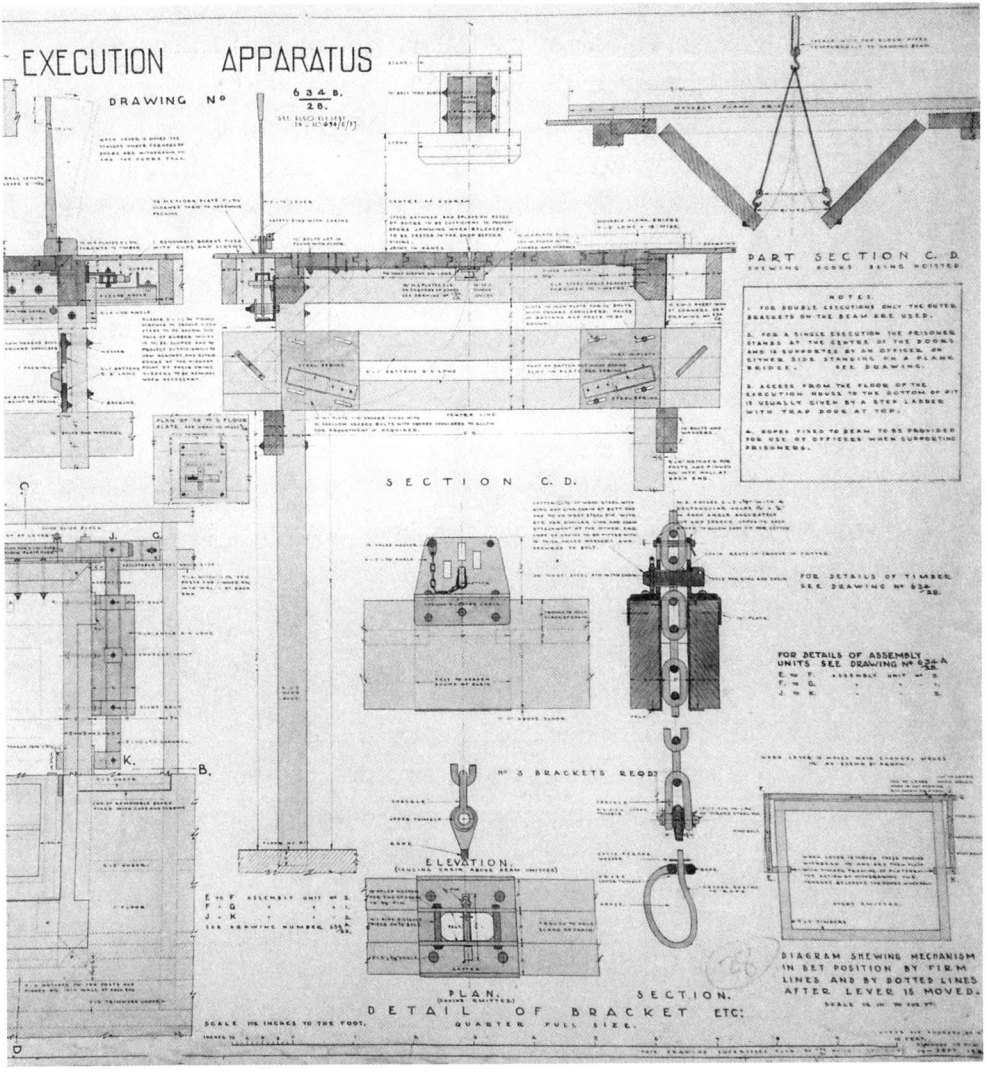

The technology of execution. This meticulous diagram describes the construction and assembly of the portable scaffold built in the 1920s at the Lower Hutt railway workshops. *ARCHIVES NEW ZEALAND, R16563581*

In 1873 Colonel Balneavis, the sheriff during the period of the wooden Stockade, wrote to the Justice Minister to plead for changes to the execution procedure to make it more efficient and less distressing for obligatory participants such as himself. At that time, a crude and temporary wooden scaffold was built to order whenever a death sentence required it. Commissioning a new scaffold was the sheriff's responsibility and one that Balneavis particularly disliked. It was 'a great difficulty,' he told his Minister, 'as many carpenters (the best) will not undertake the work'. The newly constructed scaffold then required a hangman to operate it, and engaging a suitable candidate presented Balneavis with even more pressing difficulties than finding willing carpenters.

'In this country,' he reminded his Minister, 'sheriffs depend upon the chance of getting some person from the population who may have acted [as executioner] at some prior period, or of getting some prisoner from the Gaol, who undertakes the duty merely to get his liberty ... and who is totally ignorant of what he undertakes.' The colonel then offered a proposal, based on his own experience, for making future executions less haphazard. 'The person whom I employed at the late execution was also employed some years ago at the execution of some Natives here [presumably a reference to the execution of Mokomoko and four others for murder in 1865] and has been an executioner in India. He understands all the requisites connected with such revolting matters, and is willing to accept the situation of authorised permanent executioner at a salary of £100 per annum and expenses.' Balneavis warned the Justice Minister that failure to employ such a skilled professional in this role made it certain that 'at some execution a fearful, horrible and inhuman scene will occur from the ignorance and possible want of nerve of Executioners, which will cause great discredit, dissatisfaction and comment'.[5]

He was referring to the rarely acknowledged but not uncommon circumstance when a hanging did not result in instantaneous death. The trapdoor would crash open, the condemned man would drop through it into a screened-off space beneath, and appalled witnesses could see the wrenching of the rope and hear the sounds of gradual asphyxiation. It was then the hangman's unpleasant duty to go back down the stairs, disappear behind the tarpaulins and finish off the job by adding his own bodyweight. Understandably, those obliged to witness these scenes were not inclined to describe them in detail afterwards, least of all in print, yet the careful language employed makes it clear that these executions were extremely distressing and liable to add great force to arguments to abolish the death penalty.

On this occasion, however, Balneavis's well-founded entreaty was curtly dismissed with the marginal note, possibly by the Justice Minister himself, that 'no difficulty has been experienced heretofore . . . Col. Balneavis is affected by a morbid fear he may be required to perform the duty himself.'[6] But this anonymous annotator included a further justification for refusing to engage an official executioner — that 'it is to be hoped that ere long capital punishment will be abolished'. This intriguing prediction suggests that even in the nineteenth century the practice of hanging met with some opposition, if only from those required to administer it, and that alternative forms of punishment for the gravest crimes were already envisaged. Those expectations were not fulfilled for almost a century, and only after a further 52 executions, almost half of them at Mount Eden.

Over that period, refinements were successively introduced to make the process of hanging as dignified, orderly and discreet as possible, and to reduce the risk, vividly evoked by Balneavis, of any bungling that might strengthen calls to abolish the practice. From the early twentieth century, the traditional customs of tolling the prison bell and flying a black flag from the roof on execution days were gradually discontinued.[7] These small concessions were afforded to Dennis Gunn, convicted in 1920 of murdering the postmaster in Ponsonby, Auckland. He was required to walk no more than a dozen paces from his condemned cell to the scaffold, and his hangman, although not yet the professional servant of the Crown envisaged by Balneavis, was an accomplished practitioner who had dispatched several other condemned men in the past. In short, according to one press account, 'everything of a spectacular nature was eliminated from the execution'.[8]

However, Gunn's competent hangman found, like many of his successors, that the role eventually strained the toughest constitution. When another convicted murderer, Samuel Thorn, was due to be hanged a few months later, this jaded veteran of the execution yard advised the Justice Department that he was unwilling to hang Thorn or anyone else in future. As a precaution against that eventuality Mount Eden's superintendent, Thomas Vincent, had arranged for a stand-in. That man presented himself at the prison the day before the scheduled hanging in

Above: A small crowd gathered outside the prison gates when Arthur Munn was hanged in July 1930 for poisoning his wife. ALEXANDER TURNBULL LIBRARY

Below: This 1950 image is likely to have reassured the public that Mount Eden's long-term inmates were comfortably housed. The unidentified occupant of this one-person cell can boast a furry companion, a radio, a reading light, family photos and other comforts, although not a flush toilet. NEW ZEALAND HERALD

December 1920. He had no prior experience in the role, so prison staff instructed him in the routines of operating the scaffold, placing the linen hood over the condemned man's head, adjusting the noose, and the other practices of this grisly occupation. This intensive training course apparently destroyed the novice executioner's resolve as well, and the following morning Superintendent Vincent concluded that the man was having a nervous breakdown and would be unable to discharge his duties.

This situation presented the judicial system with a severe dilemma, since custom and the law required an execution to be carried out within a week of the death sentence being passed, so the superintendent had almost no time to find a volunteer.[9] In desperation, Vincent was forced to revert to the despised and unreliable practice that had so alarmed Balneavis half a century earlier — he called on another inmate to fulfil the hangman's role. A man serving 12 months for theft, who had already helped to assemble the scaffold, agreed to execute Thorn.[10]

To the relief of the officials involved, this hanging went ahead without incident, and the Justice Department was then requested to reward the man in 'the most liberal terms'. He asked to be relieved from hard labour for the remainder of his sentence and given assistance to leave the country, and those conditions were apparently granted.[11] This was almost certainly the only occasion in the twentieth century when one New Zealand prisoner executed another. In all other instances, a fee was paid to the successful applicant from among the public, until eventually a regular state hangman was appointed to carry out this periodic duty.

Mount Eden's superintendent was required to attend every hanging during his term, so he had good reason to try to make the experience as orderly and unmemorable as possible. The year after the executions of Gunn and Thorn, a young bushman named Hakaraia Te Kahu was hanged with the help of a device invented by Superintendent Vincent 'and used for the first time, as far as is known, in the history of hanging'. This innovation was a wide belt suspended from the gallows and passed under the armpits of the condemned man to prevent him from collapsing in the final seconds as he stood on the trapdoor. Swaying visibly despite this support, Te Kahu asked, through a Māori interpreter, to send his love to his parents.[12]

Almost nothing is reliably known about those who filled the position of hangman once the Meccano Set came into use. Their identity was kept a closely guarded secret to protect against possible reprisals, and the men carried out their duties disguised beneath a hat, dark glasses and other concealing apparel. Some clues emerged in 1930, shortly after Arthur Munn was executed, when the weekly *Truth*, always readier than other papers to purvey sensationalism in the name of the public interest, ran a lengthy interview with a garrulous figure who claimed that he had pulled the lever on Munn.

The interview provided no name, description or other identifying details of this self-professed hangman, and he admitted that his friends and acquaintances would shun him if they knew of his secret profession. Nevertheless, he gave an apparently reliable account of the execution process at Mount Eden in the interwar period. He generally arrived at the prison the night before, he told the paper, and was given a bed in the hospital ward 'or whatever quarters are convenient'. From the moment the condemned man was taken from his cell, every other prisoner was kept locked up, and no one, including visitors and staff, was permitted to leave or enter the gaol until the coroner had certified the cause of death.[13]

The legal basis for state-ordered execution was the Criminal Code Act of 1893, which specified the death penalty as the only available sentence for the crimes of murder, treason and piracy.[14] The same Act authorised the punishment of flogging, a penalty that continued to be administered at Mount Eden occasionally during the early twentieth century, generally for sexual offences or robbery with violence. The device employed was a cat-o'-nine-tails, and the punishment was carried out in the same small and cheerless yard which housed the scaffold. As with executions, a carefully developed process was followed on each occasion. A medical officer first examined the victim, and his kidneys and neck were protected by heavy leather straps, as fatal consequences were to be avoided. His ankles were strapped to the legs of a large wooden triangle and his wrists to its upper point. A canvas screen, acting like a horse's blinkers, was placed behind the victim's head and shoulders to preserve the identity of the prison officer wielding the whip.[15]

|||

From a penological viewpoint, corporal punishment differed in at least one important respect from hanging. An execution undoubtedly prevented the victim from committing further crimes, but more than half of those flogged went on to re-offend, casting doubt on the punishment's alleged deterrent effect.[16] This discomforting uncertainty was aggravated during the early twentieth century by increasingly vocal assertions, especially from those in left-wing and liberal quarters, that both corporal and capital punishment were 'a grotesque and reprehensible hangover of discredited eye-for-an-eye systems of justice and punishment'.[17] The evident mental weakness of many of those sentenced to such punishments, and a number of high-profile wrongful convictions, greatly reinforced these arguments.

In the face of growing public disquiet and closer scrutiny, executions at Mount Eden nonetheless continued through the early twentieth century. They followed a clearly defined pattern, with all preparations carried out by prison staff, and only the minimum of authority left to the hangman on the day of the execution itself. In the period between a condemned prisoner's sentencing and its implementation, he (no women were ever executed at Mount Eden) was held in a special cell in the west wing, accompanied constantly by a roster of officers whose main task was to ensure that he did not cheat the gallows by killing himself. Every day he was weighed to check that the rope length was correct, and he did not learn the date of his execution until the night before. Next morning the gallows was tested with a bag of sand corresponding to his bodyweight.[18]

At the appointed time the condemned man was led from his cell, shuffling along the corridors to the east wing with straps around his arms and thighs. Often he was so heavily sedated he needed the support of prison staff to climb the scaffold. Once positioned under the beam holding the rope, his ankles were strapped, a linen bag was placed over his head, and the noose was placed around his neck with its metal eyelet facing forward. Meanwhile the hangman stood silently in the background, awaiting the sheriff's hand signal to pull the lever and release the trapdoor. The body was then left to hang in a screened enclosure beneath the gallows for an hour, after which the coroner examined it and pronounced the cause of death.

The Executive Council of government, comprising all its ministers, held the power to reprieve a death sentence and replace it with one of life imprisonment, and this power was exercised with increasing frequency as public opposition to capital punishment intensified. In 1935, however, the election of the country's first Labour government raised the prospect of ending the practice of hanging forever. Opposition to both capital and corporal punishment had been a pillar of Labour policy almost since the party's formation in 1916, yet it proved a troublesome reform for this profoundly reforming government to enact, particularly after Peter Fraser took over as prime minister. The rigidly intolerant Fraser disagreed with his Cabinet by favouring retention of the death penalty, meaning the law that imposed a mandatory death sentence for murder was not immediately repealed. Instead, in an awkwardly provisional compromise, Fraser's Executive Council exercised its prerogative of mercy over every death sentence that came before it.

In its first years of office, the government encountered little public objection to the commuting of death sentences passed on questionably convicted figures such as the bandleader Eric Mareo. In 1940 that support abruptly evaporated after a young mine worker named Cartman was convicted of the brutal murder of a woman and her son at Waikino, near Waihī. Calls for Cartman's execution were long and loud, and the Executive Council debated for several months before deciding to commute his death sentence.[19] Public outrage at this decision had not subsided when another dramatic crime kept the linked issues of capital and corporal punishment at the forefront of public debate. As noted in the previous chapter, in October 1940 five long-serving Mount Eden inmates, including one whose death sentence had been reprieved two years earlier, made a rash but determined attempt to escape. A warder who intercepted them was attacked so viciously that he was permanently disabled, both physically and mentally. The escapers were swiftly recaptured, and in February 1941 they were each given the harsh sentence of an additional 12 years' hard labour and a flogging of 20 lashes.

This case posed a deep dilemma for the Labour government's practice of remitting all sentences of corporal and capital punishment. Wellington's *Evening Post* newspaper crowed: 'The rebellious prisoners in the Auckland gaol . . . placed the government at last in a position where even the government felt ashamed to strain its discretionary sentence revision powers.'[20] At the time Fraser was overseas negotiating New Zealand's contribution to the war effort; in his absence, the firmly abolitionist Justice Minister Rex Mason introduced a bill to remove floggings from the penal code and end the death penalty for all crimes except treason.²¹ In this haphazard way the impulsively violent actions of a small group of Mount Eden inmates brought an end to hangings and floggings throughout the country after many high-principled arguments had failed to do so.

III

By late 1945, as the population at large was anticipating an enlightened postwar world, the country's maximum-security prison loomed above downtown Auckland as a baleful reminder of darker days. Its physical structure had changed very little in the half-century since Arthur Hume had designed his cheerless monument to deterrence. Both prisoners and prison officers were subjected to conditions of high humidity and stifling heat in summer, and mildew, damp and bone-chilling cold in winter. The massive walls were dauntingly resistant to modernisation, so washing and toilet facilities were antediluvian, and because most of the inmate population spent their days at hard physical work, the aroma of the prison's poorly ventilated corridors struck new arrivals with an almost physical force. More than 50 years after his first visit as a newly appointed Secretary of Justice, Bert Dallard could 'distinctly recall the revolting smell of unwashed bodies at Mount Eden . . . The ventilation of the cells was nauseating and to overcome this I had air gratings fitted at floor level and above each door.'²²

That modest improvement was no match for the effluvia generated by more than 300 men locked up for 16 hours a day without access to toilets. The prison's 'complete lack of sanitary facilities' was long remembered by waterside workers' leader Jock Barnes. Known to union members as 'the Bull' for his size, strength and forcefulness, he served two months' hard labour at Mount Eden for criticising, in typically blunt terms, the police's treatment of demonstrators during the 1951 wharf dispute. 'You were given a little enamel pisspot that you had to do everything in,' he recalled. 'Then you'd line up in the morning, you'd go along the corridor and tip them.'²³

In a gesture towards improved hygiene, from the mid-1950s inmates who worked as cooks and bakers were permitted to bathe 'when time permits and as often as they wish'.²⁴ Everyone else was limited to two showers a week, and the air in the corridors remained rank with the odour of their body and food waste, mingled with the smells of cooking and the prison's own harsh carbolic soap, made on the premises and applied widely and liberally in a futile attempt to suppress the other smells.[25]

In the aseptic and modish 1950s such conditions were a shameful anachronism, but Prisons Department officials seemed at a loss to remedy them. As the *Herald* acknowledged: 'The installation of an up-to-date plumbing system would necessitate considerable reconstruction, including the drilling of stone walls and floors several feet thick to take pipes, yet some such system appears to be urgently necessary if the present primitive arrangements are not to be perpetuated indefinitely.'[26]

These physical discomforts were accentuated by a staff shortage that Superintendent Leggett described on his retirement in 1946 as the most critical the prison had ever known. His depleted and demoralised workforce was expected to supervise an ever larger and more challenging inmate population. In the decade since executions were brought to a temporary halt, at least a dozen of the prison's cells had become the long-term homes of multiple murderers and others convicted of extremely serious crimes.[27] The armed guards who patrolled the elevated catwalks could give their colleagues little reassurance of protection from a concerted assault, since their weapons were likely to have last seen service in the New Zealand Wars and no one could be certain 'whether these firearms would actually work in an emergency'.[28]

Under the strain of these conditions, Leggett reported in May 1946, at least six of his men had suffered nervous breakdowns in the past 12 months.[29] The practice of calling in the police to assist prison officers even with routine duties became so common that the officers enlisted the support of their union, the Public Service Association, which demanded improvements to a wide range of staff amenities, and a formal training programme.[30] Salaries also improved somewhat, and a 40-hour working week was instituted in place of the gruelling earlier shifts of up to 13 hours.

But overstretched prison staff remained vulnerable. In February 1948, some officers at Mount Eden were convinced they would be attacked in the 'big yard' during one Saturday morning exercise period, 'because prisoners were overheard saying so'.[31] No attack took place but in the same month there was an uproar in the cells, allegedly provoked by a warder kicking a female prisoner, and off-duty warders and every available policeman in the city was dispatched to assist. For several hours inmates smashed their cell furniture, hurled abuse at prison authorities and warders, and regaled the neighbourhood with popular songs such as 'Pistol-packin' Momma' and 'Now Is the Hour'.[32] Local residents claimed it was the worst fracas they had known at the jail.[33] Secretary of Justice Dallard made sure that 'the press do not have access to Mount Eden, for if the prisoners discover that they are in the public eye it will take considerably longer for them to return to normal'.[34]

Into this rancorous and unsavoury institution strode Sam Barnett, the newly appointed Controller-General of the country's prisons. A lawyer by training, he arrived at this post in late 1949 after a long and illustrious career in other branches of the public service.[35] Barnett was the epitome of a postwar new broom, an impatient and determined innovator, and the very antithesis of the reactionary Colonel Arthur Hume.

He later summarised his intentions for the prison system as: 'first, to keep people out of penal institutions; and, second, so to deal with those in institutions that every wholesome and available influence is brought to bear to divert them from further offending on their release.'[36] To prepare for these challenging reforms, he travelled to the UK and US in early 1950 to observe the most recent developments in 'prison administration and modern penological treatment'.[37] He returned intent on demonstrating that his own country's prisons could eventually emulate and equal any in the world in terms of inmate education and rehabilitation.

This, he realised, would mean removing legislative leg-irons applied in the final years of the Hume period such as the habitual criminals legislation of 1906 and the 1908 Prisons Act. Accordingly, the Criminal Justice and Penal Institutions Acts were introduced in 1954, both aimed at reducing re-offending, especially among young people. Reformative detention was replaced by corrective training for an indeterminate period of up to three years. The only offenders eligible for this sentence were those aged between 21 and 30 who showed signs of embarking on a criminal career. The 'habitual criminal' provisions, which had notably failed to reduce re-offending, were replaced by preventive detention aimed at persistent criminals and recidivist child sex offenders. This sentence was also indeterminate but for three to 14 years, although with no maximum for offences against children.[38] As Mount Eden's cells came to accommodate many offenders serving such indeterminate sentences, the reformative purpose of these measures became similarly questionable.[39]

The decision on when to release inmates serving indeterminate sentences was placed in the hands of a newly created body, the Prisons Parole Board. However, judges proved reluctant to impose the sentence of corrective training, as most of those given this sentence re-offended within six years of their release. From 1954, therefore, the boards generally determined the release dates only of lifers and preventive detainees, with most other inmates eligible for remission of just a quarter of their full term.[40]

The energetic Barnett was able to push through this new legislation despite indifference to the very notion of penal reform from the Sid Holland-led Cabinet, and especially from Clifton Webb, the diminutive and grimly conservative Minister of both Police and Prisons. Other, arguably more significant, innovations did not require legislative change, and here Barnett could exercise a freer hand. From 1954 a Classification Board reviewed every inmate's case and proposed plans for their rehabilitation. In this process local sub-committees could call upon psychologists, psychiatrists, vocational guidance officers, probation officers and other specialists in determining the character and potential of each offender. Prison officers were not normally included in this consultation process — a notable shift of emphasis towards non-custodial expertise. A similar attitude lay behind the appointment of full-time chaplains, trade-training instructors and teachers to every prison. On-site medical services were expanded to include nurses and doctors, and basic dental treatment.[41]

If prison staff felt aggrieved by the appearance in their workplace of these potentially naive professionals, then their morale was bolstered by a staff training school based at Wellington Prison, where recruits were given an induction course and elementary training.[42] Their uniforms became more modern and less military, and their job title changed from 'warder' to 'prison officer'. Their work remained underpaid and poorly regarded, but they evolved a fierce esprit de corps based on mutual support in challenging surroundings, and a close-knit and communal life in barracks and prison housing.[43]

These imaginative reforms appeared, perhaps surprisingly, under the first National government, which took office in 1949 and promptly re-introduced hanging. Barnett was deeply opposed in principle to capital punishment but his Minister, Clifton Webb, was a fervent proponent of the scaffold. However, when these two very dissimilar men made

The smartly uniformed, all-male line-up in this photo from 1960 includes (front row, from left): Chaplain A. Dunn, Activities Officer Hogan, Chief Officer G. McLean, Deputy Superintendent A. Burgess, Superintendent H. V. Haywood, Chief Officer J. J. Connell, Principal Officer O'Connor, Principal Officer H. I. Eden and Principal Officer C. Tugt. DEPARTMENT OF CORRECTIONS

an exploratory visit to Mount Eden Prison in early 1950, they found themselves firmly in agreement over its future. Both men saw a pressing need to pull the irredeemable old building down. Webb said, somewhat defensively: 'The present site was doubtless quite suitable in 1872 when it was sufficiently far removed from the residential area. Now, however, it was virtually in the midst of the city and, worse still, was overlooked by three schools.'[44]

That year's Prisons Department report expressed these views concisely. The 50-year-old Mount Eden facility was 'quite unsuitable and inadequate and there are insufficient exercise yards or suitable labour facilities for modern penological treatment . . . The replacement of such an institution is a major problem but it is hoped that a solution may be found within a reasonable time.'[45] The following year's report announced unequivocally that 'Mount Eden Prison must go. We can never make radical changes to bring us in line with modern penal practice as long as we are tied to Mount Eden as our main institution.'[46]

Yet the government showed little sign of acting on its announced intention of demolishing the old eyesore and replacing it with a new maximum-security facility at Waikeria. When the local Labour MP, Warren Freer, asked a question in the House in 1953 about 'the perennial problem of moving Mount Eden prison away from the heart of the city', Webb replied that while he was still strongly in favour of that plan, he could not yet justify 'seeking the funds that would be involved even in making a beginning'.[47]

As a result, and despite Barnett's energetic upheavals at a national level, Mount Eden Prison's daily routine continued with little apparent change. The facility still held inmates of all kinds, serving sentences of simple imprisonment, reformative detention and life imprisonment, and as habitual criminals, but with few differences in their treatment apart from minor variations to their uniforms.[48] They were, however, now roughly classified according to type and length of sentences. In 1954, lifers and other long-serving men, numbering over one hundred, were held mainly in the north wing, with 30 or so habitual criminals in the south, and remand prisoners in the west. In the east wing, which also housed the execution yard, were 70-odd reformative detainees, with about 40 short-termers in its basement. Women occupied part of the north wing extension, as well as the old wooden building purpose-built for them in the 1890s.[49]

From the early 1950s Barnett's reforms instigated some badly needed advances within the prison, supposedly as immediate and interim steps before the building was finally demolished. Stanley Banyard, who had served as the prison's part-time welfare officer while employed by the Anglican Church Army, was promoted to a full-time role, with responsibility for regular duties such as mail censorship and escorting prisoners to the infirmary. He also organised many of the concerts and sports activities that were now permitted as part of the new emphasis on rehabilitation. Basketball courts and a bowling alley were marked out in the main exercise yard, and the women inmates were encouraged to play a game called tennis-quoits, using a small rope ring rather than a ball. The occasional team even arrived from outside to play against them.[50]

From 1952 the basketball and bowls teams were allowed to compete away from the prison premises, while a chess tournament took place against outsiders, and the prison's debating team won the coveted Robinson Cup, the first of many regional and national trophies it would eventually secure. Beekeeping and bridge clubs were formed, and an art class met weekly.[51] The well-known Coromandel potter Barry Brickell gave classes in his craft, and journalist John Hardingham taught a literary group whose articles appeared in national and overseas publications under the byline of a 'Special Correspondent'. For the first time in several decades, the Justice Deptartment was 'seized with a crusading zeal' to use the time inmates spent behind bars as an opportunity to reform their lives.[52]

Even unsociable and reform-resistant inmates valued changes such as the opportunity to receive food from outside. The in-house cooking also improved noticeably. The main meal was transferred to the evening, and bacon and eggs were provided twice a week — on a plate.[53] For the first time, prisoners had access to a small canteen where they could spend their modest earnings on 'tobacco, matches, sweets and shaving requisites'. Any of these privileges, it was made clear, could be withdrawn for misconduct, and none were available to short-termers serving three months or less.[54]

These innovations were introduced under the jurisdiction of the gruff and thick-set Horace Haywood, who became the prison's superintendent in 1951. This tough veteran of the country's prison system made impressive efforts to incorporate Barnett's reforms. He developed a detailed set of instructions covering almost every task and routine his staff was required to perform.[55] These indicate that Mount Eden's prisoners, among whom

In the 1950s the bakery was one of several prison enterprises which employed and trained inmates while also reducing running costs. *NEW ZEALAND HERALD*

was an ever-growing number of highly dangerous men, had far more autonomy than in the past, and that staff hoped to manage them through stringent operating procedures.

Inmates were now issued with five blankets in summer and seven in winter. Every Wednesday their sheet, pillowslip, socks and handkerchief were to be neatly folded and placed outside cell doors for collection by laundry men. Pyjamas were laundered on alternate Mondays.[56] The chapel remained the only area where inmates could meet visitors, but they were now allowed to 'kiss their wives or girlfriends when they meet and at the conclusion of a visit. Hollywood clinches [presumably a reference to full-body embraces] are barred.'[57] This was a heady freedom compared with the 1930s, when a large sign on the wall warned: 'No bodily contact between visitors and prisoners allowed.'[58]

To guard against escapes and insurrection, the night and sentry personnel were always armed with loaded weapons, and carried five rounds of ammunition. Troublesome inmates could be held in a 'separate division' of three cells in the east wing. They were strip-searched every time they entered these cells, and checked by officers at least hourly. If they were sentenced to a bread-and-water diet, they received the standard rations given to non-working inmates every fourth day. Tobacco was forbidden to them, but other inmates cleaning the corridor would sometimes thread tiny amounts of tobacco to cockroaches that were released to scuttle under the steel doors. One of the punishment cells was lined with padded canvas and used, along with restraining devices such as straitjackets, in extreme circumstances.[59]

One of the more contentious experiments in prisoner autonomy in this period was the formation of an elected Prisoners Council to liaise between inmates and the prison authorities.[60] The idea seems to have originated in 1951 with welfare officer Banyard as a way of addressing valid prisoner complaints, and of encouraging engagement and goodwill among both inmates and staff. However, many of the prison officers were ex-servicemen and utterly hostile to the idea of any power-sharing arrangement that disrupted the traditional hierarchy. 'We are in danger of consulting and considering the prisoner to the exclusion of the officer,' wrote one. 'I cannot believe that (except in the Russian Army) a Council with the powers outlined by Mr Banyard could be tolerated in any Service, and that Service survive.'[61]

Such objections forestalled progress until 1952, when an initial council of four inmates, personally selected by Banyard and Haywood, planned the formation of a larger and democratically elected body. Sam Barnett was kept closely informed of the initiative and was clearly intrigued by it, suggesting that every prisoner serving 12 months or more should be eligible to vote and to stand for membership.[62] The first election, in May 1952, had an impressive return of 86 per cent from the 163 voting papers issued.[63]

Despite this promising start, the Prisoners Council was abandoned after two years, apparently because of opposition from wary prison staff. The deputy chief officer believed that Mount Eden was entirely the wrong institution to trial such a risky experiment, 'because it contains an undue percentage of troublemakers, barrack-room lawyers and old-stagers. It is probably the least classified prison in New Zealand and has a large percentage of Maoris.' He also feared, with some justification, that the council would soon become dominated by the prison 'barons', the most domineering, influential and self-serving of its inmates.[64]

III

The short-lived Prisoners Council was one of many of Barnett's well-intentioned reforms that failed through a combination of institutional inertia and the undeniable risk of devolving power and responsibility to inmates with a record of abusing it. As staff member Donald McKenzie later put it: 'Ideas which have much to recommend them when first put forward lose the compassion that inspired their originators. Measures designed to be reformative and regenerative become routine.'[65] McKenzie was the prison's first full-time psychologist and had been appointed in 1954 to work with the schoolteacher, welfare officer, nurse and social worker.[66] His book about his time at Mount Eden is perhaps the most vivid, reliable and revealing first-person account of the prison yet published.

'The first and unforgettable impact of the prison came when the welfare officer took me into the "Dome", the central point from which three of the four wings could be watched. This was a nasal assault, an atmospheric cocktail of sweat, crude soap and urine. Inadequate ventilation and high humidity helped to increase the pungent smell.' He was immediately struck by 'the prevalence of brown-skinned prisoners'. Māori then made up about 25 per cent of the national prison population, and the proportion in the Auckland area was likely to be higher still.[67] Almost every inmate came from 'the lower social groups' and the rare exceptions were granted special treatment by staff. 'A wealthy bookmaker served his brief prison sentence in the prison hospital, wearing his own clothes and helping the staff with their racing investments.'[68]

McKenzie found that:

> Despite its 300 inmates, Mount Eden in the 1950s was, for most of the day and night, a silent place where echoes travelled far. Silence was broken when a key rasped in a lock, a steel grille banged, or a command was shouted. Only at unlock time or at lockup did the wings ring with shattering noise, iron against iron, tin plates, chamberpots, and hundreds of hobnail boots on the stone floor. Morning, midday and afternoon, human pieces moved like ill-clad grey-and-white pawns, each to his allotted place. Early unlock at 6.30am, piss pot parade, breakfast lockup, unlock, penal yard parade for muster count, lunch, lockup. One o'clock unlock, piss pot parade, penal yard muster count, back to work. 4.20 pm return from work, penal yard muster count, supper distribution, lockup. At 4.30pm silence and isolation until breakfast next day.[69]

The prison's deathly hush was due in large part to the discouragement of conversation between officers and prisoners. Any exchanges between them, beyond staff giving orders, tended to be regarded with suspicion by both parties.[70] Among themselves, prisoners talked quietly and inconspicuously out of the side of the mouth, moving their lips as little as possible.[71] Once acquired, this habit proved hard to break and even 30 years later, when prisoners were actively encouraged to communicate, old lags could still be identified by this surreptitious mode of speech.[72]

McKenzie was particularly moved by the living conditions of the 60 or so women inmates. Often already deeply humiliated by their status as prisoners, their self-esteem was further eroded by 'primitive provisions for menstrual hygiene — sanitary towels were not provided and the women had to make do with rags — washed and used again'. He found it unsurprising that many resorted to forms of self-mutilation such as wrist-slashing or swallowing pins, spoons and glass.[73]

In the mid-1950s the youngest inmate of the women's section was Juliet Hulme, one of the most unlikely and notorious individuals ever to occupy a Mount Eden cell. The murder she and her close friend Pauline Parker committed in Christchurch in 1954 later formed the subject of the film *Heavenly Creatures*, and of plays, novels and numerous books. The two girls were too young to be given the death penalty, and instead were sentenced to life and sent to separate prisons — a condition that posed great difficulties for Barnett and his officials, as Mount Eden was then the only high-security institution where women were held. Arohata, near Wellington, was still under construction and Paparua in Christchurch was suitable only for low-security prisoners.[74]

Nevertheless, Parker was sent to Paparua as a lifer, while Hulme, considered the more dominant of the two, arrived in Mount Eden in July 1954.[75] *Truth* rejoiced in relaying the announcement that both young women 'will wear the ordinary prison clothes, eat the ordinary prison food, do the ordinary prison tasks set long-sentence women prisoners and be subject to the ordinary prison discipline'.[76]

Little could have prepared Juliet Hulme, raised in comfortable surroundings as the only child of a prominent Christchurch physicist and his wife, for the rigours of prison life. Rats roamed her cellblock, which leaked so badly that water pooled on the floor. One of the toilets had a half-door and the other none at all. She too was required to wring out her menstrual cloths, and wearing them chafed her legs until they bled.[77] Three other women were also serving life for murder, all several decades older than she was.[78] Her other fellow inmates appeared to be mainly ship-girls (i.e. dockside prostitutes), and Hulme endured 'a lot of noisy Maori singing' — a novel experience for a well-bred South Islander.[79] Despite the vast gulf in their social backgrounds, she found she was not ill-treated by the other women — occasionally propositioned or grabbed, but 'I was never injured and I was never assaulted'.[80]

Donald McKenzie's observation that prison staff gave special treatment to inmates from 'good' or 'middle-class' families was borne out in the case of Hulme, whose terrible crime seemed utterly out of character. Superintendent Haywood and his wife took her into their home on weekends.[81] Captain Banyard arranged her enrolment in Correspondence

School, and she effortlessly passed exams in modern and classical languages, maths and history.[82] Just four years into her life sentence, she was transferred to the new and lower-security women's prison at Arohata, where impeccable conduct saw her released after a year.[83] Her later life was equally above reproach. Under the pen-name Anne Perry, Juliet Hulme became a celebrated crime writer, producing a string of novels that periodically recalled her formative years in 'a great cold place whose massive walls were like misery set in stone, condensation making even the inner corridors feel cold and sour. Everywhere was the smell of human sweat and stale air.'[84]

| | |

'An experience you don't ever want to have again,' Hulme wrote late in her life, 'is to be in a prison the night before they hang somebody.'[85] It was an experience she came to know well, since the last five executions carried out in New Zealand all took place at Mount Eden during her few years there. The newly formed National Party's promise to restore the death penalty had proved a vote-winner during the 1949 election campaign, when Labour leader Bob Semple prophesised grimly — and accurately — that his political opponents would 'swing to power on the hangman's rope'.[86] The Capital Punishment Act was passed just months after the election, and the ageing but still functional Meccano Set was withdrawn from storage, refurbished at Britain's Wandsworth Prison, and readied for re-use at Mount Eden's east wing yard.

Initial objections to the return of the state hangman were drowned out by a chorus of popular approval. Prison Department head Sam Barnett was profoundly opposed, in practice and on principle, to the punishment he was now required to administer, but his Minister, the lugubrious Clifton Webb, welcomed its return, and many of his parliamentary colleagues were convinced they were representing the popular will.[87] 'Most people in my electorate,' declared the member for Ōamaru, 'and indeed most people in the Dominion, are in favour of the reintroduction of capital punishment.'[88]

Some were so enthusiastically in favour that they hoped to administer the punishment themselves. Even before the Act was formally passed in December 1950, Barnett's department began receiving a flood of applications for the reinstated post of state hangman. Police weeded out applications from people of known fascist or radical persuasion and eventually three were appointed, since Barnett was aware from past experience that for every execution a main hangman and at least one stand-in was required.[89] All three appointees remained strictly anonymous and were paid £50 on each occasion their services were called upon.[90]

That proved to be a total of eight between 1952 and 1957. Over that time 22 people were sentenced to death, but Labour's practice of granting reprieves was retained in part by National's Executive Council, and 14 of those so sentenced were eventually reprieved, sometimes after lengthy and tormented months while their fate was debated.

In 1954 three bewildered Niue Islanders, all speaking little English and one aged just 18, were held in the condemned cells for the murder of the brutal Resident Commissioner Cecil Larson, the senior official who administered their tiny country on behalf of the New Zealand government.[91] Their sentences were commuted to life imprisonment following a public campaign of support and the prison's report that these were model inmates unlikely to re-offend.[92] By 1960, two of the Niueans were preparing to transfer to lower-security prisons but the third, Latoatama, opted to remain in Auckland, where his relatives could visit him. He spent a further six years in Mount Eden, an increasingly isolated, morose and obsessive figure who spent hours each night pressing his uniform and polishing his boots. 'He should have been let out years ago,' his prison officers agreed, 'but there's nothing we can do about it.' In 1966 he was moved to Waikeria and finally released after a total of 16 years — twice as long, according to historian Dick Scott, as his behaviour warranted.[93]

All hangings carried out in New Zealand under the 1950 Act took place at Mount Eden. Centralising executions in this way simplified the process in many respects. It eliminated the need to transport the scaffold, may have saved on travel for the hangman, and the perimeter wall surrounding the prison reduced the risk of unseemly public gatherings in the vicinity. It also meant that Mount Eden Prison staff and officials could gain expertise at conducting executions, sparing those at other prisons from the crushing emotional impact of this experience.[94]

Superintendent Haywood developed careful instructions for dealing with prisoners during their last days of life. He warned his staff that a shift in the condemned cell would be 'one of the most exacting duties you will be called on to perform', and only staff who volunteered for this work were expected to carry it out.[95] Once the sentence of death had been passed, the condemned cell was fitted with a special grille door so that its occupant could be clearly observed at all times. There he was under constant 24-hour guard, with prison officers sharing his cell, checking his food for contraband or poison supplied by sympathetic inmates, and cutting it into bite-sized pieces, as no condemned man could be permitted the use of a knife.[96] The east wing yard was roofed over with steel mesh, and before an execution tarpaulins were stretched over it to ensure that no glimpse of the procedure was captured by ambitious press photographers or low-flying planes. Executions were carried out there in the evening under the glare of floodlights and the mournful accompaniment of flapping canvas.[97]

The task the official hangmen were required to perform was emotionally taxing but not skilled, since all preparations up to the moment of execution were carried out by prison staff. One hangman is thought to have made a practice of covertly attending the Auckland Supreme Court on the day of a murder jury's verdict to familiarise himself with his client's stature, but given that every condemned inmate was weighed by prison staff on the days prior to his dispatch, that precaution seems scarcely necessary. It was the prison staff who shared the offender's cell in his final days, strapped his arms and legs, and administered a kindly sedative (sometimes so powerful it might almost have carried out the execution on its own). Only one condemned man, Harvey Allwood, is known to have refused this sedative. Donald McKenzie spent time with Allwood before and during his 1955 execution, and considered that 'he was a very brave man in many respects'.[98]

The executioner was required to arrive at the prison only about an hour beforehand, dress himself in an empty cell to avoid recognition (at least one favoured the Zorro mask supplied by the British Prisons Commission), and stand against the wall of the execution yard awaiting a hand signal from the sheriff, the title then given to the registrar of the Supreme Court, who was required to attend every hanging.[99] Upon this signal, the hangman pulled the lever that opened the trapdoor. On several occasions even this apparently simple action was bungled. One hangman misinterpreted the sheriff's signal and moved the lever while two prison staff were still standing on the trapdoor. Luckily another officer managed to override his action, preventing a gruesome accident, and thereafter a padlock was fitted to the lever, to be released only when the trapdoor was clear of all but its intended victim.[100]

The first man hanged under this postwar regime, in 1952, was an Urewera millworker named Silvio Fiori, a double murderer described as 'borderline feeble-minded'.[101] As this was to be the first execution at Mount Eden in 18 years, the staff resorted to subterfuges to avoid the traditional deafening chorus of shouted obscenities and hammering chamberpots during the condemned man's final walk to the gallows.[102] The cell where Fiori spent his last hours — no. 10, west wing — was at the opposite end of the prison from the execution yard and on a different level. On the appointed evening he was brought down to the east wing, supposedly for exercise and a shower. Immediately afterwards, and without warning, his arms and legs were bound, and two priests arrived to deliver the final offices.

To keep the other inmates from hearing Fiori's final walk the length of the prison, a movie was scheduled for them — a rare event which attracted almost the entire muster. As they were gazing at a screen erected in the chapel, Fiori, supported on each side by a prison officer, shuffled down empty corridors to the harshly lit courtyard where the hangman was waiting.

This strategy proved effective on that occasion, but it was clearly unrepeatable. Before the next hanging, of 23-year-old Eruera Te Rongapatahi, sections of heavy seagrass matting were laid along the corridors to muffle his footsteps.[103] The two halves of the trapdoor were also heavily padded to reduce the thunderous crash as the body fell between them. By these means Te Rongapatahi's execution, like Fiori's, proceeded without incident, although the following morning Monsignor Hyde, one of the clerics present, was so distraught he could barely stand.[104]

The remaining hangings followed the same stern and predictable pattern. On each occasion a befuddled man, usually with little education or skills, who had killed another in a moment of rage, sometimes while drunk, was led to the scaffold to pay the penalty. Thus died Harry Whiteland in December 1953. His last words to those watching were 'Merry Christmas'. That experience proved too much for the attending sheriff to bear. His two predecessors in this post had both suffered nervous breakdowns and resigned rather than witness further executions. After Whiteland's farewell salutation, this latest sheriff

This deponent being duly sworn saith:-

My name is HORACE VICTOR HAYWOOD and I am the Superintendent of Her Majesty's Prison at Mount Eden Auckland. The dead body now lying at the said Prison and which I have just viewed in the presence of Detective-Sergeant T. J. Keoghan is that of ALBERT LAWRENCE BLACK late of Auckland - a labourer by occupation and aged 20 years - who was a prisoner in the said Prison having been on the 21st. day of October 1955 convicted and sentenced to death at the Supreme Court at Auckland for the murder at Auckland on the 26th. day of July 1955 of Alan Keith Jacques.

I produce the relevant Warrants.

His Excellency the Governor-General having intimated by instrument dated the 30th. day of November 1955 that he did not intend to interfere with the said sentence of death the same was duly carried out within the walls of the said Prison this evening in my presence and in the presence of and by direction of the Sheriff John Willden Pressley.

Taken and sworn at AUCKLAND, this
5th day of December, 1955
before me—

The prison superintendent was one of several officials required to testify to the satisfactory completion of every execution. Superintendent Horace Haywood signed this form after the 1955 hanging of 20-year-old Albert 'Paddy' Black, the so-called 'jukebox killer'. *ARCHIVES NEW ZEALAND, J46 1454 COR1955/1253*

suffered severe internal haemorrhaging, took several months' sick leave and then resigned before the next hanging.[105]

The execution in August 1955 of Edward Te Whiu caused more controversy than any other, and appeared to tip public opinion firmly and finally against capital punishment. Te Whiu was a 20-year-old vagrant whose murder charge arose from a botched break-in. The lawyer appointed to his defence found him 'a good-looking youth with a friendly smile. He spoke English well and had good manners. He did not look a desperate character.'[106] Superintendent Haywood was profoundly shaken by meeting Te Whiu's parents and other members of his large family in the prison courtyard just before the young man's death.[107] After years of increasing strain from these occasions, Haywood became increasingly dependent on alcohol.[108] He developed strange fixations, began carrying a loaded pistol, and was finally removed from his post in 1963.[109]

By the time Walter Bolton, a 68-year-old Whanganui farmer, was hanged in 1957, vehemently protesting his innocence to the end, the tide of opinion had turned decisively against the death sentence. The prison doctor and other officials refused to attend any further executions, and a growing number of National MPs shared their revulsion at the practice.[110] In 1961 they were permitted a conscience vote on the issue and 10 members voted against their own party's policy, delivering a substantial majority for the abolition of capital punishment. The Meccano Set was dismantled and removed from the prison without ceremony, although the death sentence remained nominally in place for crimes such as treason until it was erased entirely from the statute book in 1989. It is one of the more peculiar paradoxes in the prison's long and lurid history that in the decade when the scaffold was the institution's 'macabre focal point' and an anachronistic vestige of outworn penal policies, the energetic Sam Barnett introduced advanced rehabilitation processes to many other areas of prison life.

| | |

One unintended and unwelcome consequence of these greater freedoms was the rise of the prison 'barons' — powerful leaders who held sway over other inmates through physical prowess, ruthlessness and cunning. In the 1950s a small number of these long-serving, elite inmates exerted remarkable influence not only over their fellow inmates but also over many of the staff. Superintendent Haywood valued the authority the barons held over other prisoners, and he rewarded them with special privileges and frequent conversations in his office. A lesser but still privileged category of prisoners were the 'trusties', identified by their blue denim trousers. Haywood advised his own officers: 'There are certain "staff" prisoners who are trusted and who are performing their duties very satisfactorily. These men are generally allowed free access to Wings.'[111] They were also allowed to take meals to the nearby officers' mess and recreation hall outside the prison walls. At least one trusty, Pat Bennett, seized the opportunity to carry on to Symonds Street several blocks away and burgle a bookstore of its stock of girlie magazines. He may not have known that the shop belonged to former inmate John A. Lee.[112]

Seasoned staff were sceptical of these freedoms. One former Mount Eden prison officer wrote a barely fictionalised memoir in which his alter ego says scathingly of the inmates under his charge, 'We're supposed to be reforming them now. It's not enough for a man to come in and do his time. We've got to send him out with a new light in his eye and soap behind his ears.'[113] But Haywood was prepared to put Barnett's innovations to the test, and he even welcomed a number of them. Haywood was especially proud of the inmates' 14-piece brass band, made up mainly of barons and trusties serving long sentences who therefore had ample opportunity to practise their instruments. Haywood's Brass Band gave several concerts each year to invited members of the public. Barnett himself was among the audience in July 1954 for the all-male 'Walled-Off Astoria Follies', featuring Hawaiian and Latin American musical numbers, a 'ballet' by a company of beautifully dressed 'girls', and an exhibition of gymnastics and weightlifting.[114]

Haywood thought so highly of the band that its members were afforded special privileges. These were often abused, and illicit drinking was known to occur during concerts.[115] However, the undeniable improvements the band and other new recreational activities produced in the attitudes of formerly sullen, withdrawn and hostile inmates ensured that the privileges associated with them remained in place for several years — until a sudden catastrophe horrified the entire country.

The band's young and competent trombonist was Edward Horton, known to fellow inmates as Slim because of his slight physique.[116] He was serving a life sentence for a particularly horrendous crime, an apparently unpremeditated rape and murder which, if it had not been committed during the Labour government's hiatus on hanging, would have certainly sent him to the scaffold. 'Our English language scarcely has words powerful enough to express the heinous nature of your crime,' declared the Chief Justice when passing sentence; indeed, the Horton case was directly instrumental in the restoration of capital punishment two years later.[117]

Slim Horton had spent much of his youth in borstal and other institutions, and for his first years at Mount Eden he was regarded by the staff as a 'lone wolf' — isolated, untrusting and untrustworthy. Performing with the band had a remarkable effect on this one-time predator and he eventually became a 'much more friendly and outgoing personality'. He began taking part in other social groups such as the indoor bowling team, and by 1955, as a model inmate with no recent disciplinary offences, was allowed to go outside the prison walls for monthly competitions against other social bowling teams.[118] In December that year, the 17-member prison team, accompanied by four officers, arrived for a regular monthly tournament at the Hibernian Hall in Mount Albert. All of them, including the staff, were out of uniform as a concession to integration and goodwill. As the evening's sport drew to a close, one shocked officer reported to his fellows that Slim Horton could not be found.

Even seven years after he committed his crimes, Horton's name and fiendish reputation could still terrify the nation. When his escape was made public, the country was gripped, as *Truth* reported, by a 'wave of terror' and the police called on reinforcements from as far away as Christchurch.[119] Despite one of the biggest manhunts to that date, he remained at large for three days until he was spotted and arrested in another Auckland suburb — tired, hungry and unresisting.[120]

The consequences for further 'reformative recreation' at Mount Eden, and every other prison, were devastating. Haywood and his senior colleagues tried to argue that Horton's disappearance was unpremeditated, out of character, and should not obscure the gains that activities such as the bowling nights had brought for other inmates. The Minister, however, was determined to win back public confidence.[121] Policies on prisoner movements were dramatically tightened, and there were no more team outings beyond Mount Eden's walls for another 20 years.[122] During that time Horton maintained the faultless conduct that had earned him his leave privileges, even after those privileges were withdrawn. After serving 23 years he was released at the age of 42.[123] For the next seven years he lived blamelessly in New Plymouth, where he married and had a child, before dying of a heart attack.[124]

In the weeks immediately following his impulsive escape, however, he sat in a punishment cell on bread and water while his team-mates fumed at the loss of liberties his action had caused them. These added to the prison's longstanding problems of inadequate staffing and overcrowding. For several years in the mid-1950s, staff shortages forced the quarry to close and large numbers of men, many of them physically tough and potentially violent, were held indoors, employed at carpentry and making steel furniture, the only trade training activities then available.[125]

The overall prison muster rose remorselessly until almost 400 inmates were crammed into a facility designed for three hundred at the most. Many cells were modified to hold three men each, and classrooms, common rooms and dining halls were converted into dormitories, but these were unquestionably unsatisfactory makeshift solutions.[126] What was to be done, asked Mount Albert MP Warren Freer, yet again, about replacing the 'sombre, grave monstrosity' in his electorate? Justice Minister John Marshall responded wearily that Mount Eden was 'one of the black spots in the prison service, and everyone would like to get rid of it'. His department would replace it as soon as possible, he insisted, but at some unspecified future date because of more pressing and appealing demands on the public purse.[127]

So the involuntary occupants of this monstrosity remained subject to its curious limitations, which included toilets without doors as a precaution against homosexual practices. Donald McKenzie found that homosexual behaviour was widespread and often non-consensual: 'Accusations of being kissed and handled were usually laughed aside [by the staff] as normal risks in prison,' he noted.[128] The chronic overcrowding was somewhat relieved from 1958 when most of the women inmates were moved out. Some were sent to the even more decrepit Dunedin gaol, built in 1851, which had been re-opened after 40 years, on a strictly temporary basis, to accommodate them. It was still in use six years later, when the Justice Department described it as 'our most congested and depressing prison and . . . quite unsuitable for housing women prisoners'.[129]

A few of the prized privileges that came with band membership

A well-appointed association cell like that occupied by members of 'Haywood's Brass Band' in 1958. *NEW ZEALAND HERALD*

survived the crackdown that followed Horton's attempted escape. A relatively comfortable 12-man dormitory cell in the east wing basement was occupied exclusively by the band members, and, almost uniquely for the prison, it was not subject to random searches.[130] Among its occupants were bandmaster Archie Banks, a prison baron whose son, John, later became a notably punitive Minister of Police, and Richard 'Maori Mac' McDonald, a 31-year-old housebreaker with a fearsome fist, who was two years into an indefinite three-to-14-year preventive-detention sentence.

In mid-1958 one of the prison's 'canaries', or 'toppers', gave Haywood the startling tipoff that men had been escaping from the band cell overnight and returning before the morning unlock. The superintendent instructed his officers to break with routine and thoroughly search the cell. Under the floorboards they found a trove of contraband including civilian clothing, a radio, quantities of cigarettes and chocolate, and that iconic artefact of 1950s indulgence, a milkshake machine.[131] This discovery represented a public safety failure almost on the scale of Horton's absconding four years earlier, and, as on that occasion, Sam Barnett raced up from Wellington to manage the departmental response. He was told by chagrined prison officers that the cell's window bars could be cut through by a serrated kitchen knife in 20 minutes. Several had been sawn off in this way and carefully replaced to appear untouched.

The formidable Maori Mac took sole responsibility for the escapes, saying that he had left the cell five times in the past few nights, between the 11 p.m. and 4 a.m. guard rounds. Using grappling hooks and an improvised ladder made from galvanised pipe in the plumbers' shop, he had been able to evade the armed guards, scale the perimeter wall and return by the same route. While on the loose he had robbed the kiosk in Parnell's famous rugby ground, Carlaw Park, and broken into several other buildings. No one else, he insisted, had accompanied him, although his cellmates had signalled that it was safe to re-enter by flashing lights from the window.[132]

This was the version of events — disturbing but not disastrous — presented to the press in the days after the breakouts were revealed. All prison staff were said to have acted appropriately, given the challenges of their obsolete workplace. Justice Minister Mason argued, rather circuitously, that '[m]en put in dormitory cells are those whose escape would not give concern to the public . . . the fact that McDonald returned after breaking out showed that he was not one of those for whom high security was required'.[133] There was no mention of the contraband goods in the official report of the incident.[134]

Auckland police were not satisfied by this explanation. There had been a wave of burglaries and car conversions around the prison in the weeks before McDonald claimed to have made his solo late-night raids. Fingerprint evidence pointed to another occupant of the band cell, but at that time it seemed impossible for an inmate of the country's maximum-security prison to have committed these offences, so the case was dropped.[135] Soon afterwards, but also before the earliest escape admitted by McDonald, a woman was gang-raped in Cornwall Park, not far from the prison. Descriptions of the attackers matched certain occupants of the band cell, but again no connection could be proved and the brutal crime remained unsolved.[136]

When the press raised these suspicions with Barnett, he flatly denied them. Maori Mac stuck to his story and told the court that his transgressions were minor compared with those of other inmates. 'I am not a dangerous criminal and have no convictions for violence . . . There are criminals in the prison worse than I'll ever be.'[137] He was given two years on top of his preventive-detention sentence and released just three years later, in June 1961.[138] Some remained convinced that he had struck a deal with prison authorities to cover up a host of other crimes and contain a far bigger scandal.[139] If so, the cover-up was successful and the consequences for the Justice Department and the prison were minimal. Horace Haywood's beloved brass band survived the setback and continued to perform for enthusiastic audiences for several more years.[140]

As usual after such a crisis, the *Herald* pronounced on the need for a new maximum-security prison: 'Whatever the state of public finances, the duty of the Government is to treat the matter seriously and start building at once. Only so can serious trouble be avoided.'[141] And, as usual, almost nothing was done apart from installing tougher window bars and floodlighting the outer walls.[142]

The security crackdown reduced the influence of prison barons on younger and more volatile inmates, and this change, coupled with the chronic overcrowding, may have contributed to an increase in assaults on staff members during 1959. On one occasion three young offenders who had been transferred from Paparua 'so that they would be subject to maximum security' set upon two instructors and an officer outside the boot shop, drenching one of them with dark leather dye.[143] 'If the officers were kinder,' the ringleader told the magistrate, 'these things wouldn't happen.'[144]

Tensions mounted steadily, and in April the following year, after six prisoners launched a sudden attack on prison officers, apparently to seize a set of keys, the staff took reprisals. The offenders were locked in separate punishment cells and then visited in succession by a group of four officers. The resulting injuries sustained by the inmates were explained by the ancient and implausible rubric that they had 'fallen down stairs'.[145]

The atmosphere throughout the prison the next day was at fever pitch. The regular morning sick parade was held, and staff discovered that a lifer, Angelo La Mattina, had vanished. The result was uproar on all sides. La Mattina was a band member and therefore well protected by the barons. He was also very popular with the general inmate population as a 'stereotypical, voluble Italian' who 'sang tenor arias with great enthusiasm in prison concerts'.[146] Prison officers carried out an inch-by-inch search of the entire prison, enduring jeers, catcalls and thunderous haka from the inmates, who on one occasion refused to return from the main yard to the wings and spent the night outside in chilly autumn rain. Meanwhile, police mounted checkpoints on every port and airport in the country. Few passengers were entirely free from suspicion, as La Mattina was a small and slender man, known for taking women's parts at prison entertainments and might therefore be disguised in women's clothing.[147]

After a week the prison's attic was minutely searched for the third time, and officers found their man huddled in a pitch-black corner of the west wing. He had reached it by crouching on top of the lift that carried meals from the basement kitchen to the first floor, then climbed hand over hand up the lift cables to the Dome where the prison wings converged, and from there through a gap in the brickwork to the attic. He had been sustained by food and blankets supplied by other prisoners, and complained later about the 'big bloody rats that ate my cheese'. In total darkness he worked away at the underside of the corrugated-iron roof, hoping to break through, then scale the outer wall and escape on an Italian liner.[148] He was finally returned to his homeland in 1968 after serving 10 and a half years.[149]

By that time Sam Barnett, instigator of remarkable developments in the prison during the 1950s, had long gone. He left office in 1960, ruefully acknowledging in his final annual report that his dreams of hauling the prison system to the forefront of international practice had come to nothing: 'We do not command international attention in the penal field. Few nations would come to learn from us. True, we have made some advances in recent years, but few could be said to be characteristic of a young country exercising independent thought, and expressing its own national attitude towards criminal offenders.'[150] Barnett remained proud of innovations such as the extension of educational, cultural and sporting activities that were initially ridiculed as 'molly-coddling' and creating 'five-star prison hotels' but later valued as beneficial.[151]

The failure of Barnett's original vision, he maintained, was not a consequence of the policies he had implemented but rather of unforeseen and uncontrollable factors: 'The rapid and unexpected increase in the rate of criminality, particularly among adolescents, and the heavy sluggishness which marks the providing of new institutions and additions to old ones, have confounded my hopes.'[152] For Mount Eden in particular, those factors produced a prison population which reached 451 in 1951, although the facility could adequately accommodate only 275.[153] An appallingly high proportion of those recent inmates were young Māori, and Barnett found this development 'the most serious and inexplicable factor in New Zealand crime'.[154]

He was clearly sympathetic to the situation of Māori in prison. 'Many of them should never have fallen into crime,' one annual report maintained. 'As a group they are certainly the most tractable and responsive prisoners we have.'[155] The staggering rise in the rate of Māori incarceration was due, Barnett felt, to unprecedented social conditions, particularly urbanisation. 'The steadying and well defined influence of the rural Maori village is rapidly broken down when the individual is faced with the new and bewildering environment of the city.' His department was struggling to respond through 'the employment of Maori officers with wide cultural backgrounds of Maori art, music, language and folklore'.[156]

Those well-intentioned efforts had no possibility of success, Barnett warned, unless action was taken on the more urgent crisis of overcrowded and antiquated prisons like Mount Eden. He had, of course, been beating this drum for years, but took the opportunity of his imminent departure to emphasise it more strongly than ever before: 'A great deal of money must be spent quickly planning and building unless there is to be a complete breakdown in the prisons, borstal and probation services.'[157]

How seriously the government treated this ominous prediction can be gauged by an exchange of letters in 1962 between Barnett's successor, John Robson, and Mount Eden's ageing and exhausted Superintendent Haywood. Following a series of assaults on his staff by young and impetuous inmates, Haywood reminded his superior of the many earlier undertakings to build a new maximum-security facility to replace his own prison: 'There is no doubt that the much needed security prison is badly needed and as quickly as possible so this young type of individual can be handled.'[158] Robson replied, 'I wish I could paint you a better picture for the future but at present I can see little hope of any substantial drop in your numbers or of any improvement in the character of your inmate population.'[159]

7:
'Burn, burn, burn'

1963–1969

'I remember it as a very foreboding place. I was sixteen, a first offender, but I was housed along with the adults. I had an uncle doing life — Les Shirtcliff. He looked after me. Made sure no one gave me a hard time.'[1] Jim Shepherd, not yet the Diamond Jim of his glory years with the Mr Asia drug syndicate in the 1980s, entered Mount Eden for the first time in early 1958. The precocious career criminal had convictions for aggravated robbery and burglary, and he spent two months in the remand unit of the country's toughest prison before serving the rest of his three-year sentence in Invercargill Borstal.

Jim was stocky, strong and quick to take offence. 'If you spoke to a prison officer, you were liable to get battered. There were a few decent ones, but it was a very primitive environment,' he recalled. He soon found himself in a fight with several officers in the exercise yard, and was sent to the solitary cells on a punishment diet. 'You got eight slices of bread and a pint of water a day. Every fourth day you got a plate of porridge in the morning and a hot meal at night. Then back to bread and water . . . They were still cracking rocks in the quarry in those days. They did the blasting at night time, and in the morning the guys would find these rocks with round holes through them where the explosive had gone in. They put iron bars through these rocks and used them for weights. Those guys were huge — muscles on their muscles.'

By his own account, over the next twenty years Jim Shepherd was in and out of prison 'like a yo-yo. What a fuckin' waste. There was no rehabilitation. They locked you in your cell about 3 or 4 p.m. and let you out again at eight the next morning. Nothing to read. It was very cold and miserable, but you adapt to it.'[2]

The son of a Pākehā father and a Northland Māori mother, raised in inner Auckland's Freemans Bay and with little evidence of any education, the teenage Jim Shepherd typified the inmate population of the day.[3] Sam Barnett's optimistic predictions of a prison workforce versed in Māori culture had yet to eventuate, and some of Mount Eden's officers deliberately provoked Māori inmates by calling them 'black bastards'. Fights in the exercise yards were frequent in the early 1960s. When one broke out, other inmates formed a ring several men deep around the brawlers, making it difficult and even dangerous for officers to intervene. However, a few officers were accomplished combatants themselves. One was a national judo champion, and Samoan-born Tuna Scanlan held

New Zealand and Commonwealth boxing titles.⁴ Prison etiquette forbade any complaints to authorities after these encounters, and injuries that could not be concealed were reported as resulting from accidents such as 'falling down the stairs'.

Officers carried batons on patrol, but after a group of inmates beat an officer with his own weapon the practice was ended. From 1961, the only armed officers were tower sentries issued with Greener riot guns (single-shot weapons that fired a cartridge loaded with light shot), and those on night watch and escort duties who carried .38 revolvers. In no other prison in the country were staff routinely armed.⁵

Imaginative and well-organised inmates upheld Mount Eden's tradition of escapes, notably in February 1961 when Trevor Nash, halfway through a seven-year sentence for a huge payroll robbery, simply strolled out of the engineering workshop where he was working. The workshop stood outside the perimeter wall but was surrounded by a three-metre barbed-wire fence — in which a hole had been conveniently cut. That night Nash became the first prison escaper to have his likeness shown to the nation on their black-and-white TV screens; previous escapers had been seen by the public only through the meatsafe grille of fuzzy newspaper photographs. Despite this unprecedented level of exposure, the nerveless safe-cracker remained at large for a record five months, longer than any other maximum-security fugitive before him. He was recaptured in Melbourne in July, smartly dressed and with his hair dyed but still apparently recognisable to a passing off-duty detective.⁶

The following year quarrying activities ceased permanently, bringing an end to more than a century of rock-breaking at the prison. The impetus for this decision seems to have been a misjudged explosion that sent a rock through the window of an adjacent Auckland Grammar School building, but prison staff were relieved that a weak link in the institution's security system had at last been eliminated.⁷ The quarry had given intending escapers a route outside the perimeter wall, as well as opportunities to acquire gelignite and detonators for more spectacular breakouts. In the final months before the quarry was shut down, Jim Shepherd was back inside Mount Eden and had gained a reputation as a skilled safe-blower. Two other inmates showed him blasting materials they had acquired, and asked for instruction in using them: 'I primed the gelignite for the sticks, and told them how long they'd got before the explosive went off. That'll never happen again. Things were pretty hectic back in those days.'[8]

Once its quarrying operations came to an end, Mount Eden changed permanently in ways both obvious and unforeseen. Fragmenting the mount's basalt rock faces had been the defining daily activity for most inmates since the prison opened, and supplied the administration with a significant stream of income to offset running costs. The ritual of forming work gangs and marching them to and from the quarry was central to the prison's routine.

After the quarry's closure, some inmates were still given training in the tailoring, bootmaking, engineering, plumbing or carpentry workshops, or assigned to duties around the prison itself, but large numbers of active young men now spent hours every day milling around cramped, wire-enclosed yards whenever they were not confined to their cells. In place of the rehabilitation programmes introduced under Haywood's superintendence and largely removed under his successor's, a new Act extended remission of sentence from a quarter to a third for inmates whose conduct had been exemplary or who had 'during his sentence performed some outstanding act of service'.[9]

In the early 1960s the overall inmate population was changing in other ways that did not bode well for the institution's peaceful functioning. The chronic overcrowding of the previous decade was somewhat relieved when lower-security accommodation became available at the Waikune and Rangipo prison farms.[10] But as the number of young and short-sentenced inmates dropped as a consequence, Mount Eden's exercise yards were increasingly dominated by long-serving hard men. The kingpins no longer exercised the same degree of authority over other inmates, and were replaced as the most respected and feared figures in the prison hierarchy by notorious criminals and high-risk escapers who spent much of their time in the back basement, the dimly lit detention unit at the end of the east wing. A thin blue seam down the side of their trousers and a white patch on the back of their jackets distinguished the occupants of this unit from other inmates, and most of them wore it as a badge of pride.

From late 1962 the 'back basement' housed a national celebrity, perhaps the best known and most widely admired criminal figure in this country's history. Then aged 25, George Wilder was a wiry whippet of a man, a skilled bushman with jug ears, a sly grin and an instinctive contempt for authority. For a felon with such a remarkable reputation, his crime sheet was distinctly modest — a few thefts, burglaries and car conversions (he favoured Jaguars), but no suggestion of violence or other very serious offences. What distinguished Wilder from other petty criminals, and earned him a cell in the back basement, was his apparently irresistible urge to make a break for the outdoors and remain there for considerable periods undetected.

He was one year into a four-year stretch at New Plymouth Prison when, in May 1962, he scaled a wall and disappeared into the Central North Island back country, a region he knew well. For eight weeks he evaded all pursuers before he was spotted and tracked down west of Lake Taupō. He arrived at Mount Eden with a further three years added to his original sentence, and was housed in the back basement security unit.[11] In January 1963 six of that unit's 14 cells were occupied, all by repeat escapers. Prison officers made half-hourly checks on them and turned over every cell daily, yet somehow Wilder managed to acquire hacksaw blades and a homemade key from inmates in other wings. Overnight, working silently between the half-hourly patrols, he cut out the lock from his cell door and went around the unit offering to release his neighbours. Frank Matich, Patrick Wiwarena and Reuben Awa, all under 30, agreed to take part in the escape attempt. They crammed into his cell, Wilder relocked their doors, and they knotted sheets into ropes while waiting for a prison officer to enter the unit.

Before 6 a.m. prison officer R. Grubb, on a routine night-shift patrol, unlocked the heavy steel grille separating the detention unit from the rest of the prison. He was promptly knocked unconscious by one of the four escapers and dragged into a toilet where he was bound and gagged. Using his keys, Wilder and his mates were able to open a further grille leading to the narrow, high-walled yard where executions had once taken place, and which was now the only place where they were permitted to exercise. By standing on each other's shoulders, the men could reach the steel mesh covering the yard and cut through it with the hacksaw blades. Clearly visible in the morning sunlight, they dodged a blast from a sentry's shotgun as they rushed for the outer wall and lowered themselves down it with their homemade ropes.[12]

Wilder's three companions were picked up within days but he, as usual, took to the bush and remained at large for an extraordinary six months. During that time his reputation for resourcefulness and non-violence, fuelled by national and even international newspaper coverage, grew to mythic dimensions. The inmates of Mount Eden cheered every new report of outwitted police search parties and jeered at their own officers, who were already humiliated by their failure to contain this homegrown Houdini. The more frustrated the police became, the more the public chose to side with this rugged and amiable outlaw.

The Australian press, true to its country's convict origins, described Wilder as 'something of a national hero' and 'a champion jailbreaker'.[13] The folksong boom was at its height in this period, and Wilder was awarded the ultimate accolade of a satirical ballad, 'The Wild(er) New Zealand Boy'. To an old tune, the Howard Morrison Quartet mockingly celebrated 'a restless man' who:

> With Matich and two Maori blokes, went missing from the can
> And George who never missed a trick, used Matich as decoy.
> They captured everyone except the Wild New Zealand Boy.[14]

Finally, a tipoff sent police to a lonely deer culler's hut on the Napier–Taupō Road, where they found Wilder comfortably installed with two rifles and plenty of fresh trout and venison. Many of the public thought he had earned the right to freedom during his six months on the run.[15] Nevertheless, he was returned to prison to serve a sentence that now extended to a daunting 13 years, longer than that imposed on most murderers.

During the early months of 1963, when Wilder was still at large, Mount Eden's superintendent, the well-intentioned but ill-fated Horace Haywood, was transferred to Paparua Prison. The move was not officially a demotion, but after eight years of presiding over executions and known to be drinking heavily, Wilder's escape may have been the final nail in the coffin of his career.[16] As his replacement, the Justice Department looked for someone capable of imposing strict discipline and rigid control over this crisis-prone institution.[17] The successful candidate, Edward Buckley, had spent his entire career in the prison service and the previous 10 years as a superintendent. He had a reputation for uncompromising toughness with both staff and inmates,

The 'Wild(er) New Zealand Boy' himself, George Wilder, seen here in an interlude between escapes. *STUFF/AUCKLAND STAR COLLECTION*

and a grim and humourless manner that earned him the unaffectionate nickname of 'Black Buckley'.[18]

He immediately announced a more punitive and inflexible regime than his predecessor's. Many of the remaining inmate privileges accumulated under Haywood were withdrawn, and education and training programmes were reduced and closely monitored. Within weeks of Buckley's takeover, this sharp reversal of policy was tested by a small-scale inmate revolt. About a hundred prisoners gathered in the main yard, refused orders to form work parties, and demanded to discuss the new and harsher conditions. Buckley, whose attitude towards inmates was consistently cold and hostile, stood firm, and the protest quickly collapsed. However, few believed that this incident marked the end of inmate unrest.[19]

Staff were at first inclined to welcome the changes Buckley introduced. They were instructed that their principal function was now the custody rather than the rehabilitation of inmates, and security systems were upgraded by improving the floodlighting of external walls and installing rolls of razor wire along the top of the perimeter.[20] In the top-security back basement, patrols were to be carried out every 15 minutes rather than half-hourly, and electronic locking and warning systems replaced the manual locks and keys.[21] Staff were forced, however, to balance these advances against the deficiencies in their new superintendent's personality and style of management. Buckley was a weak character who aimed to appear powerful by shouting, abusing and bullying his officers, often within the hearing of inmates, who relished the spectacle. It was a power structure that offered little hope of reducing the existing level of unrest.

From 1960 the innovative and occasionally incautious Sam Barnett was succeeded as Justice Secretary by a solidly scientific legal scholar, Dr John Robson.[22] He found a longstanding ally in Justice Minister Ralph Hanan, one of a handful of National Party ministers who crossed the floor in 1961 to vote to abolish the death penalty. In an impressive programme of work on new and expanded prisons, his ministry's 1961 annual report announced that a maximum-security prison would be '[o]ne of the most urgent of these new institutions' and would 'enable us to convert Mount Eden into an institution for trial, remand and short-sentence inmates . . . Mount Eden is not a full maximum security prison on modern standards.'[23] The following year a site for this state-of-the-art prison was purchased in a placid backwater north of Auckland, surrounded by orchards and market gardens, called Paremoremo.

With Mount Eden due to be downgraded to a lower-security institution, it was left largely under Buckley's control, with little attention from national office. The breakout by Wilder and his cronies in early 1963 forced a rapid reassessment of priorities. Paremoremo was not due to open until the end of the decade, and the country's most refractory prisoners seemed likely to retest the limits of their century-old establishment before then. Hanan promised to speed up work on Paremoremo; in the meantime, while acknowledging that 'the building at Mount Eden is quite unsuitable as a modern security prison', he undertook to build a new high-security unit to replace the back basement detention unit.[24] Yet even this smaller facility could not be summoned up quickly within a crowded, decaying building.

In a 1964 Justice Department report on the surging nationwide prison population, Mount Eden was described as 'the criminal terminus . . . Vicious men bent on violence, men who recognise neither discipline nor self-discipline, are housed within its walls. The dangerous psychopath, the aggressive simpleton and the periodic psychotic are also there.'[25] Allowing for the insensitive terminology of the time, this is a reasonable summation of the longest-serving and most dangerous section of the inmate population, but does not recognise the much larger number of first-offending, short-term and youthful prisoners such as Jim Shepherd who continued to be admitted.

Those inmates tended to spend only a few weeks inside the weeping stone walls of the old prison before a transfer south to newer and lower-security prison camps. That pattern, and increasing use of non-custodial penalties for young and petty offenders, meant that for the first time in some years Mount Eden's inmate numbers fell during the early 1960s. Of the smaller number who remained, more than 20 were lifers and 34 were preventative detainees. This represented a higher proportion of long-serving inmates, and of inmates with proven records of violence, than at almost any time in the past.

| | |

Buckley's term as superintendent was rocked periodically by newspaper exposés of conditions within his jail, based on information supplied by former inmates and staff. *Truth* ran a series of articles in 1963 alleging that prison officers performing random cell searches routinely found contraband, including weapons, escape equipment and alcoholic brews made from baker's yeast and almost any other fermentable food scraps. At least as disturbing were the claims that some inmates ran flourishing bookmaking businesses on the results of races broadcast over the internal speaker system. As currency, fellow inmates used the one-ounce tobacco packets known as 'figs' that were sold for threepence each in the canteen. *Truth* alleged that certain prison staff were also keen customers of these gambling rings, and conveyed large wagers and real money outside the walls on behalf of inmates.[26]

Buckley and his superiors could not credibly reject all of these revelations but maintained that they were exaggerated. They also seized on admissions in the articles that certain aspects of prison life were better than in the past, such as the declining influence of kingpins and 'standover bullies'. Even the most legendary kingpin of them all, 'Maori Mac' McDonald, eventually lost his former authority. In 1965 he was back inside serving 14 years, and the much younger Jim Shepherd, although half his size, took him on hand-to-hand in one of the corridors. McDonald, once he recovered from his astonishment, smacked the young upstart about at will, but Shepherd kept coming back for more until a kindly senior officer named Dan Cavanagh stepped in and stopped the fight. The novelty of seeing someone willing to stand up to the massive Maori Mac — and especially such a mismatched opponent — demolished the bigger man's mana in the eyes of other inmates.[27]

A year after *Truth* blew the whistle on corrupt and illegal practices inside Mount Eden, its rival weekly, the *Sunday News*, did the same. Its informants were an articulate ex-inmate identified as Kevin and a former prison officer, Graham Reddaway. In addition to the now-familiar allegations of unchecked violence between inmates, improvised weaponry and tattooing gear, and home-brewing in the workshops, they described in detail some aspects of the formerly unmentionable sexual life of the prison community. The small women's prison extending from the north wing was entirely sealed off to male prisoners, said Kevin, but the inmates managed to send written messages back and forth nonetheless. 'A slit is cut in a tennis ball and a note inserted. The ball is then belted high over the women's section where the note is read, and the reply is sent by the same method.'[28] According to psychologist Donald McKenzie, the women

The shower room, 'centre of intrigues and physical delights'. Illustration from *The Rock Orchid*, an unpublished homoerotic novel set in Mount Eden in the early 1960s. *'IN THE ORIENT' (1964–1968), C. E. R. WEBBER PAPERS, MS-3333/198/004, HOCKEN COLLECTIONS UARE TAOKA O HĀKENA, UNIVERSITY OF OTAGO*

often added a strand of pubic hair to their messages. In this way a torrid correspondence could be kept up even though neither party knew for sure which inmate they were addressing.

Both men confirmed that this hypothetical sex was not the only kind available in the prison. Male homosexuality was still illegal, so a number of inmates were serving time for having sex with other consenting adult males, and a large proportion of the rest were evidently prepared to adapt their behaviour to their current circumstances. 'In any single-sex residential establishment,' wrote McKenzie, 'homosexuality will inevitably appear. Homosexual behaviour of this kind is not necessarily an indication of permanent homosexual tendencies, but is often an adaptation to the abnormal compression and sexual frustration of an all-male or all-female population.'[29]

Kevin and Reddaway both agreed that '[h]omosexuality is rife throughout the jail, though many men who were perverts now were normal when they were sent to prison'. Kevin revealed that '[m]any of the longterm inmates have their own "boys" — or as they are called in prison jargon, "Mark Foys".' This term appears to be antipodean rhyming slang — Mark Foys was a well-known Sydney department store. 'Some longtermers have managed to get these boys as cellmates. Most of these "couples" are in the east wing, commonly known as the "married quarters".'[30]

Reddaway, after eight years on the Mount Eden staff, felt that homosexual activity, consensual or otherwise, was encouraged by the 'two men to a cell' scheme, which had been introduced in 1958–59 in response to overcrowding. He added that '[p]risoners locked up for crimes of sexual violence or who have been convicted of homosexuality are the easiest to handle in prison. They are inveterate churchgoers. The most difficult to handle are young men convicted of crimes of violence. Life prisoners and those serving preventive detention are easier to manage.'[31] The *Sunday News* editor weighed in by describing Mount Eden as a 'festering eyesore' and 'Auckland's darkest disgrace', and reiterated the tired refrain that the 'Government must put the building of the new maximum security prison at the top of its list of urgent works'.[32]

These articles provoked a much wider public reaction than *Truth*'s revelations of the previous year. One MP brandished a copy of the *Sunday News* in the House, and Justice Minister Hanan blustered that the allegations were 'highly exaggerated and in some aspects highly defamatory to certain people', but he ordered a full inquiry into them, the first Buckley had faced as superintendent. Former prison officer Reddaway told this inquiry that during his initial training course in Wellington 'we were informed . . . that homosexuality was a disease and there was no cure for it; it is something that is rife'.

Other informants were less dependable. Noel Tuohy, an influential and long-serving inmate, earnestly told the inquiry that he had heard of homosexual activity within the prison but never witnessed it himself.[33] In private he told Donald McKenzie that he was one of those fortunate inmates who had arranged to share a cell in the 'married quarters' with 'a very nice young Maori boy'.[34] Under Horace Haywood's leadership, consensual homosexual relationships had in fact been tolerated as conducive to overall harmony. One enthusiastic member of the inmates' writing class had produced a full-length (and to date unpublished) erotic novel, *The Rock Orchid*, celebrating the joys of inter-racial gay sex in the cells and during the kitchen night shift.[35]

Buckley disputed the most salacious of the *Sunday News* claims and insisted that 'I do everything in my power to transfer young offenders from Auckland Prison but there are cases when I am unsuccessful', as 'the facilities at Auckland Prison are totally inadequate for modern penal practice'. Inmates convicted for homosexual offences were kept apart from others, he said, but still managed to assert their identity by plucking their eyebrows and using black boot polish as eye shadow. Buckley said he was determined to stamp out all homosexual activity in future. The inquiry concluded that he ran the prison under a regime that was 'strict but fair', and it largely absolved him of the regulatory failings revealed by the *Sunday News*.[36]

His own staff were not so forgiving. They disliked their superintendent's high-handed and abusive manner, and after the initial lift in morale following his appointment, the old problem of rapid staff turnover reappeared. Those who remained were inclined to vent their frustrations on the inmates, who in turn seized on any opportunity to resist or retaliate. Within a year of taking over the prison with a brief to restore order and prevent further escapes, Black Buckley had isolated himself in his office in the Dome, while tension in the exercise yards ran higher than before his arrival.[37]

Down in the east wing basement, Wilder and his fellow escapers had new neighbours. Ron Jorgensen and John Gillies, both facing life for a Mafia-style sub-machinegun murder of two sly-groggers in the Auckland suburb of Remuera, had arrived in the detention unit in early 1964. The two men were celebrated underworld figures with associates at the upper levels of organised crime. In February 1965, Gillies, after a year in prison, was ready to attempt a breakout along with Wilder and another basement-dweller, Lennie Evans, serving 16 years. The key component of their plan was a sawn-off shotgun, probably smuggled into the prison in several parts.[38]

Dan Cavanagh, the grizzled veteran officer who had stepped in to break up the fight between Shepherd and Maori Mac, had just returned Evans to the security unit with two colleagues one morning when Gillies emerged from the toilet pointing the shotgun at them. He took the officers' keys and used them to release Wilder from his cell, and the three escapers ordered the officers at gunpoint to head for the stoneyard behind the prison, which had its own gate through the perimeter wall. The officer at the gate was ordered to open it, and he obeyed for fear of harming the hostages. The escapers then commandeered the only available prison vehicle, an elderly flatbed truck, and climbed aboard along with Cavanagh, the single hostage they selected to accompany them. Why they made this choice is not known, but Cavanagh had spent four years as a POW in wartime Germany and during that time had escaped himself. Few other officers are likely to have remained as calm while menaced with a firearm by desperate men.

The truck smashed through a crash barrier and out of the prison grounds, peppered by a blast of buckshot from a sentry. Until this point the escape had gone according to plan, but now it began to falter. The old truck proved an unsuitable getaway vehicle as it trundled at its stately top speed of about 40 kilometres an hour through the quiet and leafy streets surrounding the prison. With pursuit vehicles gaining, the three desperadoes pulled into the driveway of a house in Mount Eden's Horoeka Avenue, ran inside, and added its occupants, an elderly woman and her adult son, to their hostage tally.

The house was quickly surrounded by police, including members of the recently formed Armed Offenders Squad taking part in their first major operation. The escapers recognised the futility of their position and released the woman after some hours. 'I wasn't really frightened,' she told reporters later. 'They seemed quite all right. We weren't harmed.' Crawling on hands and knees to remain below the window ledges, Gillies and his two companions still hoped to win some small concessions in return for their surrender. As night approached and armed police prepared to assault using teargas, the escapers settled for cigarettes and bottles of whisky and gin provided by a considerate neighbour, then threw out the shotgun and submitted to arrest. Like his fellow hostage, Officer Cavanagh reported that apart from spending anxious hours under the twin barrels of their gun, he had suffered no ill-treatment at the hands of the three escapers: 'In fact, we were on good terms.'[39] The escapers' civil treatment of their hostages did not count for much in court, where each of them was given an extra five years. This brought Wilder's term to a total of 18 years, the longest determinate sentence imposed in New Zealand to that date.[40]

In response to this short-lived but sensational escape bid, detention unit inmates were kept in their cells for 22 hours a day, with an hour's exercise morning and night in the adjacent high-walled yard where the scaffold had stood three years earlier. Buckley also ordered one-way locks installed on the grille doors that barred access between sections of the prison — a decision that would have profound consequences for a later escape attempt. National prison authorities were also prompted to accelerate progress on both the new maximum-security prison north of the city and the stopgap high-security unit within Mount Eden itself. The site chosen for this purpose-built unit was occupied by the wooden north-wing extension built in the 1890s that housed the few women inmates who remained after most were moved to the temporarily re-opened Dunedin Prison in 1958.

In a few urgent months after the early-1965 breakout, a two-storey, free-standing building, built in the 1890s as the superintendent's house, was reconfigured into dormitory cells, and these remaining women inmates were transferred to it. The vacant women's wing, once the destination for many steamy-message-bearing tennis balls, was then demolished, and a new structure to house the high-security male inmates began to take shape in its place.[41] The construction work took nine months and the building was ready for use in March 1966.[42] This was lightning progress by past standards, yet not swift enough to contain the simmering discontent of the male inmate population and the extreme measures that some were prepared to employ.

Mount Eden's remand unit was the only area of the prison where inmates could wear their own clothes. In mid-July 1965 the unit held a new inmate who strained this degree of individuality to its limits. Daniel MacMillan, also known as Phillip Weston and by various other aliases, was a tall young man with the long beard and wild hair of a would-be magus. He wore a blanket as a poncho and was a devotee of heretical spiritual philosophies, especially Nietzsche's concept of the superman, freed of normal social constraints. MacMillan, aged 28, was held awaiting trial along with his brother David, who was seven years younger and formerly a law student at the University of Auckland. Using an Italian-made .22 revolver, these two had robbed an enormous sum from the Avondale branch of the BNZ bank, but were apprehended soon after.[43] Their father had himself been a bank manager on the North Shore, and he and his wife considered their elder son to be mentally unbalanced. Health professionals later supported this view, but his case was allowed to proceed.

Fellow inmates of the remand yard knew MacMillan as Cosmo, and he won their bemused admiration for treating the prison officers with open contempt. As his trial date approached he also spent hours noting the pattern of the officers' movements, calculating the sentries' field of view and evidently plotting an escape. His brother wanted nothing to do with it, but Daniel MacMillan formed an unlikely partnership with a solidly built career criminal named Jon Sadaraka, aged 22 and remanded for bombing a car at Western Springs. Jim Shepherd, who was then serving time in the main prison, had known Sadaraka since childhood and could recognise the bond between these two apparently dissimilar types: 'They were desperate men. MacMillan was looking at 10 years, so he was desperate to get out. Jon was sort of under his spell.'[44]

Their escape plan seems to have been modelled on the recent attempt by Wilder, Gillies and Evans, which had acquired legendary status within the prison. They therefore knew they would need cell keys and a weapon of some kind. MacMillan, for all his bizarre mannerisms, was a dedicated bank robber with access to firearms. He had travelled to Italy, where he may have obtained the revolver used for the BNZ robbery, which was not recovered when he and his brother were arrested. Sadaraka, for his part, had useful contacts on the outside, and Shepherd is confident that 'Jon got his family to smuggle the gun in for him'.[45] Both Sadaraka and MacMillan had visitors on the Saturday before their escape attempt.[46] All visits took place in the chapel, in circumstances that made it laughably easy to transfer contraband. As many as 12 inmates at once, and about 150 in the course of an afternoon, were seated along one side of a narrow trestle table, with their visitors on the other.[47] There was no barrier between them and only one officer supervising the entire room. As each visit ended, this officer was required to phone a colleague to escort the inmate out of the room, making it still more difficult for him to supervise interactions down the length of the table. Inmates were searched after each visit, but only by a 'cursory rub-down'. Presumably in this manner, Sadaraka became the possessor of a chrome-silver .22 handgun and 50 rounds of ammunition.

Remanded and sentenced prisoners were supposedly segregated in separate wings, but in practice it was not difficult for them to communicate by various illicit means. Remand inmates were not able to work in the prison training workshops, so Sadaraka is likely to have used his contacts in the sentenced section to have a cell key made in the tinsmith's workshop. Homemade keys were commonplace, and Shepherd owned a whole set: 'We used clay to copy keys that were lying around and made them up from the impressions in the workshops.'[48]

On Monday 19 July 1965, the final night before MacMillan was due to appear at his depositions hearing, the two men put their plan into effect. They were given their evening meal as usual at about 5 p.m. and locked up for the night. Both Sadaraka and MacMillan were held in cells with solid wooden doors that could not be unlocked with their homemade key, but before the lockup they gave their key to an obliging nearby inmate whose cell had a grille door. By holding a mirror through the grille, he could see when there were no guards on the catwalks. He quickly unlocked himself, and ran to Cell 16 to release Sadaraka, gave him the key and returned to his own cell.[49] Sadaraka released MacMillan from Cell 27, and because their homemade key did not fit the large grille that sealed the corridor to the main prison, they spent some tense hours waiting in a toilet for an officer to unlock it.

Just after 2 a.m. officer Ed Marchant patrolled alone towards the remand wing. He carried no weapon, as the practice of issuing revolvers to night patrols had been stopped after Wilder's escape in 1963.[50] As he unlocked the grille, he was confronted by a prison officer's worst nightmare. MacMillan emerged from the toilet wearing a balaclava and wielding an iron bar. Sadaraka, with his lower face covered by a scarf, trained the pistol on Marchant and ordered, 'Go into the toilets or we'll blow your head off.' Marchant, a robust type, refused to obey and was beaten around the head and face with the bar, yet he still managed to scream for help and blow his whistle before he was left bleeding in the corridor.

'That's when the prison came to life,' he said later. 'There were cell doors slamming and men racing all over the place.'[51] One of them was fellow officer Jock Weir, who rushed to investigate the noise. As he reached the remand wing, he was taken hostage and led at gunpoint by the two escapers towards the Dome, the prison's nerve centre, which led out to the front courtyard. Like the remand wing, the corridor to this area was closed off by locked grilles. This was the point when the prison's revamped security system began to foil the two men's plans.

Sadaraka ordered Weir to unlock the grille doors, and reinforced the command by firing a shot through a window. Even that threat could not force Weir to do as he said, because after the escape a few months earlier by Wilder and others the grilles had been fitted with locks that could only be opened from the outside. When a guard appeared on that side, Sadaraka pointed the gun through the grille and barked, 'Open up or the screw gets it.' The guard leaped sideways through an open door as Sadaraka fired twice, narrowly missing Weir. In his cell on the upper tier of the north wing, Shepherd, 'could hear the shots going off all down the wing ... After that it was chaos.'[52]

Sadaraka and MacMillan were losing control of their strategy, and feeling confused and desperate.[53] They took a second hostage, Officer Haines, who repeatedly urged Sadaraka to abandon the escape attempt and give up the gun. But 'desperate men do desperate things', says Shepherd, and the two still held out hope of forcing their way to the outside. With their two hostages they withdrew to the high-security unit in the east-wing basement, hoping that its veteran escapers might draw on their combined experience of earlier escapes and find a way to lead them to freedom. The unit's cells were forced open, and the country's most feared prisoners emerged sleepily to find themselves at large in a prison on the brink of bedlam. Over the intercom system a police inspector appealed for the two armed men to surrender. This entreaty was broadcast to the entire inmate population, who responded by creating pandemonium.

To remove the hostages from the developing melee, the prisoners locked them in one of the basement cells with their own keys. Wilder,

The prison in flames. An armed officer watches over the main exercise yard during the July 1965 riot. *STUFF/AUCKLAND STAR COLLECTION*

who carried more mana than anyone else in the prison, was placed in charge of them, and later recalled that he had 'never seen such a shaken bunch of men'.[54] His accomplices returned to the Dome and one of them used MacMillan's iron bar to smash the main switchboard, generating a volley of sparks before the whole prison was plunged into darkness. In a fateful and irreversible step, Frank Matich poured kerosene and polish on the wooden floor of the Dome, and set it alight.

The disaster dreaded since the prison's earliest days — of fire sweeping through the cellblocks — was about to begin. With the administration offices ablaze, men went to the chapel and set fire to its curtains. The tinder-dry wooden pews also burned readily, and the chapel 'went up like a bonfire on Guy Fawkes Night'. Ex-inmate and academic Greg Newbold has pointed out that it was the high-security inmates, and not the two remanded escapers, who converted an escape attempt into a devastating riot. 'Locked in their basement cells for twenty-two hours of every day, without work or recreation, their terms of solitude were indefinite . . . Their explosive behaviour when suddenly liberated requires no other explanation.'[55] Some of these men, such as Gillies and Evans, were carrying extraordinarily heavy sentences.

As the fires took hold, clouds of acrid smoke filled the corridors. Other prisoners, especially on the upper levels, feared being burned alive or suffocated, and screamed to be released. Wilder and a few other level-headed inmates immediately began to unlock as many cells doors as possible. Their improvised key was crude and difficult to use, but they persisted until their hands bled.[56] 'If it wasn't for their efforts,' Sadaraka claimed years later, 'the death toll would have been huge.'[57] Not every inmate was released unhesitatingly. According to Donald McKenzie, 'When they came to the cell of a notorious and repeated sexual offender against young girls, the men with the cell key deliberated for some time before deciding to rescue him from a grim death.'[58]

More prisoners were now able to join in the destruction, and they piled up mattresses and soaked them with anything that would burn. The solid stone walls were fire-resistant but were coated inside with layers of lead-based paint that burned freely. When the flames reached the ceilings they ignited the equally flammable kauri rafters, and fires then roared through the roofs of each of the wings. All thoughts of escape had been abandoned in favour of wanton mayhem. The knowledge that greatly respected figures such as Wilder, Gillies and Evans had begun ransacking the old building encouraged younger inmates to carry on destroying the institution that confined them.[59]

These keen arsonists were, however, only a proportion of the hundreds of inmates who now barged through the darkened wings. Many, perhaps most, of the inmates wanted nothing to do with this manic fire-raising, and a few attempted to extinguish the flames until MacMillan threatened to shoot them.

From his cell window on the north wing's upper tier, Jim Shepherd could see a stream of headlights heading towards the prison as police vehicles and fire engines arrived to surround it. It was clear to him that any prospect of escape was now out of the question, but he made sure his old mate Sadaraka released him from his cell anyway. For protection, and with the prospect of settling a few scores, Shepherd armed himself with 'a six-inch razor-sharp shiv in my right hand and a long iron bar in my left' and set out to explore the hellish interior. 'Below my cell on the first level a group of rabid prisoners surrounding the hostage prison officers were shouting "Burn, burn, burn" . . . In the eerie half-light it looked like something out of a Fellini movie . . . In all the confusion and pandemonium, the captive prison officers managed to slip away in the dark and make good their escape' — the only occupants of the prison to do so that night.[60]

A courageous group of firemen dragged their hoses through the front gate and into the Dome, but were driven back by a bombardment of crates, books, wood and cutlery from inmates on the upper landings. In one of the riot's cruel ironies, a senior fireman was knocked unconscious by a flying fire extinguisher. His colleagues withdrew to safety between the railway line and the perimeter wall, and played their hoses on the outside of the building, but to little effect.[61] The city's chief fire officer found it 'the most impossible situation he had ever been in': the old structure's design, coupled with the inmates' resistance, made effective firefighting impossible. Its barred windows broke the jets from the hoses into feeble streams, and when the most determined firemen ascended onto the roof, they found its iron sheeting screwed down so firmly that removing it was a slow and arduous task.[62] Inside the wings the heat grew so intense that toughened glass burst out of windows and inch-thick iron bars were twisted out of shape.

Less than an hour after the assault on Marchant, about a hundred police, including the Armed Offenders Squad, ringed the prison to repulse any attempt at a mass breakout. Later in the night they were joined by army personnel from Papakura military camp — more than 100 members of an artillery squadron fresh from a tour of duty in Vietnam, and an SAS ranger squadron with automatic weapons and fixed bayonets. This highly trained and galvanised force was ready to storm the prison, but level-headed senior police officers instructed them to maintain guard outside the walls.

The inmate muster that night numbered 293, and police were aware that at least two of the men at loose inside were armed and dangerous. The prison's narrow doorways meant an assault party would have to enter its darkened corridors practically in single file, and if any were captured the inmates might gain an extra hostage and his firearm.[63] This strategy of passive containment is likely to have saved lives on both sides, but later some aggrieved newspaper correspondents, such as G. Reeman of Rotorua, fiercely disagreed with it. 'Surely if the sufficient and competent security forces . . . had stormed the place at the outset, many thousands of taxpayers' money would have been saved. Perhaps a few heads would have been broken but the mutineers needed a lesson.'[64]

Within the prison the choking haze of smoke became unbearable and a group of inmates made frantic attempts to break through locked steel grilles to reach the main exercise yard. They finally succeeded by using a heavy lawn roller. Shepherd remembers 'this guy Charlie — Māori, bald-headed, he was the first guy out through the gate to the exercise yard. Burning roofing iron dropped on him from the upper levels and he was jumping around, ablaze. But it was the lesser of two evils — everyone was pouring out into the big yard.'[65]

Those inmates still confined in their cells were systematically unlocked by a group of prison officers. During the night the officers separately encountered the two MacMillan brothers, each anxious to ensure the other's safety, and removed them to cells in Auckland Central police station. It is a curious reflection on the relations between staff and inmates that throughout the riot these uniformed staff members, who included Superintendent Buckley, traversed the prison complex repeatedly without any harm or hindrance.[66] The inmates were less respectful of one another. Shepherd witnessed enthusiastic group sex in the eight-man association cells 'as fire consumed the ceilings above

Above: Fire hoses snake across the ground beneath the prison walls as firemen struggle to control the inferno inside. *STUFF/AUCKLAND STAR COLLECTION*

Below: The prison chapel stands roofless and ruined after the riot.
NEW ZEALAND HERALD

them and smoke billowing everywhere', but also brutal gang rapes of young men in the remand section. It was 'utter chaos, depravity and madness'.[67]

Daybreak revealed groups of inmates huddled in corners of the exercise yard and draped in blankets against the chilly drizzle. The local and overseas press gave front-page treatment to aerial images of a structure that resembled 'a besieged medieval castle with police, firemen and onlookers grouped around the walls and in the courtyards'.[68] Firemen had the blaze under control by mid-morning, but a heavy pall of smoke lay over the city from Mount Eden to the waterfront, clearly visible to aircraft flying overhead.[69]

The inmates, damp and cold from their night in the open, were given the opportunity to surrender, and at least 70 were eager to do so, especially the younger and short-sentenced men. They also included the once mighty Maori Mac, who may have feared retribution from his many enemies. Remaining diehards continued to roam the drenched and blackened interior of the prison, feeding fires with cooking fat and fuel oil, and setting new ones. One prisoner, as he kicked through a glass window in the north wing, was heard to call out to the crowds of press and onlookers, 'What do you think of your great Government prison now?'

Meantime, the inmates holding out in the yard ripped steel mesh off the kitchen windows, broke inside, and handed out packages of sausages and steak. The mesh was propped on chairs over a bonfire of wooden furniture and several inmates cooked a communal barbecue. 'There was no mad scramble for food,' says Jim Shepherd. 'All the men lined up and waited patiently.'[70] The midwinter weather made the prospect of a second bleak night in the yard uninviting, even for the most defiant. Nevertheless, they dragged mattresses into sheltered doorways or bedded down in corridors and the least damaged cells in the east and northern wings. One elderly Aucklander is reported to have rung police to say she was concerned about the prisoners' welfare, and offered accommodation for three of them at her home for the night.[71]

After darkness fell, the bonfires in the yard were kept alight with broken furniture, and the shrouded figures around them spent some of the night singing to the accompaniment of three guitars and a mouth organ. A few of the most persistent used a grappling hook to claw rolls of barbed wire from the top of the perimeter wall and attempted to climb it on a

The atrium of a cellblock in the aftermath of the riot. *NEW ZEALAND HERALD*

precarious tower of broken furniture. By then the Auckland Electric Power Board had installed powerful floodlights that bathed the exercise yard in harsh white light, and the climbers were easily repelled by warning shots and jets from a fire hose.[72]

The following morning the two hundred-odd men who remained in the yard were hungry, chilled, short of sleep and ready to surrender. 'Prisoners are very regimented,' says Shepherd. 'You get used to a routine. It's when you break it that the trouble starts.'[73] Lifer Ron Jorgensen approached the police stationed in the Dome and asked if he and the other inmates could keep their personal property if they gave themselves up. This was agreed to, but the terms of surrender were otherwise unconditional.

By 11 a.m. the last of the inmates had been accounted for. 'One by one, with our hands above our heads', Shepherd and his fellow inmates filed out of the main exercise yard and through a cordon of armed police lining both sides of the corridor linking the Dome with the front entrance. As they emerged they were closely searched by prison staff and taken to unroofed yards at the back of the prison. There they spent two more cold and miserable nights with no shelter and little food as authorities desperately juggled national prison musters to create space for them all.

During those days prison staff, Justice Department officials and police made a solemn inspection of the smoking shell that was the country's only maximum-security prison, and in the process discovered Sadaraka's loaded revolver and various improvised weapons. The rugged stone walls had suffered little damage but almost nothing else remained intact. In some places the ceiling and roofing iron had crashed into the passageway between tiers of cells in a mound of charred beams and twisted ironwork.[74] More than 60 cells had been set alight, and the kitchen, chapel, bakehouse, storerooms and watch-house destroyed.[75] The administration offices in the Dome were gutted and their contents, including many inmate files, burned or ruined by water damage.[76]

Water continued to pour into the lower floors and basement, and the stench of smoke was overpowering. The main exercise yard was a scene of squalid intemperance, with uncooked sausages and bacon strewn among damp bedding and sodden clothing; lying in the middle of the yard was a huge double bass from the prison band. One journalist, a veteran of foreign assignments, had 'never seen anything like this since Korea'.[77]

The carnival is over. One of the prison band's instruments lies in the middle of the main yard. *NEW ZEALAND HERALD*

Among the men squatting miserably in the rear yards were 22 lifers and 34 preventive detainees. Paremoremo was specially designed to receive such inmates but was still several years away from completion. In desperation, the men were categorised according to their perceived security risk and dispersed accordingly. About 40 short-termers were kept behind to help with the clean-up, and were accommodated in the least damaged sections of the prison. Another 30 were sent to minimum-security prison farms, and others to Mount Crawford in Wellington and Paparua in Christchurch. There they proved disruptive, especially at Paparua where a minor riot soon took place, and teargas was needed to subdue them. The newly built psychiatric hospital at Lake Alice was temporarily designated a prison to receive those considered more dangerous.

To make room for the remaining long-sentenced, escape-prone and violent men, including Shepherd, 60 borstal boys were transferred from Waikeria to Invercargill. The 10 regarded as the most dangerous of all, including MacMillan, Sadaraka and Wilder, were held in a new high-security unit at Waikeria which, by chance, had just been completed. Many found their time there very uncomfortable: conditions and routines were unfamiliar, and staff treated them with great suspicion. One later recalled: 'We were let out for maybe ten minutes each day. In those few minutes we had to have a shower and clean our cell out . . . We were more or less living like animals. About eleven chaps were sent to mental hospital from there. Several fellows cut their wrists.'[78]

In the heat of the riot, Maori Mac had been among the first to hand himself in to police. He then volunteered information to them about conditions inside, and later cooperated with a commission of inquiry by providing evidence against riot leaders. Those actions made him an outcast at Waikeria, and he was transferred to Mount Crawford for his own safety.[79] The other high-risk inmates spent nine months in Waikeria's high-security unit while the work of building a similar stand-alone prison-within-a-prison at Mount Eden itself was accelerated. Just a week after the riot concrete was poured for the floor.

Similar urgency was accorded to the long-promised maximum-security prison north of the city. The Christchurch *Star* pointed out that there was currently 'no maximum security prison anywhere in New Zealand', and demanded 'the utmost urgency to build a new prison which would remedy this fundamental defect'.[80] Some suggested that by forcing the fast-tracking of this project, the rioters had inadvertently performed a service to the country.[81]

III

An inquiry into the largest and most destructive prison riot in the country's history delivered its report at the end of 1965, and again Superintendent Buckley was absolved of direct responsibility for the carnage.[82] The locks on the corridor grilles, installed after Wilder's escape attempt in February, were found to have been the crucial factor in containing Sadaraka and MacMillan. 'Without security locks on all outside doors I am sure there would have been a mass breakout,' said Officer Haines, one of the hostages, in a radio interview.[83] Both inmates and prison staff were commended by the inquiry for their courage in releasing inmates from their cells and helping to ensure that no deaths and few injuries resulted.

Yet the inquiry also found serious lapses in prison procedures that enabled the ringleaders to obtain the revolver and cell key, and later allowed remand inmates to link up with sentenced prisoners, to devastating effect. The riot might have been entirely prevented, thought the inquiry, if stringent searches had located either the revolver or the key.[84] It found that failure to adequately supervise visits, or search inmates afterwards, was due primarily to an acute staff shortage, with some officers required to work for 13 successive days without a break.[85]

Twenty-four inmates were charged with offences arising from the riot, including assault, attempting to escape and setting fire to prison property. They were dealt with leniently by the court, and even Sadaraka and MacMillan, who received the heaviest sentences, successfully appealed them. The press was inclined to agree that pursuing severe legal remedies against the rioters could 'foster wide resentment and so spark further trouble'.[86] However, the subsequent careers of the two ringleaders suggest that they themselves failed to appreciate this example of official pragmatism.

MacMillan was returned to maximum security after his escape attempt, and a few weeks later was declared insane and transferred to a mental hospital. He spent seven years there until considered eligible for parole. He then left the country for Australia and resumed his interrupted career as a bank robber, pulling off several armed robberies before his spectacularly violent death in 1979, in a machine-gun battle with New South Wales police. Sadaraka completed his original sentence for the car-bombing, but in 1975 was given 10 years in Paremoremo for assault and robbery. He was paroled in 1980 and also headed to Australia, where he murdered his brother-in-law during a furious argument. He served 14 years in maximum security and was then deported back to New Zealand. Just six months later, and aged in his 50s, he was back in Paremoremo for the murder of a Hokianga drug dealer.[87]

In late July 1965, Mount Eden's inmate muster stood at just 13, the lowest in its long history. The long-debated issue of demolishing the charred, derelict and barely habitable prison seemed finally capable of resolution. For years before the riot, Justice Minister Hanan had favoured tearing down this looming physical rebuke to liberal penal practice, and Auckland's local politicians and residents, especially those who lived nearby, avidly supported its demolition. Yet there remained the question of the prison's new maximum-security unit, already under construction and intended to house the country's worst offenders until Paremoremo was completed a few years hence.

Hanan was also acutely conscious that the country's other prisons could not long absorb the several hundred displaced inmates. A few weeks after the riot he announced that the burnt-out building would be partially rebuilt to house 150 remand, short-term and medium-security inmates on a strictly temporary basis.[88] Later, as those renovations were underway, he emphasised that 'Mount Eden will be completely demolished, and not a vestige of the existing institution will remain, except for the new security unit being built now, for fourteen men'.[89]

Like a continually reprieved inmate of its own condemned cells, the indomitable old building won yet another stay of execution. By mid-August, with the worst of the debris cleaned out of the wings, the inmate muster had already risen to one hundred, with some of the men housed in cells whose ceilings leaked badly. Buckley acknowledged, 'It will be a bit unfortunate for some of them if it rains . . . they will just have to put up with it.'[90] As with the original stone structure, much of the rebuilding work was carried out by inmates themselves. Burnt-out timber roof trusses were replaced with steel beams, new roofing iron was laid down, and the kitchen and west and south wings were rebuilt. The other two wings were

A burned-out workshop destroyed in the 1965 riot.
NEW ZEALAND HERALD GLASS PLATE COLLECTION, AUCKLAND LIBRARIES, 1370-39-4-2; PHOTOGRAPHER BILL ROWNTREE

left largely untouched and marked for demolition.[91] The renovations went far beyond restoration to produce substantial alterations throughout the prison — more extensive than any since it was built, or subsequently.[92]

By Christmas most former inmates, such as those sent to Lake Alice, were returned to the renovated cells. The partially rebuilt and barely functional prison already housed more inmates than the 150 it was designed to hold.[93] They found their conditions significantly worse than before the riot. Inmates were now confined to cells for up to 17 hours a day except on weekends, when it was compulsory to go out into the yard even on wet days. They were no longer allowed newspapers, hobbies or recreation materials, apart from library books. Weekly visits were tightly monitored, with no physical contact allowed of any kind, let alone 'Hollywood clinches'. According to one officer, Buckley had 'all the inmates running at double time and snapping to attention like bloody soldiers'.[94]

Demolition of the sealed-off and unrestored east and north wings began in early 1966, when inmates removed the first sections of ornamental stonework from the crenellated towers. Whether by accident or otherwise, these heavy pieces of carved stone damaged the paving and drains as they were lowered to the ground, and Justice Minister Hanan halted the project until it could be carried out 'by people experienced in demolition work'. The perimeter wall of the prison also had to remain in place 'since the building had to be kept secure to hold remand prisoners until a new remand centre could be built'.[95]

III

Nine months after the riot, in March 1966, the brand-new Mount Eden high-security unit was ready to receive the hardest cases sent to Waikeria. Jim Shepherd was among the 12 who were driven back to Auckland in a specially reinforced bus, with a group of armed officers behind barriers at its front and rear, and an escort of four carloads of armed police.[96] The new unit was a miniature version of the state-of-the-art facility under construction at Paremoremo. Each of its 14 cells was a six-by-three-metre steel box that proved uncomfortably hot and stuffy in summer. All strategic points were controlled by electronic switches, and visits were made in locked booths behind shatterproof glass. The unit's occupants were confined to their cells for more than 18 hours a day, including all meal times. Twice a day they were escorted into a dayroom in groups of three to carry out simple work projects. Exercise was allowed for two hours in the afternoon in a small cage-like enclosure, again in groups of three. No other association privileges were allowed.[97]

Shepherd remembers the unit as 'virtually an underground concrete and steel bunker. The doors were solid steel with mesh panels top and bottom so officers could see inside at all times. Our food was passed through a small opening.' During his three years there, he says, 'we were subject to torture — lights on all night, gates going every 20 minutes. You couldn't sleep. The screws would bang on the cell doors with their batons just to be smartarses. There's nothing before or since to compare with that place. I realised later that it did a lot of damage to me psychologically. None of us came out in good shape.'[98]

The single event he could look forward to was the weekly visit from the Catholic priest, Father Leo Downey. Although not a Catholic, Shepherd, in common with many other Mount Eden inmates, regarded the priest as 'a real gentleman. No one had any dealings with the Anglican padre — he was considered on the side of the authorities.'[99] After some persuasion, Shepherd was allowed to complete his minimal high school education by correspondence, and while still inside he gained a University Entrance qualification, possibly the first Mount Eden inmate to do so.

Two fellow inmates, Ron Jorgensen and George Wilder, were gifted and enthusiastic visual artists and conducted a years-long campaign to be allowed to pursue this interest from their cells. Shepherd, who had first met Wilder some years before the riot, regarded him as 'a lovely bloke — not a violent bone in his body'.[100] Yet Wilder was serving a crushingly long sentence among very violent men, and he hoped to spend some of that time creating artwork. In a rare piece of good fortune for him, the Justice Department asked a volunteer prison visitor, Grace Shaw, to meet with Wilder. She then appealed to luminaries of Auckland arts and culture such as novelist Maurice Shadbolt, historian E. H. McCormick and artist Colin McCahon for help in providing the caged folk hero with outlets for creative expression.[101]

In late 1965 Wilder's advocates began asking prison authorities to allow him the use of drawing paper, pencils and charcoal in solitary, and these materials were reluctantly permitted a year later.[102] Labour MPs took up his case and convinced Justice Minister Hanan to allow Wilder oil paints, brushes and an easel.[103] 'If we are to rehabilitate even the most difficult prisoners,' said MP Colin Moyle, 'we should do our utmost to see they are gainfully employed as much as possible.'[104]

Buckley, however, refused to allow Wilder to have these materials in his cell, so his art-making was restricted to the few hours spent each day in the dayroom. In protest at this and other petty restrictions, all 12 prisoners in the security unit went on hunger strike in September 1967. Some held out for six days and the Justice Department considered force-feeding them, until Labour MP Martyn Finlay visited the unit and agreed to take up their case.[105] His intervention saw small improvements — meals were served on a table instead of on the cell floor — but Buckley continued to obstruct Wilder's artistic ambitions.

Colin McCahon, then a lecturer at the Elam School of Fine Arts, visited Wilder at the high-security unit weekly, and attempted to offer constructive critiques through two sheets of bulletproof glass.[106] Wilder's skilful, somewhat romanticised charcoal portraits and landscapes were exhibited in Auckland to some acclaim, and an art school in Connecticut, in the US, awarded him a correspondence course.[107] These encouraging steps towards rehabilitation saw him transferred to Paparua Prison, Christchurch, in 1968. There he proved an exemplary inmate, working hard as a Braille transcriber and a budding short story writer, and he was released on parole the following year after serving eight years of his 19-year sentence.[108] 'I'd put a gun to my head rather than go back there,' he told a reporter soon after his release.[109]

The remaining inmates of Mount Eden's high-security unit were transferred in 1969 to the newly finished D Block at Paremoremo. This block, described as 'a longterm isolation facility', was the most secure section of a no-expense-spared maximum-security institution, the most advanced prison the country had yet seen.[110] Yet its clinically clean interior, all electronically controlled sliding panels and automatic warning systems, appeared to its first occupants like a hotel in comparison with the cells they had left behind. Shepherd was in no doubt that '[i]t was good to get out of Mount Eden' and equally clear that 'cruel and brutal conditions breed cruel and brutal men'.[111]

After serving his time at Paremoremo, Shepherd called on contacts and expertise accumulated at both prisons, and joined the increasingly brutal Mr Asia heroin-smuggling syndicate, which made millions of dollars before an international police operation caught up with them in 1986. Shepherd was given 25 years' hard labour without parole, and served almost 15 of them, mainly at 'supermax' prisons such as Goulbourn, south of Sydney, a nineteenth-century stone-built cousin to Mount Eden.[112]

No other single event in Mount Eden Prison's long history has had the same far-reaching effects as the 1965 riot. In the most dramatic way possible, it confirmed to politicians and ministerial officials that a maximum-security institution built to leading international standards regardless of expense could be postponed no longer.[113] This realisation dismantled any remaining arguments that the old prison could still contain high-risk inmates while meeting modern expectations for penal management.[114] After 1969, Mount Eden became redundant in terms of its original function as the country's maximum-security prison. It would remain in use for many more years, but would never again command the same authority and significance within New Zealand's justice system and wider society.[115]

8:
Death on remand
1970–2011

The prison that once loomed in splendid isolation over Auckland City was engulfed by housing and light industry from the 1920s. In the late 1960s its setting suffered a further indignity, and one which created a new and ongoing security risk. New on- and off-ramps at Khyber Pass Road on Auckland's southern motorway swept within metres of the prison at the height of its perimeter wall. The main exercise yard, tramped daily by at least 200 inmates, was suddenly within a stone's throw of any Aucklander prepared to breach the highway code. On a warm Sunday afternoon in late 1970, a noisy hundred-strong crowd, including several children, took this opportunity. They were led by the Progressive Youth Movement (PYM), the shock troops of New Zealand radical activism, and set out for the prison on foot from Albert Park in the city centre.

The country's most recognisable radical activist, the shaggy-haired, charismatic face of youth rebellion, Tim Shadbolt, had been admitted to Mount Eden a few days earlier — not for using the word 'bullshit' in public, as many of the protesters believed, but for refusing to pay an accumulation of fines for this and various other minor offences. The protest march was intended to show support for him and other political activists held in the prison around the same time, especially Bob van Ruyssevelt and John Bower, serving four and five years respectively for bombing a Parnell air force depot storing equipment for use in the Vietnam War. A solitary traffic officer made a token effort to stop the marchers from swarming onto the motorway, and was brushed aside.

They climbed onto a metre-high crash barrier to gain a better vantage point, and began tossing packets of cigarettes, bags of sweets and other prohibited delights to the inmates in the yard. The prison's newly appointed superintendent, Jack Hobson, reported the inmates 'fought amongst themselves to get possession' of them. When prison officers managed to force the inmates out of reach of this rain of treasure, the protesters threw lighted firecrackers instead. Portable megaphones amplified fiery speeches about the injustices of the prison system and songs promising to 'blow up the walls'.

Superintendent Hobson had replaced Buckley the year before, with instructions to restore the partially rebuilt prison to an orderly and well-managed state. This protest was one of the first acts of mass insubordination he had faced. 'It was impossible to clear the yard,' he told Justice Secretary Robson, 'and had we attempted to do so we would have had a first-class disturbance on our hands.'¹ Nor were the police much help at controlling the protesters. 'We were caught on the hop by this one,' admitted Senior Sergeant Rains. 'I could only muster two constables and didn't get to the prison until 3.40 p.m.' The marchers had clearly committed an offence by walking on the motorway but they were unlikely to be charged or deterred from repeating it, since traffic officers had no powers of arrest and could only take the offenders' names, 'which are usually fictitious'.

In fact, an identical action took place the following month, when five dozen cans of beer were flung into the exercise yard as an early Christmas present for the inmates. 'About half burst on impact,' reported Hobson, 'but the rest were consumed in record time by those lucky enough to get a can in the general melee.' Such lightning demonstrations might appear fairly harmless, he told Robson, but they provided an opportunity for more dangerous contraband, such as drugs and firearms, to be delivered to inmates. 'To be quite truthful, there is no knowing just what has been introduced during the last three such demonstrations.'² A barbed-wire fence was erected to prevent public access to the on-ramp, and Hobson hoped to forestall further protests by removing some of the instigators from his prison. He regarded the Parnell bombers Bower and van Ruyssevelt as 'very prominent anarchist prisoners', and 'it would be in the interests of discipline to transfer them'.³

Bob van Ruyssevelt, then aged 22, had no prior experience of imprisonment and found it 'initially quite scary . . . I was put in a cell with a man who they say had sex with a sheep and then cut its throat. He did nothing to me but showed me a knife he had under his mattress.' After several months van Ruyssevelt was transferred to Paparua Prison near Christchurch, which appeared little better. Looking back on this time after a half-century with no further convictions, van Ruyssevelt believes that 'Mount Eden should be bulldozed. Doubling up in cells should not be allowed. There need to be more alternatives to prison such as restorative justice, more mental health support, more education and decriminalisation of drug use.'⁴

Tim Shadbolt had the highest public profile of the three young activists held in Mount Eden at this time but was not transferred elsewhere, partly because he was serving a much shorter sentence but also because a fellow inmate intervened with Jack Hobson to lessen the impact of his presence on the prison's functioning. The PYM protesters who first surged up the motorway on-ramp in November had alerted Shadbolt to their plans beforehand, and expected him to be waiting in the exercise yard when they arrived and then to launch into one of his trademark orations denouncing the prison system and calling for solidarity between inmates and other social dissidents. Instead, on that afternoon he was down in the 'pound', the punishment cells, where he found himself in the company of long-serving criminals George Wilder and Trevor Nash, an experience the young radical found unexpectedly enjoyable and informative.

Wilder had been released on probation the year before, swearing never to set foot in a prison again. He had spent his first weeks of freedom in the Titirangi, West Auckland, home of Maurice Shadbolt, his loyal supporter and writing mentor (and, coincidentally, Tim's cousin).[5] Like all long-serving ex-inmates, Wilder struggled to adapt to an unfamiliar world with rules of conduct that he had to learn by breaking them. He was well known to Auckland police, and claimed they would not even allow him to linger on a street corner without harassing him. After several months he met up with Trevor Nash, a fellow professional criminal who was then also between sentences. Nash convinced him to improve their finances with a quick illegal enterprise, and both men soon faced a variety of charges including receiving stolen goods.[6] The judge felt enough sympathy for Wilder that, for once, no extra term was added to his previous sentence, but he was returned to Mount Eden to serve out the nine years that remained of it.

The legendary escaper was initially wary of the articulate young celebrity installed in an adjacent punishment cell, but for want of other company the two soon forged a friendship and spent every minute of their precious exercise periods in the former execution yard, playing a ferociously competitive version of squash using only their hands and a tennis ball. Shadbolt was younger, fit and naturally athletic, but 'I never won a single game. He could climb up a wall virtually, and whack that ball back at me.'[7] Wilder also enthralled Shadbolt with stories of his days on the run from police. He described evading a manhunt that had surrounded him in a small area of swamp. He sank under the peaty brown water and, in classic prison-break fashion, breathed through a hollow reed, managing to remain undetected even when a police dog trampled over his stomach. Shadbolt offered to help with writing and publishing this picaresque life story, and arranged a sizeable advance on the royalties. Wilder was initially tempted but changed his mind

Heading for the highway. Progressive Youth Movement members and supporters (left) take the motorway off-ramp to protest the imprisonment of Auckland radical Tim Shadbolt. From the ramp they were able to toss cans of beer to the prisoners in the exercise yard (below). *BARRY LEE COLLECTION*

and returned the publisher's cheque, saying that he planned to avoid all public attention once he was finally released.

Nash, the career bank robber who had staged a celebrated walk-away escape in 1961, was a very different figure. To Shadbolt, Nash seemed 'like a caged tiger. He just paced up and down completely naked in his cell.' He tried to strike up conversation with this intimidating villain, and offered to publicise his experiences, too, in the interests of prison reform. Nash's response was bluntly unfavourable. 'He said something like, "You bloody little twat. I'm a criminal. I rob banks. This is how the system works. I make a lot of money for my wife and five kids. I get caught now and again and I do my time. Prison reform? What sort of wanker's idea is that?"'[8]

Tim Shadbolt spent almost his entire month-long sentence in the pound with these two, and despite suffering Nash's contempt, considered himself fortunate to have done so. In fact, he owed this experience to one of Mount Eden's most unforgettable inmates, the former Māori Battalion commander, Auckland City councillor and expert on traditional weaponry, Colonel Pita Awatere DSO, MC. The year before Shadbolt arrived, Awatere began serving life for the murder of his wife's lover, and immediately created a lasting impression on fellow inmates and staff, including Superintendent Hobson.

One of those inmates was 17-year-old Te Rangikaheke Kiripātea, who in 1969 was serving his first prison sentence in a large 10-bunk cell in the prison's south wing. He heard of Awatere's impending arrival some days before the celebrated, silver-haired figure appeared:

> When he first stepped into the wing — aroha, eh? An emotional wave reached out to him. I remember he was quite dark-skinned, very handsome, had a giant presence. He had a lot of dignity even in those circumstances. He was a lot older than the rest of us Māoris . . . That was when I had an awakening of things Māori — I was hungry for it. We knew that he had this wealth of knowledge, and we'd walk the yards together constantly.[9]

As well as mentoring young Māori, Awatere, who spoke several ancient and modern languages and could quote Shakespeare by the hour, worked as the prison librarian. In that role he admired Shadbolt's efforts to encourage other inmates to express themselves in writing. When he learned of the imminent PYM march and Shadbolt's intention to declaim on criminal justice from the exercise yard, he intervened with prison staff to forestall such naive and foolhardy action. Shadbolt recalls: 'He knew there'd be a riotous situation and said "Get rid of that student radical", and they put me in the pound.'[10]

Superintendent Jack Hobson, in particular, had a very high regard for the polymathic and courteous Awatere, and recognised that his presence in the prison provided an opportunity to address a disturbing trend in the inmate population. By 1970 the proportion of Māori in prison had soared to five times that in the general population, an unprecedented situation due mainly, the government admitted, to 'the social, economic and cultural pressures associated with migration to an urban metropolis'.[11]

The exploding number of young Māori inmates placed especially heavy stress on Mount Eden Prison, sited in the heart of the nation's biggest city and near major Māori centres of population. Hobson therefore gave his uniquely authoritative new resident every encouragement to pass on elements of his traditional knowledge to eager young inmates such as Kiripātea. Awatere eventually held regular classes for at least 30 students in the arts of whaikōrero, taiaha and te reo, and also spoke on behalf of the hosts at welcome ceremonies for visiting Māori. 'He was obviously the kaumātua of the prison,' says Kiripātea. 'In the eyes of the Justice Department, he was the only one who could do that in that situation.'[12]

Superintendent Hobson was a humane and insightful man who won the admiration of both inmates and Justice Department officials. He hoped that once memories of the 1965 riot began to fade, he could relax the harsh security measures imposed under Buckley, and extend recreation and education programmes for both Māori and non-Māori. Once again, those expectations were thwarted by remorselessly rising inmate numbers. The prison had been renovated to hold just over two hundred inmates, and by early 1971 the muster reached 375. E. A. Missen, the new Secretary for Justice, drew up a 10-year plan that included replacing Mount Eden with a new remand and short-sentence facility, but not, he made clear, 'as an immediate priority'.[13]

So, in yet another stopgap measure, the department planned to repair the prison's two most badly damaged wings, still standing vacant six years after the riot, to cope with the latest crisis in inmate numbers. This vague intention suddenly became much firmer in March 1971, when another riot broke out. It was short-lived and caused little damage, but focused official attention very sharply on the security risks inherent in a grossly overcrowded, understaffed and imperfectly repaired prison.

On 21 March, a Saturday, the two hundred-odd inmates in the main yard were called in from the afternoon exercise period as usual, but about half of them refused to return to their wings. They presented Hobson with a list of demands and grievances that included perennial complaints of poor food and inadequate recreational and medical facilities, but also more imaginative suggestions such as improving the system of payment for prison work, and receiving two clean bedsheets rather than one each week. Hobson promised to forward the list to Wellington, but the rebels were not appeased and threatened to stay out in the yard all night if necessary. After some hours they began to smash its seats and other wooden structures, and some men armed themselves with broken lengths of wood as batons. Hobson later told his superiors that he could do nothing but contain the situation. 'I just did not have the staff. We would have needed 100 officers', and his complement was only about half that number.[14]

As darkness fell the rioters broke into a locked tunnel and acquired a drum of diesel fuel that rekindled their bonfire but also spread burning oil towards cells occupied by other inmates, who then had to be dragged away through the flames by staff. When an attempt was made to break into the kitchen, which might have supplied provisions for an indefinite siege, Hobson abruptly abandoned his hands-off approach. As a newly appointed superintendent, he decided that his response to this revolt would determine his relations with the inmates for the rest of his term. Accordingly, he ordered handguns issued to his officers and instructed them to aim either high or low.

In the volley of gunfire that followed, two inmates were hit by bullets, neither fatally, and the rest surrendered soon afterwards. Five prison staff required treatment for injuries, and for at least one of them, the tenacious officer Ed Marchant, the mounds of charred wreckage left in the exercise yard evoked uncomfortable memories of the 1965 riot. He had been badly beaten on that occasion by Sadaraka and MacMillan, the two young remand prisoners whose escape attempt had precipitated the earlier uprising.

Those considered to be the ringleaders of the latest revolt were transferred to Paremoremo. They included Kiripātea, then aged 19, who remembers 'having to walk a gauntlet of officers as we went back in. Then they kicked us down the stairs.'[15] All the grievances presented to Hobson were dismissed, with Justice Minister Dan Riddiford describing the request for two bedsheets a week as ridiculous.[16] With an alacrity typically shown only after such incidents of serious disorder, Cabinet approved plans to repair the prison's derelict north and east wings, and they were re-opened later that year, providing an extra 143 beds.[17] To refute fears that this was a retrograde step, Riddiford added that 'the need to quit the prison altogether was accepted as an urgent priority', and he predicted that it would be entirely vacated by 1977.[18] Its site would then be used for the promised 'modern short-term and remand prison', a premature glimpse of what would take almost 40 more years to come to pass.[19]

Hobson's firm and strategic handling of the 1971 riot was admired by both his department and politicians.[20] They showed their appreciation by placing him in charge of Paremoremo the following year, where he immediately earned the respect of the hard men of D Block by releasing them from their cells, and walking among them alone and unarmed.[21] His replacement at Mount Eden was Jack Rogers, an Englishman who had worked at similarly antiquated high-security prisons in his homeland, such as Pentonville, before moving to New Zealand in the 1950s with a desire to reform rather than replicate such institutions.

III

Rogers took charge of a prison that was both overcrowded and critically run-down. Even basic toilet facilities were inadequate and a single washbasin might be shared by 48 inmates. All the earlier reform initiatives appeared to have stagnated into a narrow concern for security and rigid regulation. Each weekly tobacco ration, for example, was issued with a single match, though Rogers found that craving inmates managed to use this up to 16 times by splitting it carefully into tiny slivers. 'It can be done ... You dampen the match head first.'[22]

The only organised recreational activity was a weightlifting class, formed in 1970 by prison officer Mike O'Donnell, who had previously represented Ireland at the sport. After some years at Mount Eden he realised that although the inmates prized physical strength, they had no legitimate way to exert themselves since the closure of the quarry. O'Donnell converted an unused workshop into a crude gym, and equipped it with basic weights and benches made on the premises. He then served as instructor, helped by visiting experts such as the diminutive Commonwealth gold medallist Precious McKenzie.[23] The gym remained hugely popular 25 years later, when O'Donnell had become the prison's longest-serving officer.[24]

Following the 1965 riot most of the trade-training workshops, such as the cabinetmaking, tailoring, canvas goods and bootmaking shops, were transferred to Paremoremo, and the few that remained produced tubular-steel furniture for government departments, and plastic and paper bags. They could employ only a small number of inmates; the others spent their weekdays in idleness, unable to earn the two-dollar weekly wage that was partly paid out as credit at the canteen and otherwise accumulated for the date of release.[25] To increase employment opportunities, Rogers sent about a hundred of the lowest-security inmates — those with short sentences and considered at low risk of escaping or violence — outside the prison walls every weekday on work parties. Some travelled by bus, accompanied by several officers, to work in the large gardens at Paremoremo, where the produce, and the bread from its bakery, fed both prisons.[26]

Other inmates maintained and painted prison housing and other government buildings, or worked in carpentry, engineering and spray-painting shops alongside the prison. A much smaller number who were soon to complete their sentences were granted the exceptional privilege of pre-release parole, spending weekends away from the prison and returning to it voluntarily on Monday morning. While on parole they were forbidden to drink or drive a car, and remained in the care of an approved sponsor such as a spouse, parent or prison visitor.[27] Eventually this scheme expanded to become work-parole, and a select group of inmates was able to hold down jobs outside the prison as part of their reintegration into the community before release. They were housed in a stand-alone unit of modern design and materials, with its own toilet and washing facilities and a tiny kitchen. Its 20 cells were somewhat larger and considerably warmer than those in the main block, especially as they enjoyed an abundance of natural light. The pre-release unit had its own access to the outside world, sparing its occupants the need to pass through the great front gates.[28]

Soon after Rogers took over, Tim Shadbolt was back inside, once again for refusing, on principle, to pay the various fines he had accumulated. The period between his first and second sentences had been spent in the relative seclusion of a commune on the shores of the Manukau Harbour, and he discovered that over that time his public profile had much diminished, and other inmates were no longer inclined to pay the same regard to his political provocations: 'I was just a smartarse young hippie trying to interfere with their life.' On his second day inside he heard a group of inmates singing in Māori and greeted them through the cell door. 'I said, "Great singing, fellas. I know I'm just a bed and breakfast boy [short-sentenced inmate] but I'd love to join in."'

Their sour reaction told him instantly that he had made a serious mistake. Later he encountered two of the singers serving up dinner, and found that he would get nothing to eat that night. 'The queue was building up behind me and I thought, "Man, I'm going to get a hiding. I'm not safe here at all."' Shadbolt promptly sought out the prison social worker and asked if any member of the public had offered to pay his outstanding fines. He was told that several people were prepared to repay the $200 owing. 'I said, "Just pick one and say yes please," so an hour later I was out of there. I was only in for maybe a couple of nights. It was a sudden dose of reality.'[29]

This helpful intervention by the prison's newly appointed social worker was an outcome of Rogers' determination to revive progress towards rehabilitative measures. Social workers and psychologists now supported the prison chaplain, and the general staff were given training in shifting from 'a purely custodial role to that of people with the understanding and ability to determine causative factors which made inmates act the way they did'.[30]

Dr Miriam Jackson (later Saphira) began working as a prison psychologist in late 1975, and remained at Mount Eden for more than a decade. She recalls, 'I was very conscious of the spiritual nature of the prison. It was full of pain, so you had to adjust with compassion. I can also remember fearing the surly prison officers. On a bad day they would wind some prisoner up and then send him to see us. But I never had any problems with those men — they were always in tears within a few minutes. Many men there had been raped as little boys — I hadn't expected that.'[31]

Each day Dr Jackson had to be escorted through eight locked gates to reach her office, where the only toilet facility was a men's cubicle with no door. 'Whenever I used it they had to put a trusted inmate on guard with his back to me. He was always very polite. The whole place was damp and my joints ached from arthritis, but some of the men came from much worse conditions outside.' One inmate made a point of offering cups of tea to Jackson and the other psychologists, and of staying to converse with them. 'He was very educated and interesting to talk to.'[32] This was Colonel Awatere, who died unexpectedly in the prison in early 1976, just months before he was due for parole, apparently of complications from diabetes.

| | |

Dr Jackson found mental health issues were almost universal among the prison's women inmates. 'I could see the benefits of having a much more therapeutic prison regime where they could learn to deal with their emotions at the moment and heal their childhood backgrounds.'[33] For more than 20 years the assistant matron, and then matron, of the women's prison was Dot Costar. She recalled: 'We used to ring a bell at 7 each morning to unlock the cells, then breakfast was brought over on trays from the men's prison . . . At 8am we had a muster, and the sentenced women were given their jobs for the day. They were all domestic duties like laundry, cleaning the rooms, sewing. Every prisoner could get a free issue of tobacco in those days, and some of the women used to make up these little packs of tobacco for the whole prison.'

The only personal possession women inmates were allowed to keep after sentencing was a wedding ring. 'They were issued with two complete sets of clothing, right down to underwear.' These uniforms were a type of long smock for day wear and a lighter one, known as the 'party frock', to wear in the evenings and other free time. 'Even their sanitary towels were all numbered, and the women had to wash them out, then dry them by carrying them around on their belts during the day.' Evenings were spent watching TV in the recreation room until the 9 p.m. lockup, then listening to the radio in their cells until lights-out at eleven.[34]

A young remand inmate of the women's prison in this period recalls that almost all of her fellow prisoners were Māori and 'lots of them couldn't read. They had to get other people to read their mail.' The most terrifying of her fellow inmates was 'a big woman they called Cochise. She was over six foot and very strong — full of rage and anger. If you saw her coming down the corridor you'd turn and run. She spent most of her time down in "the hole", where you had to live with the smell of your chamberpot.' For this terrified first-time inmate, the week's highlight was the arrival of the 'special mothers', voluntary female prison visitors. 'They were each allocated to four or five of us, and they came and talked to us in our cells. Mine was a lovely Indian lady. It was good to see a face that wasn't glowering at me.'[35]

In the following decade a high-profile activist entered the women's prison. Sandra Coney was an editor of the feminist magazine *Broadsheet*, which had notably published a treatise on Māori sovereignty by Colonel Awatere's daughter Donna, a psychologist who had worked at Mount Eden. Coney was arrested along with many others on Waitangi Day 1982, during protests at the Treaty grounds. 'I had some eggs in my pocket. I hit the Governor-General, Sir David Beattie, twice. He had his plumed hat on.' She was refused bail — 'they thought I was dangerous' — and remanded to the century-old former superintendent's house alongside the prison, which had housed its female inmates since the chaos of 1965. 'It seemed to me like a nineteenth-century workhouse. There was absolutely nothing useful to do and nowhere to exercise — just a small yard with a high wall around it. The women had a much worse deal than the men who had far more facilities, such as a gym.' Sandra Coney remembers the 10 days she spent in this neglected appendage to the main prison as 'extremely boring. We were only allowed to carry out completely meaningless activity, like putting a tablespoon of sugar into a plastic bag and sealing it with heat. And the food was really terrible. It was cooked in the men's prison and delivered to us — we weren't even allowed to do our own cooking.'[36]

She made use of the enforced idleness by keeping a prison diary, later published in *Broadsheet*:

> The women's prison is a two-storied late-Victorian wooden house at the end of Lauder Road. Nestled at the foot of the mammoth stone walls of the men's prison, its honey-bricked exterior looks deceptively homely and innocuous... Upstairs are three cells of 6–8 beds in bunks. One solitary cell is for women on murder charges. Each cell has a lavatory and handbasin behind a partition. Windows are curtainless and kept permanently open. Consequently it is bitterly cold as

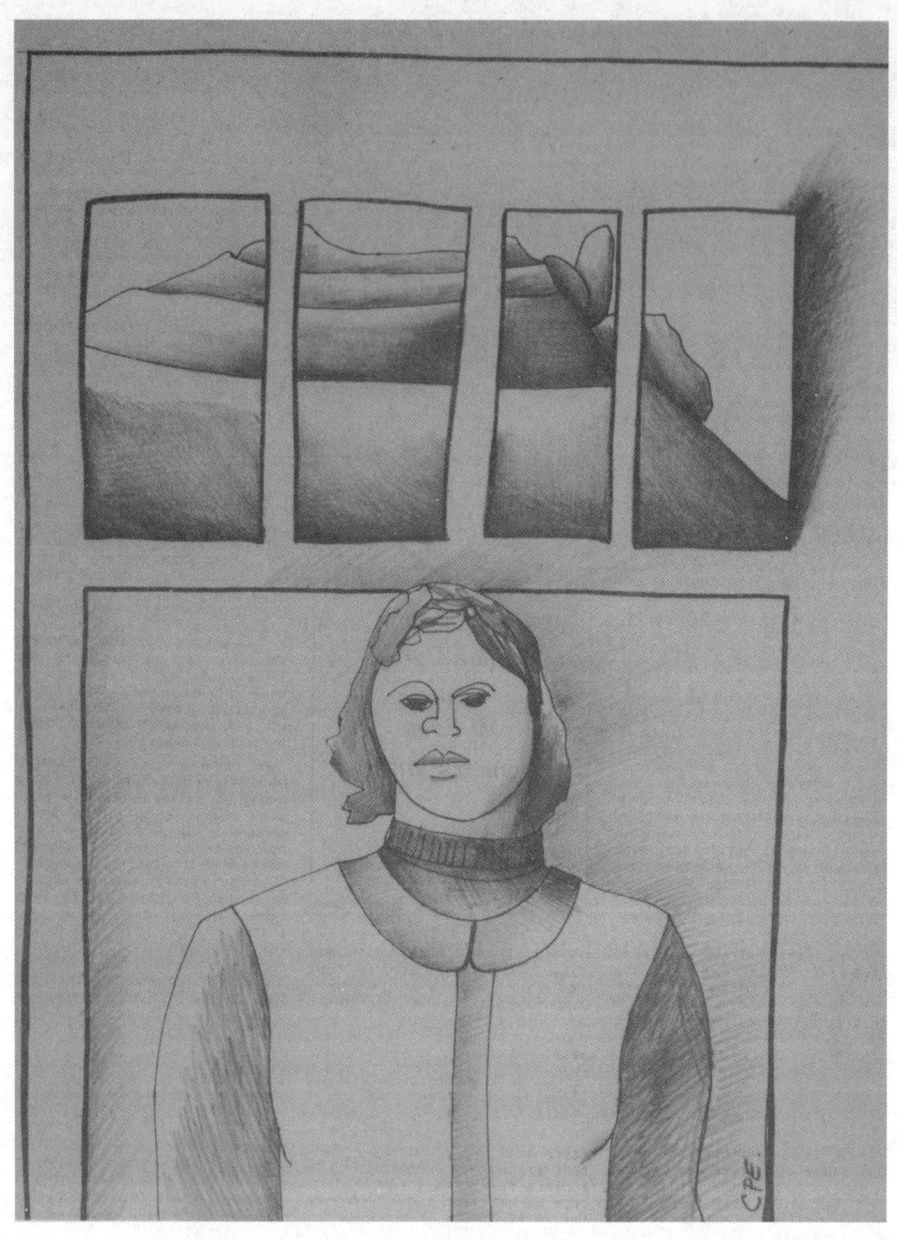

The drawing by Claudia Pond Eyley that accompanied Sandra Coney's 1982 prison diary published in *Broadsheet*. COURTESY OF CLAUDIA POND EYLEY

winter sets in. Remands are locked together in their cells from 5pm till 6.30 in the morning . . . Boredom hangs around the place, an unwelcome but inevitable visitor. Mornings spent dry-scrubbing floors and afternoons spent embroidering prison numbers on old sheets and packing rations of sugar leave the mind aching for stimulation. Backs ache from long sitting in stiff vinyl chairs; bodies dull and sluggish from lack of exercise . . . Although Mount Eden is a remand and short-stay institution, women can spend up to eight months there. One woman in my cell had been on remand since January waiting for trial. There were three very pregnant women, one a week away from confinement . . . All my preconceptions about my fellow inmates proved groundless. They accepted me, shared their knowledge with me and were interested in me and my politics.[37]

The racial imbalance in this small community was even more marked than in the larger one alongside. 'Just about every other woman there was a Māori or Pacific Islander,' Coney remembers. 'I was a complete abnormal, but they were perfectly friendly.'[38]

The run-down women's prison briefly housed another high-profile prisoner a few years later. For her part in the 1985 bombing of the Greenpeace ship *Rainbow Warrior* in Auckland Harbour, Dominique Prieur, a French military intelligence officer, was fortunate to be placed in one of the single cells normally reserved for murderers. Her co-conspirator, Alain Mafart, was in the main prison alongside, and apparently found its conditions so primitive that he requested a transfer to the higher-security Paremoremo.[39] Prieur succeeded in improving her own surroundings by persuading staff to provide her with a television, and dumbbells for weightlifting, in her cell. These privileges later became available to other inmates.[40]

Both the Justice Department and the Ombudsman's Office had received many complaints about facilities in the women's section, and work on a new and larger women's unit, with extra cells and the kitchen and dining facilities that Coney hoped for, began soon after Prieur's transfer into French custody. It was opened in 1988 and enlarged several years later to accommodate 54 women.[41] Even so, by 1997 the library in the women's prison was just 'a trolley with a few books on it', according to one inmate. 'If you were fast enough, you could grab a Mills & Boon.' Two years later the reading matter was greatly improved through the efforts of a volunteer, Lynn Dawson, who taught remedial reading to the women inmates. 'It's had such a positive effect on so many women,' she said. 'You see them come in and they can hardly read and they've got no confidence. It's amazing the difference it makes when they can read better.'[42]

Another eagerly awaited group of women volunteers gave monthly talks in the men's prison on sex education. As volunteer Mary Woodward explained: 'Our family planning talks were part of a pre-release programme run by Prisoners Aid. We gave an hour lecture once a month in the prison chapel for those in the pre-release group who chose to attend, usually between 10 or 20 inmates.' One of her colleagues had to overcome her nervousness at

> the noisy unlocking and locking of heavy doors as we progressed through the prison to the chapel, and certainly we could expect catcalls and remarks from prisoners in their cells on the few occasions they got a peep at us ... Our brief was to concentrate on relationship matters often arising from the difficulty or inability many men had in discussing this sort of issue with their partners ... While there were often laughs as men opened up about their sexual preferences, the conversations were at times protracted beyond the hour as inmates welcomed the opportunity for straight talk with open-minded females who listened as well as spoke.[43]

At this time, and for many years afterwards, the Department of Corrections refused to issue condoms to inmates to avoid condoning any form of sexual activity among them. Irrepressible but prudent sexual partners were forced to improvise with alternatives such as 'a bread bag and butter', until condoms were eventually supplied by medical staff.[44]

| | |

By 1976 the creaking institution held 430 inmates, the greatest number in its history to that date and more than any other prison in the country. Staff were obliged to work 'six days a week, sometimes seven' and their union, the PSA, was 'gravely disturbed at the failure of successive governments to solve the problem of overcrowding in the prison and the workload on officers'.[45] Yet the incumbent government appeared no closer to finding a replacement for the prison than any of its predecessors. In early 1977, the year in which Justice Minister Riddiford had promised that the prison would be permanently shut, its inmates were hard at work repairing battlements that his predecessor had ordered demolished after the 1965 riot. The old prison, Superintendent Rogers surmised with accuracy, 'will be with us for a fair while yet'.[46]

In line with international penological practice, Rogers introduced pets to encourage tender feelings among the inmates: a fish tank in the lending library and budgerigars in the pre-release hostel.[47] Inmates were also known to feed the pigeons that perched on the ledges of cell windows, but eventually grilles were placed over the ledges to end the practice.[48] The daily menu now ran to scrambled eggs at breakfast, with curried sausages and steamed chocolate pudding at night. The improvement that inmates probably valued most was an increased number of showers. They still, of course, had to use chamberpots in their cells at night, since even a vigorous reformer like Rogers could not negotiate the cost of installing modern toilets in cells made from solid stone. Most cells also lacked glass in their heavily barred windows and were therefore bitterly cold in winter.[49]

Through the 1970s and 1980s, drug use proved an ever-increasing problem. Whether or not their original offence was drug-related, large numbers of inmates were now admitted showing symptoms of recent drug use and withdrawal, and once inside they displayed great determination and ingenuity at smuggling in drugs and paraphernalia such as hypodermic syringes, and at hoarding, swapping and selling prescribed medication.[50] Extra vigilance was demanded from staff to manage behaviour and symptoms associated with drug use, including attempted suicide, self-mutilation and sudden decline in physical health, which occasionally proved fatal.

British-born musician Tommy Adderley was admitted for supplying morphine to a persistent acquaintance who proved to be an undercover cop. Adderley had enthusiastically indulged in the cheap Thai heroin that began entering the country from the mid-1970s, and he was a regular user by the time of his arrest.[51] He arrived at the prison in August 1981, and a few months later sent friends one of the more insouciant accounts of Mount Eden Prison life on record:

> I'm attached to the kitchen and I'm in charge of the prison bread shop. I'm more or less my own boss and work unsupervised most of the time and at my own speed. I start at 5 am until I'm finished. My cell is right next door to the kitchen and in fact the whole kitchen is quite isolated from the rest of the jail. We have our own messroom and TV, plus our own pool and table-tennis tables. We get clean clothes every day, a great hot shower, plus our meals are always fresh and hot. We eat what we like and the tea billy is boiling all day long.[52]

Adderley maintained that the experience of imprisonment had ended his addiction, but other inmates found no difficulty in sustaining their habits inside. At times the smell of marijuana in the corridors was so strong 'you could get stoned just walking around', says former officer Zane Paine. Methamphetamine, or P, later became the drug of choice, as it was easy to conceal inside body cavities and its users could be detected only by problematic behaviour changes. 'They become violent — erratic would be the word. Even more so when they're coming down off it.'[53]

The perennial issue of mental illness among inmates was greatly worsened by the rise in drug use. Rogers gave the example of an inmate returned to the prison from Oakley Mental Hospital who, the following day, 'stands in the main yard in the midst of the bulk of inmates and threatens to fight all and sundry. It takes six officers to restrain this inmate and place him in a special observation cell. By Sunday, although under medication, he is smashing up his cell and assaulting staff whenever his cell door is opened.'[54] For such eventualities a special medical unit was created in the remand wing, with resuscitation equipment and drug antidotes. The hospital had an isolation unit added for infectious patients, and in 1976 Rogers reported: 'We've had three lepers, and a case of hepatitis.'[55] As well as three doctors on call and a visiting dentist, the staff grew to include five psychologists, a forensic psychiatrist and a female social worker.

| | |

Drug-addled and mentally disordered criminals drew little sympathy from the general public, but from the mid-1970s the country was shaken to learn that Mount Eden's inmates included children as young as 13, placed there on remand from the Children's Court. Exposing this practice and campaigning to end it was largely the work of ACORD, the Auckland Committee on Racism and Discrimination, whose members included a public-spirited scientist named Oliver Sutherland:

> We had a reasonable relationship with the superintendent of the prison and he let me go in and meet the kids held on remand. I found it a very forbidding place and it horrified me to meet young kids in there, 15-year-olds, who had no idea what was going on. The prison staff didn't like it. They said it was a hassle for them because they couldn't keep them separate from the adults. There were stories of these kids sharing cells with deranged drug addicts.[56]

In 1974 ACORD publicised the case of Kahu W., a 14-year-old Rarotongan schoolboy who was arrested on Auckland's Queen Street. He had never been in trouble with police before, but because he had no money he was charged with being 'idle and disorderly'. Lacking legal representation, he pleaded guilty 'because a police officer told him to', and was remanded to Mount Eden for a week before being acquitted.[57] A stream of ACORD press releases and reports on cases like this, backed by multiracial demonstrations outside the prison gates by concerned Aucklanders including future prime minister David Lange, produced damning newspaper headlines and drove the Justice Department to launch an inquiry headed by Judge Augusta Wallace, who concluded that, 'Young people should not be remanded to Auckland's Mount Eden Prison.'[58] The inquiry brought no change to sentencing policy, however, and all teenaged offenders from the upper North Island who were remanded in custody were routinely sent there.

ACORD was one of many organisations drawing attention to racial inequity, an issue glaringly apparent in a prison whose muster was now overwhelmingly Polynesian. In 1981 the government's determination to host a tour by South Africa's racially selected national rugby team proved a uniting force for these organisations, and their vigorous opposition to the tour gave a number of their members first-hand experience of Mount Eden's racial imbalance. 'Initially the prisoners were on the side of rugby,' remembers Tim Shadbolt, 'because listening to sport was their escape

Auckland criminal lawyer and future PM David Lange (at back, obscured) is among the placard-holders at this 1976 protest organised by ACORD (Auckland Committee on Racism and Discrimination) against the practice of remanding children to Mount Eden Prison. AUCKLAND LIBRARIES HERITAGE COLLECTIONS, NZMS 521-347-7

from the misery of being locked up. But once the numbers of protesters built up and they started to talk about why they were in there, they won the other guys over to their side.'[59] Tigilau Ness, of the anti-racist group Polynesian Panthers, served nine months with four other anti-tour protesters. 'I was lucky to have a protector,' he said, 'a Polynesian Panther who looked after the five of us. I'd wake up and he'd be at the foot of my bed, guarding us.'[60]

In 1983 the prison was split into three self-contained divisions: a general, a remand and a women's prison, each with its own youth section. This meant subdividing the exercise yards into eight smaller areas bounded by wire fencing (and later by concrete walls), which at last enabled the complete segregation of remand, sentenced and young inmates. A nine-bed medical wing opened in place of the old infirmary.[61] The basement of the north wing was converted into observation cells for psychiatrically disturbed inmates, whose number increased sharply after the city's psychiatric hospitals introduced new admissions criteria. This, said one prison officer, 'practically negates the provision for disturbed inmates to be transferred' from the prison.[62]

Although it had lost its maximum-security status, the reconfigured Mount Eden sometimes held as many as 20 inmates on murder charges, and the 22 cells in the high-security block, known as the 'separates division', were often insufficient for the prison's needs. Among their occupants were escapers from both Mount Eden and other institutions, the very disruptive, those who had asked to be kept apart from others, and 'certain transvestites and active effeminate homosexuals who have to be segregated from the mainstream of the inmate community'.[63] An ever-increasing number of inmates asked to be held in the separates division, generally because they had been charged with the sexual assault of children. The incidence of those crimes increased from 1989, when children were permitted to give evidence in court in the form of video interviews.[64]

Members of rival gangs such as the Mongrel Mob and Black Power also had to be kept apart from each other as much as possible, as 'inevitably there is ill feeling between the various groups'.[65] The Mongrel Mob, regarded by staff as 'the toughest of the tough', were first isolated in E Block but were still able to intimidate other inmates, such as remand prisoners wearing prized footwear or warm clothing.[66] They also upheld the prison's sorry reputation for insecurity that had earned it the nickname of the Outward Bound School.

In September 1983, four gang members on remand sawed though the bars of their cell before dawn with a smuggled hacksaw blade. They climbed onto the roof of the former security block, then over the perimeter wall using plaited blankets.[67] Two years later, a bloody brawl erupted in one of the exercise yards as more than 30 members of the rival Mongrel Mob and Black Power gangs fought with iron bars, chisels from hobby carving activities and other improvised weapons. Three were hospitalised and others treated within the prison.[68]

Finally, in 1987, general manager Brendan Moynihan cracked down on gang culture, and placed members of the same gang in different wings. This may have reduced their ability to exercise dominance over specific areas of the prison, but they remained a formidable threat. Just three years after the crackdown, six Mongrel Mob members pulled off an evidently well-planned escape. During the evening recreation period, when sentenced inmates from two blocks were allowed to mingle, they stabbed one officer with a knife and bashed two more with metal table legs to acquire a set of keys. With these they opened a series of doors, and reached an exterior yard where a long ladder was waiting for them. They climbed the perimeter wall and dropped the considerable distance onto a grass verge. A heavy wire fence still separated them from freedom, but a hole had been cut in it and a gold Ford Falcon was parked across the road. At high speed the six headed north, pursued through the back roads by a convoy of police vehicles. Prison staff blamed the escape, with good reason, on relentless staff cuts. Only four prison officers were on duty in the block where the attack took place, down from eight three months earlier.[69]

The actions of ungovernable prison inmates like these tended to overshadow incidents of generosity and compassion. When Peter Mauriri, a popular officer with 14 years' service, died suddenly on duty in 1987, almost every one of the 354 inmates contributed towards a koha from their minimal weekly allowance. They collected this sum at their own initiative as a sign of their respect for Mauriri and sympathy for his wife and children. 'Peter Mauriri got on very well with everyone,' said Gerry Guy, the chair of the Mount Eden group of the Prison Officers Association, which had largely replaced the PSA as the staff's representative body. 'The inmates' collection was a measure of the respect they had for the man.'[70]

III

The prison had become a short-term holding pen where, typically, inmates were classified and then moved to a more suitable institution elsewhere, usually staying for no more than a fortnight. Most were on remand or awaiting transfer to longer-stay institutions. The smaller number of sentenced prisoners served no more than six months and half their term was routinely remitted for good behaviour.[71] After their evening meal they had a few hours to watch TV, lift weights, and play pool, darts and chess. Christmas Day was the highlight of the year. Cultural groups arrived from around the city to perform and lead the inmates in singing, and they had a choice of two feature films.[72]

Only sentenced inmates wore the dark-blue prison uniform and were allocated jobs in the furniture-making workshops or servicing the prison facilities. Since nothing in the way of trade training or pre-release experience could be expected in the relatively short period they spent there, the limited range of jobs was keenly contested. The kitchen was preferred to the laundry, which handled all the sheets, towels and uniforms. The laundry's moist atmosphere, however, suited the flax used for traditional weaving, and large bunches of it hung from the ceiling. At times inmates were able to contribute to community projects beyond the prison walls. In an echo of the track-cutting project on Rangitoto Island 70 years earlier, hundreds of native seedlings were raised with the help of the Forest and Bird Society, and planted out by low-security prisoners on the Meola Reef public reserve, a former rubbish tip near Westmere.[73]

The staff, once populated by implacable ex-servicemen or failed candidates for the police force, were giving way to younger people and, to the alarm of the older officers, to women. In 1986, at least a decade after North America, Britain and Australia had broken this barrier, the first woman officer was employed to work in the men's division. Linda Brougham did not have to carry out full-body searches, but her duties were otherwise no different from those of her colleagues. The inmates 'have been very respectful', she reported, 'and have probably toned down their behaviour'.[74]

In time, it became apparent that female officers could bring distinctive qualities to their work. 'Male inmates will talk to a female officer about things that they would never discuss with a male,' one of them found, 'like they'll talk about their families and their relationships. They'll discuss their personal problems.'⁷⁵ Cathalena Sinclair, a Samoan-born mother of six, joined the staff in 1989. 'I'm a Pacific Islander and we can have an impact on our people ... We sort of put a calm on them here and so they feel a bit more relaxed while they're doing their time.'⁷⁶ Zane Paine, longtime Mount Eden corrections officer and union delegate, said that 'having women in the [men's] prison was one of the most positive changes I saw'.⁷⁷

By the time Beth McLeod joined the staff around the end of the century, she was one of 20 women officers in the men's prison. As an out lesbian she had chosen not to work in the women's prison where she might be 'at much greater risk of false accusations' of sexual harassment. When she first arrived at her new workplace, she recalls, 'I was struck by the testosterone smell. There's very little natural light and you're enclosed in the walls like an inmate ... In the prison culture you encounter a lot of sexualisation, and you need to have a very good sense of humour.' As it happened, some of her own colleagues proved at least as challenging as the inmates, and in 1998 she won $12,000 compensation from the Auckland Employment Tribunal after her unit manager was found to have harassed her about her sexual orientation.⁷⁸

McLeod learned that the job also required a highly tuned instinct for imminent violence. 'You might be watching a yard from the bridge, with ninety inmates all walking around. There's a stereo going, someone's kicking a ball, it's a nice sunny day. Suddenly the music stops and the men stop walking. You know something's going to happen but you don't know what. Could it be a riot? A mass escape or a fight? Or will some of them jump up on the bridge and take you hostage? When an inmate eyeballs you and says, "I'm going to kill you," to feel love, empathy and compassion in that moment is quite difficult.'⁷⁹

That very situation confronted her colleague Raewyn Abbott, the remand unit manager, in 1996. She was approached in her office by two inmates who suddenly produced improvised knives made from razor blades melted into the plastic handles of cutlery, and held them at her throat. To hamper her movement they took her shoes off, cut down the front of her shirt and tied her hands behind her back. They then took her car keys and, with an arm linked through each of hers and their blades against her neck, ordered her to walk with them to the front gate. That journey took them through the visitors' room and down a flight of stairs, passing numerous staff on the way.

Some thought she was the victim of a practical joke, as she was due to be married two days later. Other staff recognised an escape attempt but did not intervene for fear that the highly agitated men would carry out their threat to fatally slash their colleague. Once through the main gates, the two men unlocked her car; staff surrounded it, but watched helplessly as she was pushed onto the back seat with one man straddled on top of her. Then came a moment of fortuitous confusion as the other hostage-taker was unable to start the car. In that time Abbott succeeded in freeing her hands and unlocking a rear door. Another officer gave the signal to lunge at the kidnappers, and Abbott was rescued unharmed. Remarkably, she returned to work three months later. 'I didn't want those guys to affect the rest of my life,' she said, and at the time of writing she continues to work with the Department of Corrections.[80]

Abbot's experience resulted in several new protocols for dealing with crises in the prison. Emergency flipcharts were developed to guide staff through critical decisions, and specialist debriefing was made available to those traumatised by life-threatening events. Staff were no longer expected simply to 'harden up' after terrifying ordeals like hers.

At least as transformative as the influence of women officers on the culture of the prison was the gradual recognition that Māori culture was inherent to the institution. Just as in wider society, this was an uneven and troubled process that brought dissension and obstruction as well as goodwill. An important step came in 1985 when Reverend Nehe Dewes, from a prominent East Coast family, was appointed prison chaplain, the first Māori to hold this post in the prison's hundred-year history. He introduced services in both Māori and English, and hoped one day to see a Māori cultural centre.[81] More immediately, however, Reverend Dewes became concerned at the rising rate of suicide attempts, bizarre behaviour and violent disorder among the inmates, and particularly among the Māori majority.

In the year he arrived there were eight suicides at the prison. In 1986, on three successive weeks, inmates climbed to the roof of the main building to protest the conditions of their confinement. Since they were in full view of passing vehicles, and provided striking press and TV images, their actions were widely publicised. The last of these episodes of 'roof-walking' was made by two young remand inmates, Gary Hobson and Jackie Waru, who spent an 18-hour vigil on adjacent turrets. Their demands for toilets and washbasins in cells, extra time out of cells in summer, and better facilities and food for remand inmates were not granted. Instead, the prison announced that protruding metal collars would be attached to the drainpipes in the exercise yards to prevent further rooftop sit-ins, and until those were installed the pipes would be kept well greased.[82]

The Justice Department was inclined to attribute the sharp increase in these incidents of disorder and suicide to the growing number of people with psychiatric problems admitted to the prison, and to an increase in suicide in the general population. Others, however, saw them as symptoms of spiritual unrest, especially in the case of Māori inmates psychically damaged by confinement in a site of concentrated suffering. Attention was drawn to the row of gravestones marking where execution victims were buried. Dr Ranginui Walker, chair of the Auckland District Maori Council, pointed out that Māori inmates were, 'in effect, living in an urupa (sacred burial ground) which is a grievous transgression of Maori custom'.[83]

Ethnologist David Simmons claimed that Māori inmates generally, and especially those from Whakatōhea, the tribe to which some of the executed men had belonged, were in spiritual danger. 'I think it would be a wise move on behalf of the Justice Department to move Maori people . . . from the prison until a tohunga-matakite [priestly seer] says it is safe.'[84] These views were at first strongly opposed by the newly appointed prison superintendent, Humphrey Stroud, who considered that, 'this thing has been blown out of proportion . . . We are very alert to the Maori side of things and we are very aware of the needs of different people.' He doubted that anyone could reliably identify those who lay beneath his prison's asphalt. 'They have been there for more than 100 years and people have been walking on them ever since.'[85]

Stroud had first entered Mount Eden as a junior officer in 1956, and after the 1965 riot was decorated for heroism in rescuing trapped inmates from the flames. He was appointed superintendent in 1984 and resisted efforts to exhume the buried bodies for the next five years. Stroud was finally overruled in 1989, when the all-night exhumation described in the introduction to this book was permitted to take place. That pivotal event marked a distinct break with the policies and practices of the past. Mount Eden no longer fulfilled a secondary function as a historic cemetery, and the bodies lying there were granted the long-overdue dignity of reburial in sites where they were welcomed. By finally acknowledging differing cultural practices, and attempting to reckon with historic injustice, the macabre yet moving exhumation ceremony may have relieved some of Mount Eden's accumulated burden of spiritual anguish.

Although Superintendent Stroud was reluctant to accept such arguments, he welcomed multi-million-dollar renovations that the Justice Department hoped would 'shake off the place's forbidding reputation'.[86] The urgency of this work was undeniable. The electrical wiring had become so old and faulty that an electrician was permanently employed just to keep circuits operating. Sewage leaked from damaged pipes into the exercise yards, and on occasion flowed down a ramp towards the basement kitchen in E Block, where inmates struggled to repel it with brooms and fire hoses. Rats heard rustling in the walls proved to be the size of cats, too fat to fit through clay drainpipes.[87]

For inmates, the most eagerly welcomed refurbishment carried out on Stroud's watch was the once-unimaginable luxury of flushing toilets in every cell. High-powered drills bored through solid basalt walls, producing a deafening din that caused entire rows of cells to be temporarily vacated, but as soon as their toilets were functioning, inmates clamoured to be transferred to them, ending the morning ritual of emptying pisspots into a reeking stainless-steel drain.

Even these costly renovations proved incapable of elevating a listed historic building to modern standards, especially as it was consistently overcrowded and understaffed. During 1987 prison staff repeatedly resorted to short-term industrial action and refused to accept further inmates until the 'muster' fell below 366, the largest number they believed could be held securely and humanely. These actions were coordinated with the staff of Carrington psychiatric hospital, a symbiotic institution whose patients were regularly transferred to and from Mount Eden. In September 1987, Carrington staff refused to take further patients referred by the courts, while prison officers banned new admissions until 21 psychiatrically disturbed inmates could be held separately from the main body. This calculated stalemate was resolved by building a new psychiatric wing on the site of the former work-parole unit for day-release inmates, which was moved elsewhere.[88] In addition to these stopgap measures, Missen's 1971 plan for a purpose-built

Auckland Regional Prison was given new priority, and the department promised that a five-storey medium-security prison for 120 male and female inmates would be ready for use by 1989.[89] This and later deadlines came and went with no sign of construction activity.

| | |

Even as the superannuated prison entered its drawn-out final phase of life, it continued to reassert its reputation as 'the hardest jail in New Zealand — worse than Parry'.[90] Career bank robber Simon Kerr made national news in 1994 when he and fellow inmate Shane Thorne climbed up a new ventilation shaft and set up camp in the turret, using mailbags and plastic sheeting for shelter.[91] Kerr says they made their protest after seeing a friend, Tamati Gray, dragged down to the punishment cells with a broken arm. Thorne came down from the roof after a week, but Kerr held out for 13 days until, in an operation that gained maximum media coverage, a mobile crane swung a cageload of prison officers in riot gear above his barricade. In full view of TV cameras, they leaped down on Kerr. 'I fought them to the end,' he says, but he was hauled into the cage and, battered but defiant, sent to solitary for three months.[92]

Kerr had spent several earlier terms in the prison, starting at age 16, and had already escaped from it twice.[93] Mount Eden was evidently unsuitable for such high-risk remand inmates, but all other prisons were too distant from inmates' families, lawyers, probation officers and courthouses. Paradoxically, the long-sentenced inmates of Paremoremo may have posed fewer risks than those facing serious charges on remand since, according to one officer, 'remands are more tense because they're not sure what sentence they're looking at, so they're quick to react to anything'.[94]

In yet another security upgrade, banks of remote-controlled cameras were installed, monitored from offices beneath the Dome, and unsightly rolls of razor wire topped the outer walls to discourage escapes.[95] For many years inmates and their visitors spoke through a clear screen running down the middle of a long table. The screen was removed in the early nineties, but inmates thereafter greeted their visitors attired in close-fitting orange jumpsuits, elasticised at wrists and ankles and with a zip at the back to discourage concealment of contraband such as drugs and cellphones.

Sentenced prisoners were confined in the south wing. They could use a small gym in the east wing exercise yard once used for executions, and the condemned cells were replaced by a kitchen that offered cereal and toast for breakfast, sandwiches and filled rolls for lunch, and a varying menu for dinner. In a development unimaginable a few decades earlier, the kitchen catered for vegan, vegetarian and pork-free diets.[96]

For remand inmates, who were denied work duties, the days passed monotonously and were spent mainly in cramped cells with twin steel bunks. The only natural light came from a small barred window in the back wall, and the lack of heating meant bone-chilling cold in winter, when the infirmary was thronged with cases of colds and flu. These patients were issued with extra blankets and their families could bring them warm clothes, although these might immediately be requisitioned by heavies in the exercise yards.[97] Three hours each morning and afternoon were spent in these barren enclosures, playing bruising games of basketball and 'crash' — a cross between rugby and bullrush. During scorching midsummer weather, the water cannons in the watchtowers were occasionally turned on to provide relief for inmates, although the city council complained that this caused the water pressure in the surrounding area to drop markedly.[98]

For young and first-time inmates the yard could be a terrifying place, dominated by gang members.[99] Requiring juvenile inmates to mix with adults breached a 1993 United Nations convention, but was enforced at Mount Eden on the doubtful grounds that older inmates exercised 'a stabilising effect on younger ones'.[100] Under this regime, and despite a growing awareness of the particular mental health needs of its most vulnerable inmates, Mount Eden gained the dire status of the prison with the highest rate of suicide in the country.[101] Ten inmates killed themselves in 1997 alone. Most were on remand, young, Māori or Polynesian, or all three.

David Tufala, just 15 years old, killed himself while inmates in adjoining cells were frantically ringing their cell alarms and calling for guards. The alarms failed to register at the prison's control centre due to a problem with the power supply. A few months later, 18-year-old Eruera Maaka, who had begged the sentencing judge not to remand him to Mount Eden, was also dead. In a letter to his family two days earlier, he wrote that 'the kingpin wants to smash me . . . I really have nowhere to run. I might as well stay here and get gangbashed.'[102]

Most suicides chose the same method — threading plaited bedsheets around the bars of their cell window, then slumping down until their bodyweight caused them to stop breathing. Losing consciousness was believed to take about 45 seconds.[103] Corrections officers grew accustomed to opening the heavy cell doors and finding a body to be cut down. Eventually, whether the victim was Māori or Pākehā, prison authorities established the practice of asking a local kaumātua to deliver incantations in the cell before a new inmate was placed there.

The primary suicide-prevention tool available to the prison authorities was a risk-assessment form. All inmates filled this in when assessed on admission, and if they gave two or more positive answers to questions about drug and alcohol use or family problems, they were sent to a 16-bed 'special unit' whose cells had no sharp corners, non-rip sheets and no bars to tie them to, and 24-hour video surveillance. Three of the cells, for 'highly active suicidals', were entirely bare apart from a small metal drain in the corner; their occupants wore special 'suicide gowns' made from non-rip material and without zips or buttons. The flaw in this vetting process was the pride that teenage offenders took in appearing 'staunch' and refusing to admit to vulnerabilities.[104] The prison's suicide rate remained appalling, and in 1998 the Howard League for Penal Reform held a protest meeting to condemn it. Over 300 people called for legislation making it illegal for young people to be held in Mount Eden, and for its urgent demolition or closure.[105]

Neither of these demands was met for more than a decade, but as the twenty-first century began a few prison staff introduced a more compassionate approach to engaging with inmates that eventually brought a noticeable lifting of the oppressive atmosphere. The longstanding practice among senior staff, in particular, had been to treat both inmates and each other with a distant and heartless severity, and some officers competed to write up the greatest number of misconduct reports. The routine response to inmates struggling to cope with prison life was 'Harden up — do your lag'. That harsh ethos proved damaging to the domestic lives of the officers themselves, and their profession had a dismal record for marital stability. 'If guys are calling out to you at work all day,' said one divorced officer, 'when you get home the last thing you want to do is talk.'[106]

Younger staff began instead to treat inmates as individuals rather than adversaries. A new system of sentence planning was introduced, with

Peter Williams QC, president of the Howard League for Penal Reform, called for improved conditions for remand inmates during the 1994 rooftop protest by Simon Kerr and Shane Thorne, who are shown in the background of this photograph. *NEW ZEALAND HERALD*

each prison officer assigned a group of up to eight inmates to monitor and support. The officers then developed individual sentence plans for those on remand, and these became rehabilitation plans if the inmates were sentenced. Beth McLeod, an advocate of this approach, said she and her like-minded colleagues had become 'like social workers, because we're there to help them, to rehabilitate them'.[107] The old guard responded by referring to these officers as 'tree-huggers', and insisted that inmates would exploit any sign of weakness or loss of authority among the staff. That risk, however, had always been present, and was eventually addressed by a separate training programme to alert staff to exploitation by inmates.

Sentence planning proved less effective at Mount Eden than in other prisons around the country because inmates were not held there long enough to develop a constructive rapport with their assigned officers. Even so, the early results were so encouraging that staff who initially disparaged the new system began to adopt it. By that time, however, construction had begun in earnest on the long-promised remand prison, and disused outbuildings were demolished to make way for the floor slab of the brand-new structure. No one in the durable old relic alongside could doubt that the death sentence imposed on the prison decades earlier would soon be carried out. All thoughts of sentence planning and other policy initiatives were swept aside, and a drawn-out but inexorable shutdown began.

The inmate muster had reached more than 500, and every one of them had to be securely relocated to a prison elsewhere in the country or to the brand-new Auckland Central Remand Prison (ACRP) standing alongside their own. This $40 million facility, housing 250 remand inmates, opened in July 2000 and became the main reception prison for newly remanded male prisoners in the Auckland region. As each of its gleaming new wings was completed, it was rapidly occupied by Mount Eden inmates, escorted in groups along a temporary elevated tunnel that linked the old and new buildings. Not all inmates welcomed the chance to leave an iconic institution which, for all its discomfort and inconvenience, held a reputation and prestige that its replacement could never match. 'Hey boss, the Rock's the Rock,' these unwilling evacuees told Neville Mark who, as Mount Eden's last prison manager, was charged with managing the shutdown.[108]

Mount Eden's remaining women inmates were moved in 2006 to a new purpose-built women's prison in Manukau City, and their former

The 'honey-brick' prison superintendent's house was built c.1894, near the main prison buildings. The house became the women's prison in 1923 and was vacated by 1988, when a new women's prison was built. The building was demolished in the first years of the twenty-first century to make room for a new Auckland Central Remand Prison. *DEPARTMENT OF CORRECTIONS*

accommodation became a reintegration unit for low-risk sentenced prisoners who were approaching the date of their release.[109]

For all its state-of-the-art equipment and polished appearance, ACRP soon acquired a notoriety to rival its incorrigible neighbour. Mount Eden was the first prison in New Zealand to be administered by a private company, initially the Australian-based GEO Group. A new Labour government was elected in 1999 with a commitment to return it to state operation, but the fee for breaking the management contract obliged them to wait until the contract came up for renewal in 2005. Five years later the National Party was in coalition government, and the prison was re-privatised, with the contract awarded to the British conglomerate Serco. This proved a fraught relationship, and after inmates were found to be running 'fight clubs', allegedly with staff taking bets on the outcome, Serco's contract was revoked in 2015.

The last 50 or so sentenced inmates in Mount Eden spent their final days in the prison repainting its interior walls, and cleaning everything as thoroughly as the antiquated decor allowed. The gloomy, subterranean kitchen had been closed down, so meals were brought over to them from the immaculate facility next door. A supply of 50 mattresses and other bedding was kept in storage for unspecified future requirements. 'We had to mothball the place,' said Mark, 'but at the same time keep it ready to re-open at six months' notice depending on the national prisoner muster, or in case of an emergency like a riot at another prison.'[110] Some of the remand prison's innovative security measures could be enforced across both institutions, helping to keep Mount Eden's final years almost trouble-free. All people and vehicles entering either prison now had to pass through a single entranceway where they could be checked by sniffer dogs for drugs, weapons and other forbidden items such as unauthorised mail.[111]

As the inmate numbers steadily dropped, Mount Eden's resident rat population did likewise. With less food and other comforts available to them, the rats proved more willing to sample the poison baits that for decades had been routinely laid around the corridors. 'Rats know not to eat a bait except when a place is closing,' Mark discovered. He also noticed that the pigeons fluttering around the turrets and upper windows grew much bolder and came up the front steps and into the Dome offices every morning. 'It was as though they were taking back their own property.'

A series of valedictory barbecues and other muted celebrations were held for both inmates and staff in the final weeks. They had been told that soon after the shutdown, part of the old building was likely to reopen as highly distinctive office space for Department of Corrections administrative staff, and there were also rumours of a small museum of the country's penal system. As a result, the formal closing ceremony on 8 July 2011 was a quiet and low-key occasion. After so many strident demands over the previous century for the prison to close, the reality was greeted not with rejoicing but with a mild and nostalgic regret by the skeleton staff present. The national flag flying above the main gates was solemnly lowered, then ceremonially folded and passed to a succession of senior staff, along with the keys to the prison.

'There wasn't a great sense of finality,' Mark recalled, 'because quite a few of us had already started working in the new prison next door and some of the others expected to be back at Mount Eden once it reopened as regional office space. But even so, there was a real sense of sadness that day. The staff would have loved to stay on. For them it felt like leaving home.'

More than 150 years after the first convicts were delivered to the Stockade, and almost a century after the last stones were laid for the building that replaced it, the old prison's walls no longer confined those sentenced for breaking the law. By then it had outlasted so much vilification, and survived so many calls for its demolition, that to those who knew it best the building seemed almost benign, and reassuringly abiding. The old villain had finally been rehabilitated, and its sentence planners looked forward to its future after a long life of crime.

Epilogue
Releasing the ghosts

'Mt Eden Prison is a death trap and an eyesore . . . an awful place, haunted by the ghosts of those who have died within its grim, sunless spaces. It has really bad vibes, the worst of any place I have visited, including the centuries-old slave forts and castles of Ghana.'

These are strong words, especially from an architect. Colin MacGillivray went still further and condemned the old prison as an earthquake risk that 'contributes nothing to the streetscape because it is ugly and largely hidden from view'.[1] He was writing in Auckland's newspaper of record in 2004, several years after the new remand prison had opened alongside Mount Eden and was siphoning off its inmates in batches. By that time the old prison was likely to be closed in the near future and Auckland especially was humming with speculation about its fate. MacGillivray may have offered the most vividly expressed argument for the physical destruction of Mount Eden, but he was writing in a long and vituperative tradition.

In 1971 a Wellington newspaper opined that this 'bleak monument to nineteenth century unenlightened penal policies' would not be mourned when it disappeared. As soon as Paremoremo was ready to receive its first inmates, the *Dominion* predicted confidently, 'that anachronism and disgrace to enlightened society, Mt Eden, can finally be reduced to dust'. The Mount Eden Borough Council, with a particularly close interest in the fate of the prison buildings, made it clear that it would be delighted when the 'antique and archaic monstrosity' was removed from its otherwise tranquil neighbourhood.[2]

In 1973 Labour's Justice Minister, Martyn Finlay, gave the latest in a long series of undertakings to do so, with the qualification that the planned new remand and short-sentence prison must be ready for use before the old one was pulled down.[3] 'Once again Mount Eden Prison is under sentence of death,' intoned the *Herald*. 'But the grey stone walls have survived 34 years of Government attempts to shut it down.'[4] Why those walls remained standing for at least 45 more years is a tale of broken political promises and repeated failure to provide humane and adequate inmate care, but also of slowly evolving recognition of the prison's historic significance and iconic stature.

Just two years after vigorously demanding its removal, the Borough Council revised its position and proposed that after the prison buildings were decommissioned they should be taken over by the Historic Places Trust (later renamed Heritage New Zealand) 'and used in some community capacity, such as a museum'. The Trust's Auckland committee was cautiously supportive. 'It is an historic building in its own right, made from permanent materials, and it would be a serious loss to the community if it was pulled down.'[5] This appears to be the earliest serious indication that the grimy old fortress might have significant heritage and community value once it was no longer in use as a penal facility. Until that point it had not been deemed worthy of preservation, and its eventual demolition was both assumed and widely welcomed. Suddenly, its craggy yet oddly picturesque stone towers appeared too notable to destroy.

In 1976, when National's Justice Minister announced that Auckland must endure the prison for at least another 10 years and that a large sum would be spent upgrading it, the *Herald* continued to press for 'demolition of that monstrous stone edifice'.[6] In 1983, however, the monstrous edifice received a Category 1 classification from the Historic Places Trust. This did not totally protect it from future demolition but empowered the Trust to place a protection order on it if necessary. The building 'has considerable architectural merit', said the Trust. 'Enclosed behind a massive wall the prison has a medieval character incorporating square castellated towers and Gothic windows . . . [it] is an impressive, albeit forbidding, landmark in the Mt Eden district and it is an important record of penal building in the nineteenth century.'[7]

Almost a century after its foundations were laid, and after innumerable promises to raze it, 'the Mount' had acquired the aura of age and endurance, with educational and commercial value in its visual grandeur and lurid past. It was also, of course, still in constant use as a place of incarceration, and its obsolete facilities and inadequacy for any form of rehabilitation were ever more apparent. In the same year the Historic Places Trust awarded the building its highest heritage rating, a group of Labour MPs, including future prime minister Helen Clark, made a tour of inspection and posed, rather unwisely, for a lighthearted press photo behind a barred gateway. Their impressions belied that cheerful image.

Waitākere MP Ralph Maxwell found the prison 'appalling. The conditions that exist, with the cold stone walls and the lack of facilities in most cells, are a world apart from more modern prisons.' He noted that its location had become utterly unsuited to a penal institution with a record of frequent escapes. 'When inmates go over the wall, everything they need is close at hand. Shops and homes to be burgled for money, clothes and food. Cars to be stolen for transport. Perhaps even hostages for the most desperate escapers to use in striking bargains with the police.'[8] The four Opposition MPs criticised the government for its lack of forward planning for a replacement prison, but their own party soon proved little more effective.

Three years later, Labour's Geoffrey Palmer was Minister of Justice, and although he conceded that Mount Eden was 'probably the most unpleasant of all the nation's jails', said that it would nevertheless remain fully occupied. 'The law would not permit animals to be kept in such a place,' retorted the Auckland *Star*. 'It is a blot on New Zealand's justice system and an affront to human dignity. Mr Palmer should reconsider the plans to retain it.'[9] Sir Clinton Roper, a retired High Court judge who chaired a sweeping inquiry into the country's prison system, was equally insistent that Mount Eden should not merely be closed but pulled down altogether.[10]

In defiance of near-universal public opinion, the embattled penitentiary survived both fates, seemingly sustained by a shaky combination of historical momentum and political inertia. The Auckland legal community was a further powerful factor in ensuring its mysterious longevity. Criminal lawyers were determined to keep clients close at hand, where they could be visited quickly, easily and economically, and sometimes persuaded judges to order a long-term remand inmate to be returned there from a more distant prison. A former Corrections officer pointed out: 'A lawyer who has to travel through Auckland to say Springhill [near Meremere], and then try to visit another [client] at Pare [Paremoremo] would spend a couple of hours in traffic. By having all your clients at a central city site you can be done and dusted with prisoner matters and be ready by 10 at the court.'[11] Legal aid lawyers did not lessen their pressure to keep Mount Eden operating until a new remand prison was under construction alongside it.

By the end of the century the Mount Eden muster had nearly doubled since the early 1970s but its facilities had not increased in proportion, so inmates and staff were all placed under worsening conditions. In only a few relatively minor respects could improvements be noted. While the new heritage classification prevented any significant modification to

New paint over century-old stonework — a cellblock atrium in the 1990s. *STUFF LIMITED*

the external structure, some of the gloomy interior walls experienced a remarkable transformation, unthinkable at any earlier period, when talented inmate Dave Bradley covered them in large murals, including a reproduction of Lindauer's *Ana Rupene and Child* in the south wing, and nautical scenes in the visiting room.[12]

When the smart Auckland Central Remand Prison (later the Mount Eden Corrections Facility) opened in 2000, the dreary stone structure alongside appeared even more superannuated. Its long-term future remained indeterminate, and a growing chorus called for its inspired repurposing for public use. The *Herald*'s editorials, which had advocated demolition for decades, now changed course and declared: 'Mt Eden should not be pulled down; it should be combined into a historical and cultural centre which would provide a natural, if at times morbid, attraction.'[13]

This view was supported by a notable former inmate, Arthur Allan Thomas, who had spent nine years in the prison after his wrongful conviction for murdering his neighbours. He remembered the experience with disgust. 'We got up in the morning and emptied our pee pots; the smell was absolutely unbelievable. I still remember it. I couldn't eat my breakfast a lot of mornings.' Yet even he agreed that his unsavoury former residence was too symbolically important to simply destroy. A museum, he thought, would be the most appropriate use for it.[14]

Epsom MP Richard Worth pointed to Tasmania and Alcatraz, near San Francisco, where similar relics of a harsh penal system had been converted into profitable tourist attractions. He hoped the Auckland City Council would keep the 'most forbidding' parts of the building, such as the punishment block and exercise yards, and demolish the 'less architecturally interesting bits'. The income earned from tourists, he felt, could then be put to worthy ends such as providing reading matter in other prisons.[15]

Some continued to press for the building's demolition on the grounds that its past was so discreditable that it should not be allowed to survive as a permanent reminder of official inhumanity. Phil Warren, chair of the Auckland Regional Council, thoughtfully disposed of those arguments. 'The prison has become notorious,' he admitted, 'because of its conditions, and the deaths and suicides that have occurred there', but he suggested that those were the very reasons why its preservation was in the public interest.

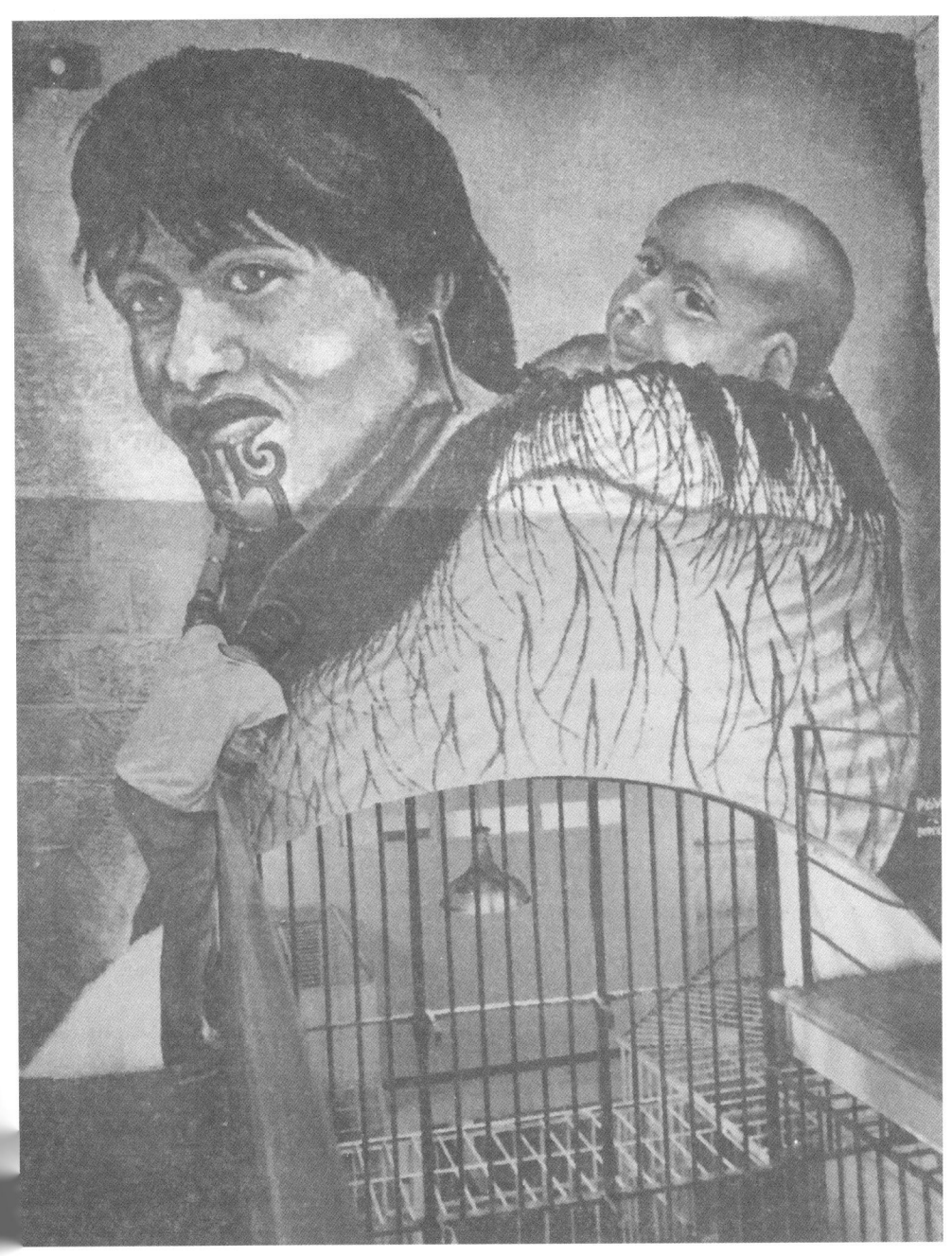

Inmate and artist Dave Bradley puts the finishing touches to his reproduction of Lindauer's 1878 painting *Ana Rupene and Child* in the prison's south wing in 1996. 'It gives the boys something to think about,' he said. 'A lot of them have families and children.' SUNDAY STAR-TIMES

Arthur Allan Thomas spent nine years in Mount Eden for a double murder before he was found to have been wrongfully convicted in 1980. Eighteen years later, when this photo was taken, the sight of the prison could still make him shudder. *NEW ZEALAND HERALD*

We should look to preserve the prison so it can serve as both a lesson and source of history for the next generation. Like it or not, Mt Eden Prison is one of Auckland's most distinctive and best-known historic landmarks . . . It has the potential, if preserved and adapted for reuse, to enhance public understanding of New Zealand's penal system. It has, after all, been one of the main focal points for the concepts of justice, punishment and rehabilitation in the Auckland region since the 1850s.[16]

Neil Smith spent five years in Mount Eden as a conscientious objector during World War Two, and he later lived almost alongside it during a long career as a community adviser for the Auckland City Council. Like Warren, he thought the old building should be preserved in a form that consciously commemorated its former purpose. 'I have long thought that when it does close as a prison it should be gifted to the city or the regional council with the view of enhancing community spirit and understanding of our past and past culture . . . What better place to learn about our past justice system than to take a stroll within its very walls.' Smith was concerned that the Department of Corrections, which had assumed control of the country's prisons from the Justice Department in 1995, seemed to have no clear plans for the building's future, and he feared that because it stood on some of the most valuable real estate in the country the site might be sold to the highest bidder.[17]

Even the most enthusiastic advocates for transforming the prison into a more respectable public institution admitted that it would be a difficult and costly exercise. On top of the fundamental deficiencies built into the original structure under Colonel Hume, subsequent neglect and underfunding had rendered the building a health and safety nightmare. A devastating 2004 Department of Corrections report revealed that the renovations carried out since the 1970s had merely papered over the cracks of larger structural problems, and the building had become so squalid and run-down that much of it failed to comply with current building codes. Vital infrastructure such as sewerage, wiring and fire protection systems were on the brink of failure. The levels of natural light, ventilation and heating were all well below minimum acceptable standards, and facilities for the disabled were almost non-existent.

In a suburb acutely conscious of real-estate values, this Boston Road address was surely the only property at imminent risk of being condemned as dangerous or insanitary under Auckland City Council bylaws, by its staff under recent health and safety legislation, and by its inmates on human rights grounds. 'Options for the future of this facility have been presented over successive Budget cycles to successive governments,' the report noted.[18] Its findings were a hollow echo of the last years of the decrepit Queen Street Gaol, which remained in use for almost 10 years after the opening of its replacement, the Stockade.

The number of people required to endure these shameful conditions was, fortunately, dropping steadily as inmates were transferred elsewhere, and fewer staff were needed to supervise those who remained. Public opinion now conclusively favoured retaining at least part of the prison, but government ministers were unenthusiastic about committing to the massive cost of deferred maintenance. In December 2004 Cabinet approved the plan to expand the new remand centre by at least another 400 beds, finally enabling Mount Eden to be shut down. The government's preferred option for the old prison's subsequent use was to preserve a third of it 'for heritage purposes' but, somewhat improbably, to convert the remainder into administration offices for the Department of Corrections' Auckland staff.[19] That plan did not long survive the process of budgeting for the costs of conversion, or the unenthusiastic reaction of the staff themselves. The *Herald* pointed out that 'the barren nature of the structure means that few in the Corrections Department will queue to work there'.[20] The department opted to rent downtown office space for them instead.

The long list of drawbacks to running a regional office from this distinctive but impractical workplace included not only the expense of renovations but also the many ghosts said to inhabit it. Architect Colin MacGillivray claimed that the prison was haunted by the spirits of those who had died within its walls, and although theirs is a notably stoical and level-headed profession, many former prison officers say they have experienced the presence of supernatural phenomena. From minor oddities, such as a loudspeaker continuing to broadcast eerie voices after it was disconnected from the public-address system, or heavy doors opening suddenly under no apparent impulse, through to more disturbing manifestations, many people familiar with the recesses of the prison describe experiences that defy easy explanation.

The subterranean kitchen in the east wing adjoins the former execution yard, and one newly appointed officer was required to walk through it several times a night during his shift. 'I suddenly felt a cold draught from nowhere, and then I could feel hands rubbing my back. The first time it happened I was so shook up that I told two older officers on the next floor. They said, "It's just haunted, that's all."'[21] Another wing of the building held a battered piano, and for years a succession of nightshift staff reported hearing it playing jaunty dance tunes from the 1920s. If they raced to apprehend the nocturnal performer, the music stopped before they arrived, and they found no sign of any disturbance. Finally the prison manager ordered the piano thrown out, but his staff continued periodically to file reports of mysterious midnight music, always cheery tunes from the same era and from the same remote corridor.

These accounts may seem quaintly implausible on paper; they seem less so when recounted in the first person by people of evident sincerity and commonsense. Perhaps these apparitions are best understood as collective memories of extreme emotional states, psychic expressions of the very real accumulated anguish and violence experienced within the prison walls.

A second wave of major construction began in 2008 when new accommodation blocks and support facilities were added to the remand centre, more than doubling the number of beds it provided. The *Herald* rejoiced that this substantial infrastructure project, costing more than $200 million, would also provide 'a definitive opportunity to rid Auckland of the unloved Victorian edifice' right next door. This time the paper backtracked somewhat on its own earlier suggestion that part of the old prison should be reopened to the public. The *Herald* now claimed that since Mount Eden was surrounded and overshadowed by newer buildings, it would have little visual presence from the street compared with other Victorian-era prisons repurposed as tourist attractions, such as Alcatraz, which is sited magnificently on its own island in San Francisco Bay. As a compromise, proposed the paper:

> Selected sections of the stone wall that was built around the jail in the mid-1870s by prisoners could be retained and incorporated appropriately into the new prison. This would ensure a slice of the site's history was preserved, without

going down the unnecessarily extravagant and inappropriate course of transforming much of the old prison. Many would welcome such a move. Some structures are so forbidding that society breathes a sigh of relief when they are gone. Mt Eden Prison is one.[22]

Three years later the prison stood entirely empty, but four years after that, in 2017, the national inmate muster spiked suddenly, and the recidivist option of re-opening it for emergency prisoner accommodation was briefly canvassed. The Department of Corrections urgently needed 200 extra beds, and its vacated facility in Mount Eden could provide at least that many, in cells which still had working locks on the doors. To the relief of those expected to implement this resurrection, logistical obstacles scuppered the plan at an early stage. 'It would cost several million dollars, and deliver far and away the worst quality [prison] beds nationally,' said Charlie Post, a senior Corrections official responsible for capacity provision. 'Plus the buildings have several ligature points where it's very difficult to control inmates, and there are no rooms for rehabilitation programmes.'[23] His department somehow found space for a second new prison on the closely confined Mount Eden site, and construction of its 245-bed building, at a cost of $140 million, was due to begin at the time of writing.

When completed, that seven-storey structure will overlook a steadily deteriorating heritage building that has lain unused and vacant for at least a decade. Weeds are beginning to push through the cracked tarmac of the exercise yards, and even the seemingly indestructible perimeter wall is showing signs of neglect and decay. Without decisive action to preserve it, the prison's already alarming repair bill will climb higher still, until age and attrition render the building's future moot. Post hopes this outcome can be avoided. 'I firmly believe that Mount Eden has many stories to relate, and it should be telling them. I think there's a significant appetite for a publicly accessible museum.' He believes the cost of that project could be considerably reduced by 'demolishing the less visible and less historically interesting parts of the prison, like the southern and eastern wings, and keeping the rest'.[24]

By repurposing its most notorious prison as a museum, New Zealand would be following proven international practice. Not only Alcatraz but also other former prisons such as Robben Island in South Africa and Fremantle and Melbourne Prisons in Australia have been reopened as compelling interactive museums of their respective penal systems. Even in a reduced form, Mount Eden's looming towers and grim corridors could cater to this universal public appetite for the macabre. And as a national museum of the country's history of crime and punishment, the prison could present that history not in facsimile but in irrefutably solid form for generations to come.

Mount Eden Prison's remarkable longevity makes it a unique stage on which to present some of the most dramatic and significant events of our colonial past. No matter how unappealing or shameful those events may be, nothing is to be gained by continuing to overlook them. When, in recent years, other historically contentious subjects, once misrepresented or ignored, have been opened for examination and debate, the result has been enhanced engagement and redemption in public life.

One intriguing question such a national museum might address is why New Zealand's penal system, although based on the United Kingdom's, has a rate of incarceration almost 50 per cent higher, at 214 per 100,000 citizens, compared with 145. Among OECD countries, New Zealand's rate is surpassed only by the markedly more repressive countries of Chile (233), Lithuania (235), Israel (236) and Turkey (288), while the United States (655) remains the undisputed champion in this field.

Just as the bodies of execution victims, buried for more than a century in the prison grounds, were reverentially exhumed, identified and reburied where they properly belonged, so the many other stories and personal histories embedded in and around the prison's basalt walls are worthy of recording and reconsidering in the light of the present. The ghosts that are said to haunt the prison seem unlikely to be released from it, or from our national consciousness, by tearing down the walls they inhabit.

Notes

Introduction: Bringing up the bodies

1. Interview with Te Kahautu Maxwell, 10 September 2017.
2. Reverend Nehe Dewes, appendix to H. P. Baker, *The Strongest God*, Auckland: Cape Catley, 1990, 236.
3. Personal communication, S. Best, 3 October 2017.
4. Interview with Te Kahautu Maxwell.
5. Dewes, appendix to Baker, *The Strongest God*, 237.
6. Interview with Te Kahautu Maxwell.
7. Personal communication, P. Lister, 5 March 2019.

1: Feculent hovel: 1841–1865

1. J. Coates to Colonial Secretary, 9 April 1842, 1A 1 1842/622, Archives NZ.
2. *Blue Book* 1841, 195, 1A 12 02, Archives NZ.
3. *Daily Southern Cross*, 10 December 1862, 3 (supp.).
4. *New Zealand Herald and Auckland Gazette*, 17 July 1841, 3.
5. Police Magistrate, Auckland to Lieutenant-Governor Hobson, 4 May 1841, IA1 1841/504, Archives NZ.
6. *New Zealand Herald and Auckland Gazette*, 13 October 1841, 3.
7. Percival Berrey, Sheriff, to Colonial Secretary, 4 November 1843, 1A1 28 1844/465, 1843/2010, Archives NZ.
8. J. R. Phillips, 'A Social History of Auckland 1840–1853', MA thesis, University of Auckland, 1966, 188.
9. Una Platts, *The Lively Capital*, Christchurch: Avon Fine Prints, 1971, 70.
10. *New Zealand Herald and Auckland Gazette*, February 1842, quoted in Platts, *The Lively Capital*, 79.
11. Felton Mathew to Colonial Secretary, Auckland, 28 January 1842, 1A 1 1842/168, Archives NZ.
12. IA 1 1842/1132, Archives NZ.
13. *Daily Southern Cross*, 10 December 1862, 3 (supp.).
14. *New Zealand Herald and Auckland Gazette*, 9 October 1841, 2.
15. *New Zealand Herald*, 24 December 1897, 1 (supp.).
16. Ibid., 24 December 1884, 2 (supp.).
17. *New Zealand Gazette and Wellington Spectator*, 26 March 1842, 3.
18. lA 1 42/623, Archives NZ.
19. 'Acts and Proceedings', Auckland Provincial Government, XIV 1862, App. A, no. 11.
20. Richard Hill, *Policing the Colonial Frontier: The Theory and Practice of Coercive Social and Racial Control in New Zealand, 1767–1867*, vol. 1, Wellington: Department of Internal Affairs, Historical Publications Branch, 1986, 179.

21 Platts, *The Lively Capital*, 74.
22 'Kaumatua' (William Porter), *New Zealand Herald*, 24 December 1897, 1 (supp).
23 *New Zealander*, 12 July 1845, 3.
24 Sadly, no further details of this intriguing legal action could be found.
25 Platts, *The Lively Capital*, 76.
26 J. Johnson, Colonial Surgeon, to Governor Hobson, 9 May 1842, 1A 1 1842/633, Archives NZ.
27 J. Coates to Colonial Secretary, 18 May 1842, 1A 1 1842/633, Archives NZ.
28 See, for example, *Daily Southern Cross*, 20 May 1843, 3.
29 *New Zealand Herald and Auckland Gazette*, 25 December 1841, 2.
30 'A Convict's Story: Transportation to Norfolk Island', *Lyttelton Times*, 25 April 1853, 4.
31 Rev. J. F. Churton to Colonial Secretary, Auckland, 4 October 1842, 1A1 16 1842/1980, Archives NZ.
32 Sheriff's office to Governor Shortland, Auckland, 14 November 1842, 1A1 16 1842/1980, Archives NZ.
33 *Daily Southern Cross*, 20 May 1843, 3.
34 William Phelps Pickering, 'Indents of Convicts Locally Convicted or Transported from Other Colonies, Hobart', CON16/1/2, 48, Tasmanian Archives and Heritage Office.
35 Greg Newbold, *The Problem of Prisons: Corrections Reform in New Zealand Since 1840*, Wellington: Dunmore Publishing, 2007, 30.
36 Marginalia to Sheriff's office to Governor Shortland, Auckland, 14 November 1842, 1A1 16 1842/1980, Archives NZ.
37 Happily for Pickering, after four years in Van Diemen's Land he was pardoned, married and returned to New Zealand. There he found work as a government clerk and eventually owned numerous properties in the Wellington region, including a hotel in Tinakori Road. For this information I am grateful for the research of Dr Kristyn Harman, University of Tasmania.
38 P. J. Coleman, *'A Blot on the Statute Book' — Imprisonment for Debt in New Zealand 1840–1990*, Wellington: NZHistoryJock, 2016, 13.
39 Simon Best, 'The Queen Street Gaol: Auckland's First Courthouse, Common Gaol and House of Correction (Site R11/1559)', Auckland: Department of Conservation, Auckland Conservancy, 1992, 25.
40 IA 143/2010, Archives NZ.
41 Percival Berrey, Sheriff, to Colonial Secretary, 18 May 1846, 1A1 50 1846/1026, Archives NZ.
42 Ashworth quoted in Platts, *The Lively Capital*, 76.

43 P. Buddee, *The Fate of the Artful Dodger: Parkhurst Boys Transported to Australia and New Zealand 1842–1852*, Perth: St George Books, 1984, 58–59, 74.
44 *Daily Southern Cross*, 25 November 1843, 2.
45 Ibid.
46 Ibid., 14 September 1844, 2.
47 Ibid., 3 February 1844, 2.
48 *New Zealand Gazette and Wellington Spectator*, 30 September 1844.
49 *New Zealander*, 16 August 1849, 2.
50 Johnson to Colonial Secretary, 19 June 1844, 1A1, 1844/1437, Archives NZ.
51 *Daily Southern Cross*, 2 December 1842, 2.
52 Ibid., 9 December 1843, 3.
53 *Blue Book* 1843, 215, IA 12 05, Archives NZ.
54 Newbold, *The Problem of Prisons*, 220.
55 1A1 1844/720, Archives NZ.
56 'Rules and Regulations of the Auckland Gaol', *Blue Book* 1850, 198, Archives NZ.
57 1A1 1844/484, Archives NZ.
58 'Auckland Gaol — rules and regulations for Crown Prison', *Blue Book* 1844, 197, Archives NZ.
59 Quoted in Best, 'The Queen Street Gaol', 47.
60 Percival Berrey, Sheriff, Auckland, to Colonial Secretary, Auckland, 24 July 1848, IA1 70 1848/1635, Archives NZ.
61 J. Dunn, 'An Enquiry into the New Zealand Prison System 1840–1880', MA thesis, Victoria University of Wellington, 1947, 12–13.
62 P. Berrey to Colonial Secretary, 8 June 1846, 1A1 1847/1964, Archives NZ.
63 Superintendent of Works to Colonial Secretary, 19 October 1843, 1A1 28 1844/465, 1843/2010, Archives NZ.
64 '1844 Rules and Regulations for Auckland Gaol', *Blue Book* 1844, 204, Archives NZ.
65 Sheriff Berrey to Colonial Secretary, 4 November 1843, 1A1 28 1844/465, Archives NZ.
66 C. Bridge RM to Colonial Secretary, 28 September 1848, 1A1 102/1852/456 Archives NZ.
67 *New Zealand Herald*, 24 December 1884, 2 (supp.).
68 *Daily Southern Cross*, 31 August 1875, 5.
69 *New Zealand Herald*, 24 December 1884, 2 (supp.).
70 See, for example, 'Return of sick prisoners treated within the gaol hospital', *Blue Book* 1854, 372, Archives NZ.

71 John Johnson MD to Colonial Secretary, 19 June 1844, 1A 1 44/1437 Archives NZ.
72 F. Thatcher, Superintendent of Public Works, 5 July 1845, 1A1 43/1845/1072, Archives NZ.
73 Cotton quoted in Platts, *The Lively Capital*, 124.
74 Platts, *The Lively Capital*, 79.
75 Resident Magistrates Outward Letterbook 1848–55, 1858, quoted in Best, 'The Queen Street Gaol', 100.
76 P. Berrey to Colonial Secretary, 18 October 1847, 1A1 62 1847/1964, Archives NZ.
77 Quoted in Coleman, *'A Blot on the Statute Book'*, 15.
78 *Daily Southern Cross*, 24 February 1844, 2.
79 1A1 69 1848/1362, Archives NZ.
80 Native Secretary to Governor, 20 March 1856, 1A1 170 1856/2084, Archives NZ.
81 Ordinance for the Regulation of Prisons 1846, s. 9, 13, qPam 1846 NZ 20, Alexander Turnbull Library (ATL).
82 *New Zealander*, 3 June 1848, 2.
83 Ibid., 27 October 1847, 2.
84 Ibid., 21 June 1848, 2.
85 Quoted in Robert Burnett, *Penal Transportation: An Episode in New Zealand History,* Occasional papers in criminology no. 9, Wellington: Victoria University of Wellington, 1978, 29.
86 As with William Pickering, Margaret Reardon's life took a kinder course after her transportation. She married an ex-convict in Australia and raised two children before her death at the age of 80. www.eoe.convictwomenspress.com.au/index.php/biographical-dictionary/22-r/144-reardon-margaret.
87 William Davies, Colonial Surgeon, 5 May 1849, 1A1 79 1849/1214, Archives NZ.
88 Percival Berrey to Colonial Secretary, 7 March 1851, 1A1 1851/421, Archives NZ.
89 G. J. Arney, 'Memorandum Concerning the Gaols at Auckland,' *Appendices to the Journals of the House of Representatives (AJHR)*, 1861, D-2A, 11.
90 Ibid., 10.
91 Ibid., 9.
92 1A 1 1852/2629, Archives NZ.
93 *Daily Southern Cross*, 21 January 1853, 2.
94 Arney, 'Memorandum Concerning the Gaols at Auckland', 9.

95 Quoted in Alan G. L. Shaw, *Convicts and the Colonies: A Study of Penal Transportation from Great Britain and Ireland to Australia and Other Parts of the British Empire*, London: Faber & Faber, 1966, 33.
96 *New Zealander*, 16 August 1849, 2.
97 Quoted in Burnett, *Penal Transportation*, 19.
98 Burnett, *Penal Transportation*, 20–21.
99 Percival Berrey, Sheriff, to Colonial Secretary, Auckland, 13 May 1846, 1A1 50 1846/1026, Archives NZ.
100 William Davies, Surgeon, to Sheriff, 18 May 1846, 1A1 50 1846/1026, Archives NZ.
101 Secondary Punishment Act 1854, s. 9.
102 Burnett, *Penal Transportation*, 44.
103 *Maori Messenger*, 1 January 1855, 10.
104 1A 12/15 pp. 351-4, Archives NZ.
105 *Blue Book* 1852, 170; 1854, 348, Archives NZ.
106 Arney, 'Memorandum Concerning the Gaols at Auckland', 11.
107 *Daily Southern Cross*, 18 September 1855, 3.
108 L. O'Brien, Sheriff, to William Brown, Superintendent, Auckland, 17 September 1855, ACGO 8333 1A1/158 1855/3094, Archives NZ.
109 T. M. Philson Casebook, 'Return of Sickness Treated in City Gaol', 1858, Auckland University Library special collections MSS & Archives, 2004/5.
110 Auckland Provincial Council Votes and Proceedings 1862, Report A, No. 11, quoted in Best, 'The Queen Street Gaol', 26.
111 G. Arney, 'Report on Auckland Gaols', J1 1861/447, Archives NZ.
112 *New Zealander*, 8 June 1861, 5.
113 *Daily Southern Cross*, 2 September 1864, 5.
114 *New Zealander*, 21 December 1864, 4; 23 December 1864, 5; 2 March 1865, 3.
115 Ibid., 20 December 1864, 4.
116 *New Zealand Herald*, 24 December 1884, 2 (supp.).
117 Ibid., 21 December 1863, 2.
118 Ibid.
119 *Daily Southern Cross*, 22 November 1865, 4.
120 *New Zealand Herald*, 19 November 1866, 4.

2: Paste-board gaol: 1855–1876

1 W. Mason, Provincial Architect, to Superintendent, Auckland, 16 November 1855, IA1 159 1855/3847, Archives NZ.
2 Jennifer Wilkins, 'Eden in Auckland', *New Zealand Geographic*, no. 140, July–Aug 2016, 88–103.

3   C. J. Martin, 'Memorandum on Draft Report of Committee on Secondary Punishment in Lieu of Transportation', *Appendices to the Journals of the House of Representatives (AJHR)*, 1854, 1–2.
4   Ibid., 8–9.
5   Quoted in André Brett, *Acknowledge No Frontier: The Creation and Demise of New Zealand's Provinces, 1853–76*, Dunedin: Otago University Press, 2016, 85.
6   *Daily Southern Cross*, 17 April 1855, 2; 2 October 1855, 3.
7   *New Zealander*, 12 April 1856, 3; *Auckland Provincial Gazette*, 30 July 1856, 144.
8   R. I. M. Burnett, *'Hard Labour, Hard Fare and a Hard Bed': New Zealand's Search for its Own Penal Philosophy*, Occasional Monographs Series no. 1, Wellington: National Archives of New Zealand, 1995 18; *Weekly News*, 27 August 1864, 6.
9   'Provincial Council Session', *New Zealander*, 25 January 1862, 5.
10 *Daily Southern Cross*, 7 November 1867, 3.
11 *New Zealander*, 11 October 1856, 3.
12 *Daily Southern Cross*, 26 August 1856, 2.
13 Ibid., 2 December 1856, 3; 12 December 1856, 3.
14 Ibid., 25 August 1864, 5.
15 *New Zealand Government Gazette*, 8 September 1856.
16 Dr McGauran, 1 June 1857, 1A1 1857/894, Archives NZ; *New Zealand Government Gazette*, 26 June 1857.
17 Evidence of Dr Philson, 'Board to inquire and report on matters connected with the prisons of the Province', 20 June 1861, NZ MSS595, Auckland Provincial Council records, Auckland Public Library.
18 *New Zealander*, 7 December 1861, 5.
19 'Board to inquire and report on matters connected with the prisons of the Province', 20 June 1861, NZ MSS 595, Auckland Provincial Council records, Auckland Public Library.
20 *New Zealander*, 4 May 1865, 2.
21 *Auckland Provincial Government Gazette*, vol. 7, no. 7, 12 March 1858, 4.
22 *New Zealand Herald*, 19 July 1864, 3.
23 *Auckland Star*, 17 March 1877, 2.
24 '1855 Regulations, Auckland Gaol', ACGO 8333 1A1/158 1855/3291, Archives NZ.
25 *New Zealander*, 8 June 1861, 5.
26 'Reports and Memoranda of the Judges of the Supreme Court of New Zealand', *AJHR*, 1861, D2-A, 5–8.
27 Ibid., 8.

28 *Daily Southern Cross*, 2 December 1862, 3.
29 Ibid., 2 September 1864, 5.
30 George McElwain, gaoler, 31 March 1862, NZ MSS 595, Auckland Provincial Council Records, Auckland Public Library.
31 *New Zealander*, 19 April 1862, 2.
32 Ibid., 4 June 1862, 3.
33 Ibid., 22 October 1864, 4.
34 *Daily Southern Cross*, 23 September 1863, 3.
35 Ibid., 25 August 1864, 5.
36 *New Zealand Herald*, 22 November 1865, 4.
37 Ibid., 19 April 1864, 4.
38 *New Zealander*, 13 April 1864, 3.
39 *New Zealand Herald*, 16 April 1864, 4.
40 Ibid.
41 *New Zealander*, 21 April 1864, 3.
42 *Daily Southern Cross*, 16 June 1864, 3.
43 *New Zealand Herald*, 19 July 1864, 3.
44 *Daily Southern Cross*, 24 August 1864, 4.
45 'Report Furnished by the Inspectors of Gaols and Prisons for the Province of Auckland, on the subject of granting "class" or "exertion" money to prisoners at the Mount Eden Gaol, 14 May 1867', Auckland Provincial Council records, Auckland Public Library.
46 *Daily Southern Cross*, 26 November 1866, 6.
47 *New Zealand Herald*, 22 November 1865, 4.
48 *New Zealander*, 27 April 1865, 2.
49 *New Zealand Herald*, 4 March 1865, 5.
50 *New Zealander*, 4 May 1865, 2.
51 *Daily Southern Cross*, 4 March 1865, 4.
52 Ibid., 21 November 1866, 5.
53 *New Zealand Herald*, 15 February 1867, 4.
54 Ibid., 6 February 1867, 4.
55 *Daily Southern Cross*, 16 March 1865, 4.
56 Ibid., 12 April 1865, 4.
57 Ibid., 16 March 1865, 4.
58 *New Zealander*, 10 April 1865, 3.
59 Ibid., 4 May 1865, 2.
60 Ibid.
61 *New Zealand Herald*, 9 February 1867, 5.
62 *Daily Southern Cross*, 11 October 1864, 4.
63 *New Zealander*, 4 May 1865, 2.

64 B. Maclean, Annual Report on Mount Eden Gaol, 15 January 1875; inwards letters, 22 February 1875, AP2 27 521/75, Archives NZ.
65 Evidence of Mrs Andrewartha, *New Zealand Herald,* 20 February 1867, 3.
66 *New Zealand Herald,* 22 November 1865, 4; 'Report of Mount Eden Goal Enquiry Committee', *Journal of the Auckland Provincial Council,* Sess. XX 1866–7, A-10, 55; Robyn Anderson, '"The Hardened Frail Ones": Women and Crime in Auckland, 1845–1870', MA thesis, University of Auckland, 1981, 186.
67 *Daily Southern Cross,* 2 December 1865, 5.
68 *New Zealand Government Gazette,* no. 39, 29 June 1866, 26; Anderson, '"The Hardened Frail Ones"', 182.
69 Ibid., 175; 'Report of Mount Eden Gaol Enquiry Committee', 53–54.
70 *New Zealand Herald,* 20 February 1867, 3.
71 Ibid., 14 February 1867, 4.
72 Ibid., 24 January 1866, 5.
73 Jenny Coleman, *Polly Plum: A Firm and Earnest Woman's Advocate: Mary Ann Colclough 1836–1885,* Dunedin: Otago University Press, 2017, 85.
74 *Daily Southern Cross,* 6 December 1871, 3.
75 Coleman, *Polly Plum,* 122.
76 See, for example, J. Broadhead, 'An Enquiry into the New Zealand Prison System 1840–1880', MA thesis, Victoria University of Wellington, 1947, 96–102; Anderson, '"The Hardened Frail Ones"', 179.
77 *New Zealand Herald,* 2 March 1867, 5; 20 September 1866, 3.
78 *Daily Southern Cross,* 2 December 1865, 5.
79 *Auckland Weekly News,* 11 August 1866, 15.
80 Report of Penal Establishment Committee, *AJHR, 1866,* F-14, 3.
81 *Daily Southern Cross,* 6 February 1866, 5.
82 Ibid., 6 April 1866, 4.
83 Ibid., 5 April 1865, 5.
84 *New Zealand Herald,* 9 April 1866, 4.
85 Ibid., 7 May 1866, 6.
86 *Daily Southern Cross,* 18 May 1866, 3.
87 Ibid., 4 August 1866, 4.
88 Ibid., 18 May 1866, 3.
89 *New Zealander,* 4 May 1865, 2.
90 *Daily Southern Cross,* 4 August 1866, 4.
91 Report from Visiting Justices, 28 February 1866, *Journals of the Auckland Provincial Council,* Sess. XI, 165–66, A-14; *Daily Southern Cross,* 9 July 1866, 5.
92 *New Zealand Herald,* 5 December 1866, 5.

93 *Colonist*, 23 October 1866, 2.
94 *Daily Southern Cross*, 19 November 1866, 5.
95 Ibid., 26 November 1866, 6.
96 AJHR, 1854, Appendix A to Report of Secondary Punishment Committee, 2.
97 *New Zealand Herald*, 7 February 1867, 6.
98 Ibid., 16 February 1867, 6.
99 Ibid., 18 February 1867, 3.
100 Ibid., 6 February 1867, 4.
101 Ibid., 5.
102 1A1 2191 1867/1955, Archives NZ.
103 *New Zealand Herald*, 15 February 1867, 4.
104 Quoted in J. Dunn, 'An Enquiry into the New Zealand Prison System', MA thesis, Victoria University of Wellington, 1947, 75.
105 *New Zealand Herald*, 6 February 1867, 5.
106 Ibid., 14 February 1867, 4.
107 Ibid., 18 February 1867, 3.
108 Ibid., 19 February 1867, 4.
109 Ibid., 22 February 1867, 4.
110 Ibid., 5 March 1867, 5.
111 Ibid., 28 February 1867, 3.
112 *Daily Southern Cross*, 31 January 1867, 6.
113 Annual report of B. Maclean, Visiting Justice, 15 January 1875, AFCM 8180 A1627 AP2 27/ 521/75, Archives NZ.
114 *New Zealand Herald*, 22 November 1865, p4.
115 'Return, furnished by the Governor and Gaoler [R. A. Eyre], showing the number of Male Prisoners attending the school at Mount Eden Gaol from June to December 1868, their state of education, and the progress made, 20 January 1869', Auckland Provincial Council records, Auckland Public Library.
116 *Auckland Provincial Government Gazette*, 4 May 1867, no. 22, 152.
117 Ibid.
118 'Reports of Royal Commission on Prisons', *AJHR*, 1868, A-12, 3.
119 Ibid., 18.
120 *Daily Southern Cross*, 6 February 1867, 3.
121 *New Zealand Herald*, 4 March 1869, 4.
122 *Daily Southern Cross*, 29 September 1868, 4.
123 *New Zealand Herald*, 17 March 1869, 3.
124 Ibid.; *Dictionary of New Zealand Biography*, www.teara.govt.nz/en/biographies/2t32/te-wake-heremia

125 Brent McAlister, *From Farms and Flats: The History of Land Use in Mount Eden*, Auckland: Mount Eden Borough Council, 1983, 20.
126 *Daily Southern Cross*, 8 January 1863, 3.
127 *Auckland Star*, 17 September 1872, 2.
128 R. Clough et. al, *Mt Eden Prison Monitoring: Progress Report, Wall*, Wellington: Department of Corrections, 2009, 6.
129 *Auckland Star*, 17 September 1872, 2.
130 Ibid., 21 March 1872, 2.
131 *Daily Southern Cross*, 1 April 1872, 2.
132 *Auckland Star*, 11 May 1872, 2.
133 Ibid., 9 August 1872, 2.
134 'Report of the Auckland Gaol Commissioners and correspondence thereon', *AJHR*, 1877, H-30, 2.
135 Report of B. Maclean, Visiting Justice, 1874, AFCM 8180 A1627 AP2 27/521/75, Archives NZ.
136 *Auckland Star*, 13 January 1873, 2.
137 Quoted in Anderson, '"The Hardened Frail Ones"', 111.
138 R. Ayre, Governor and gaoler, to Provincial Secretary George Jeffrey, 27 January 1874, 1A1 361 1874/397, Archives NZ.
139 Wardress Mt Eden Gaol, 30 April 1874, Gaoler, HM Gaol, Auckland, to Superintendent, Auckland, AP2 46 734/76, Archives NZ.
140 'Reports and memoranda of the Justices of the Supreme Court of New Zealand', *AJHR*, 1861, D-2a, 7.
141 'Reports of the Royal Commission on Prisons', *AJHR*, 1868, A-12, 15, 29.
142 'Application from officers of the Mount Eden Gaol for increased salary and relaxation of present hours of duty', *Auckland Provincial Council Journal*, Sess. XXIX, 1874.
143 *Auckland Provincial Gazette*, 10 October 1876, 427.

3: Stone Jug: 1877–1909

1 *Auckland Star*, 19 December 1876, 3.
2 Ibid., 22 December 1876, 2.
3 Ibid., 4 January 1877, 3.
4 'Report of the Auckland Gaol Commissioners and correspondence thereon', *Appendices to the Journals of the House of Representatives (AJHR)*, 1877, H-30, 4; *New Zealand Herald*, 2 October 1877, 2; *AJHR*, 1878, I-4, 27.
5 *New Zealand Herald*, 5 March 1870, 5; *Daily Southern Cross*, 1 April 1870, 7.
6 *Auckland Star*, 11 February 1878, 3.

7   *New Zealand Herald*, 2 October 1877, 2.
8   Report of Visiting Justice Thomas Cheeseman, 19 January 1877, Reports on Auckland (Mt Eden) prison including prison plans; gaol commission report; statistical and financial returns of gaol for 1876; J1 259 m 1880/413, Archives NZ.
9   Mr Barstow, Visiting Justice, to Minister of Justice, 6 September 1879, ibid.
10 Ibid.
11 L. O'Brien, Governor and gaoler, report to Minister of Justice, 1 January 1880, ibid.
12 O'Brien to Under-Secretary, Justice Department, 29 December 1877, ibid.
13 *New Zealand Herald*, 2 October 1877, 2.
14 L. O'Brien, Governor and gaoler, to Visiting Justices, 13 February 1878, Reports on Auckland (Mt Eden) prison including prison plans; gaol commission report; statistical and financial returns of gaol for 1876; J1 259 m 1880/413, Archives NZ.
15 Memorandum for acting Colonial Architect, 11 November 1878, ibid.
16 'Report of the Auckland Gaol Commissioners and correspondence thereon', *AJHR*, 1877, H-30, 1.
17 Ibid., 4.
18 'Reports on Auckland prison including prison plans', J1 259 m 1880/413, Archives NZ.
19 *New Zealand Herald*, 14 May 1879, 4.
20 *AJHR*, 1878, I-4, i.
21 *New Zealand Herald*, 3 February 1881, 4.
22 'Appointment of Inspector of Prisons,' *AJHR*, 1881 H-4A, 4.
23 M. P. Mayhew, *The Prison System of New Zealand 1840–1824*, Wellington: Department of Justice, 1959, 39.
24 *Observer*, 26 November 1881, 12.
25 'Report of Inspector of Prisons', *AJHR*, 1881, H-4, 1–2.
26 *Observer*, 27 November 1881, 162.
27 *Auckland Star*, 29 November 1882, 2.
28 Thomas Y. Wilson, 'New Zealand Prisons 1880–1909: The Administration of Colonel Arthur Hume', MA thesis, Victoria University of Wellington, 1970, 101.
29 Ibid., 102.
30 *New Zealand Herald*, 2 October 1877, 2.
31 Wilson, 'New Zealand Prisons 1880–1909', 68.
32 *Auckland Star*, 20 February 1878, 2.

33 Patricia Webb, *A History of Custodial and Related Penalties in New Zealand*, Wellington: Government Printer, 1982, 112–13 and ch. 5.
34 'Report of Gaols Management', *AJHR*, 1878, I-4, 28.
35 John Pratt, *Punishment in a Perfect Society: The New Zealand Penal System 1840–1939*, Wellington: Victoria University Press, 1992, 139.
36 Auckland Prison regulations in 'Prison file of Thomas Hall, murderer', DAHB 5861 A1282 1/, Archives NZ.
37 'CE Mackay inmate file (1920-26)', W2636 J17313 /6 1920/3112, Archives NZ. I am grateful to Paul Diamond, the biographer of Mount Eden inmate Charles Mackay, for this information.
38 *Auckland Star*, 30 June 1887, 8.
39 'Prison file of Thomas Hall, murderer', DAHB 5861 A1282 1/, Archives NZ.
40 *Auckland Star*, 21 April 1884, 2.
41 New Zealand Parliamentary Debates (*NZPD*), vol. 47, 23 June 1884, 278.
42 *Auckland Star*, 18 April 1878, 4.
43 Tristan Egarr, 'Discipline and Defence: Military Influence on Policing and Imprisonment c. 1870–1913', MA thesis, Victoria University of Wellington, 2010, 25.
44 Mayhew, *The Prison System of New Zealand*, 43, 53.
45 *AJHR*, 1884, H-5, 4; 1886, H-4, 4.
46 Clough and Associates, *Doing Time at the Mount: Archaeological Investigations at Mt Eden Prison Final Report*, Wellington: Department of Corrections, 2008, 20.
47 *New Zealand Herald*, 21 November 1882, 6.
48 Ibid.
49 *New Zealand Herald*, 2 November 1886, 4.
50 Ibid., 26 September 1892, 6.
51 Personal communication, Charlie Post, 29 March 2019.
52 Felix Timmerman, 'Construction Report, Mt Eden Prison Building', Department of Corrections, undated.
53 *Auckland Star*, 21 March 1889, 5; *Evening Star*, 17 June 1909, 2.
54 *Auckland Star*, 2 January 1896, 5.
55 *New Zealand Herald*, 7 January 1896, 5.
56 *NZPD*, vol. 83, 3 July 1894, 195.
57 *Auckland Star*, 26 June 1909, 13.
58 *New Zealand Herald*, 2 June 1879, 5.
59 *Auckland Star*, 26 June 1909, 13.
60 Ibid.
61 Ibid.
62 Sandra Coney, *Standing in the Sunshine: A Social History of*

New Zealand Women Since They Won the Vote, Auckland: Penguin, 1993, 122. I am grateful to Sandra Coney for referring me to this information.

63 *Auckland Star*, 27 June 1893, 1.
64 Ibid., 22 March 1886, 4.
65 J. Dunn, 'An Inquiry into the New Zealand Prison System 1840–1880', MA thesis, Victoria University of Wellington, 1947, 74–76.
66 'Report of Inspector of Prisons', *AJHR*, 1882, H-6, 2.
67 Bronwyn Dalley, 'Prisons Without Men: The Development of a Separate Women's Prison in New Zealand', *New Zealand Journal of History*, vol. 27, no. 1, 1993, 41–42.
68 Department of Justice, Prisons Branch, *AJHR*, 1907, H-20, 5.
69 A. Friend, *A Faithful Standard Bearer: Life of Duncan MacPherson*, Auckland: Clark & Matheson, 1914, 115.
70 *New Zealand Herald*, 24 March 1890, 6.
71 Department of Justice, Prisons Branch, *AJHR*, 1890 H-4, 4.
72 *AJHR*, 1895, H-20, 5.
73 The industrial school housed boys convicted of minor crimes, or without adequate adult support. They were given some basic schooling, carried out most of the routine work of washing, cleaning and cooking, and were sent out to work as apprentices, messenger boys and the like whenever a position could be found for them. Their wage was paid to the school, which kept a little back for them on their release but put most of the money towards their upkeep.
74 *New Zealand Herald*, 4 November 1886, 3.
75 P. J. Whelan, 'Care of Destitute, Neglected and Criminal Children 1840–1900', MA thesis, Victoria University of Wellington, 1956, 142.
76 'Auckland Prison gaoler's report', *AJHR*, 1902, H-20, 9; 1907, H-20, 5.
77 'Inspector of Prisons report', *AJHR*, 1904, H-20, 3; 1905, H-20, 4.
78 'Inspector of Prisons report', *AJHR*, 1886, H-7, 4.
79 'Auckland Prison gaoler's report', *AJHR*, 1907 H-20, 4.
80 *Observer*, 2 May 1891, 6.
81 *AJHR*, 1901, H-20, 4.
82 *Auckland Star*, 23 May 1903, 4.
83 *AJHR*, 1901, H-20, 4.
84 *New Zealand Herald*, 13 February 1892, 1 (supp.).
85 *Auckland Star*, 2 September 1892, 4.
86 Ibid., 17 September 1909, 6.
87 Ibid.
88 *New Zealand Herald*, 11 January 1888, 4.

89   Ibid., 26 September 1892, 6.
90   *Observer*, 21 September 1889, 11.
91   *New Zealand Herald*, 5 August 1882, 5.
92   *Auckland Star*, 21 February 1887, 2.
93   *New Zealand Herald*, 23 May 1893, 5.
94   *AJHR*, 1905, H-20, 3.
95   *NZPD*, vol. 121, 5 August 1902, 181.
96   *Observer*, 25 March 1905, 3.
97   *Evening Star*, 22 July 1905, 8.
98   *Observer*, 25 March 1905, 3.
99   *AJHR*, 1905, H-20, 3.
100 *Observer*, 25 March 1905, 3.
101 *New Zealand Herald*, 28 August 1906, 4.
102 *AJHR*, 1909, H-20, 4; Webb, *A History of Custodial and Related Penalties in New Zealand*, 16–18.
103 Quoted in David Gee, *The Devil's Own Brigade: A History of the Lyttelton Gaol 1860–1920*, Wellington: Millward Press, 1975, 38.
104 Quoted in Mayhew, *The Prison System of New Zealand,* 95.
105 *NZPD*, vol. 150, 1910, 349.
106 *Auckland Star,* 3 March 1909, 8.
107 Ibid., 11 August 1909, 4.
108 James L. A. Kayll, *A Plea for the Criminal*, Invercargill: W. Smith Commercial Printers, 1905, 77.
109 Whelan, 'Care of Destitute, Neglected and Criminal Children', 91.
110 *Auckland Star,* 3 March 1909, 8.
111 Hon. Dr Findlay, 22 October 1909, *NZPD*, vol. 147, 1909, 458–59.

4: Brutal Bastille: 1910–1922

1   Jack Perkins (producer), 'Men of Broad Arrow' (pt. 1), Spectrum documentary, Radio NZ, 1974.
2   J. A. Lee, *Delinquent Days*, Auckland: Collins, 1967, 118.
3   Ibid.
4   *Otago Daily Times*, 12 April 1911, 5.
5   *New Zealand Herald*, 2 May 1912, 8.
6   Lee, *Delinquent Days*, 23; *New Zealand Herald*, 31 January 1918, 4; *Auckland Star*, 8 November 1924, 12.
7   Perkins, 'Men of Broad Arrow'.
8   Ibid.
9   Lee, *Delinquent Days*, 118.
10 Ibid., 120.

11 Perkins, 'Men of Broad Arrow'.
12 Lee, *Delinquent Days*, 122.
13 'Prison Life of a Striker', *Maoriland Worker*, 10 January 1913, 8.
14 *Maoriland Worker*, 15 November 1912, 2; *Auckland Star*, 19 September 1912, 5.
15 Perkins, 'Men of Broad Arrow'.
16 Lee, *Delinquent Days*, 122.
17 From Kendrick Smithyman, '1912', in Kendrick Smithyman, *Imperial Vistas Family Fictions*, Auckland: Auckland University Press, 2002, 73. I am grateful to Smithyman's anthologist, Scott Hamilton, for drawing my attention to this poem.
18 Patricia Mayhew, *The Penal System of New Zealand, 1840–1924*, Wellington: Department of Justice, 1959, 105.
19 *New Zealand Herald*, 9 March 1974, sec. 2, 3.
20 Lee, *Delinquent Days*, 122.
21 'Prison Life of a Striker', 8.
22 W. Parry to T. Franklin, 2 September 1912, 09/02/2060, Capper Collection, Waihī Museum.
23 *New Zealand Herald*, 15 November 1912, 8.
24 Lee, *Delinquent Days*, 125.
25 Perkins, 'Men of Broad Arrow'.
26 *Evening Post*, 21 June 1911, 7.
27 Perkins, 'Men of Broad Arrow'.
28 Lee, *Delinquent Days*, 120.
29 *Auckland Star*, 16 March 1914, 6.
30 Ibid.
31 Ibid.
32 *Appendices to the Journals of the House of Representatives (AJHR)*, 1913, H-20, 5.
33 District Engineer, Public Works Department, to Under-Secretary Public Works Department, 5 May 1916, 'Mt Eden Prison, Auckland', AAQB 889 W3950 596/ 25/69 pt 2, Archives NZ.
34 'Plans of south wing extension, 1913', BBAD A717 24137, Box F86, Archives NZ.
35 Under-Secretary, Department of Justice to Under-Secretary, Public Works Department, 19 June 1914, 'Mt Eden Prison, Auckland', AAQB 889 W3950 596/ 25/69 pt 1, Archives NZ.
36 *AJHR*, 1913, H-20, 5.
37 Ibid., 8.
38 Ibid., 1915, H-20, 9.

39 Ibid., 1918, H-20, 2.
40 Ibid., 1917, H-20, 10.
41 Ibid., 1918, H-20, 2.
42 Ibid., 1917, H-20, 3.
43 Mayhew, *The Penal System of New Zealand*, 111–12.
44 *New Zealand Herald*, 28 March 1911, 8.
45 *Auckland Star*, 10 May 1912, 8.
46 *Maoriland Worker*, 6 September 1912, 3.
47 Henry Holland, *Armageddon or Calvary?: The Conscientious Objectors of New Zealand and 'The Process of Their Conversion'*, Wellington: Maoriland Worker Printing and Publishing Co., 1919, 106.
48 *Auckland Star*, 27 April 1917, 2; 30 April 1917, 6.
49 *AJHR*, 1918, H-20, 2.
50 Ibid., 1915 H-20, 9.
51 Holland, *Armageddon or Calvary?*, 115; *New Zealand Herald*, 14 January 1918, 4.
52 Mayhew, *Prison System of New Zealand*, 112.
53 *Maoriland Worker*, 3 January 1917, 4; 10 January 1917, 4.
54 *Grey River Argus*, 24 May 1917, 3.
55 Mayhew, *The Penal System of New Zealand*, 112.
56 *Grey River Argus*, 3 October 1917, 4.
57 *AJHR*, 1918, H-20, 2.
58 Holland, *Armageddon or Calvary?*, 116.
59 Ibid.
60 Paul Baker, *King and Country Call: New Zealanders, Conscription and the Great War*, Auckland: Auckland University Press, 1988, 178.
61 *N.Z. Truth*, 8 August 1914, 12.
62 *Sunday Star-Times*, 18 December 2016, 1.
63 Athol Jackson interview, Tape 2, OHC 7389_PM_S_01, Quaker Oral History Project (OHColl-0427), ATL, interviewer Katherine Knight, 20 April 1990.
64 'Distribution of pamphlet "Guilty" amongst conscientious objectors', J40 W1190 262 1918/19/10, Archives NZ.
65 Secretary of State for the Colonies to Governor-General, 19 June 1918, G1 233 1918/2261, Archives NZ.
66 Lowell Thomas, *The Sea Devil's Fo'c'sle*, London: William Heinemann, 1930, 250–51.
67 Robin Hyde, *Nor the Years Condemn*, Dunedin: Otago University Press, 1995 (1st edn 1938), 194.
68 Thomas, *The Sea Devil's Fo'c'sle*, 254–55.

69 *Auckland Star*, 7 August 1916, 3; 3 August 1916, 5.
70 *New Zealand Herald*, 28 September 1916, 6.
71 Professor Taiarahia Black, personal communication, 6 April 2018.
72 Translation by Prof. Taiarahia Black.
73 *New Zealand Herald*, 14 January 1918, 4.
74 Quoted in Monty Soutar, *Whitiki Whiti! Whiti! E!: Māori in the First World War*, Auckland: David Bateman, 2019, 268–70.
75 Quoted in Michael King, *Te Puea*, Auckland: Hodder & Stoughton, 1982, 94.
76 Ibid.
77 *Dominion*, 29 May 1919, 6.
78 Quoted in Soutar, *Whitiki Whiti! Whiti! E!*, 268–70.
79 Baker, *King and Country Call*, 201.
80 H. Urquhart to C. E. Matthews, 10 March 1919, 'Re list submitted by the Defence Department of Conscientious Objectors, 1919', J40 Box 206, 1919/14/1, Archives NZ.
81 Jim McAloon, 'Thorn, James', *Dictionary of New Zealand Biography*, www.teara.govt.nz/en/biographies/4t15/thorn-james.

5: Rock College: 1923–1946

1 *Auckland Star*, 15 August 1922, 2.
2 Ibid., 24 April 1923, 5.
3 Ibid., 23 August 1919, 15.
4 Ibid., 8 November 1924, 19.
5 Anonymous, *Five Years for Fraud*, London: Sampson Low, Marston & Co., 1936, 16.
6 'Reminiscences of Mount Eden Prison', H. E. Thatcher papers, University of Auckland manuscript A53, folder 5, 8.
7 *New Zealand Herald*, 20 September 1923, 8.
8 Robin Hyde, *Journalese*, Auckland: National Printing Co., 1934, 208.
9 *N.Z. Truth*, 12 December 1929, 10.
10 *Auckland Star*, 23 August 1919, 15.
11 Ibid., 26 August 1919, 11; 20 February 1920, 5.
12 *New Zealand Herald*, 21 September 1923, 9.
13 Ibid., 20 August 1919, 9.
14 *Auckland Star*, 9 March 1921, 7.
15 *Appendices to the Journals of the House of Representatives (AJHR)*, 1937, H-20, 11.
16 *New Zealand Herald*, 20 September 1923, 8; *Auckland Star*, 4 November 1931, 6.
17 Ibid., 22 May 1924, 7.

18 Ibid., 19 July 1921, 2.
19 Donald F. McKenzie, *While We Have Prisons*, Auckland: Methuen NZ, 1980, 47.
20 Ibid.
21 *AJHR*, 1920, H-20, 5–6.
22 *Auckland Star*, 13 June 1925, 15.
23 'Reminiscences of Mount Eden Prison', 25.
24 *New Zealand Herald*, 5 June 1935, 14.
25 Ibid., 20 December 1934, 23.
26 *Auckland Star*, 26 November 1925, 10.
27 *AJHR*, 1924, H-20, 8.
28 *Auckland Star*, 9 November 1920, 5.
29 Ibid., 7 July 1925, 5.
30 Ibid., 20 February 1920, 5.
31 Ibid., 7 September 1934, 3.
32 *AJHR*, 1931, H-20, 3–4.
33 *New Zealand Herald*, 13 April 1932, 13.
34 *Auckland Star*, 29 September 1932, 8.
35 *AJHR*, 1932, H-20, 12–13; *New Zealand Herald*, 29 September 1932, 13.
36 *New Zealand Herald*, 21 September 1923, 9.
37 Ibid., 10 July 1921, 6; *Auckland Star*, 27 July 1921, 2.
38 *New Zealand Herald*, 1 July 1927, 14. The league was formed in Britain in the nineteenth century and named for an eighteenth-century pioneer of penal reform. The New Zealand branch remains active.
39 Alan Mulgan, 'B. E. Baughan: Some Memories', *Landfall*, vol. 12, no. 4, December 1958, 333–35. I am indebted to Carol Markwell for this reference from her forthcoming biography of Blanche Baughan.
40 See, for example, *New Zealand Herald*, 9 November 1922, 6; *N.Z. Truth*, 22 December 1922, 7.
41 *New Zealand Herald*, 20 December 1928, 13.
42 Quoted in Michael Field, *Mau: Samoa's Struggle for Independence*, Auckland: Polynesian Press, 1991 (1st edn 1984), 131.
43 *Evening Star*, 9 February 1929, 18.
44 Field, *Mau*, 132.
45 *Auckland Star*, 26 January 1929, 13.
46 Ibid., 30 December 1929, 7.
47 Field, *Mau*, 142.
48 *Auckland Star*, 30 December 1929, 7.
49 *AJHR*, 1933, H-20, 2.
50 See, for example, *Auckland Star*, 13 February 1934, 3.
51 *New Zealand Herald*, 6 April 1945, 7.

52 'Reminiscences of Mount Eden Prison', 33–34. I am grateful to Scott Hamilton for drawing my attention to this useful resource.
53 Ibid., 6.
54 *New Zealand Herald*, 27 January 1931, 12.
55 'Reminiscences of Mount Eden Prison', 8.
56 *Auckland Star*, 28 September 1931, 8.
57 Melville Harcourt, *A Parson in Prison*, Auckland: Whitcombe & Tombs 1942, 270–75.
58 Charles Farrell and Rebecca Ellis, *The Trials of Eric Mareo*, Wellington: Victoria University Press, 2002, 110, 214–15.
59 Ibid., 153.
60 *AJHR*, 1925, H-20, 12; Marie Gray, *About Time: Biography of a Prison Chaplain*, Wellington: Moana Press, 1991, 71.
61 *New Zealand Herald*, 2 February 1931, 10.
62 Conrad Bollinger, *Against the Wind: The Story of the New Zealand Seamen's Union*, Wellington: New Zealand Seamen's Union, 1968, 155.
63 'Reminiscences of Mount Eden Prison', 27.
64 *New Zealand Herald*, 23 October 1925, 10; 30 October 1925, 10.
65 Graeme Dunstall, 'Governments, Police and the Left, 1912–51', in P. Maloney and K. Taylor (eds), *On the Left: Essays on Socialism in New Zealand, Dunedin:* Otago University Press, 2002, 94–95.
66 *Auckland Star*, 12 October 1925, 8.
67 *New Zealand Herald*, 20 August 1919, 9.
68 Ibid., 22 September 1923, 6.
69 Harcourt, *A Parson in Prison*, 288–89.
70 *New Zealand Herald*, 8 September 1919, 9.
71 *Auckland Star*, 20 February 1920, 5.
72 New Zealand Parliamentary Debates (*NZPD*), vol. 217, 24 July 1928, 689.
73 *New Zealand Herald*, 13 August 1932, 12.
74 *AJHR*, 1929, H-20, 8.
75 *New Zealand Herald*, 1 July 1927, 14.
76 *AJHR*, 1929, H-20, 8; *New Zealand Herald*, 21 August 1929, 12.
77 Hyde, *Journalese*, 208.
78 *Auckland Star*, 11 October 1921, 5.
79 Ibid., 2 May 1936, 10.
80 *New Zealand Herald*, 21 December 1926, 16.
81 I am grateful to Mackay's biographer, Paul Diamond, for sharing his researches on this cruelly maligned figure, including the intriguing information that the riot in which Mackay was killed featured in a 2017 historical TV drama series, *Babylon Berlin*.

82   'Reminiscences of Mount Eden Prison', 19.
83   *New Zealand Herald*, 10 January 1931, 6.
84   *N.Z. Truth*, 10 January 1929, 3; quoted in Harcourt, *A Parson in Prison*, 184.
85   *Auckland Star*, 4 May 1925, 8.
86   Ibid., 25 August 1932, 7.
87   Ibid., 20 November 1929, 7.
88   Ibid., 18 July 1928, 9.
89   *New Zealand Herald*, 21 September 1929, 10.
90   Ibid., 9 October 1935, 16.
91   *Auckland Star,* 30 July 1918, 6.
92   *New Zealand Herald*, 5 October 1926, 12.
93   *Auckland Star*, 9 September 1927, 9.
94   *New Zealand Herald*, 29 August 1928, 12.
95   Ibid., 11 October 1929, 15.
96   *New Zealand Observer*, 26 March 1931, 3–4.
97   *New Zealand Herald*, 4 October 1940, 9.
98   *Auckland Star*, 23 October 1940, 11.
99   Fraser, Semple and other Labour MPs were held at other prisons than Mount Eden.
100 James Edwards, *Waiting for the Revolution, Auckland:* David Ling Publishing, 1998, 133.
101 *Evening Post*, 26 July 1932, 8.
102 *New Zealand Herald*, 31 December 1932, 11.
103 *New Zealand Observer*, 4 October 1932, 5.
104 Edwards, *Waiting for the Revolution*, 139.
105 *Auckland Star*, 27 April 1936, 8.
106 Ibid., 28 April 1936, 8.
107 *AJHR*, 1936, H-20, 7.
108 S. Heydon, 'McMillan, David Gervan', *Dictionary of New Zealand Biography*, www.teara.govt.nz/en/biographies/4m25/mcmillan-david-gervan
109 *AJHR*, 1939, H-20, 6.
110 *Auckland Star*, 28 April 1937, 8; *AJHR*, 1938, H-20, 8.
111 *Auckland Star,* 29 March 1932, 8.
112 Ibid., 2 October 1940, 9.
113 *New Zealand Herald,* 9 October 1940, 8.
114 Heydon, 'McMillan, David Gervan'.
115 *Evening Post*, 16 November 1943, 3.
116 Ian Hamilton, *Till Human Voices Wake Us*, Auckland: Ian Hamilton, 1953, 116.
117 Ibid., 104.

118 *New Zealand Herald,* 17 October 1941, 6.
119 Harcourt, *A Parson in Prison,* 182.
120 Ibid., 144.
121 Ibid., 172–73.
122 *Evening Post,* 19 November 1942, 3.
123 *Auckland Star,* 21 November 1942, 6.
124 David Grant, *Out in the Cold: Pacifists and Conscientious Objectors in New Zealand During World War II,* Auckland: Reed Methuen, 1986, 94.
125 *New Zealand Herald,* 4 October 1941, 12.
126 Superintendent Leggett to Dallard, Controller-General of Prisons, 28 November 1941, 'Naval and military defaulters — general', ACGS 16211 J1 12/2/10, Archives NZ.
127 E. Wright to Dallard, Controller-General of Prisons, 6 November 1941; Acting Superintendent to Controller-General of Prisons, 26 November 1941, 'Naval and military defaulters — general'.
128 Paul Ostereicher, '"They Would Not Fight": A Survey of Conscientious Objection During World War II', MA thesis, Victoria University of Wellington, 1955, 124–25.
129 *Auckland Star,* 9 July 1942, 4.
130 *Evening Post,* 3 March 1945, 6.
131 *New Zealand Howard League for Penal Reform,* pamphlet, Roth collection, 83-247-15, Alexander Turnbull Library, 7.
132 *AJHR,* 1945, H-20, 6.
133 Ibid., 4.
134 Ibid., 6.
135 *Evening Post,* 11 July 1944, 7.
136 Ibid., 4 August 1944, 4; Bruce Morris, *Jailbreak: Violent Episodes in New Zealand Prisons,* Auckland: Wilson and Horton, 1975, 7–9.
137 *Press,* 20 February 1945, 6; Ostereicher, '"They Would Not Fight"', 128.
138 'Recalcitrant defaulters in prison', Memo for Minister of Justice, 16 February 1945, 'Naval and military defaulters — general'.
139 *New Zealand Herald,* 7 April 1945, 9.
140 Ibid., 10 March 1945, 6.
141 *Auckland Star,* 12 September 1945, 7.
142 Hamilton, *Till Human Voices Wake Us,* 82.
143 Ibid., 110.
144 B. L. Dallard, Controller-General of Prisons to Superintendent Auckland Prison, 15 November 1945, 'Naval and military defaulters — general'.
145 *New Zealand Herald,* 15 January 1946, 6.
146 Ibid.; Ostereicher, '"They Would Not Fight"', 168.

6: The Meccano Set: 1947–1962

1. *N.Z. Truth*, 26 April 1924, 7.
2. Meccano was a brand of children's construction toy, very popular in the 1950s, made of metal strips connected by bolts and screws.
3. Donald F. McKenzie, *While We Have Prisons*, Auckland: Methuen NZ, 1980, 73.
4. Pauline Engel, *The Abolition of Capital Punishment in New Zealand 1935–1961*, Wellington: Department of Justice, 1977, 1–2.
5. Colonel Balneavis, Sheriff, Auckland, to Minister of Justice, 15 September 1873, 'Suggestions as to conducting executions of criminals', ACGS 16211 J1 146/bd 1873/2554, Archives NZ.
6. Ibid., marginalia.
7. *New Zealand Herald*, 23 June 1920, 6.
8. *New Zealand Times*, 23 June 1920, 4.
9. Criminals Execution Act 1883, s. 5.
10. Controller-General of Prisons to Thomas Vincent, Superintendent, Auckland Prison, 15 December 1920; T. Vincent to Controller-General of Prisons, 24 December 1920, ACGS 16211 J1 980/ 1920/805, Archives NZ.
11. A. Stubbs to Under-Secretary of Justice, 20 December 1920, ACGS 16211 J1 980/ 1920/805, Archives NZ.
12. *Auckland Star*, 10 October 1921, 7.
13. *N.Z. Truth*, 7 August 1930, 1.
14. Criminal Code Act 1893, ss. 77, 106, 167.
15. Berkeley Dallard, *Fettered Freedom: A Symbiotic Society or Anarchy?*, Wellington: Department of Justice, 1980, 112
16. Department of Justice, *Crime in New Zealand*, Wellington: Government Printing Office, 1968, 234.
17. Engel, *The Abolition of Capital Punishment*, 4–6.
18. McKenzie, *While We Have Prisons*, 75, 80.
19. Engel, *The Abolition of Capital Punishment*, 13.
20. *Evening Post*, 12 September 1941, 4.
21. Engel, *The Abolition of Capital Punishment*, 10.
22. Dallard, *Fettered Freedom*, 55–56.
23. Jock Barnes, interviewed in *Shattered Dreams*, dir. Francis Wevers, 1990, accessed Ngā Taonga — Sound and Vision, Wellington.
24. 'Auckland Prison — breakdown of routine duties', BBAF 1390 A528 1/a, Archives NZ.
25. McKenzie, *While We Have Prisons*, 13–14.
26. *New Zealand Herald*, 10 April 1945, 7.

27 Greg Newbold, *Punishment and Politics: The Maximum Security Prison in New Zealand*, Auckland: Oxford University Press, 1989, 41.
28 *New Zealand Observer*, 25 February 1948, 6.
29 *New Zealand Herald*, 4 May 1946, 6.
30 Newbold, *Punishment and Politics*, 13.
31 Deputy Controller-General of Prisons to Controller-General, 11 February 1948, 'Auckland Prison Mt Eden Pt. 1 1940-49', ACGS 16211 J1/1409 11/11/2 pt 1, Archives NZ.
32 *Dominion*, 2 February 1948, 8.
33 Newbold, *Punishment and Politics*, 12.
34 *New Zealand Herald*, 3 February 1948, 6.
35 Newbold, *Punishment and Politics*, 18–19.
36 *Appendices to the Journals of the House of Representatives (AJHR)*, 1959, H-20, 20.
37 Ibid., 1950, H-20, 9.
38 Newbold, *Punishment and Politics*, 43.
39 J. L. Robson, *Sacred Cows and Rogue Elephants: Policy Development in the New Zealand Justice Department*, Wellington: Government Printing Office, 1987, 58–59.
40 Newbold, *Punishment and Politics*, 44.
41 Andrea G. Napier, 'Each Day Is Different: Prison Officers and Their Work', MA thesis, Victoria University of Wellington, 2012, 113.
42 *AJHR*, 1950, H-20, 11.
43 Napier, 'Each Day Is Different', 112.
44 *New Zealand Herald*, 27 March 1950, 6; 2 November 1950, 8.
45 *AJHR*, 1950, H-20, 9.
46 Ibid., 1951 H-20, 12.
47 *New Zealand Parliamentary Debates (NZPD)*, vol. 300, 20 October 1953, 1886–87.
48 McKenzie, *While We Have Prisons*, 21–22.
49 Newbold, *Punishment and Politics*, 23.
50 *AJHR*, 1950, H-20, 17.
51 *New Zealand Herald*, 2 July 1952, 5; Newbold, *Punishment and Politics*, 37.
52 McKenzie, *While We Have Prisons*, 25.
53 Newbold, *Punishment and Politics*, 31–32.
54 Ibid., 38.
55 'Auckland Prison — breakdown of routine duties', BBAF 1390 A528 1/a, Archives NZ.
56 Ibid.
57 Ibid.

58 James Edwards, *Waiting for the Revolution*, Auckland: David Ling Publishing, 1998, 135.
59 McKenzie, *While We Have Prisons*, 44.
60 'Formation of prisoners' council at Auckland Prison, 1952', ACHS 16211 J1/1602 21/2/26, Archives NZ.
61 Memo, 12 July 1951, ACHS 16211 J1/1602 21/2/26, Archives NZ.
62 Barnett, Secretary for Justice, reply to Haywood, Superintendent, 21 August 1952, ACHS 16211 J1/1602 21/2/26, Archives NZ.
63 Prison Council report, from inauguration 14/2/1952 to 10/6/1952, in ibid.
64 Deputy Chief Prison Officer, Minute Sheet, 20 November 1952, in ibid.
65 McKenzie, *While We Have Prisons*, 20.
66 Department of Justice, *Crime and the Community: A Survey of Penal Policy in New Zealand*, Wellington: Government Printer, 1964, 66.
67 Newbold, *Punishment and Politics*, 22.
68 McKenzie, *While We Have Prisons*, 11.
69 Ibid., 48.
70 Ibid., 15–16.
71 Newbold, *Punishment and Politics*, 25.
72 McKenzie, *While We Have Prisons*, 67.
73 Ibid., 22.
74 Julie Glamuzina and Alison J. Laurie, *Parker and Hulme: A Lesbian View*, Auckland: New Women's Press, 1990, 100.
75 Ibid., 101.
76 *N.Z. Truth*, 8 September 1954, 21.
77 Peter Graham, *So Brilliantly Clever: Parker, Hulme and the Murder That Shocked the World*, Wellington: Awa Press, 2011, 249.
78 Joanne Drayton, *The Search for Anne Perry*, Auckland: HarperCollins, 2012, 285.
79 Graham, *So Brilliantly Clever*, 246.
80 Quoted in Drayton, *The Search for Anne Perry*, 284.
81 Glamuzina and Laurie, *Parker and Hulme*, 104.
82 Drayton, *The Search for Anne Perry*, 280.
83 Graham, *So Brilliantly Clever*, 259.
84 Anne Perry, *Silence in Hanover Close*, London: Grafton, 1988, 296.
85 Quoted in Drayton, *The Search for Anne Perry*, fn 60, 288.
86 Quoted in Engel, *The Abolition of Capital Punishment*, fn 41, 35.
87 Ibid., 27–28, 55.
88 *NZPD*, vol. 293, 21 November 1950, 4389.
89 *N.Z. Truth*, 7 February 1951, 9.
90 McKenzie, *While We Have Prisons*, 74.

91   Robson, *Sacred Cows and Rogue Elephants*, 94.
92   Dick Scott, *Would a Good Man Die?: New Zealand, Niue and the Late Mr Larsen*, Auckland: Hodder & Stoughton/Southern Cross Books, 1993, 142.
93   Ibid., 151.
94   Sherwood Young, *Guilty on the Gallows: Famous Capital Crimes of New Zealand*, Wellington: Grantham House, 1999, 9–10.
95   'Auckland Prison — breakdown of routine duties', BBAF 1390 A528 1/a, Archives NZ; Newbold, *Punishment and Politics*, 104.
96   'Auckland Prison — breakdown of routine duties'.
97   McKenzie, *While We Have Prisons*, 73.
98   *New Zealand Herald*, 30 August 1986, sec. 2, 2.
99   Young, *Guilty on the Gallows*, 14.
100 Robson, *Sacred Cows and Rogue Elephants*, 154.
101 Department of Justice, *Crime in New Zealand*, 65.
102 McKenzie, *While We Have Prisons*, 76.
103 Newbold, *Punishment and Politics*, 100.
104 Ibid., 103.
105 McKenzie, *While We Have Prisons*, 76–77.
106 Leonard P. Leary QC, *Not Entirely Legal*, Auckland: Whitcoulls, 1977, 174–75.
107 Engel, *The Abolition of Capital Punishment*, 58; Newbold, *Punishment and Politics*, 105.
108 McKenzie, *While We Have Prisons*, 80.
109 Newbold, *Punishment and Politics*, 113–14.
110 Robson, *Sacred Cows and Rogue Elephants*, 164.
111 'Auckland Prison — breakdown of routine duties'; Newbold, *Punishment and Politics*, 74.
112 Newbold, *Punishment and Politics*, 76.
113 Michael Burgess, *Mister*, London: New Authors Ltd no. 44, 1964, 81.
114 *New Zealand Herald*, 23 July 1954, 11.
115 Newbold, *Punishment and Politics*, 88.
116 *New Zealand Herald*, 6 July 1954, 11.
117 Robson, *Sacred Cows and Rogue Elephants*, 67.
118 McKenzie, *While We Have Prisons*, 57.
119 *N.Z. Truth*, 14 December 1955, 1.
120 *New Zealand Herald*, 17 December 1955, 14.
121 Robson, *Sacred Cows and Rogue Elephants*, 71.
122 Newbold, *Punishment and Politics*, 54.
123 McKenzie, *While We Have Prisons*, 54.
124 *Western Leader*, 6 December 2005, 7.

125 McKenzie, *While We Have Prisons*, 49.
126 Newbold, *Punishment and Politics*, 65–66.
127 *NZPD*, vol. 313, 13 September 1957, 2405, 2407.
128 McKenzie, *While We Have Prisons*, 13–14.
129 *AJHR*, 1964, H-20, 6–7.
130 Newbold, *Punishment and Politics*, 89.
131 Ibid., 93.
132 Ibid., 92.
133 *New Zealand Herald*, 15 June 1958, 8.
134 Newbold, *Punishment and Politics*, 95.
135 McKenzie, *While We Have Prisons*, 35–36.
136 Ibid., 59–60.
137 *New Zealand Herald*, 15 June 1958, 8.
138 Newbold, *Punishment and Politics*, 95.
139 McKenzie, *While We Have Prisons*, 59–60.
140 *New Zealand Herald*, 21 November 1962, 3.
141 Ibid., 14 June 1958, 12.
142 Newbold, *Punishment and Politics*, 96.
143 *N.Z. Truth*, 30 June 1959, 41.
144 *New Zealand Herald*, 23 June 1959, 15.
145 *N.Z. Truth*, 19 July 1960, 5.
146 McKenzie, *While We Have Prisons*, 58–59.
147 Bruce Morris, *Jailbreak: Violent Episodes in New Zealand Prisons*, Auckland: Wilson & Horton, 1975, 11–14.
148 Ibid.
149 McKenzie, *While We Have Prisons*, 58–59.
150 *AJHR*, 1959, H-20, 5.
151 Ibid., 27.
152 Ibid., 1960, H-20, 9.
153 Ibid., 13.
154 Ibid., 10.
155 Ibid., 11.
156 Ibid., 21.
157 Ibid., 1959, H-20, 5.
158 H. Haywood, Superintendent, to Secretary for Justice, 17 April 1962, 'Auckland Prison, riots and behaviour of prisoners', ACGS 16211 J1/1420 12/6/4 1A, Archives NZ.
159 J. Robson, Secretary for Justice, to Superintendent, Auckland Prison, 26 April 1962, ACGS 16211 J1/1420 12/6/4 1A, Archives NZ.

7: 'Burn, burn, burn': 1963–1969

1. Jim Shepherd interview, 19 September 2018.
2. Ibid.
3. Jim Shepherd, *Mr Asia: Last Man Standing*, Sydney: Macmillan, 2010, 6–8.
4. Greg Newbold, *Punishment and Politics: The Maximum Security Prison in New Zealand*, Auckland: Oxford University Press, 1989, 79.
5. Ibid., 127.
6. Bruce Morris, *Jailbreak: Violent Episodes in New Zealand Prisons*, Auckland: Wilson & Horton, 1975, 19.
7. 'Mt Eden Prison — quarry 1960-1967', BBAD A463 1054, Box 524 a 10/4 2, Archives NZ.
8. Jim Shepherd interview.
9. Penal Institutions Amendment Act 1964, s. 2.
10. Newbold, *Punishment and Politics*, 124.
11. *Auckland Star*, 18 July 1963, 1.
12. *N.Z. Truth*, 30 April 1963, 20.
13. *Auckland Star*, 18 July 1963, 1.
14. Howard Morrison Quartet, 'The Wild(er) New Zealand Boy', La Gloria, 1963.
15. *New Zealand Parliamentary Debates (NZPD)*, vol. 331, 17 August 1962, 1521.
16. Newbold, *Punishment and Politics*, 114.
17. Ibid., 131.
18. Ibid., 132.
19. Ibid., 135.
20. *New Zealand Herald*, 20 July 1963, 1; 22 July 1963, 1.
21. Morris, *Jailbreak*, 27–32.
22. Newbold, *Punishment and Politics*, 117.
23. *Appendices to the Journals of the House of Representatives (AJHR)*, 1961, H-20, 13.
24. *NZPD*, vol. 335, 27 June 1963, 88.
25. Department of Justice, *Crime and the Community: A Survey of Penal Policy in New Zealand*, Wellington: Government Printer, 1964, 67.
26. *N.Z. Truth*, 23 April 1963, 20.
27. Shepherd, *Mr Asia*, 20.
28. *Sunday News*, 30 August 1964, 3.
29. Donald F. McKenzie, *While We Have Prisons*, Auckland: Methuen NZ, 1980, 69.
30. Ibid.
31. *Sunday News*, 6 September 1964, 2–3.
32. Ibid.

33 'Notes of evidence of enquiry into alleged happenings at Auckland Prison, 21 October 1964' in 'Prisoner — General — Auckland Prison — insubordinate behaviour of prisoners', ACGS 16211 J1 W2304/31 12/6/4 2, Archives NZ.
34 McKenzie, *While We Have Prisons*, 38.
35 B. Pimley, *The Rock Orchid*, in Webber, Cyril Ernie Richard: Papers (MS-3333/197 and 198) Hocken Collections, University of Otago.
36 'Notes of evidence of enquiry into alleged happenings at Auckland Prison, 21 October 1964', 14.
37 McKenzie, *While We Have Prisons*, 26.
38 Newbold, *Punishment and Politics*, 140.
39 Quoted in Morris, *Jailbreak*, 33–37.
40 Owen J. Cherrett, *'Without Fear or Favour': 150 Years Policing Auckland 1840–1990*, Auckland: New Zealand Police, 1989, 311; 'Enquiry into escape of John Frederick Gillies, Leonard Edwin Evans and George Wilder from Mt. Eden — 4 February 1965 — Report of A. A. Coates S.M.', ACGS 16251 J68/1, Archives NZ.
41 Newbold, *Punishment and Politics,* 22.
42 Ibid., 142.
43 *Western Leader*, 21 July 2005, 6.
44 Shepherd interview.
45 Ibid. Police, however, later suspected that a former prison officer had smuggled the gun but were unable to prove it; *N.Z. Truth*, 1 March 1966, 48.
46 *Auckland Star*, 21 December 1965, 1, 3.
47 Ibid.
48 Shepherd interview.
49 Newbold, *Punishment and Politics,* 148.
50 Ibid., 127.
51 *8 O'Clock*, 20 July 1974, 53.
52 Shepherd interview.
53 Newbold, *Punishment and Politics*, 148.
54 Tim Shadbolt interview, 6 October 2017.
55 Newbold, *Punishment and Politics*, 161.
56 'Inquiry into prison riots and fire at Mt Eden [Auckland Prison] on 20-21 July 1965', 12, BADW 11459 A1426 1/, Archives NZ.
57 *Sunday Star-Times*, 16 July 1995, C6.
58 McKenzie, *While We Have Prisons*, 71.
59 Newbold, *Punishment and Politics*, 162.
60 Shepherd, *Mr Asia*, 28–29.
61 Newbold, *Punishment and Politics*, 150.

62 *Evening Post*, 20 July 1965, 18.
63 Newbold, *Punishment and Politics*, 149.
64 Letters to the editor, *New Zealand Herald*, 27 July 1965, 6.
65 Shepherd interview.
66 *Evening Post*, 20 July 1965, 18.
67 Shepherd, *Mr Asia*, 31.
68 MOVIETONE NEWS A2158: 'Auckland; riots and fires in NZ prison drama; catalogue ref. F59438 personal record, Cunningham, Gordon Hamilton, Mt Eden Gaol fire', catalogue ref. F47854, accessed Ngā Taonga — Sound and Vision, Wellington.
69 *Evening Post*, 20 July 1965, 18.
70 Shepherd, *Mr Asia*, 32.
71 'Report by David Scott on Mount Eden prison riot, July 1965', catalogue ref. 237328, accessed Ngā Taonga — Sound and Vision, Wellington.
72 Newbold, *Punishment and Politics*, 152.
73 Shepherd interview.
74 *Evening Post*, 20 July 1965, 18.
75 *Sunday Star-Times*, 16 July 1995, C6.
76 Cherrett, *'Without Fear or Favour'*, 312–13.
77 'Report by David Scott on Mount Eden prison riot, July 1965'.
78 James McNeish, catalogue ref. 27314, RNZ Sound Archives.
79 Newbold, *Punishment and Politics*, 169; Shepherd interview.
80 *Star* (Christchurch), 24 July 1965, 1.
81 NZPD, vol. 332, 14 October 1965, 3563.
82 Commission of Inquiry (1965a), *Report into Disturbance at Auckland Prison on 20–21 July, 1965*, Wellington: Department of Prisons, 1965, 18.
83 'Coverage of Mt Eden Riot, 1965', catalogue ref. 216066, RNZ Sound Archives.
84 Commission of Inquiry, *Report into Disturbance at Auckland Prison*.
85 *Auckland Star*, 21 December 1965, 1, 3.
86 *New Zealand Herald*, 27 July 1965, 6.
87 Newbold, *Punishment and Politics*, 147.
88 J. L. Robson, *Sacred Cows and Rogue Elephants: Policy Development in the New Zealand Justice Department*, Wellington: Government Printing Office Publishing, 1987, 9.
89 NZPD, vol. 332, 15 October 1965, 3563.
90 *New Zealand Herald*, 9 August 1965, 1.
91 *Sunday Star-Times*, 16 July 1995, C6.
92 NZPD, vol. 343, 27 July 1965, 1416–33.
93 Newbold, *Punishment and Politics*, 159.

94 Quoted in ibid., 158.
95 *New Zealand Herald,* 10 February 1969, 14.
96 Shepherd interview.
97 Newbold, *Punishment and Politics,* 171; Report of enquiry in hunger strike in security section, by F. McCarthy, SM, 21 November 1967, in 'Prisoners — General — Auckland Prison — insubordinate behaviour of prisoners', ACGS 16211 J1 W2304/31 12/6/4 2, Archives NZ.
98 Shepherd interview.
99 Ibid.
100 Ibid.
101 *Sunday Times,* 3 January 1971, 11. I am grateful to Tim Balme, creator of a one-man show based on George Wilder's life, for sharing his extensive research on this complex and elusive figure.
102 *Evening Post,* 15 August 1967, 12.
103 *Dominion Sunday Times,* 15 October 1967, 11.
104 *New Zealand Herald,* 16 August 1967, 1.
105 Newbold, *Punishment and Politics,* 172; *New Zealand Herald,* 14 September 1967, 1.
106 *Sunday Times,* 20 August 1967, 5.
107 *Eve,* August 1969, 11.
108 *New Zealand Herald,* 4 May 1969, 7, magazines.
109 *Sunday Times,* 9 August 1970, 5.
110 Robson, *Sacred Cows and Rogue Elephants,* 195.
111 Shepherd interview.
112 Shepherd, *Mr Asia,* 1–2.
113 Robson, *Sacred Cows and Rogue Elephants,* 195
114 Newbold, *Punishment and Politics,* 163.
115 Robson, *Sacred Cows and Rogue Elephants,* 195.

8: Death on remand: 1970–2011

1 J. Hobson, Superintendent, to Secretary for Justice, 30 November 1970, in 'Prisoners — General — Auckland Prison — insubordinate behaviour of prisoners', ACGS 16211 J1 W2304/31 12/6/4 2, Archives NZ.
2 J. Hobson, Superintendent, to Secretary for Justice, 22 December 1970, ACGS 16211 J1 W2304/31 12/6/4 2, Archives NZ.
3 J. Hobson, Superintendent, to Secretary for Justice, 30 November 1970, ACGS 16211 J1 W2304/31 12/6/4 2, Archives NZ.
4 Bob van Ruyssevelt interview, 2 April 2018.
5 *Sunday Times,* 16 August 1970, 13.
6 *New Zealand Herald,* 7 November 1970, 4.

7   Tim Shadbolt interview, 6 October 2017.
8   Ibid.
9   Te Rangikaheke Kiripātea interview, 8 September 2017.
10 Shadbolt interview.
11 *Appendices to the Journals of the House of Representatives (AJHR)*, 1971, H-20, 27.
12 Te Puna Wai Korero, 'Teaching Maori in Prisons', 1977, catalogue ref. 45358, NZ Sound Archive.
13 *New Zealand Herald*, 30 December 1970, 3; *AJHR*, 1970, H-20, 24.
14 Ibid., 21 March 1971, 1.
15 Kiripātea interview.
16 *New Zealand Herald*, 8 April 1971, 5.
17 *AJHR*, 1972, H-20, 3.
18 *New Zealand Herald*, 8 April 1971, 5.
19 Ibid., 21 March 1971, 1.
20 *New Zealand Parliamentary Debates (NZPD)*, vol. 371, 23 March 1971, 635.
21 Greg Newbold, 'What Works in Prison Management: Effects of Administrative Change in New Zealand', *Federal Probation*, vol. 56, December 1992, 56.
22 *New Zealand Herald*, 28 January 1978, 2.
23 *Evening Post*, 28 January 1984, 8.
24 *New Zealand Herald*, 15 October 1988, 12; 1 December 1993, 9.
25 *AJHR*, 1970, H-20, 13; Neil Darragh, 'Social Relations of Prison Inmates', MA anthropology thesis, University of Auckland, 1973, 36.
26 *New Zealand Herald*, 17 April 1971, 14.
27 *Auckland Star*, 26 January 1974, Weekender, 4.
28 *New Zealand Herald*, 22 January 1986, 2.
29 Shadbolt interview.
30 *New Zealand Herald*, 28 January 1978, sec. 2, 2.
31 Miriam Saphira interview, 9 January 2018.
32 Ibid.
33 Ibid.
34 Dorothy Costar interview, OHColl-0549/1, Alexander Turnbull Library.
35 Anonymous interview, 3 July 2016.
36 Sandra Coney interview, 28 November 2017.
37 Sandra Coney, *Broadsheet*, July/August 1982, 58–61.
38 Coney interview.
39 *New Zealand Herald*, 8 November 1985, 1.
40 Raewyn Abbott interview, 11 November 2019.
41 *Dominion*, 6 December 1991, 3.

42 *New Zealand Woman's Weekly*, 11 October 1999, 34.
43 Mary Woodward interview, 22 January 2018.
44 *Express*, 11 September 2002, 7–8.
45 *New Zealand Herald*, 2 September 1976, 3.
46 Ibid., 27 October 1976, 1.
47 *Auckland Star*, 2 October 1976, 17.
48 Zane Paine interview, 9 October 2019.
49 *Auckland Star*, 7 January 1978, 5.
50 J. Rogers, Superintendent to Secretary for Justice, 27 July 1977, in 'Prisoners — General — Auckland Prison — insubordinate behaviour of prisoners', ACGS 16211 J1 W2304/31 12/6/4 2, Archives NZ.
51 Christine Mintrom, *Tommy Adderley 1940–1993: The Man and His Contribution to Pop, Jazz and Rock Music in New Zealand*, New York: iUniverse, 2003, 111,113.
52 Quoted in ibid., 117.
53 *Metro*, October 2008, 54–59.
54 J. Rogers, Superintendent to Secretary for Justice, 27 July 1977, in 'Prisoners — General — Auckland Prison — insubordinate behaviour of prisoners', ACGS 16211 J1 W2304/31 12/6/4 2, Archives NZ.
55 Auckland Star, 2 October 1976, 17.
56 Oliver Sutherland interview, 10 January 2018.
57 ACORD, *Children in State Custody*, Auckland: ACORD, 1979 (rev. edn 1981), 3–4; Submissions on Children's and Young Person's Bill, 1974, xii.
58 *Auckland Star*, 2 December 1984, A3.
59 Shadbolt interview.
60 *New Zealand Herald*, 22 Nov. 2016, A34.
61 Ibid., 14 August 1984, 11.
62 A. J. Hardie, First Officer, Remand Division, to Secretary for Justice, 17 January 1985, in 'Prisoners — General — Auckland Prison — insubordinate behaviour of prisoners', ACGS 16211 J1 W2304/31 12/6/4 2, Archives NZ.
63 Ibid.
64 Saphira interview.
65 J. Rogers, Superintendent, to Secretary for Justice, 27 July 1977, in 'Prisoners — General — Auckland Prison — insubordinate behaviour of prisoners'.
66 Paine interview.
67 *New Zealand Herald*, 12 September 1983, sec. 1, 1.
68 Ibid., 21 May 1985, sec. 1, 1.
69 Ibid., 31 January 1990, sec. 1, 1.

70 Ibid., 12 October 1987, 1.
71 Ibid., 29 December 1990, sec. 2, 1.
72 *Central Leader*, 20 December 1983, 4.
73 Ibid., 26 August 1994, 1.
74 *New Zealand Herald*, 31 October 1986, 2; Greg Newbold, 'Women Officers Working in Men's Prisons', *Social Policy Journal of New Zealand*, no. 25, July 2005, 107.
75 Quoted in Newbold, 'Women Officers Working in Men's Prisons', 111.
76 'No Joy in Eden', *PSA Journal*, June 1989, 5.
77 Paine interview.
78 *New Zealand Truth*, 10 July 1998, 4.
79 *Express*, 11 September 2002, 7–8.
80 Abbott interview.
81 *Auckland Star,* 14 December 1985, B9.
82 *New Zealand Herald*, 16 May 1986, 15.
83 Ibid., 30 August 1982, S2, 2; 16 February 1987, 8.
84 Ibid., 5 August 1986, 3.
85 Ibid., 4 August 1986, 1.
86 Ibid., 8 June 1987, 5.
87 Paine interview.
88 *Auckland Star*, 21 October 1987, 3.
89 Ibid., 4 June 1987, 3.
90 Anonymous interview, 21 October 2019.
91 *Dominion*, 16 August 1994, 3.
92 Simon Kerr interview, 16 October 2019.
93 *Dominion*, 18 June 1990, 1.
94 Anonymous interview, 1 November 2019.
95 *New Zealand Herald,* 23 May 1998, H3.
96 *Central Leader*, 1 August 2008, 15.
97 *Metro*, October 2008, 54–59.
98 Neville Mark interview, 28 August 2019.
99 *New Zealand Herald,* 23 May 1998, H3.
100 Ibid., 21 May 1994, sec. 2, 1.
101 *Metro*, October 2008, 48–53.
102 *New Zealand Listener*, 14 March 1998, 18–22.
103 *New Zealand Herald,* 23 May 1998, H3.
104 *New Zealand Listener*, 14 March 1998, 18–22.
105 Ibid.
106 Anonymous interview.
107 *Express*, 11 September 2002, 7–8.

108 Mark interview.
109 'Mt Eden Prison Site Redevelopment Project', 18 May 2007, Cabinet paper PM7/P13/25/33/3, 3.
110 Mark interview.
111 *Central Leader,* 25 June 2010, 10.

Epilogue: Releasing the ghosts

1   *New Zealand Herald,* 13 May 2004, A15.
2   *Dominion* (editorial), 13 April 1971, 12.
3   *New Zealand Herald,* 12 December 1973, 3.
4   Ibid., 18 May 1974, sec. 2, 3.
5   Ibid., 12 December 1973, 3.
6   Ibid., 2 September 1976, 6 (editorial).
7   List entry record no. 88, Heritage NZ Pouhere Taonga.
8   *Auckland Star,* 16 August 1984, 3.
9   Ibid., 4 June 1987, 8.
10 *New Zealand Herald,* 4 August 1988, 5.
11 P. Lister, personal communication, 17 December 2019.
12 *Sunday Star-Times,* 18 August 1993, A3.
13 *New Zealand Herald,* 6 May 1998, A14 (editorial).
14 Ibid., 8 May 1998, 1.
15 *Central Leader,* 25 August 2000, 5.
16 *New Zealand Herald,* 31 August 2000, A13.
17 *Central Leader,* 18 October 2000, 1.
18 *New Zealand Herald,* 27 February 2006, A4.
19 'Mt Eden Prison Site Redevelopment Project', 18 May 2007, Cabinet paper PM7/P13/25/33/3.
20 *New Zealand Herald,* 9 May 2008, A10.
21 Anonymous interview.
22 *New Zealand Herald,* 7 May 2008, A7; 9 May 2008, A10 (editorial).
23 Charlie Post interview, 29 March 2019.
24 Ibid.

Bibliography

Official publications

Appendices to the Journals of the House of Representatives (AJHR)
Auckland Provincial Government Gazette
Journal of the Auckland Provincial Council
Blue Book of Statistics — Colony of New Zealand (Blue Book)
New Zealand Gazette
New Zealand Parliamentary Debates (NZPD)

Books

Anonymous, *Five Years for Fraud*, London: Sampson Low, Marston & Co., 1936.
Baker, H. P., *The Strongest God*, Auckland: Cape Catley, 1990.
Baker, Paul, *King and Country Call: New Zealanders, Conscription and the Great War*, Auckland: Auckland University Press, 1988.
Bollinger, Conrad, *Against the Wind: The Story of the New Zealand Seamen's Union*, Wellington: New Zealand Seamen's Union, 1968.
Brett, André, *Acknowledge No Frontier: The Creation and Demise of New Zealand's Provinces, 1853–76*, Dunedin: Otago University Press, 2016.
Buddee, Paul, *The Fate of the Artful Dodger: Parkhurst Boys Transported to Australia and New Zealand 1842–1852*, Perth: St George Books, 1984.
Burgess, Michael, *Mister*, London: New Authors Ltd, no. 44, 1964.
Burnett, Robert, *Penal Transportation: An Episode in New Zealand History*, Occasional papers in criminology no. 9. Wellington: Victoria University of Wellington, 1978.
Burnett R. I. M., *'Hard Labour, Hard Fare and a Hard Bed': New Zealand's Search for its Own Penal Philosophy*, Occasional Monographs Series no. 1. Wellington: National Archives of New Zealand, 1995.
Cherrett, O. J., *'Without Fear or Favour': 150 Years of Policing Auckland 1840–1990*, Wellington: New Zealand Police, 1989.
Coleman, Jenny, *Polly Plum: A Firm and Earnest Woman's Advocate: Mary Ann Colclough 1836–1885*, Dunedin: Otago University Press, 2017.
Coleman, P. J., *'A Blot on the Statute Book': Imprisonment for Debt in New Zealand 1840–1990*, Wellington: NZHistoryJock, 2016.
Coney, Sandra, *Standing in the Sunshine: A Social History of New Zealand Women Since They Won the Vote*, Auckland: Penguin, 1993.
Dallard, Berkeley, *Fettered Freedom: A Symbiotic Society or Anarchy?*, Wellington: Department of Justice, 1980.
Drayton, Joanne, *The Search for Anne Perry*, Auckland: HarperCollins, 2012.
Edwards, James, *Waiting for the Revolution*, Auckland: David Ling Publishing, 1998.

Farrell, Charles and Rebecca Ellis, *The Trials of Eric Mareo*, Wellington: Victoria University Press, 2002.
Field, Michael, *Mau: Samoa's Struggle for Independence*, Auckland: Polynesian Press, 1991 (1st edn 1984).
Glamuzina, Julie and Alison J. Laurie, *Parker and Hulme: A Lesbian view*, Auckland: New Women's Press, 1991.
Graham, Peter, *So Brilliantly Clever: Parker, Hulme and the Murder That Shocked the World*, Wellington: Awa Press, 2011.
Grant, David, *Out in the Cold: Pacifists and Conscientious Objectors in New Zealand During World War II*, Auckland: Reed Methuen, 1986.
Gray, Marie, *About Time: Biography of a Prison Chaplain*, Wellington: Moana Press, 1991.
Hamilton, Ian, *Till Human Voices Wake Us*, Auckland: Ian Hamilton, 1953.
Harcourt, Melville, *A Parson in Prison*, Auckland: Whitcombe & Tombs, 1942.
Hill, Richard, *Policing the Colonial Frontier: The Theory and Practice of Coercive Social and Racial Control in New Zealand, 1767–1867*, vol. 1., Wellington: Department of Internal Affairs, Historical Publications Branch, 1986.
Holland, Henry, *Armageddon or Calvary?: The Conscientious Objectors of New Zealand and 'The Process of Their Conversion'*, Wellington: Maoriland Worker Printing and Publishing Co., 1919.
Hyde, Robin, *Journalese*, Auckland: National Printing Co., 1934.
—— *Nor the Years Condemn*, Dunedin: Otago University Press, 1995 (1st edn 1938).
Kayll, James L. A., *A Plea for the Criminal*, Invercargill: W. Smith Commercial Printers, 1905.
King, Michael, *Te Puea*, Auckland: Hodder & Stoughton, 1982.
Leary, Leonard P. QC, *Not Entirely Legal*, Auckland: Whitcoulls, 1977.
Lee, John A., *Delinquent Days*, Auckland: Collins, 1967.
Mayhew, M. P., *The Prison System of New Zealand 1840–1824*, Wellington: Department of Justice, 1959.
McAlister, Brent, *From Farms and Flats: The History of Land Use in Mount Eden*, Auckland: Mount Eden Borough Council, 1983.
McKenzie, Donald F., *While We Have Prisons*, Auckland: Methuen NZ, 1980.
Mintrom, Christine, *Tommy Adderley 1940–1993, The Man and His Contributions to Pop, Jazz, and Rock Music in New Zealand*, New York: iUniverse, 2003.
Monro, George B., *A Faithful Standard Bearer: Life of Duncan MacPherson*. Auckland: Clark & Matheson, 1914.

Morris, Bruce, *Jailbreak: Violent Episodes in New Zealand*, Auckland: Wilson & Horton, 1975.

Newbold, Greg, *Punishment and Politics: The Maximum Security Prison in New Zealand*, Auckland: Oxford University Press, 1989.

—— *The Problem of Prisons: Corrections Reform in New Zealand Since 1840*, Wellington: Dunmore Publishing, 2007.

Perry, Anne, *Silence in Hanover Close*, London: Grafton, 1988.

Platts, Una, *The Lively Capital*, Christchurch: Avon Fine Prints, 1971.

Pratt, John, *Punishment in a Perfect Society: The New Zealand Penal System 1840–1939*, Wellington: Victoria University Press, 1992.

Robson, J. L., *Sacred Cows and Rogue Elephants: Policy Development in the New Zealand Justice Department*, Wellington: Government Printing Office, 1987.

Scott, Dick, *Would a Good Man Die?: New Zealand, Niue and the late Mr Larsen*, Auckland: Hodder & Stoughton/Southern Cross Books, 1993.

Shaw, Alan G. L., *Convicts and the Colonies: A Study of Penal Transportation from Great Britain and Ireland to Australia and Other Parts of the British Empire*, London: Faber & Faber, 1966.

Shepherd, Jim, *Mr Asia: Last Man Standing*, Sydney: Macmillan, 2010.

Smithyman, Kendrick, *Imperial Vistas Family Fictions*, Auckland: Auckland University Press, 2002.

Soutar, Monty, *Whitiki Whiti! Whiti! E!: Māori in the First World War*, Auckland: Bateman, 2019.

Thomas, Lowell, *The Sea Devil's Fo'c'sle*, London: William Heinemann, 1930.

Young, Sherwood, *Guilty on the Gallows: Famous Capital Crimes of New Zealand*, Wellington: Grantham House Publishing, 1999.

Webb, Patricia, *A History of Custodial and Related Penalties in New Zealand*, Wellington: Government Printer, 1982.

Pamphlets and reports

ACORD, *Children in State Custody*. ACORD 1979, rev. edn 1981.

Best, Simon, *The Queen St Gaol: Auckland's First Courthouse, Common Gaol and House of Correction (Site R11/1559)*, Department of Conservation, Auckland Conservancy, 1992.

Clough and Associates, *Doing Time at the Mount: Archaeological Investigations at Mt Eden Prison* final report, Wellington: Department of Corrections, 2008.

Clough, Rod et al., *Mt Eden Prison Monitoring: Progress Report, Wall*, Department of Corrections, 2009.

Commission of Inquiry, *Report Into Disturbance at Auckland Prison on 20–21*

July, 1965, Wellington: Department of Prisons, 1965.
Department of Justice, *Crime in New Zealand: A Survey of Penal Policy in New Zealand*, Wellington: Government Printing Office, 1968.
Engel, Pauline, *The Abolition of Capital Punishment in New Zealand 1935–1961*, Wellington: Department of Justice, 1977.
Timmerman, Felix, 'Construction Report, Mt Eden Prison Building', Department of Corrections, n.d.
New Zealand Howard League for Penal Reform, pamphlet, Roth collection, 83-247-15 ATL.

Journal articles

Anon, 'No Joy in Eden', *PSA Journal*, June 1989, 5.
Coney, Sandra, *Broadsheet*, July/August 1982, 58–61.
Dalley, Bronwyn, 'Prisons without Men: The Development of a Separate Women's Prison in New Zealand', *New Zealand Journal of History* 27, no. 1, 1993, 37–60.
Dunstall, Graeme, 'Governments, Police and the Left, 1912–51', in P. Maloney and K. Taylor (eds), *On the Left: Essays on Socialism in New Zealand*, Dunedin: Otago University Press, 2002.
Mulgan, Alan, 'B. E. Baughan: Some Memories', *Landfall* 12, no. 4, December 1958, 333–35.
Newbold, Greg, 'Women Officers Working in Men's Prisons', *Social Policy Journal of New Zealand*, no. 25, July 2005, 105–17.
Wilkins, Jennifer, 'Eden in Auckland', *New Zealand Geographic*, no. 140, July–August 2016, 88–103.

Audio and video

Costar, Dorothy interview, OHColl-0549/1, Alexander Turnbull Library (ATL).
'Coverage of Mt Eden riot, 1965', catalogue ref. 216066 RNZ Sound Archives.
Howard Morrison Quartet, 45rpm recording, 'The Wild(er) New Zealand Boy', La Gloria, 1963.
Jackson, Athol, interview Tape 2, OHC 7389_PM_S_01, Quaker Oral History Project (OHColl-0427) ATL, interviewer, Katherine Knight, 20 April 1990.
McNeish, James, catalogue ref. 27314, Radio NZ Sound archive.
MOVIETONE NEWS A2158: 'Auckland; riots and fires in NZ prison drama; catalogue ref. F59438 personal record, Cunningham, Gordon Hamilton, Mt Eden Gaol fire', catalogue ref. F47854 accessed Nga Taonga — Sound and Vision, Wellington.
Perkins, Jack (producer), 'Men of Broad Arrow' (pt. 1), 1974, Spectrum documentary, Radio NZ.

Quaker Oral History Project (OHColl-0427), ATL.
Scott, David, 'Report on Mount Eden Prison Riot, July 1965', catalogue ref. 237328, accessed Ngā Taonga Sound and Vision, Wellington.
Te Puna Wai Korero, 'Teaching Maori in Prisons', 1977, catalogue ref. 45358 NZ Sound Archive.
Wevers, Francis (director), *Shattered Dreams,* 1990, accessed Ngā Taonga Sound and Vision, Wellington.

Periodicals

Auckland Star
Auckland Weekly News
Central Leader
Colonist
Daily Southern Cross
Dominion
Evening Post
Evening Star
Grey River Argus
Lyttelton Times
Maori Messenger
Maoriland Worker
New Zealand Gazette and Wellington Spectator
New Zealand Herald
New Zealand Herald and Auckland Gazette
New Zealander
N.Z. Truth
Observer
Press (Christchurch)
Sunday News
Sunday Star-Times
Western Leader

Theses and dissertations

Anderson, Robyn. '"The Hardened Frail Ones": Women and Crime in Auckland, 1845–1870', MA thesis, University of Auckland, 1981.
Darragh, Neil, 'Social relations of prison inmates', MA thesis, University of Auckland, 1973.
Dunn, J., 'An Enquiry into the New Zealand Prison System 1840–1880', MA thesis, Victoria University of Wellington, 1947.

Egarr, Tristan, 'Discipline and Defence: Military Influence on Policing and Imprisonment c.1870–1913', MA thesis, Victoria University of Wellington, 2010.
Mansill, Douglas B., 'A Civil and Ecclesiastical Union? The Development of Prison Chaplaincy in Aotearoa — New Zealand', MPhil thesis, Auckland University of Technology, 2008.
McLellan, John M., 'Soldiers and Colonists: Imperial Soldiers as Settlers in Nineteenth-century New Zealand', MA thesis, Victoria University of Wellington, 2017.
Napier, Andrea G., 'Each Day is Different: Prison Officers and their Work', MA thesis, Victoria University of Wellington, 2012.
Ostereicher, Paul, '"They Would Not Fight": Survey of Conscientious Objection during World War II', MA thesis, Victoria University of Wellington, 1955.
Phillips J. R., 'A Social History of Auckland 1840–1853', MA thesis, University of Auckland, 1966.
Whelan, P. J., 'Care of Destitute, Neglected and Criminal Children 1840–1900', MA thesis, Victoria University of Wellington, 1956.
Wilson, Thomas Y., 'NZ Prisons 1880–1909: The Administration of Colonel Arthur Hume', MA thesis, Victoria University of Wellington, 1970.

Archives and records

Archives and Heritage Office, Tasmania, Australia
Archives New Zealand (Archives NZ)
Auckland Provincial Council records, Auckland Public Library
Capper Collection, Waihī Museum
H. E. Thatcher papers, University of Auckland
T. M. Philson Casebook, Auckland University Library special collections
Webber, Cyil Ernie Richard: Papers (MS-3333/197 and 198), Hocken Collections Uare Taoka o Hākena, University of Otago

Interviews

Jeanette Abbott
Tim Balme
Simon Best
Taiarahia Black
Sandra Coney
Zane Paine
Simon Kerr
Te Rangikaheke Kiripātea

Barry and Anna Lee
Phil Lister
Neville Mark
Te Kahautu Maxwell
Charlie Post
Bob van Ruyssevelt
Miriam Saphira
Tim Shadbolt
Jim Shepherd
Pete Smith
Oliver Sutherland
Mary Woodward

Websites

www.teara.govt.nz/en/biographies/
www.tvnz.co.nz

Acknowledgements

The author gratefully acknowledges an initial research grant from the New Zealand History Research Trust Fund (Ministry for Culture and Heritage), and a grant in aid of publication from the Peace Education Fund (Religious Society of Friends Aotearoa / New Zealand.)

An earlier version of chapter two, 'Feculent Hovel', co-written with Warwick Tie, appeared in the journal *Counterfutures: Left Thought and Practice Aotearoa*, no. 3, 2017, 23–55.

An earlier version of the material on imprisoned World War One dissenters was presented to the conference 'Dissent in the First World War', hosted by the Stout Research Centre for New Zealand Studies, Victoria University of Wellington, 31 August–2 September 2017.

Staff of the following institutions have given invaluable support: National Library of New Zealand Te Puna Mātauranga o Aotearoa, Te Rua Mahara o te Kāwanatanga Archives New Zealand, Ngā Taonga Sound and Vision, Auckland Libraries Ngā Pataka Kōrero o Tāmaki Makaurau, Tāmaki Paenga Hira Auckland War Memorial Museum.

Thanks also to my fellow members of the Wellington History Writers Group, and to Robbie Burton, Nicky Hager, Scott Hamilton, Mark Hanson, Tame Iti, Jenny and George Packard, Jeremy Rose, Jane Tolerton, Sir Kim Workman and Petra at Good Dixie's café, Lyall Bay.

Special thanks to man of letters, lifelong friend and cater-cousin Roger Steele for raising the idea for this book. At its final stages, editor Jane Parkin and the team at Massey University Press have been consistently expert and enjoyable to work with.

Living with a writer is never easy and seldom rewarding, and I am endlessly grateful to my fellow communards, and above all to Erin for backing me.

About the author

Mark Derby is a New Zealand writer and historian whose work has also been published in Britain, Spain and the US. His previous publications include *Ragnar Redbeard: The Antipodean Origins of Radical Fabulist Arthur Desmond* (Steele Roberts, 2017), *Petals and Bullets: Dorothy Morris: New Zealand Nurse in the Spanish Civil War* (Sussex Academic Press/Potton & Burton, 2015), *White-collar Radical: Dan Long and the Rise of the White-collar Unions* (Craig Potton Publishing, 2013), *The Prophet and the Policeman: The Story of Rua Kenana and John Cullen* (Craig Potton Publishing, 2009), *Kiwi Compañeros: New Zealand and the Spanish Civil War* (Canterbury University Press, 2009; Spanish-language edition published 2011 in association with the University of Castilla-La Mancha, Spain).

He has been jailed but never imprisoned, and lives on Wellington's south coast with three generations of his family.

Index

Page numbers in **bold** refer to images

A

Abbott, Raewyn 282–83
ACORD (Auckland Committee on Racism and Discrimination) 277, **278**
Adderley, Tommy 275–76
Addington women's prison, Christchurch 156, 165
Albert Barracks, Auckland 40, 60
Alexandra Barracks, Wellington 100
Allen, James 146
Allen, Stephen 158
Alley (prison escapee) 108
Allwood, Harvey 209
Andrewartha, Mrs 70, 72
Armed Offenders Squad 236, 244
Arney, Sir George 43–44, 45, 49, 50, 62, **63**, 64, 70, 73, 88
Arohata prison 206, 207
Asian prisoners 157
Auckland
see also courthouse, Auckland; Mount Eden Prison; Queen Street Gaol; Stockade (Auckland Gaol)
 grog shops 26
 impact of New Zealand Wars 64
 map, January 1842 **25**
 temporary raupō lockup, 1840 23, 24
Auckland Central Remand Prison (ACRP, later Mount Eden Corrections Facility) 290, 291, 292, 296, 298, 300
Auckland Gaol see Mount Eden Prison; Paremoremo Prison; Queen Street Gaol; Stockade (Auckland Gaol)
Auckland Provincial Council 47, 48, 50, 56, 60, 64, 67, 68, 69, 73–74, 79, 81, 86, 88
Auckland Regional Prison proposal 265, 285–86, 290
Awa, Reuben 227
Awatere, Donna 272
Awatere, Pita 264–65, 270
Ayre, Robert 81

B

Balneavis, Henry 188–89, 191
Banks, Archie 217
Banks, John 217
Banyard, Stanley 201, 203, 204, 206–07
Barnes, Jock 195
Barnett, Sam 197, 198, 200, 201, 204, 206, 207–08, 212, 213, 217, 218, 219–21, 230
Barstow, Mr (Visiting Justice) 94
Baughan, Blanche 157
Bay of Islands 27–28, 30, 31, 46, 66
Bay of Plenty 12, 14, 74, 76
Bayley, John 176
Beattie, Sir David 272
Beckham, Thomas 77, 79, 80, 83
Bennett, Pat 213
Berrey, Percival 36, 37, 38–39, 40, 41, 44, 46–47
Best, Simon 13
Black, Albert 'Paddy' ('jukebox killer') 211
Black Power 14, 279, 280
Bolton, Walter 212
Bourbeau, Oswald 162, 164
Bower, John 260, 261
Bradley, Dave 300
Brailsford, John 139
bread-and-water diet 38, 48, 70, 72, 103, 164, 177, 203, 215, 224
Brickell, Barry 201
Brougham, Linda 281
Brown, Thomas 24
Brutal Bastille, name for Mount Eden Prison 141
Buchanan, Alexander 76
Buckley, Edward 228, 230, 231–32, 235, 237, 244, 251, 252, 254, 256, 261, 265
Buckley, John 168–69
Budd, E. C. 164
Bull, Thomas 27
Burgess, A. **199**
Burke, Daniel 81
Burns, Joseph 42
Burrows, P. F. 105, 107

C

Calder, Jasper 166
Caldwell, James 98, 99
capital punishment 16, 119–20, 173, 186, 189, 192, 193–95, 198, 214, 230
  see also hanging
Capital Punishment Act 1950 207, 208
Carleton, Hugh 77
Carrington psychiatric hospital 285
Cartman, Douglas Herbert 194
Cavanagh, Dan 232, 236, 237
cells
  association (communal or dormitory) cells 159–60, **216**, 217–18, 244, 246
  cellblock atrium, 1990s **299**
  flowers and pictures in cells 172
  flushing toilets 285
  foul air and smells 57, 129, 195, 300
  lack of glass in windows 275
  lighting 119, 122, 132, 151, 255
  Mount Eden cell, 1950 **190**
  Mount Eden high-security unit 254
  observation cells for psychiatrically disturbed inmates 279
  punishment cell (dummy) 70, 76, 164, 176, 178, 203, 215, 219, 262
  remand inmates 187
  silent system 99
  suicide prevention 288
  two men to a cell 234, 261
censorship of mail 102, 168, 201
chaplains 115, 122–23, 164, 166, 171, 173, 175, 198, 269
  Māori 283
Cheeseman, Thomas 93
Chemis, Louis 117–18
children 16, 70, 73, 77, 115–16, 276–77, 278
  non-custodial sentences 116
  sexual offences against 279
choir 160
Christie, John 127
Christmas Day 281
Churton, John 31, 32
Clark, Helen 297
Classification Board 198
Coates, James 22–23, 28–29, 31, 32, 33, 36
Colclough, Mary **71**, 72–73
Communist Party 162, 164
Compulsory Military Training Act 1911 137–38
Coney, Sandra 271
  diary, published in Broadsheet **272**, 271–72
Connell, J. J. **199**
Connor, Arthur 46–47
conscientious objectors 16, 137–42, 146, 147, 151, 175–78, **179**, **180**, 181
  Māori 143–47
Contagious Diseases Act 1869 112–13
Cooper, Jeremiah 46
Cooper, Whina 84
corporal punishment 173, 193, 194–95
  flogging 79, 103–04, 121, 127, 164, 170, 173, 192–93, 193, 194, 195
  whipping 36, 61, 76, 77, 79, 99, 103
Costar, Dot 271
courthouse, Auckland **25**, **26**, 26–27, 29, 50
  conditions for jurors 29
  first trial, 1842 27–28
  women's cells beneath courthouse 43–44, 50
Cresswell, D'Arcy 166, 167
Crichton, Jack 178, 181
Criminal Code Act 1893 192
Criminal Justice Act 1954 197

D

Dallard, Bert 178, 195, 197
Davis, Sir Ernest 132, 170
Dawson, Gilbert 24
Dawson, Lynn 274
debtors 16, 33, 41, 49, 58, 70, 73, 86, 105
dentists 198, 276
Department of Corrections 17, 19, 274, 283, 288, 293, 303, 304, 306
Department of Prisons 95, 139, 156, 157, 159, 164, 196, 200, 207–08
depressions
  early 1930s 156, 159
  long depression, 1890s 115
detention camps for military defaulters 176, 177, 178
Dewes, Nehe 283
Dickison, Jim 152, 170
doctors 49, 80, 112, 141, 176–77, 198, 212, 276
Downey, Leo 255

draft resisters 16
Dreardon, George 79, 80
drug use 261, 275, 276, 288, 292
drunkenness, as an offence 16, 22, 24, 26, 29, 44, 49, 70, 87, 113, 115, 116–17, 166
Dumfrey, Richard 68
Dunedin Prison 86, 98, 215, 237
Dunn, A. 199

E

Eden, H. I. 199
education of prisoners 98, 99, 123, 261
  Mount Eden Prison 99, 136–37, 153, 154, 162, 198, 220, 265
  Queen Street Gaol, proposed literacy classes 31–32
  Stockade (Auckland Gaol) 81, 83, 87
Edwards, Jim 170, 171
Eggerton, Mary Alice 113
employment of prisoners 60, 153–54, 281
  see also quarrying and stonework; tree-planting camps
  blacksmithing 60, 100, 144
  boot and shoe making 60, 67, 100, 154, 156, 226
  carpentry 60, 100, 102, 215, 226
  carving figures from bullock horn 61
  domestic work 60, 70–71, 92, 100, 157, 276, 281
  gardening 155
  Mount Eden bakery 202
  payment 67, 86–87, 88, 100, 102, 154, 175, 266, 268
  skills of little use after discharge 155–56
  tailoring 60, 153, 154, 156, 226
  trade training 102, 123, 198, 215, 226, 268, 281
  work parties outside prison 154–55, 268, 281
  work-parole 268
escapes and breakouts 15–16, 106, 108, 121, 168, 231, 279, 298
  band members 217–18
  Buckley 168–69
  gang members 280
  Horton 214
  Kelly gang 172–73, 194
  MacMillan and Sadaraka 238–40, 242
  Nash 225
  prevention and discouragement 61, 237, 240, 286
  Queen Street Gaol 47, 48–49
  Raewyn Abbott taken hostage 282–83
  Stockade (Auckland Gaol) 59, 61, 62, 68–69, 76–77, 78, 84, 85–86
  Westlake's escape demonstration 150–51
  Wilder 226–28, 231
  Wilder, Gillies and Evans 236–37
Evans, Lennie 236–37, 242, 243
Execution of Criminals Act 1858 64
executions see capital punishment
exhumation of bodies of men buried in prison grounds
  Mount Eden Prison 12–15, 66, 76, 284–85, 307
  Queen Street Gaol 28, 51
Eyley, Claudia Pond, drawing 272

F

Federation of Labour 139
Findlay, John 122, 123, 165
Finlay, Martyn 256, 296
Finney, Jeannie 72, 73
Fiori, Silvio 210
fire and riot at Mount Eden Prison, 1965 241, 242–44, 245, 246, 247, 248, 249, 250–52, 253, 254, 256, 265, 266, 284
First Offenders' Probation Act 1886 116
Fisher, Francis 30
FitzRoy, Robert 40, 46
Flynn (Stockade governor) 67, 69
food and water for prisoners 119, 152, 172, 201, 266, 275, 287
  hard-labour diet 59–60, 126, 141
  Hume's views on diet 98, 115
  Queen Street Gaol 36–37, 40
  remand and non-workers' rations 126, 129
  special diets 287
  Stockade (Auckland Gaol) 57, 59–60, 68, 76
  warders' duties 134
  women 156–57, 271
forensic psychiatrist 276
Forest and Bird Society 281
Fort Cautley, Auckland 132
Fraser, Peter 170, 194
Freer, Warren 200, 215
Fulloon, James 12, 74

G

gagging 79
gangs 279–80, 287
GEO Group 292
German civilian prisoners, World War I 142
Gillies, John 236–37, 242, 243
Goodward, Henry 103–04
Gould, Robert 139
governors 99, 122
Graham, Doug 15
Gray, Tamati 286
Grey, George 41–42, 45–46, 104
Grey, Henry George, 3rd Earl Grey 56
Grubb, R. 227
guards *see* prison officers
Gunn, Dennis 189
Guy, Gerry 280

H

habitual criminals' and offenders' legislation 121–22, 171, 197
Habitual Drunkards Act 1906 117
Haines (prison officer) 240, 251
Hale, Joseph 29–30
Hall, Thomas 102–03
Hamilton, Ian 173
Hanan, Ralph 230, 231, 234–35, 252, 254, 255
hanging 164, 170, **185**
   Harper 64–66
   Māori 28, 51, 66–67, 74–76, 191, 210, 212
   'Meccano Set' portable scaffold 184, 186, **187**, 191, 207, 212
   Mount Eden Prison 120, 132, 134, 185, 188–89, **190**, 191–92, 193, 207–12
   prison inmates as hangmen 191
   Queen Street Gaol 28, 42, 50, 51
   scaffold, Auckland **27**, 28
   Stockade (Auckland Gaol) 64–67
Hansen, Harold 178
hard labour 30, 31, 32, 37–38, 40, 41, 43, 49–50, 98, 137, 165, 170, 173, 176, 177, 194
   see also quarrying and stonework
   construction of prison buildings 104–06
   financial returns 68
   penal servitude 47, 48, 49, 68, 100
   public works 24, 35, 38, 47, 48, 56, 86
Hardingham, John 201

Harper, Richard 64–66, 76
Hay, Frank 122
Haywood, Horace **199**, 201, 206, 208–09, 211, 212, 213, 217, 218, 221, 226, 228, 235
Haywood's Brass Band 213–14, 216, 217, 218, 219, 248, **249**
Hill, Reverend 115
Historic Places Trust (later Heritage New Zealand) 297
Hobson, Gary 284
Hobson, Jack 260–61, 265, 266, 267
Hobson, William 22, 24, 26, 29, 51
Hogan (Activities Officer) **199**
Holland, Harry 141, 170
Holland, Sid 198
homosexual activity 160, 165, 166, 215, 234, 235, 279
The Rock Orchid **233**, 235
Hood, Joseph 108
Horomona Poropiti 12, 13, 14, 75
Horton, Edward 'Slim' 213–15, 217
hospital and medical services 136, 152, 158, 176, 201, 266, 276, 279
   Queen Street Gaol 43
   Stockade (Auckland Gaol) 94–95
Hospital for the Insane, Auckland 41, 45, 67
Howard League for Penal Reform 157, 165, 288, 289
Hulme, Juliet 206
Hume, Arthur 96, **97**, 98–100, 102, 103, 104–05, 110, 113, 115–17, 118, 120, 121, 122, 128, 175, 195, 197, 303
hunger strikes 139, 177–78, **179**, **180**, 256
Huntly coalminers' strike 140
Hutchinson, Mrs (Prison Gate Brigade) 113
Hyde, Monsignor 210
hygiene and sanitation 57, 68, 94, 98, 106, 129, 136, 151, 152, 195–96, **233**, 250, 275, 285

I

Imprisonment for Debt Abolition Act 1874 86
incarceration rate, New Zealand 307
industrial schools 116
Inspector of Prisons 96, 98–100, 102, 103, 104–05, 113, 115–17, 118, 120, 121, 122–23, 128
Ironside (chief gaoler/superintendent) 136, 155–56, 164

J

Jackson, Athol 142
Jackson, Miriam (later Saphira) 269, 270
Jacques, Alan Keith 211
Johns, Arthur 139
Johnson, John 22, 29, 35–36, 37, 40, 41, 43
Jones, John 140
Jorgensen, Ron 236, 248, 255

K

Kahupaea, Heremita 13, 75
Kaka, Tahi 132, 134
Kane, Mary Ann 92–93
Kayll, James 122–23
Kean, William 24, 26
Kelly gang 172–73
Kerr, Simon 286, **289**
Killey, John 50
Kīngitanga movement 144
Kirimangu, Mikaere 12, 75
Kiripātea, Te Rangikaheke 264, 265, 267
Kohimarama industrial training school 116
Kororāreka (Russell) 23, 40

L

La Mattina, Angelo 219
Lake Alice psychiatric hospital 250, 254
Lamb, Alfred 168
Lang, Patrick 59
Lange, David 277, **278**
Larson, Cecil 208
Latoatama 208
Lee, Ernest 153
Lee, John A. 126–30, **131**, 132, 134, 147, 169, 170, 186, 213
Leggett, Thomas 170, 177, **178**, 181, 196
leg-irons 31, 38, 61, 68, 76, 80
letter-writing by prisoners 61, 102–03, 132, 151, 158, 287
    illicit letters 168
library, Mount Eden Prison 119, 122, 130, 132, 151, 162, 254, 264
    women's prison 273–74
life imprisonment 102, 103, 117, 126, 143, 151, 166, 168, 198, 200, 206, 214, 224, 231, 234, 250, 264
    commuted death sentence 84, 160, 193, 208
    Stockade (Auckland Gaol) 57, 86

Ligar Canal 40, 44
Lindauer, *Ana Rupene and Child* 300, **301**
Lister, Phil 15
Lock Hospital 112–13

M

Maaka, Eruera 287
MacGillivray, Colin 296, 304
Mackay, Charles 166, **167**
MacMillan, Daniel (aka Phillip Weston) 238–40, 242, 244, 250, 251–52, 266
MacMillan, David 238, 244
MacPherson, Duncan 115
Mafart, Alain 273
Mahoney, Edward 93, 94–95, 96, 101, 105
Maketu Wharetotara 27–28, 51
Maniapoto, Rewi 110
Māori
    Albert Barracks construction 40
    British penal system 28
    hired to help haul drunks off to gaol 26
    language 62
    New Zealand Wars 64, 74
    refusal to enlist, World War I 143–46
    tribal justice processes 27, 28
    urbanisation 16, 159, 220, 265
Māori in prisons 38, 62, 110, 112, 158–59, 204, 264–65, 277, 279, 283–84
    attitudes of prison staff 224
    Awatere's classes 265
    destruction of letters written in Māori 102
    'dog tax' prisoners 112
    education 83, 136–37
    efforts to allow for cultural practices 41–42, 66, 284–85
    exhumation of bodies of men buried in prison grounds 12–15, 28, 51, 66, 76, 284–85, 307
    hangings 28, 51, 66–67, 74–76, 191, 210, 212
    illness 41–42, 48, 74, 80, 112
    language 62, 80, 102
    military defaulters 143–47
    Pai Mārire or Hauhau followers 74–76
    prison officers 220
    proportion of inmates 16, 110, 159, 204–05, 220, 265, 277
    spiritual unrest 284–85

suicide 16, 283, 284, 287
'the Pa,' Stockade 110
women 270–71, 273
Marchant, Ed 239–40, 266
Mareo, Eric 160, 162, 194
Mareo, Thelma 160
Mark, Neville 290, 292, 293
Marshall, John 215
Martin, Maria 88
Martin, William 42, 46, 56, 77
Mason, Henry 164–65
Mason, Rex 175, 179, **180**, 194–95, 217–18
Mason, William 54, 56
Massey, Bill 129, 134, 136
Mathew, Felton 24, 26, 29
Matich, Frank 227, 228, 242
matrons 70, 72, 88, 157, 270
Matthews, Charles E. 122
Matthews, Kit 152–53
Mauriri, Peter 280
Maxwell, 'Diesel Dick' 13
Maxwell, Ralph 297–98
Maxwell, Te Kahautu 12, 13, 14
McAuley, Harold 178, 179, 180
McCabe, Owen 59
McCahon, Colin 255, 256
McCormick, E. H. 255
McDonald, Richard 'Maori Mac' 217–18, 232, 236, 246, 250
McElwain, George 22, 24, 29, 43, 64
McKenzie, Donald 19, 204–06, 209, 215, 232, 234, 242
McKenzie, Precious 268
McLean, Ellen 72, 73
McLean, G. **199**
McLeod, Beth 282, 290
McManus, Kate and Mary 87
McMillan, Girvan 170, 171, 172, 173
McNaughton, Donald 24
mental health 261
  effect of drug use 276
  imprisonment of mentally ill patients 16, 29–30, 39, 45, 115, 116, 118, 152–53, 157
  psychiatrically disturbed inmates 279, 284, 285
  women inmates 271
Meola Reef public reserve plantings 281
military prisoners 41, 64, 74–76, 137–40, 175–78, **179**, **180**, 181

Mills, R. J. 169
Missen, E. A. 265, 285–86
Mokena, Here 145
Mokomoko 13, 14, 15, 16, 75, 76
Mongrel Mob 279–80
Moreton, George 164
  A Parson in Prison 173, 175
Motuarohia Island, Bay of Islands 27–28
Mount Cook prison, Wellington 99–100, 123
Mount Crawford Prison, Wellington 186, 250
Mount Eden Borough Council 296–97
Mount Eden Corrections Facility (formerly Auckland Central Remand Prison) 300, 305
  see also Auckland Central Remand Prison (ACRP, later Mount Eden Corrections Facility)
Mount Eden (Maungawhau) 51, 54, **55**, 60
Mount Eden Prison 15–17, **18**
  see also cells; escapes and breakouts; hospital and medical services; library; prison officers; prisoners; punishments; riots and uproars; Stockade (Auckland Gaol)
  admittance and management routines 118–19
  aerial view, 1930 **161**
  armoury 119
  Auckland Star articles, 1919 151–52
  bakery **202**
  break-in, 1889 108
  canteen 201
  chapel 160, 162, **163**, 239, 242, **245**, 274
  closing ceremony 17, 293
  criticism of facilities and practices 169–70, 173, 175
  dangerous and insanitary condition, 2004 303–04
  decommissioning 15, 17, 290, 292–93, 296–97
  detention unit (back basement) 226, 227, 230, 231, 235–36, 237, 240
  'hardest jail in New Zealand' 16, 286–88, 290
  Haywood's instructions 201, 203
  heritage classification 17, 297, 298, 300
  high-security unit 231, 237, 240, 242, 250, 252, 254–55, 256, 279
  insect infestations 119, 129, 145

maximum-security institution 15–16, 118, 121, 165, 168, 195, 218, 219, 230–31, 257, 279
names 7
new 245-bed building under construction 2020 306
'only purely penal prison' 165
'Outward Bound School' 280
pre-release unit 268
preservation and repurposing as museum 17, 303–04, 305–07
Prisoners Council 203–04
reconfiguration into three divisions, 1983 279
reformative function 155–56
regulations 102, 178, 267
relocation proposals 169–70, 200, 218, 220–21, 267, 285–86
remand and short-term prison 230, 252, 265, 267, 273, 281
remand unit 224, 238, 239, 240, 246, 279 (*see also* Auckland Central Remand Prison; Mount Eden Corrections Facility)
renovations, 1987 285
repair of north and east wings, 1971 265–66, 267
south wing **135**, 136, 137
stone prison buildings ('Stone Jug') 93–96, 98, **101**, 105–06, **107**, 108, **109**, 110, **111**, 118–23, 126, 134, 136, 137
Sunday News articles, 1964 232, 234–35
supernatural phenomena 304–05, 307
Truth articles, 1963 231–32
unhealthy conditions 106, 129, 151, 154, 195–96, 206, 207, 267
Mount Eden suburb 169
Moyle, Colin 256
Moynihan, Brendan 280
Mr Asia drug syndicate 224, 256–57
Munn, Arthur 190, 192
murals painted by Dave Bradley 300, **301**
murder 42, 74, 117, 143, 152–53, 166, 172, 186, 189, 192, 194, 196, 209, 214, 279
  abolition of capital punishment 210–12
  exhumation of bodies of men hanged for murder 12–15, 13, 66, 76, 284–85, 307
  'Great Barrier Island murderers' 120
  by Harper 64–66, 76
  by Hulme and Parker 206–07
  by Jorgensen and Gillies 236
  by Māori 12, 13, 66, 75–76, 84, 120, 132, 188, 210, 212, 264
  Motuarohia murders 27, 28
  by Niueans 208
  by Sadaraka 252
  by women 271

N

Napier, William 120
Nash, Karl 79
Nash, Trevor 225, 262, 264
National Council of Women 113
Naughton, James 83
Neill, William 60
Ness, Tigilau 279
New Zealand South Seas International Exhibition, 1925 155
New Zealand Wars 64, 86, 196
Newall, Sir Cyril 173
Newbold, Greg 19, 242
Ngāpuhi 12, 13, 28, 84
Ngāti Awa 12, 14
Ngāti Whātua 41, 54, 66–67, 83
Ngatihoko 74
Niueans in prison 208
Noble, John 49
nurses 43, 67, 198, 204

O

O'Brien, Loughlin 49, 60–61, 93, 94, 95, 99, 100, 101
O'Connor (Principal Officer) **199**
O'Donnell, Mike 267–68
Okeroa 66
Ordinance for the Regulation of Prisons 1846 42
Ostler, Sir Hubert 173

P

Pacific Islands prisoners 16, 157–58, 273, 277, 279, 282, 287
pacifists *see* conscientious objectors; religious pacifists
Paine, Zane 276, 282
Pakatoa Island, retreat for 'inebriates' 117
Palmer, Geoffrey 298
Papakura military camp 176, 244
Paparua Prison, Christchurch 206, 216, 218, 228, 250, 256, 261

Paraharahara 80
Paremoremo Prison 230, 231, 237, 250–51, 252, 254, 256, 267, 268, 286, 296, 298
Parihaka 12
Parker, Pauline 206
Parkhurst boys 33, 35–36, 45
parole 198
  pre-release parole 268
  work-parole 268
Parry, Bill 129, **131**, 132, 140, 147, 170
Patterson, Colonel 145
Peacocke, Ponsonby 83
Penal Institutions Act 1954 197
penal policies 16, 17, 62
  commission of inquiry into New Zealand gaols, 1878 96
  early 20th century 118, 128
  government inspection 96, 98–100, 103, 104–05
  inquiries into suitability of existing prisons for a national prison 74, 83–84
  national high-security prison 99–100, 121, 169–70, 200, 218, 221–22, 230, 231, 234, 237, 250–51, 256, 257
  parliamentary report on prison management, 1854 56
  principle of lesser privilege 115
  private management of prisons 292
  reformative policies 122–23, 129, 147, 155, 165, 170, 171–72, 175, 197–98, 200, 201, 203–04, 213, 219–21, 267
penal servitude sentence 47–48, 49, 68, 84, 86, 100, 106, 128
penal system, British 28, 56, 99, 105, 307
pets 275
Phillips, Celicia 76
Philson, Thomas Moore 60, 72, 79, 112
Pickering, William Phelps 30–31, 32, 33, 45
Plummer, Frederick 77, 78, 86
Pointon, Thomas 122, 150
political prisoners 16, 45, 110, 129, 158, 162, 164, 166, 170–71, 260, 269, 273
Polynesian Panthers 279
Post, Charlie 306
Poulton, Jane 157
preventive detention 197, 217, 218, 231, 234, 250
Prieur, Dominique 273
principle of lesser privilege 115

prison farms 118, 165, 226
  see also Rangipo prison farm; Waikeria prison farm; Waikune prison farm
Prison Gate Brigade, Salvation Army 113, 115
prison officers 67, 81, 82, **88**, 105, 106, **114**, 128, **131**, 141, 150, 155, 166, 169, 171, 172, 194, 195, 196, **199**, 281
  see also psychologists; specialist staff, e.g. nurses
  assaults by inmates 121, 172, 173, 194, 218–19, 221, 225, 227, 240, 251, 266, 282–83
  assaults on, and harsh treatment of, inmates 127, 219, 224–25, 255
  attitudes to corporal punishment 77, 79, 103, 104
  attitudes to Māori inmates 224
  compassionate approach 288, 290
  condemned cell duties 208–09
  conditions and wages 68, 88, 104, 134, 136, 175, 196, 198, 274–75
  custodial function 230, 269
  dormitory, the Stockade 77
  firearms 61, 69, 86, 106, 203, 225, 266
  Hume's views and reforms 99, 104
  incentive payments 75, 79
  Māori 220
  matrons 70, 72, 88, 157, 270
  prisoner advocacy 79, 80
  proportion of prisoners to staff 88, 266, 280
  recruitment from the armed forces 99, 104, 122
  sentry and patrol duty 69, 106
  shortages 176–77, 196, 215, 235, 251, 280, 285
  training 104, 175, 196, 198, 290
  women 281–83
Prison Officers Association 280
prisoners
  see also Asian prisoners; education of prisoners; employment of prisoners; food and water for prisoners; letter-writing by prisoners; Māori in prisons; military prisoners; Pacific Islands prisoners; political prisoners; privileges; punishments; recreation; remand prisoners; sexual activity of prisoners; visitors; women and girls in prisons; young offenders

'barons' 204, 212–13, 218–19, 226, 232
classification 38, 61, 102, 119, 121, 137, 154, 165, 168, 200, 204, 281
clothing and footwear 36, 37, 61, 64, 67, 100, 102, 151–52, 153, 203, 270, 276, 279, 281, 286, 287
criminal activity while in prison 168
deaths 127, 128, 141, 146–47
discipline 36, 61, 69, 76, 77, 79, 81, 87, 96, 99, 103, 116, 122, 171, 177, 206, 228, 230 (*see also* punishments; riots and uproars)
discouragement of conversation 205
duties 37, 60
exercise 46, 72, 76, 94, 99, 119, 137, 139, 161, 162, 166, 172, **174**, 177, 237, 254, 255, 262, 287
fights 224–25, 232, 280, 292
firearms 236, 237, 238–40, 248, 251, 261
grievances 170–72, 174, **174** (*see also* riots and uproars)
hair cropping 61, 72, 87
health 37, 38, 40, 41–42, 43, 44, 49, 57, 59–60, 61, 68, 152, 275
homeless 115
overcrowding 40, 44, 48, 49, 50, 59, 68, 86, 87, 92, 94, 162, 215, 218, 220, 265, 267, 274–75, 285, 298
pre-release 274
'trusties' 213
unjust treatment 42
Prisoners Aid 274
Prisoners Council 203–04
Prisoner's Hill, Mount Eden 60
Prisons Act 1883 103
Prisons Act 1908 197
Prisons Board 165, 166, 171, 173
Prisons Parole Board 198
privileges 43, 119, 156–57, 164, 201, 230, 255, 268, 273
  band members 213, 215, 217
  classes of prisoners 61, 102
  loss of privileges 61, 103, 129, 164, 201, 203
  tobacco 151, 164
probation 116, 159, 165, 221, 262
Progressive Youth Movement (PYM) 260–62, 265
prostitution 26, 49, 87, 94, 112–13, 206
protests and demonstrations 260–62, **263**

psychologists 19, 198, 204, 232, 269, 270, 271, 276
Public Service Association (PSA) 196, 274–75, 280
punishments
  see also capital punishment; corporal punishment; hard labour; sentences
  bread-and-water diet 38, 48, 70, 72, 103, 164, 177, 203, 215, 224
  brutal punishments, the Stockade 79–81
  gagging 79
  leg-irons 31, 38, 61, 68, 76, 80
  loss of privileges 61, 103, 129, 164, 201, 203
  objective of judicial system 56, 61
  for offences committed while in prison 164
  policies 122
  punishment cell (dummy) 70, 76, 164, 176, 178, 203, 215, 219, 262
  solitary confinement 37, 38–39, 48, 59, 61, 79, 80, 103, 139, 177, 224, 286
  stocks **26**, 29
  treadmill punishment proposal 39
  women 72

Q

Quakers 141–42
quarrying and stonework 59–60, 69, 106, 126, 138, 141, 155, 159, 170, 224
  closure of quarry 225–26, 268
  diet for labouring men 59–60
  difficulties of working with scoria 60, 86–87
  injuries 154
  mechanised equipment 67, 136, 154
  payment 86–87, 100, 154
  road metal 156
  stone cutting and shaping 76–77, 86–87, 106, 126, 127
Queen Street Gaol 16, 22–24, **25**, 26, **26–27**, 28–29, 30–31, 33
  see also cells; escapes and breakouts; hospital and medical services; prison officers; prisoners; punishments
  1855 ground plan 34
  convicts waiting for transportation 46, 47–48
  decrepit state, 1850s 48–49, 50–51, 64, 304

expansion 39
mentally ill inmates 29–30, 39, 45
pound 39
regulations and routines 36–39
transfer of prisoners to the Stockade 57, 59, 69–70
unhealthy conditions 40, 44–45, 49
Queen Street riots 170–71

R

racial inequity 277, 279
Rainbow Warrior bombing 273
Rains, Senior Sergeant 261
Ramsey, Thomas 120–21
Rangipo prison farm 226
Rangitoto Island roads, walking tracks and construction work 154–55, 281
Rātana faith 160
Reardon, Margaret 42
recreation 166, 175, 177, 214, 220, 254, 265, 266, 276, 281
  arts 201, 255–56
  beekeeping 201
  bowling 201, 214
  chess 201, 281
  competitions away from prison premises 201
  debating 162, 201
  'instructive talks' 162, 172, 274
  literary group 201
  movies 162, 210
  music and concerts 172, 201, 213–14, 218, 219
  pets 275
  radio broadcasts 172, 175, 270
  reading 119, 122, 164, 274, 300
  sports 175, 201
  TV 270, 273, 276, 281
  weightlifting 267–68, 273, 281
Reddaway, Graham 232, 234
reformers 113
  Blanche Baughan 157
  Howard League for Penal Reform 157, 165
  Mary Colclough 71, 72–73
  Mrs Hutchinson 113
rehabilitation 16, 17, 62, 81, 100, 102, 157, 198, 201, 212, 224, 226, 269, 306
  rehabilitation plans 290
religion

see also chaplains
prayer services 38
Sunday services 31, 32, 38, 160
Religious Objectors Advisory Board 146, 147
religious pacifists 138, 139, 141–42, 146
see also conscientious objectors
remand prisoners 200, 224, 230, 239, 246, 251, 252, 254, 279, 281, 286
see also Auckland Central Remand Prison (ACRP)
  conditions 87, 151, 166, 238, 273, 279, 284, 289, 297
  diet 126, 129
  Māori 74
  Queen Street Gaol 38, 48–49
  sentence plans 290
  Stockade (Auckland Gaol) 58, 70, 74, 87, 93–94, 95, 126
  suicide 287
  women 93–94, 270–71, 273
  young offenders 277
restorative justice 261
Riddiford, Dan 267, 275
Ringatū faith 12, 112
riots and uproars 16, 265, 292
  1904 120–21
  1948 196–97
  1965 17, **241**, 242–44, **245**, 246, **247**, 248, **249**, 250–52, **253**, 254, 256, 265, 266, 284
  1971 266–67
  revolts and protests 139, 177–78, **179**, **180**, 230, 256, 283–84, 286
Robinson, Isaac 76–77, 79, 85–86
Robson, John 221, 230, 260
Rogers, Jack 267, 268, 269, 275
Roper, Sir Clinton 298
Rotoroa Island, retreat for 'inebriates' 117
Rua Kēnana 143–44
Ruaki 41
Ruarangi 66
Ruatoria 13

S

Sadaraka, Jon 238–40, 242, 248, 250, 251, 252, 266
Salvation Army
  Prison Gate Brigade 113, 115
  retreats for 'inebriates' 117

Samoan prisoners 158
sanitation and hygiene 57, 68, 94, 98, 106, 129, 136, 151, 152, 195–96, **233**, 250, 275, 285
Sayers, Edward 43
scaffolding work by prisoners 128–29, 130
Scanlan, Tuna 224
Scott, Alexander 120
Scott, Dick 208
Seckington (prison escapee) 168
Secondary Punishment Act 1854 47, 54
security measures and equipment 60–61, 177, 230, 237, 240, 251, 265, 266, 267, 286, 292
Seddon, Richard 108
sedition 162, 164
self-harm 275
Semple, Bob **131**, 170, 207
sentence planning 288, 290
sentences
    see also capital punishment; hard labour; life imprisonment; parole; punishments; transportation of offenders
    corrective training 197, 198
    penal servitude 47–48, 49, 68, 84, 86, 100, 106, 128
    preventive detention 197, 217, 218, 231, 234, 250
    probation 116, 159, 165, 221, 262
    reformative detention 165–66, 197, 200
    remittances 86, 102, 173, 194, 226, 281
Serco 292
Severne, Francis 116, 117, 118
sexual activity of prisoners 49, 160, 165, 166, 215, 232, **233**, 234–35, 244, 246, 274
sex education 140–41
sexual offences 103, 104, 165, 166, 192, 197, 214, 218, 234, 242, 246, 269, 279
Shadbolt, Maurice 255, 262
Shadbolt, Tim 260, 261–62, 264–65, 269, 277, 279
Sharkey, Patrick 24
Shaw, Grace 255
Shepherd, Jim 224, 225–26, 231, 232, 236, 238, 243, 244, 246, 248, 250, 255, 256–57
Shirtcliffe, Les 224
Shortland, Willoughby 29, 31, 32, 35
Simmons, David 284

Sinclair, Cathalena 282
Smith, Neil 176, 303
Smith, William 92–93
Smithyman, Kendrick 130
social workers 269, 276
solitary confinement 37, 38–39, 48, 59, 61, 79, 80, 103, 139, 177, 224, 286
Somerville, Thomas 36
Springbok rugby tour, 1981 277, 279
Stack, James 74–75, 76
staff see prison officers
Staley, Mildred 165
Stockade (Auckland Gaol) 15, 48, 51, 54, **55**, 56–57, **58**, 110, **111**, 118, 126, 137
see also cells; escapes and breakouts; hospital and medical services; Mount Eden Prison; prison officers; prisoners; punishments; riots and uproars
    1870s 86–88
    Arney's reports and views 62, 64, 73, 88
    Auckland Provincial Council inquiry into condition and management 69
    boundary fence 57, 59, 62, 68
    commission of inquiry, 1877 95, 96
    fire risk 57, 95, 119
    government inspection 96, 98–99, 102
    inquiry into brutal treatment and Visiting Judges, 1867 79–81, 83
    Provincial Council plans for new gaol, 1860s 73–74
    regulations and routines 60–62, 67, 79–80, 102–03, 104, 134, 136
    school 81, 83, 87
    staff status raised by Hume 104
    stone boundary wall 77, 85–86, **89**, 95
    transfer of prisoners from Queen Street Gaol 57, 59, 69–70
    unhealthy conditions 57, 68, 94–95, 98, 134
stocks, Auckland **26**, 29
stonework see quarrying and stonework
Stout, Sir Robert 169
strikes
    Homeboat Strike, 1925 162, 164
    Huntly coalminers' strike 140
    Waihī strikers 128–30, **131**, 132, 139
Stroud, Humphrey 284–85
suicide and attempted suicide 15, 16, 117–18, 250, 275, 283, 284, 287–88, 300
    prevention 153, 288

Sunday News articles, 1964 232, 234–35
Supreme Court, Auckland **26**, 27, 43–44, 50, 62, 164, 209, 211
Sutherland, Oliver 277

T

Taiwhakaea Marae, Whakatāne 14
Tamasese 158
Tarawairu 48
Tasmania
  see also transportation of offenders
  Port Arthur penal colony 45–46
Te Arawa 146
Te Atairangikaahu, Te Arikinui Dame 14
Te Kahu, Hakaraia 191
Te Kooti Arikirangi Te Tūruki 112
Te Mahuki 110, 112
Te Puea Hērangi, Princess 145–46
Te Rahui, Hakaraia 13, 75
Te Rarawa 84
Te Rongapatahi, Eruera 210
Te Waere 41–42
Te Wake, Heremia 84
Te Whiu, Edward 212
teachers 32, 81, 83, 136, 198, 204
'Temenia' 41
Thatcher, Herbert 159, 160, 166, 168
Thomas, Arthur Allan 300, **302**
Thomas, Evan 162, 164
Thomas, John 66–67, 83
Thorn, James 139–41, 147
Thorn, Samuel 189, 191
Thorne, Shane 286, **289**
tobacco 36, 70, 87, 103, 108, 119, 129–30, 151, 156, 160, 164, 172, 201, 203, 232, 262, 267, 270
transportation of offenders 30–31, 32, 45–47
  abolition 47–48, 54, 56
  Māori 12
  Margaret Reardon, only woman 12, 42
transported convicts from Britain and Ireland 33, 35–36, 45–46
treadmill punishment proposal 39
Treaty of Waitangi 27–28, 146
tree-planting camps 118, 128
Truth articles, 1963 231–32
Tucker, Abner 46
Tuckwell, Joseph 67, 69–70, 76, 77, 78, 81, 103
Tufala, David 287

Tugt, C. **199**
Tuhaere, Paora 67, 83
Tūhoe 12, 143–44
Tūrangawaewae 14

U

Urquhart, Harry 138, 147

V

Vagrant Act 1866 94
Van Diemen's Land *see* transportation of offenders
van Ruyssevelt, Bob 260, 261
Vincent, Thomas 189, 191
violent offenders 15, 118, 120–21, 143, 152, 177, 192, 231, 234, 255
Visiting Justices 72, 77, 79–81, 83, 87, 93–94, 98, 154, 164, 178
  women 113
visitors 56, 61, 102, 103, 108, 140, 151, 164, 203, 238–39, 251, 254
  prison visitors 255, 268, 271
  visitors to women 70
Vogel, Sir Julius 96, 98
Völkner, Carl 13, 15, 74
volunteers
  prison visitors 255, 262, 271
  remedial reading teacher 274
  sex education talks 274
Von Luckner, Count Felix 142–43

W

Waiaua Marae 15
Waihī strikers 128–30, **131**, 132, 139
Waihorotiu Creek 23–24, 33
Waikato iwi 144–47
Waikeria high-security unit 139, 200, 208, 250, 254
Waikeria prison farm 152, 153, 156
Waikune prison farm 226
Waiohua confederation of tribes 54
Waitākere ranges, suggested prison site 169
Waite, Arin 24, 26
Waite, Flora 157
Walker, Ranginui 284
Wallace, Augusta 277
'Walled-Off Astoria Follies' concert 213
warders *see* prison officers
Warren, Phil 300, 303

Waru, Jackie 284
Webb, Clifton 198, 200, 207
Weir, Jock 240
welfare officer 201, 203, 204
Wellington women's reformatory 156
Westlake, Tom 150–51, 153
Whakatāne 14, 66
Whakatōhea 12, 13, 15, 75, 76, 80, 284
whipping 36, 61, 76, 77, 79, 99
White, William 141
Whiteland, Harry 210
Wilder, George 226–28, **229**, 231, 235, 236–37, 240, 242, 243, 250, 251, 255–56, 261, 262, 264
Wilford, Superintendent 144
Williams, Peter **289**
Wilson, John 177
Winiata, Taurangaika 120
Wiwarena, Patrick 227
women and girls
  industrial school for delinquent girls, Auckland 115
  in the stocks 29
women and girls in prisons 156–57, 165, 200, 215, 237, 271–74
  charged with drunkenness or vagrancy 16, 26, 72, 87, 94, 113
  children 16, 70, 73, 77
  conditions 43–44, 50, 72–73, 77, 86, 92, 93–94, 205–06
  contact with male prisoners 232, 234
  domestic work 37, 70, 92, 100, 157, 270, 273
  Hume's views 113, 115
  Juliet Hulme 206–07
  mental health 271
  payment 100
  pregnancy and childbirth 72, 94, 157, 273
  Prison Gate Brigade, Salvation Army 113, 115
  prison officers 281–83
  schoolroom and Women's Home proposals 72–73
  separation from male prisoners 38, 70, 73, 77, 92, 105, 160, 232, 279
  sports 201
  Stockade (Auckland Gaol) 16, 58, 70–71, 72–73, 77, 86, 92–94, 113, 232, 234, 237
  visitors 70
  vulnerability to abuse 24, 26, 196

Women's Christian Temperance Union 113
women's prisons 113
  Addington 156, 165
  Arohata 206, 207
  Manukau City 290
  Mount Eden Prison 200, 232, 237, 270, 271–74, 290, **291**, 292
  Stockade (Auckland Gaol) **58**
Woodward, Mary 274
World War One 137–47
World War Two 160, 175–81
Worth, Richard 300
Wright, John 79
Wynyard, Lieutenant-Colonel 43

Y

Yates, William 39
young offenders
  see also children
  Auckland Gaol 33, 35–36, 49–50
  borstal or probation 165
  mixing with adults 287
  Mount Eden Prison 115–16, 132, 134, 220, 226, 231, 277, 279, 287
  Stockade (Auckland Gaol) 76, 77, 79, 86, 220
  suicide 287, 288
Young, Thomas 79, 80

First published in 2020 by Massey University Press
Private Bag 102904, North Shore Mail Centre
Auckland 0745, New Zealand
www.masseypress.ac.nz

Text copyright © Mark Derby, 2020
Images copyright © as credited, 2020

Design by Megan van Staden
Cover photographs by Auckland Libraries Heritage Collections, 7_A1855 (front), *New Zealand Herald* (back, top), Auckland Libraries Heritage Collections, 7-A17598 (back, middle), *Stuff/Auckland Star* Collection (back, below), Auckland Libraries Heritage Collections, 4-1068 (case)

The moral right of the author has been asserted

All rights reserved. Except as provided by the Copyright Act 1994, no part of this book may be reproduced, stored in or introduced into a retrieval system or transmitted in any form or by any means (electronic, mechanical, photocopying, recording or otherwise) without the prior written permission of both the copyright owner(s) and the publisher.

A catalogue record for this book is available from the National Library of New Zealand

Printed and bound in China by Everbest Investment Ltd

ISBN: 978-0-9951318-5-9
eISBN: 978-0-9951378-5-1

The assistance of Creative New Zealand is gratefully acknowledged by the publisher